12: Globalization is propagated by wealthy countries w[...] [...]onors.
actually more for their own benefit in the end. At [...]

13: Globalization not good for poor country's sovere[...] [...]ir
agendas to sync move w/ agendas of donor coun[...] [...]v.
[...]rkers)

13/14: Also increases accountability of country's govt. to civil society

The Globalizers which can lead to decentralization of power and more civilian control over govt.

↳ "To what extent are powerful institutions (global or local) held responsible for their actions?"

p.15: 5 key Propositions: · Global agendas usually trump local agendas
· Local agendas succeed only if they can "plug into a global agenda
· Honduras receives some benefit for following globalization agenda
· Potential draw backs/damage of development are glossed over/ignored
· Donor countries that promote globalization are often larger recipients of globalization-related benefits than recipient countries.

p.17: "Development" obscures the complexity of political economic projects.

p.19: Development as "globalization subsidy" and "political influence buyer"

Ch.2: p.29: 17% of Honduran 正攺府 income is from "fondos externos", or outside funds.
39: large wealth disparity btwn. 正攺府 & development agencies,
· Most powerful/influential agencies promote capitalist growth + neoliberal political reform.
· WB + USAID bring local NGO's into the fold, setting up "dummy NGO's" like
(pg.32) FORRIDEH3, which gives $ to NGO's and is funded by USAID.

43/44: "re-engineering" and "results packages" mean there is more accountability
since the impact of development projects are now measured: is a school being used? etc.
49: USAID is Not for "appropriate technology" such as co-ops, more for privatisation.
50/51: USAID "consultants" call shots + influence Honduran govt. to adopt globalization policies.
Lamar is afraid to admit USAID is "running things"
52: USAID funds a project a pseudo-lobbying group that drafts laws + advocates legislation
66: Donor countries don't train people how to be "experts" in recipient countries because that
way they lose the ability to influence decisions in that country - leverage that determines
which crop they export or grow, or which companies can be based there, or constructing military bases.
71: Donor country monopolization of developing country-related knowledge through reports + articles.
U.S. Policy is based off of these articles, despite the fact they are written by outsiders (often).

85/86: "Mixed accountability", where one works to help local govt., but is only accountable to
the organization they work for, not the 当地 正攺府

93/94: Global inequality being perpetuated w/in these development agencies w/ 2-tiered pay
scales as their experts as some more experience while recipient countries are not given
equal chance to implement globalization-styled policies under aid orgs.
100: Help to Honduras always comes from training beyond its borders, whether Hondurans who go
abroad for college or high school, or international workers coming in from other countries.

107: "Internal brain drain" of govt. → development agencies

113/114: there is tension due to asymmetrical salaries coupled w/
asymmetrical levels of expertise and local experience w/ certain issues.

Johns Hopkins Studies in Globalization

Christopher Chase-Dunn, *Series Editor*

Consulting editors: Volker Bornschier, Christine Gailey, Walter L. Goldfrank, Su-Hoon Lee, William R. Thompson, Immanuel Wallerstein, and David Wilkinson

The Globalizers

Development Workers in Action

Jeffrey T. Jackson

125: Foreign aid org.s always want to be the "teachers", never relinquishing control of their organization to a local.

133: Definitions of "power"

☆ 136: Globalization does not minimize or degrade the power/role of the state, but rather causes it to modify its function to fill a role of pursuing global agendas through supranational institutions like G8, WTO, the U.N, etc.

138: Globalizers seek to transform recipient countries into "neo-liberal stts" w/3 functions:
INFRA STRUCTURE: construct & maintain infrastructure for global economic activity (airports, highways etc.)
NEO-LIBERAL REFORMS: encourage monetary policy that allows foreign investment and export-led growth
SOCIAL WELFARE: provide social order & stability to ensure prior 2 functions can be carried out

141: What aren't the globalizers doing? They manage or influence almost every aspect of life in Honduras. They don't want to "overwrite" govt. institutions w/ their own, just change their structures + influence their behavior to align w/ "global governance" policies.

☆ 142 & 144: Much effort is spent convincing countries to grant organizations a "carte blanché" for implementing programs in their country, just as steps are taken to insure that orgs. don't govern a place, but rather finessé govt. to adapt the policies recommended by them and their teams of foreign consultants or "development experts"

146: 145/ Saying yes (or being told to say yes) to an organization is tacitly buying into their particular agenda.

El Cajón
150: Proof for Small is Beautiful as seen by El Cajón dam.

151/152: The importance of appropriate technology and scale, proven by #'s.

154: Development banks provide "global govt. subsidies" to the world's largest dam-building firms.

The Johns Hopkins University Press

Baltimore

154/155: Drawbacks to Huge Dams in Poor Countries.

161: Feasibility studies failed to consider human costs of forced migration or added stressors; infrastructure of places they would be moved, or cost of acquiring new skills if farming wasn't an option, or the costs of lost topsoil plantion... vs it

Photographs on pages 22, 128, and 148 are by the author.

Johns Hopkins Paperback edition, 2007
9 8 7 6 5 4 3 2 1

The Johns Hopkins University Press
2715 North Charles Street
Baltimore, Maryland 21218-4363
www.press.jhu.edu

The Library of Congress has catalogued the hardcover edition of this book as follows:

Jackson, Jeffrey T., 1966–
    The globalizers : development workers in action / Jeffrey T. Jackson.
        p.   cm.—(Johns Hopkins studies in globalization)
    Includes bibliographical references and index.
    ISBN 0-8018-8123-4 (hardcover : alk. paper)
    1. Community development personnel—Honduras. 2. Rural develop-
ment personnel—Honduras.   3. Globalization—Political aspects—Honduras. I. Title. II. Series.
HN160.Z9C647 2005
307.1'412'097283—dc22   2004026039

ISBN 13: 978-8018-8758-1
ISBN 10: 0-8018-8758-5

A catalog record for this book is available from the British Library.

⭐194/195: Accountability not taken by WB or IDB, but by Honduran institutions instead!

199: Inadequacy of "top-down" style of decision-making favored by global orgs (WB, IDB). Accountability lays with orgs. who hired contractors.

Maquiladoras

211: Reasons for U.S. construction of offshore industrial processing zones.

For my mentors:

Ross Gandy, Gideon Sjoberg, Thomas Skidmore, and David Stark

212: The "real reasons" why the U.S. was so interested i potential # for subcontracting U.S. companies.

214: US AID was able to change the laws of a country to make a more friendly climate for potential investors in the country.

216: In < 3 mo.s, USAID had teamed up w/ Honduran (also AID-funded) orgs to create a dummy organization like FOPRIDEH (p.32) to fund maquilas.

223/224: How USAID authored a law that was passed by Honduran congress, a sign that AID had garnered "sufficient consent" and was now "along for the ride"

234: B/c rights of Honduran workers were not laid out up front, many violations such as child labor, forced overtime, limited bathroom breaks, locked fire exits, etc. occurred.

235: Conflicting of global agendas.

247: Clash of the NGO's: N.L.C. and UNITE from America worked w/ local Honduran labor unions to gather evidence of workplace abuse + unfair conditions, then used info to expose maquila practices on news shows.

248: NLC & CODEH represent competing global agenda to USAID + maquiladora-creators.

251: By funding the ILO, the U.S. govt. was using *more* aid # to solve the problems created by the use of past aid #.

253: Gap & other clothes companies circumvented local Honduran government as it was seen to be "untrustworthy" and insufficient for protecting the rights of laborers. It hired an independent monitor to insure fair practices were being implemented in the Z.I.P.s

⭐254: Summary of maquiladora process spearheaded by USAID

Contents

List of Tables and Figures   *ix*

Preface   *xi*

Acknowledgments   *xvii*

List of Abbreviations   *xxi*

INTRODUCTION: The Globalizers in Honduras   1

PART I: Who Are the Globalizers?

1   The Institutions   23
2   The People   57
3   The Expats   73
4   The Locals   97

PART II: The Globalizers in Action

5   Global Governance   131
6   Building Dams   149
7   Fixing Dams   179
8   Making *Maquiladoras*   207
9   Legitimating *Maquiladoras*   233
10 Rebuilding after Hurricane Mitch   259

CONCLUSION: Maintaining Global Governance   301

Notes   *311*

Bibliography   *345*

Index   *351*

Tables and Figures

Tables

1	Bilateral Institutions in Honduras	27
2	Multilateral Institutions in Honduras	28
3	NGOs in Honduras	34
4	Consequences of Hurricane Mitch in Honduras	260

Figures

1	Map of Honduras	4
2	ODA to Honduras	25
3	ODA Relative to GDP	26
4	ODA by Source of Donor	30
5	Number of NGOs in Honduras	32
6	Geographical Location of the Globalizers in Tegucigalpa	36
7	Robinson's Model of the Transnational State Apparatus	137
8	The Global Government in Honduras	143
9	Cartoon, by Sergio Chiuz	183
10	How the Dam Was Saved	188
11	FIDE Ads Promoting ZIPs	226
12	Honduran Apparel Exports to the United States	230

Preface

This book is about nation building. Whose nation is being built and who is doing the building are not neutral issues. In practice, nation building occurs in what is generally referred to as "the developing world." It is the "less-developed" countries in Latin America, Asia, Africa, and the Middle East whose nations are targeted for political construction. And it is the wealthy, "advanced" countries of the world that take on the role of architects and engineers. Typically, these "nations of the North" (or Western nations, depending on your vantage point) operate together in various international forums (such as the Group of Eight) that are governed by agreed upon frameworks of rules and expectations. Often referred to as donor countries, these nations provide large amounts of financial assistance for economic and political development. As I will show, an international body of institutions and professional development workers has emerged that does the nation building for developing countries throughout the world. These individuals and institutions operate globally to create new political structures; in this sense, therefore, nation building is about global governance.

The book explores global governance in the developing world through a case study of how the international organizations of the donor countries operate in one such developing nation: Honduras. My analysis is based upon my own experiences living and conducting fieldwork in Honduras during ten months in 1995–96. In addition, I returned in the summer of 2001 to spend another month doing a follow-up investigation. During both visits, I learned a great deal about the various development organizations operating there. Some of this information was available through newspapers or the development organizations' own brochures, publications, and files. Most of what I learned, however, came from interviews I conducted with development workers themselves. I tried as much as possible to enter their world. I spoke with a wide variety of development professionals, both Honduran and expatriate, including everyone from the unpaid volunteer to the most well-known directors. I also interviewed a number of Honduran government officials (including ministers) whose work was integrally connected to development assistance.

When I began the project in 1995, my intention was to carry out an in-depth ethnography of development workers in a particular setting. I quickly realized, however, that "doing development" in Honduras was but a small piece in the much larger puzzle of globalization. Development workers were not simply administrators of "aid" from donor countries; they were promoters of global agendas and builders of transnational institutions of governance. Therefore, my conceptualization of them shifted from "international development professionals" to "globalizers" as I began to see their work as integral to global politics.

Although these international development professionals in Honduras work for a wide variety of development organizations, they form, together with their Honduran governmental and nongovernmental counterparts, a close-knit coalition of policy makers: an international body of governance that some might even refer to as a global government. These professionals and institutions in Honduras work together to mold the Honduran nation-state to more closely conform to international expectations and norms, and to better integrate the Honduran nation-state into transnational structures of governance (such as the United Nations and the International Monetary Fund, or IMF). In other words, the globalizers and their Honduran counterparts are not only giving the Honduran political system an overhaul, they are also erecting a new global government. I explore this process empirically by examining the experiences of individual development workers as they pursue various political initiatives in Honduras.

Examining the international development profession in Honduras reveals how global governance works. I contend we need to *see* global government to understand it. We need to know its institutions and its actors. The goal of this book is to make these globalizers visible. At the center of my analysis are four main concerns that have yet to be fully explored in the globalization literature: First, I am interested in the mechanisms of power that the globalizers have at their disposal. Most globalization scholars trace global power to the transnational capitalist class. While I agree that global capitalists hold much more power than other groups in the operation of global government, the way in which this power is exercised is much more complex than most scholars suggest. Capitalists are certainly trying to set up the new global political structures to their advantage, but the new transnational institutions of governance are not at their beck and call: capitalists do not provide the money for nation building or global governance, governments do; and, in particular, the governments of what is called the donor community provide the international aid money that drives global politics. The power of the globalizers thus lies principally in the large bureaucratic institutions the donor nations have invented to coordinate and disburse this aid. I therefore place these international development organizations at the center of my analysis, and it is from this central position the mechanisms of power must be identified.

Second, global politics is not just about brute force. Even if recent history, such as U.S. nation building in Iraq, would lead us to believe that military intervention is a precursor to nation building, historically this is not often the case. Scientific and technical knowledge, techniques of bureaucratic management, and professional expertise are also a large part of the picture. Global governance works through the mobilization of not only capital and military force but also experts and their expertise. Transnational institutions of governance are staffed and supported by a diverse array of professionals trained in the modern academies of donor countries and guided by their technical training. The state-of-the-art professional expertise in economics, social science, political science, medicine, education, business, and engineering forms the knowledge base from which the nation builders operate and make policy prescriptions and recommendations throughout the world.

Third, it is important to emphasize here the *agency* that the globalizers have as they operate within transnational institutions. Because the new rules of global governance are being created by human beings, I place these human agents at the heart of my analysis. How the globalizers negotiate conflicts between diverse local interests and global interests within the context of powerful bureaucracies is complex. Although this agency is largely unexplored in the globalization literature, ultimately much of the power that will determine the shape of the future transnational global political arrangements lies here.

Fourth, it is the donor countries that benefit most from development assistance and nation building in the developing world. These benefits are largely invisible if you examine only the public record (newspaper, TV, and magazine news). This is because donor countries refer to this process as "aid." Cloaked behind this term, nation building and global governance are spun as "helping" and "generosity," and few people know of the real benefits that donor countries receive. I give these economic and political dividends a central place in my analysis and, as I shall make clear, the benefits to donor countries far outweigh the costs.

These four features of global governance—the mechanisms of power at the disposal of development agencies, the expertise embedded in the individuals and institutions administering development aid, the agency of development workers, and the benefits that accrue to the donor countries—have largely been overlooked in globalization literature, which tends to focus more on global economic phenomena than global politics. My hope is that, by sketching a portrait of the globalizers in Honduras, I can offer some understanding of not only the political dynamics of globalization in one Central American country, but also the history of our present circumstances and the conditions of globalization in which we find ourselves.

Summary of the Book

In part 1 of the book, "Who Are the Globalizers?" I introduce the international development profession in Honduras by describing the institutions and people that carry out development projects in the country. We will take a tour of Tegucigalpa, the capital city, and visit the various development agencies that are prominent in what I call the "development landscape" (chap. 1). Exploring where these institutions are situated geographically and politically in relation to the Honduran national government, this chapter illustrates just how significant these globalizers have become over the last thirty years. In particular, I trace the flow of money into Honduras from donor countries in the form of "official development assistance" and what it means for carrying out various agendas, both global and local, throughout Honduras.

Chapters 2, 3, and 4 discuss the development workers employed by the various agencies. Here you will meet the globalizers. Through an examination of both foreign (chap. 3) and local (chap. 4) development workers' career paths, I argue that international development workers constitute a growing profession with its own subculture, socialization practices, career ladder, and legitimating ideologies. Although the profession is available to both Hondurans and foreigners, entrée differs between the two groups, and the reward structure provides much greater benefits to expatriates. This allows expatriate development workers to "live like royalty" while they carry out their work in Honduras, and this gap is a source of tension between expatriate and Honduran development workers. These chapters explore how development professionals view these issues and the potential problems they raise.

By examining specific development projects in Honduras, part 2, "The Globalizers in Action," addresses how the institutions and individuals presented in part 1 shape Honduran society. First, in chapter 5, I briefly explore the wide range of projects carried out in Honduras by the international development profession. I argue that, although the institutions, professionals, and areas of expertise differed for each project, the fundamental political process involving these international organizations and the Honduran nation-state is the same in each case. In particular, I build upon previous scholarship and contend that the international development organizations and their Honduran counterparts make up an emerging "transnational state apparatus"—a global government—that has increasing power and influence in shaping public policy in the country. This chapter provides a framework for understanding the mechanisms of power at the globalizers' disposal. Specifically, it points out how the globalizers insert themselves into the local political process, conduct surveillance in order to gather information useful for their purposes, and garner the consent of Hondurans in various institutions in order to carry out their global political agendas.

Chapters 6 through 10 illustrate this process of insertion, surveillance, and garnering consent by exploring in detail three significant Honduran development projects. In chapters 6 and 7, I present an overview of the largest development project ever carried out in Honduras: the construction of the El Cajón hydroelectric dam. The history of the dam is significant not only because of the role of international development experts in its design and construction (chap. 6), but also because its failure in 1994 was largely responsible for the severe energy crisis Honduras experienced that year, requiring extensive work by the globalizers to restore the dam to working condition (chap. 7). I examine the issues of blame and accountability that arose as a result of its failure. In particular, I argue that within the nascent global polity there appear to be no formal mechanisms through which developing countries can air grievances or seek compensation for development projects that fail. Implications of this finding for both the international development profession and the Honduran citizenry are discussed. In chapters 8 and 9, I explore the creation and promotion of *maquiladoras* (offshore assembly zones) in Honduras. I present the development profession's role in the creation of export processing zones in the 1980s (chap. 8) as well as their involvement in mitigating the damage to the developing maquiladora industry caused when international nongovernmental organizations (NGOs) began to criticize the new Honduran factories for labor violations (chap. 9). Finally, Chapter 10 examines the manner in which the globalizers and the growing transnational state apparatus sprang into action after Hurricane Mitch devastated the country in 1998. I discuss the significant part played by international development institutions in the relief, recovery, and reconstruction efforts following the disaster.

In the concluding chapter, "Maintaining Global Governance," I address the problems facing international development agencies and their employees as they seek to maintain hegemony in the developing world; in particular, the problems of inefficiency, Honduran national sovereignty, accountability, transparency, and the lack of local control over the globalization process. The globalizers are active in confronting these concerns through various strategies. These strategies reinforce the flow of development funds into the development profession and foster its legitimacy in developing countries. In the closing paragraphs, I analyze the problems associated with each strategy and the questions they raise for the future of Honduras in the context of globalization. I also offer my thoughts regarding the overall role of the globalizers in Honduras and what it can tell us about globalization processes throughout the world.

Acknowledgments

Books are not written by single individuals. They are the product of countless interactions between many people over time. I am deeply indebted to the following, without whom this book would not exist:

I thank the Andrew W. Mellon Fellowship in Latin American Sociology from the Department of Sociology at the University of Texas for the two years of support for my original dissertation work in 1995. I am also extremely grateful to the Croft Institute for International Studies, the Department of Sociology and Anthropology, the College of Liberal Arts, and the Office of Research at the University of Mississippi for their financial support of this project. In particular, their assistance allowed me to return to Honduras in 2001 to conduct follow-up fieldwork on the Hurricane Mitch recovery that became the basis for chapter 10. This support also provided important writing time during the summer months. I am fortunate to be at an institution that encourages and supports junior faculty research.

I am even more grateful for the colleagues and friends whose help, support, advice, guidance, criticism, and love have sustained this project when it might otherwise have languished in file drawers as a heap of disconnected notes and undeveloped ideas. Antonio Ugalde, Bryan Roberts, Larry Graham, and Doug Foley got the project off the ground and gave it a push in the right direction. Christine Williams helped keep it aloft with moral support, publication advice, and key editorial suggestions on early versions of the manuscript. I truly appreciate her continued encouragement. Gideon Sjoberg deserves special thanks for his unwavering support of this study from the very beginning. I admire him not only for his intellectual abilities and his contagious enthusiasm for sociology, but also for his exceptional talents as a patient listener and as a thoughtful provider of "humble suggestions." I cannot thank him enough for the telephone conversations and the encouraging words of support that sustained me and guided me through many moments of feeling lost or uncertain. I will always look to him as an example of what it means to be a mentor.

I thank the development workers in Honduras who took the time to speak with a "nosy sociologist" about their work and their lives. Without their willingness to engage in conversations regarding some of the more difficult aspects of their work, this book would not have been possible. Special thanks go to a number of individuals who helped me make contacts and who allowed me to observe them at work. Thanks to Judy and Rainer for the dinners and conversations out on the porch, to Tito and Kathy for the wine, the television, and for teaching me some art, and to David for his belief in my project and for being such a great travel companion. Thanks also to Victoria, Humberto, Magnus, Kristine, Ana, Toki, Kathy, Xiomara, Carmen, Guillermo, Lucy, and Cristina for making my fieldwork in Honduras such an enjoyable and rewarding experience. I would also like to thank Lizeth Angélica Reyes in Honduras and Laura Asberry in Austin for transcribing the Spanish-language interview tapes.

Alejandro Portes, Peter Evans, and Susan Eckstein offered extremely valuable advice and criticism early on, as did my friends Tim Dunn, Dag MacLeod, and Patti Richards. I am grateful to them all for nudging me toward the difficult questions. I would like to thank William Robinson for his published work on the transnational state, which helped me tremendously in clarifying my own theoretical framework, and also for his kind words of encouragement in Oxford and Anaheim. I thank Christopher Chase-Dunn for helping me understand what was important about this project when it was still a dissertation and for his enthusiastic support once it developed into its current form. Walter Goldfrank gave close attention to the first manuscript version and I owe him a tremendous debt of gratitude for his critical eye and his extremely helpful suggestions. I also thank my editor, Henry Tom, and the Johns Hopkins University Press. This book has benefited tremendously from Henry's professionalism and diligence and I appreciate his belief in this project as well as his skilled guidance in getting it to press.

I thank Joe Ward for showing me the publishing industry ropes, for his insistence that I was ready to submit a proposal, and for his editing help on early versions of the first two chapters. Jay Johnson and Gary Long also read early versions of manuscript chapters and I thank them for their advice and encouragement. Thanks to: Robbie Ethridge for blazing the trail; Max Williams, Michael Metcalf, and David Swanson for believing in the research; Holly Reynolds, Doug Sullivan-Gonzalez, Katsuaki Terasawa, and Mark Healy for stimulating exchanges and friendly suggestions; and Joel Ellwanger, Chip Wells, Jenny McFarlane, Patti Giuffre, Grant Mallie, Michelle Ronda, Dennis Grady,

Chuck Ross, Minjoo Oh, Hyun Park, Gabe Wrobel, Kevin McCarthy, Marty McCarthy, Denton Marcotte, Ted Ownby, Nancy Bercaw, Scott Kreeger, and Sue Grayzel for demonstrating that friendship and intellectual conversations go hand in hand.

I would like to thank my family for their love and encouragement. While they have sometimes wondered aloud, "What is taking so long?" they have never wavered in their support for me. I would particularly like to thank Chris Jackson and Thomas Dellinger, the two engineers in my family, for their help on the El Cajón material.

Four people, above all others, helped me make this book what it is today. First, I would like to thank two members of "the Institute," Tracy Citeroni and Alejandro Cervantes-Carson, for nurturing this book in its infancy, for feeding it healthy doses of critical theory in its youth, and for supporting it from afar as it came of age by sending it care packages of theory and chocolate at just the right moments. Their encouragement has meant more to me than I could hope to express.

Finally, I owe my deepest thanks to two wonderful friends who founded YOHG—our "Year of High Gear" tenure support and reading group—and who have been down in the trenches with me as I have cranked this manuscript out. Thanks to Laurie Cozad, who patiently and persistently helped me through each draft of each chapter of this book. Each time I was faced with a logjam, Laurie helped me see the big picture and offered constructive writing guidance to get me back on track, all while helping keep my spirits up with stiff drinks and good times. I benefited tremendously from her sharp editorial eye, intellectual perspective, and ability to see what's important.

Most of all, I thank my soul mate and life partner, Kirsten Dellinger. As a member of YOHG, she also read every single word of every single version of this manuscript, offering painstaking editing and rewriting help. From the very beginning of this project and through all its phases—fieldwork, long-distance phone calls, deadlines, dead ends, late nights, writer's block, fatigue, and doubt—she responded with encouragement, energy, affirmation, time, constructive criticism, meals, back rubs, love, and hope. I wouldn't have been able to write this book without her.

Abbreviations

ACDI	L'Agence Canadienne de Développement International (Canadian International Development Agency)
AECI	Agencia Española de Cooperación Internacional (Spanish Agency of International Cooperation)
AHM	Asociación Hondureña de Maquiladores (Honduran Manufacturers Association)
AID (USAID)	Agency for International Development (same as USAID)
AMA	American Management Associations
ANDI	Asociación Nacional de Industriales de Honduras (National Association of Industrialists)
ANEXHON	Asociación Nacional de Exportadores de Honduras (National Association of Honduran Exporters)
APEC	Asia-Pacific Economic Cooperation
APSO	Agency for Personal Service Overseas (Ireland)
ASDI	Agencia Sueca de Cooperación Internacional para el Desarrollo (Swedish International Development Cooperation Agency)

ASONOG	Asociación de Organismos No Gubernamentales de Honduras (Association of Honduran Nongovernmental Organizations)
BID	Banco Interamericano de Desarrollo (Inter-American Development Bank)
BPE	Bureau of Private Enterprise (USAID)
CABEI	Central American Bank for Economic Integration
CADERH	Centro Asesor para el Desarrollo de los Recursos Humanos de Honduras (Advisory Council on Human Resources Development)
CARE	Cooperative for Assistance and Relief Everywhere
CBI	Caribbean Basin Initiative
CDC	Commonwealth Development Corporation (U.K.)
CECLA	Concorcio El Cajón (El Cajón Consortium)
CEPAL	Comisión Económica Para America Latina y El Caribe (Economic Commission for Latin America and the Caribbean, UN)
CIDA	Canadian International Development Agency (same as ACDI)
CIMEQH	Colegio de Ingeneiros Mecánicos y Eléctricos de Honduras (Honduran Society of Civil Engineers)
CODEH	Comisionado de Derechos Humanos de Honduras (Honduran Human Rights Commission)
CODHEFOR	Comisionado Hondureño Forestal (Honduran Forestry Commission, GOH)
COHEP	Consejo Hondureño de la Empresa Privada (Honduran Council of Private Enterprise)
CONICA	Concorcio Internacional El Cajón (El Cajón International Consortium)
COPECO	Comisión Permanente de Contingencias (Permanent Emergency Contingency Commission, GOH)
CRS	Catholic Relief Services
ENEE	Empresa Nacional de Energía Eléctrica (National Electrical Energy Company, GOH)
ESF	Economic Support Fund (U.S.)
EU	European Union
FAO	Food and Agriculture Organization (UN)

FESITRANH	Federación Sindical de Trabajadores Nacionales de Honduras (Federation of Unions of National Workers of Honduras)
FHIA	Fondo Hondureño de Inversión Agrícola (Honduran Agricultural Investment Fund)
FHIS	Fondo Hondureño de Inversión Social (Honduran Social Investment Fund)
FIDE	Foundation for Investment and Development of Exports
FONAC	Foro Nacional de Covergencia (National Convergence Forum)
FOPRIDEH	Foro de Organizaciones Privadas de Desarrollo de Honduras (Forum of Private Development Organizations of Honduras)
FUHRIL	Fundación Hondureña de Rehabilitación e Integración del Limitado (Honduran Foundation for the Rehabilitation and Integration of the Disabled)
FUNDEMUN	Fundación para el Desarrollo Municipal (Foundation for Municipal Development)
G7	Group of Seven
G22	Group of Twenty-two (OECD member nations)
GAO	General Accounting Office (United States)
GDP	gross domestic product
GEMAH	Gerentes y Empresarios Asociados de Honduras (Honduran Management Association)
GOH	Government of Honduras
GTZ	Deutsche Gesellschaft für Technische Zusammenarbeit (Germany)
HAMCHAM	Honduran-American Chamber of Commerce
IDB	Inter-American Development Bank
IESC	International Executive Service Corps
ILO	International Labor Organization (UN)
IMF	International Monetary Fund
INA	Instituto Nacional Agrario (National Agrarian Institute, GOH)
JICA	Japan International Cooperation Agency
m.a.s.l.	meters above sea level
MONENCO	Montreal Engineering Company

NAFTA	North American Free Trade Agreement
NGO	nongovernmental organization
NLC	National Labor Committee
ODA	official development assistance
OECD	Organisation for Economic Co-operation and Development
PAHO	Pan American Health Organization
PRODEPAH	Proyecto de Desarrollo de Políticas Agrícolas en Honduras (Honduran Agricultural Policy Development Project)
SANAA	Honduran Ministry of Water and Sanitation
SECPLAN	Secretaría de Planificación (GOH)
SETCO	Secretaría Técnica y de Cooperación Internacional (GOH)
SIDA	Swedish International Development Cooperation Agency (same as ASDI)
SOPTRAVI	Secretaría de Obras Públicas Transporte y Vivienda (Ministry of Public Works, Transportation, and Housing, GOH)
TCC	transnational capitalist class
TDP	Trade and Development Program (USAID)
TNC	transnational corporation
TNS	transnational state
UN	United Nations
UNAT	Unidad de Apoyo Técnico (National Unit for Technical Support, GOH)
UNDP	United Nations Development Programme
UNICEF	United Nations Children's Fund
UPSA	Unidad de Planificación Sectorial Agrícola (Agricultural Sector Planning Unit, GOH)
USAID	United States Agency for International Development
WB	World Bank
WFP	World Food Programme (UN)
WOLA	Washington Office on Latin America
WTO	World Trade Organization
ZIP	Zona Industrial de Procesamiento (Export Processing Zone)

The Globalizers

The Globalizers in Honduras

What is this all about? What is this massive internationalist intervention, aimed at a country that surely does not appear to be of especially great economic or strategic importance?

—JAMES FERGUSON,
THE ANTI-POLITICS MACHINE, 1990

In the late 1970s and early 1980s, anthropologist James Ferguson identified a pervasive and powerful force that was operating in the small African country of Lesotho. This force had the ability to create and implement political projects at will, even when the likelihood of failure was high. It could carry out these projects in the face of local opposition, often with little regard for local governmental procedures. It could even change these governmental procedures for its own purposes.

What was this omnipotent force? It was the "development industry" (what he called the "development apparatus"), made up of the many international agencies funded from abroad that were operating in Lesotho in the name of promoting development. In 1979, Lesotho received $49 in the form of development assistance for every man, woman, and child in the country. These funds came from twenty-four different donor countries and were administered under the auspices of more than seventy-five development organizations. Throughout his analysis, Ferguson wondered why this activity was taking place with such intensity, but his conclusion raised more questions than it answered. He argued that the development apparatus appeared to be about "expanding the power of the state" in some way.[1] But it remained unclear to him *whose* state was being expanded because numerous foreign states were implementing these projects within Lesotho. Ferguson ended by suggesting that the results from Lesotho were unclear and wondering about the extent to which such a force may be operating in other countries.[2] And if it is, why?

In the 1990s, I found a similar force operating half a world away in the small Central American country of Honduras. In 1995, Honduras received $67 per citizen in development assistance from abroad and, like Lesotho, was swarming with international aid agencies and expatriate "experts." In addressing Ferguson's question "What is this all about?" I believe the answer is much clearer now than it was when he conducted his research: it is about globalization. Development agencies exist in developing countries such as Lesotho and Honduras to advance the interests of donor countries. The agencies create a framework of global governance that develops and maintains the policies necessary to promote their various global agendas throughout the world. They constitute a "global government" that promotes the interests of the world's wealthiest nations and buttresses the capitalist world economy. In other words, development agencies are the "globalizers." The purpose of this book is to provide a concrete illustration of how this new system of global governance works.

The Globalizers

Globalization has become a buzzword. But how many times have you heard someone talk about a "globalizer"? Although hundreds of books and articles on globalization have been published in the last ten years or so, outlining the features of this profound, worldwide transformation, none have used "globalizer" to describe what is going on.

Current scholarship on globalization has emphasized the *structure* of globalization but has paid little attention to the human *agents* involved in its development. Much of the globalization literature gives the impression that globalization is occurring all by itself, that it consists of transformations that are bigger than us and processes that have taken on a life of their own. Like a natural law of social or economic evolution, globalization is made to seem a monolithic and unstoppable juggernaut that is imposing itself upon all of humanity. Some scholars argue that it is largely a product of unprecedented technological advances, such as jet travel and instantaneous electronic communication.[3] Others suggest it is a new phase of capitalist expansion, following the logic of capitalist development.[4] Still other scholars contend that globalization is the spread of common ideological orientations such as modernity and universalism across the planet.[5]

Although scholars have helped us understand the architecture of globalization by identifying its key elements and processes, I would argue that globalization is more than a macrolevel phenomenon. Globalization is also a concrete series of actions, initiatives, and decisions made by human beings within the organizations they have invented. The architecture of globalization has *architects*. Globalization is occurring in our world because people actively create it, nurture it, and promote it.

The late French sociologist Pierre Bourdieu offered what I believe is the best definition of globalization in this regard. He defined it as "*an economic politics* seeking to unify the economic field by means of a whole group of legal-political measures destined to beat down all the limits to this unification." Although Bourdieu's focus was primarily on economic globalization (which, as I argue below, is only one of many globalization agendas, albeit a significant one), he also emphasized globalization as a *political* process driven by *political actors*. He wrote: "'globalization' is not a mechanical effect of laws of the economy or technology, but *the product of a politics put to work by an ensemble of agents and institutions* and the result of the application of deliberately created rules to specific ends."[6]

But who are these agents and institutions? I consider the members of the international development profession to be the most significant globalizers in the world today. Development workers and the institutions that employ them have been largely taken for granted[7] or overlooked[8] in the globalization literature, which tends to depict transnational corporations and the transnational capitalist class as the primary agents of globalization. They are certainly important players, but this book casts the spotlight instead upon professionals who enter the developing world in order to create the conditions necessary for the transnational corporations to do what they do. It is the story of hardworking men and women who travel regularly across international borders to implement policies designed to foster global trade and build the world economy. It is the story of how a particular group of individuals, equipped with professional expertise and vast institutional resources, engage in the economic politics of the developing world and, in so doing, promote various global agendas. This book examines how one country—Honduras—is becoming more deeply integrated into the global system and the key part played by the international development profession in that process.

The Case of Honduras

Honduras is a mountainous, tropical country of just over 6 million people. It is roughly the size of Ohio and located in the middle of the Central American isthmus, two thousand miles south of New Orleans. In terms of gross domestic product per capita, Honduras is the second-poorest nation in the Western Hemisphere and has a narrow, agriculturally based economy heavily dependent upon the export of coffee and bananas. It is a small country.

Some might think that the experiences of such a small, "insignificant" place would offer few lessons about globalization. But in countries such as Honduras, the agenda of globalization is most actively promoted and most strongly felt owing to the large presence of international aid agencies and development workers.

Honduras has a long history of external influence and intervention in its national affairs. From Spanish colonialism and the European presence of the seventeenth century to U.S. neocolonialism under "manifest destiny" and the

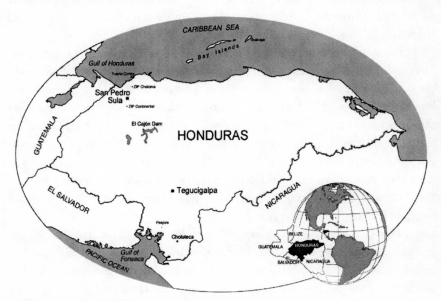

Figure 1. Map of Honduras

cold war, Honduran history is a lesson in dependency. In this sense, Honduras has always had agents of modernization and development from one or more powerful nations "helping" it to become more prosperous and, most importantly, more readily exploited. In this regard, Honduras (like Ferguson's case of Lesotho) is an extreme case that was chosen to place in sharpest focus the structures of global governance. The precise configuration of the transnational state apparatus, I assume, varies greatly from country to country. And I would predict that the power of the development industry in heavily aid-dependent countries (such as Honduras) will be much greater than in larger, less dependent countries (e.g., Mexico). I believe the basic outline of this apparatus is similar in all countries receiving significant amounts of development assistance and that the case of Honduras provides a good indication of what this basic outline entails. The extent to which this outline holds for other aid-recipient nations depends upon future comparative analysis and empirical assessment. The generalizability of the Honduran case is an issue I consider further in the concluding chapter.

I am not suggesting, therefore, that the external influence called globalization is occurring for the first time. My point is that the institutional-political structure of global governance that is the subject of this book largely came into being during the last fifty years (mainly in the 1980s and 1990s). The form it has taken *is* new, and my examination here takes the 1950s as its rough historical starting point. A longer-term historical analysis taking into full account Honduras's engagement with the capitalist world system is beyond the scope of my analysis.[9]

Honduras is today a heavily aid-dependent country. From the Honduran point of view, the development organizations bringing this aid are highly significant in shaping the political and economic realities of the country. In addition, they are seen as advancing the globalization agenda. These agencies are large (such as the World Bank, United Nations Development Programme, and United States Agency for International Development) and small (such as Cosude, the Swiss development assistance agency, Catholic Relief Services, and Save the Children). They are in some cases the providers of official development assistance (ODA) funds often amounting to tens of millions of dollars a year (such as JICA, the Japanese International Cooperation Agency, UNICEF, and GTZ, the German development agency), and in others, nongovernmental organizations (NGOs) providing much smaller, private funds while nonetheless maintaining a prominent position on the local scene (such as CARE, World Vision, and Covenant House).

Staffed by highly trained professionals from throughout the world and operating with budgets that often dwarf their Honduran government counterparts, these development organizations are ubiquitous in Honduran society. They work in every social sector—agriculture, commerce, education, energy, forestry, health care, transportation, urban planning, water and sanitation—and deal with every social problem facing Honduras: homelessness, illiteracy, AIDS, deforestation, unemployment, infant mortality, teen drug abuse, malnutrition. Their many projects dot the Honduran countryside and their logo-emblazoned vehicles are recognized far and wide. As such, their presence is widely known and deeply felt by all Hondurans. Both the investment banker and the taxi driver read about their activities in the daily newspaper. The upwardly mobile entrepreneur and the landless peasant attend their seminars.

The stated mission of the people and institutions constituting this *international development profession* is to bring development to Honduras. The strategies by which development is pursued have varied since the birth of this profession in the 1960s. In the past, there were often strong disagreements regarding what the proper path to national development entailed. Today, however, there is a growing consensus about what development means and a growing convergence of approaches that development organizations take.

Increasingly, the international development profession subscribes to the logic of globalization. The idea is that, in order to alleviate poverty and develop economically, politically, and socially, Honduras should "go global" and link into the world system. It should open up to the outside world and let in investors, products, and ideas. It should tailor its production to the global marketplace, exporting its culture and products in response to global demand. In addition, Honduras should adopt roughly the same political and economic strategies, and the same technology, that the developed countries apply to their problems. In other words, Honduras should run itself the way the developed world runs itself. The international development profession carries out this agenda through the projects it funds and implements. This is how development workers are *globalizers*.

Making the International Development Profession Visible

The idea that the international development profession is an important agent of globalization has not been fully explored in the new arena of globalization studies. While none have used the term *globalizer*, most scholars of globalization have identified the principal agent of globalization in the world today as the transnational corporation (TNC) or, more to the point, the individual entrepreneurs of the transnational capitalist class (TCC).[10] The typical globalization story is about selling Coca-Cola in the Kalahari. It's about Nike producing Air Jordans in Indonesia. It's about McDonalds selling Big Macs in Beijing. These global giants (along with SONY, Phillip Morris, Disney, General Motors, Wal-Mart, Citibank, and hundreds of other TNCs) are almost universally cited as the main engine of the globalization machine. It is this economic motor of transnational capitalist expansion (along with the transnational institutions and treaties supporting it—such as the World Trade Organization, or WTO, and the North American Free Trade Agreement) that has received the most attention from social scientists.[11] According to these scholars, "it's the global economy!" and not much else that should be the focus of attention. The power that TNCs and the TCC have in promoting globalization has led most commentators to conclude that the process is inevitable and unstoppable.[12] This largely economic process is often referred to as globalization from above.[13] According to this view, globalization is occurring because the most powerful interests on the planet—large, wealthy corporations located in the world's wealthiest and most powerful nations—want it to happen.

Much attention has also been paid to globalization from below.[14] Some scholars, for instance, have examined the migration of workers across national borders.[15] Others have looked at how popular social movements in various regions of the world have garnered international support for their cause and, in so doing, more effectively brought about social change in their own locale.[16] This has been the case particularly with those studying so-called civil society and NGOs. Still others have focused on religious, ethnic, and cultural resistance to globalization. In each instance, globalization from below is to be seen in the actions of the less powerful (vis-à-vis transnational capital) as they attempt to negotiate, adapt to, resist, and reform the world around them by "going global" themselves. The argument is that there is a growing opposition to the actions of TNCs and their allies in promoting globalization. These "discontents" (such as the Zapatistas in Chiapas, Mexico, and the WTO protesters in Seattle) oppose globalization in its current form and seek to build a more just and democratic global society.[17] Whether the subject is transnational labor migration, international NGOs, international labor solidarity, international human rights, the global environmental movement, international women's rights, international children's rights, indigenous rights, religious fundamentalism, civil society, or terrorism, the scholarship focusing on globalization from below seems to share the view that all of these processes are more or less counter-reactions or backlashes to the agendas of powerful transnational capitalism.[18]

With so much attention being paid to globalization from above and globalization from below, an obvious question emerges: What is going on in the middle? These other perspectives are important and necessary, but they overlook a vital link: What is the relationship between the economic imperatives from above and the political conflicts from below? Where exactly do the economic politics Bourdieu referred to take place? In particular, how do those existing outside the processes of globalization become integrated into the global system? And how are those who might be critical of globalization incorporated as well? There must be a middle space where the advocates and agents of globalization from above come together with the "discontents" from below.

Development institutions exist within this middle space, and international development workers and the institutions employing them thus offer an excellent opportunity to study globalization in action. These institutions operate globally at the nexus between the developed world (and its globalization agendas) and the developing world (which is generally becoming integrated into the global capitalist system). Those who work within these institutions are ideally situated to observe globalization at all levels. The motives of these individuals are not necessarily consistent with the views of those above or below them but incorporate elements of each. Development workers are operating within a context of multiple agendas.

Global Agendas

Globalization is about advancing the economic and political interests of the TCC resident mainly in the wealthy countries of the world. To achieve this, these wealthy nations provide incentives to poorer nations to go along with their agenda. The incentives are called development assistance, and the agenda is called opening up to the international free-market system.[19] The wealthy nations promote this agenda using their globalization missionaries: development workers. These globalizers create the conditions under which capitalist globalization can proceed.

How can a transnational corporation produce its wares in an underdeveloped country if the laws of that country make it difficult to do so? Enter the development professional to consult with country officials and offer advice regarding legal policy changes for setting up offshore assembly zones and fostering a better environment for foreign investment. (See chapters 8 and 9.) In this way, the globalizer knocks down any impediments to offshore production. How does a transnational corporation make sure its offshore assembly workers are well trained and healthy? Again, the development professional steps in to offer financial and technical assistance to the ministries of education and public health, providing new textbooks, teacher training, and an overhaul of the public health system. (See chapter 5.) The globalizer thus ensures a healthy, educated workforce.

And how does a transnational corporation manage to efficiently move supplies and products over long distances and across national boundaries if roads and ports are in poor condition or if tariffs make it difficult to do so? The development professional once more comes in to fund, design, and build better roads and ports and offer advice for reducing trade barriers in the interests of national development. (See chapter 5.) In this manner, the globalizer eliminates the obstacles to the mobility of goods and services.

The primary role of the globalizer, then, is to lay the groundwork on which global capitalism can expand and develop. The global economy is growing in our world because people and institutions are actively fostering it. The architecture of economic globalization has, as I have stressed, its architects (and engineers, and construction workers, et al.). Advancing global capitalism is not, however, the only role of the globalizers; they have other agendas as well. And this is something often overlooked by scholars focusing primarily on the economic nature of globalization.[20]

A Multiplicity of Agendas

Globalization is not simply a single agenda (i.e., promoting capitalism) or even a monolithic set of agendas (i.e., neoliberalism). Rather, it is a multiplicity of agendas. Some are dominant or hegemonic and others are peripheral. Sociologists John Boli and George Thomas refer to these agendas as global cultural scripts, the various recipes, rules, and frames of reference that define and constrain how independent nation-states can operate in the global context.[21] These scholars emphasize the role of the world polity as opposed to the world economy. They argue that globalization entails nations following the same recipes (more or less) for how societies should function: general welfare rights for all citizens regardless of race, religion, or sex; universal public education: human rights; environmental protection. The recipes are created not by the independent nation-states, according to this view, but by transnational institutions such as the United Nations (UN) and the World Bank (WB) that have come into being during the past fifty years or so.

I argue that development organizations are the main promoters of these global scripts in the developing world as they carry out a broad range of programs pertaining to issues of universal concern. Everything from protecting the environment, to enhancing the rights of women, quelling the spread of AIDS, defending children's rights, building democracy, and improving adult literacy (not to mention promoting global capitalism) falls into the globalizers' domain. It is as if to say, "If your country has a problem—any problem—there is a global script that can provide the solution. And we are the ones who know the recipe."

Taken as a whole, the multiplicity of agendas that the globalizers pursue in the developing world involve them in every facet of human life; no issue of human concern is beyond their reach. The overarching agenda of the globalizers is to advance global capitalism while promoting other "universally" accepted principles throughout the world. In this way, principle by principle, piece by piece, the globalizers put into place the numerous components of a global society.

Agendas in Conflict

There is considerable disagreement in the world regarding what these so-called universal principles should be. I do not argue that the various global scripts are created on high and forced upon the citizens of the world. There is no top-down global government setting the agenda and running the entire planet. On the contrary, there are many debates and disputes about what the various agendas and global scripts should consist of. It is important to examine how development workers actively negotiate, reinforce, and resist these agendas as they carry out their work. Some agendas become prominent and influential (such as the call for a reduction in greenhouse gases) while others meet with resistance, fall out of fashion, or sink into the background (e.g., nuclear disarmament). These global disputes ebb and flow and the principles have yet to become fully established in any coherent institutional framework or unified treatise of global law.

In addition, not all agendas are equal. Some are tied to more powerful interests than others and are therefore more widely promoted, disseminated, and implemented. Within the international development profession there is a hierarchy of agendas in which some global scripts matter more than others. The dominant agendas are largely determined by the donor countries and, benefiting from greater financial support for their implementation, achieve hegemonic status within the development profession. As a result, these "big-time" agendas (as one development worker I interviewed described them) have a much greater impact in the developing world. In contrast, other global scripts are relatively "small potatoes" (quoting again the development worker). Attracting less donor interest and, as a result, lower priority within the development profession, they become peripheral to the central mission of development organizations.[22]

Ultimately, our global society will be shaped by the manner in which global agendas are opposed or supported by the globalizers. Agendas are sometimes mutually reinforcing and other times in conflict with one another. As a result, development professionals variously operate in lockstep with one another or at loggerheads. In the following chapters, I present examples of how development workers actively negotiate these competing agendas at all levels of policy making and project implementation.

What holds this hierarchy of multiple agendas together are the donors. The overarching globalization agenda is determined mainly by the wealthiest nations. Canada, France, Germany, Italy, Japan, the United States, and the United Kingdom make up the Group of Seven nations (G7). Their representatives meet regularly to discuss various common interests, including how to administer ODA to developing countries. The G7 accounts for 75 percent of all bilateral (country-to-country) aid to the developing world.[23] These same seven countries provide the overwhelming majority of funds to finance multilateral aid through organizations such as the WB and the UN. In addition, the Organisation for Economic Co-operation and Development (OECD, Paris) recognizes a total of twenty-two donor countries that provide economic assistance to the developing world. Often referred to as the Group of Twenty-two (G22), this body of large, industrialized nations, which includes the G7, dominates the decision-making process within the WB, International Monetary Fund, and the WTO.[24] Most important, these donor countries set the priorities and make important policy decisions regarding which agendas to pursue within the globalization effort.

Despite the multiplicity of agendas, in the 1980s and 1990s there was an increasing convergence of agendas as the developed nations began subscribing to the same development paradigm for the developing world: promote neo-liberal reforms and market-based strategies in order to expand free enterprise through foreign investment, with an emphasis on producing exports for the global marketplace, and, where possible, promote various global scripts deemed significant by the international community. As a result of this convergence (especially in the post-Soviet era in which there are few competing economic models), wealthy nations and the global institutions they support have come to define and shape the globalization agenda.[25]

Development assistance and the international development profession are the primary mechanisms through which the imposition of this agenda occurs. By means of the development apparatus, donor countries are able to impose specific agendas upon recipient countries that ultimately serve the donor countries' interests. They are able to do this because they are paying the tab. By giving tens of billions of dollars each year to the developing world, donor countries can set the terms under which that money is spent and define the projects that are carried out.[26] In the long run, these projects benefit the donor countries to a greater extent than the so-called recipients.

Globalization is thus a process promoted and maintained by the wealthy countries for their benefit under the guise of helping the poorer countries. This is not the typical view of development assistance. Most people assume that the wealthy nations of the world are giving aid to poor nations because it is the generous thing to do. The shiny veneer of beneficence covering development assistance has made this perception common. The veneer is the public image development organizations cultivate in order to present themselves as pursuing the greater moral good: helping those less fortunate. All development organizations engage in advertising campaigns and public relations to create the image of doing good work. The aim of such promotion is to engender the belief that donating to these organizations will help the less fortunate—feeding the hungry, fighting poverty, clothing the naked, educating the illiterate, healing the sick.

An institution's claim that it is doing good doesn't mean, of course, that it is. Ascertaining whether the WB, for example, is doing good would require examining its actual practices in the world. We would need to look beyond the veneer. Critics of development practice have pointed out that the veneer of helping is more than just an optimistic spin: it is a distortion.[27] They argue that it conceals the truth about development practice as an exercise of power. Help usually comes with strings attached that ultimately serve the interests of the helper far more than those of the helped. With its accompanying conditions, development assistance has become what one critic has called "an instrument of the perfect—that is, elegant—exercise of power."[28]

Understanding the "elegant power" development institutions wield in their work is important for perceiving the nature of capitalist globalization. For it is under the benign halo of helping that the globalizers enter the developing world to advance their multiple agendas.

The Role of the Recipient Country

Poorer countries such as Honduras try to negotiate the best possible deal for themselves in relation to the globalizers' multiple agendas. Various groups within developing countries can exploit, accommodate, or resist the global agendas that the globalizers bring across their borders. If they choose not to go along with the globalization program, they can try to oppose it by, in effect, kicking the globalizers out. This option, however, is not easy to pursue because the globalizers bring significant amounts of money and international credit with them.[29] But it can be done.[30] Yet, more often than not, developing countries consent to the agendas of the globalizers and, in return, receive some benefits. This certainly appears to be the case in Honduras. The goal of many Hondurans who negotiate this process is to maximize these benefits. In addition, we must recognize that there are multiple interests in Honduras, too. Therefore, throughout this book the multiplicity of local agendas will also be taken into consideration.

Accountability versus Sovereignty

What does it mean for an international institution to carry out its agenda within the borders of a sovereign nation? As I will show in the coming chapters, this is a difficult issue to interpret. The manner in which Honduran national sovereignty is able to coexist alongside the activities of the globalizers is still unclear at this point since it is an issue that is only beginning to emerge within the current historical context of globalization. On the one hand, globalization undermines Honduran national sovereignty by transforming Honduran political institutions themselves into agents that carry out the agendas of the globalizers in general and of the donor countries in particular. On the other, globalization enhances the capacity of Honduran government institutions to be politically accountable to civil society in ways that foster democratic processes (such as civilian control of the military, fair and open elections at the regional and national levels, and freedom of the press), which can result in increased local control over political decisions throughout the country. In other words, globalization is both tearing down and building up the Honduran nation-state. Nevertheless, if we were to compare the amount of political control held by the Honduran government and that held by the globalizers, I think we could reasonably conclude that the globalizers appear to be gaining power and, in many cases, may even have the upper hand in many political decisions.

Whether we are talking about the globalizers or the Honduran government as decision maker, I believe the crucial issue for developing countries confronting globalization is: To what extent are powerful institutions (global or local) held responsible for their actions? In other words, the key issue is not only national sovereignty but also accountability, and, in examining the activities and actions of the globalizers in Honduras, I view them through this lens.[31] I attempt to show how (and if) international development organizations are held accountable for the projects they carry out and the agendas they advance. Unfortunately, the conclusions in regard to this question are not encouraging. It would seem that there are very few formal mechanisms through which the globalizers are held responsible for their actions. This is the biggest challenge facing the international development profession and it threatens to undermine the globalization system. Of course, development organizations realize this and are actively pursuing strategies to enhance their legitimacy in the developing world.

The Globalizers in Honduras: Five Propositions to Guide the Analysis

The current clash between global agendas and local interests in Honduras is a dynamic, evolving process. The interaction between the globalizers and the national actors in Honduras unfolds through many negotiations and alliances created by multiple groups with multiple agendas. Some groups in Honduras are already moving in the same direction as the global agendas and eagerly join the globalizers. Others, despite their initial opposition, succumb to the globalizers' agendas in a process of cooptation or accommodation. Still others maintain their opposition. The global-local linkages being forged between the globalizers and various Honduran groups throughout the nation are creating a new, transnational social arrangement; this new social arrangement *is* globalization. In particular, it is the globalization of politics and the emergence of global governance. In the following chapters, I will focus on five propositions that characterize this new social arrangement:

First, global agendas tend to win out over local agendas most of the time. This is because international development institutions are effective, well-funded organizations staffed by highly trained professionals. The institutional wherewithal that development organizations are able to bring to bear upon any Honduran social issue outweighs, in most cases, that of most Honduran national institutions and organizations. Likewise, the highly trained experts these development institutions employ are able to exert their professional authority in a context where professional training is at a premium. Because professional expertise tends to reside in international development organizations, it is their agendas that are most effectively (and with the least resistance) carried out. This is in contrast to the Honduran national institutions, which are often unable to recruit and retain professionals with technical expertise due to the relatively lower salaries and benefits they are able to offer. *promoting a "we know best" approach to development.*

Second, local agendas succeed only as they are capable of linking into the global agendas. Honduran organizations, business groups, NGOs, and social movements are most often successful when they are able to gain the support of the international community. Honduran interests unable or unwilling to "go global" in pursuit of their efforts tend to weaken over time and, in the context of globalization, ultimately become second-class players to their globalizing counterparts.

Third, Honduran institutions (and Honduras as a whole) receive some benefits from participating in the globalization agenda. The incentives for joining the globalizers in their plans are often quite strong. Honduran organizations that link up to global agendas can usually expect financial support that dramatically surpasses what is available on the national scene. In addition, Honduran professionals who themselves become globalizers enjoy higher salaries (often paid in dollars) and greater occupational prestige. Honduran institutions also achieve greater political power in the local policy-making process as they are able to bring their influential global ally to the table. The globalizers are aware of this and take great pains to spell out to Hondurans the potential benefits associated with any global agenda. There is no development project without "recipient benefits" highlighted in great detail. These benefits can be as small as "running water for a few hundred families" or as large as "millions of dollars in increased wood exports." Whatever the case, there is always something to be gained by Honduras within the globalizers' agenda. Failure to participate in these global agendas, therefore, often seems ludicrous or irrational since the benefits are so self-evident. As one development worker I spoke with put it, "these projects sell themselves." Bearing in mind Honduras, in fact, receives new roads, electric power, bridges, latrines, increased agricultural output, running water, sanitation, health care, education (the list is long) from the international development profession, it would be foolish to argue that Honduras receives nothing out of this global arrangement; it gains a lot. Whether receiving these benefits can be considered "development" or whether, by their receipt, poverty is on the decline in Honduras are empirical questions that are beyond the scope of this analysis.

Fourth, the negative consequences or potential drawbacks of development projects are downplayed or ignored. The international development profession promotes its projects in Honduras by accentuating the benefits they will bring and by utilizing terms such as "aid," "assistance," or "help." The long-term risks and costs of these projects, on the other hand, are often obscured or minimized. This is a major problem because these projects are often costly, especially when it comes to development loans, which must be paid back by the recipient country with interest (albeit low interest). They are also riskier and more likely to fail than the development profession is willing to admit.

In short, development organizations obscure the risks and costs of their projects behind the rhetoric of helping. Crucial in this stratagem is the usage of the term *development.* Most of the international and transnational institutions operating in Honduras refer to themselves as development institutions or make the claim that development is central to their mission. For these reasons, the notion of "development" is key to my analysis. I believe "development" is the ideological motivation behind the activities of these institutions as well as the ideological justification used to give these activities the appearance of legitimacy within the local political process. Development is a chimera. It obscures the true agenda of these institutions behind an emperor's cloak of shifting meanings. The true agenda is globalization.

I do not wish to imply that there is some sort of conspiracy to keep this "true mission" hidden. The goals of the globalizers in Honduras are in plain sight. They are printed on mission statements and disseminated in press releases, public reports, and Web pages. Yet, "development" is the ideology that disguises this agenda of globalization. The halo of development puts a positive spin on their practices (which might otherwise be more strongly questioned or challenged) and transforms any political project they might propose into "the right thing to do." Development is the Midas touch, turning to gold whatever it is attached to. In the name of development, deforestation and exploitation of old-growth hardwood forests turns into taking advantage of natural resources for national economic growth. In the name of development, *maquiladoras* and the exploitation of workers by transnational corporations become job opportunities for the poor. This process holds true for any project—hydroelectric dams, legal reforms, or reducing trade barriers. Development turns any agenda into a good agenda by hiding it behind the shiny veneer of beneficence. Moreover, "development" makes global agendas (and, by extension, international development organizations) immune to criticism. Why would anyone want to criticize an organization whose goals are to help the poor? Who could be against improving the lives of women and children in the developing world? Who can fault the WB when it claims, "Our dream is a world without poverty"?[32]

Logging or maquiladoras or hydroelectric dams are not inherently evil. Third world countries are not being duped into accepting a bill of goods that offers them no opportunities for advancement or improvement. Logging and maquiladoras can (and do) contribute to both economic growth and job opportunities. They also have real drawbacks, risks, and downsides. My point is not that the discourse of development presents inherently flawed political economic projects as wholly good, that "development" tricks countries into accepting things not in their best interest. Rather, "development" obscures the complexity of political economic projects.[33] It accentuates the positive and avoids the downside. It also allows large bureaucratic organizations that operate under the development moniker to easily dismiss the criticisms of their actions. Most importantly, it shields the globalizers from explaining how the projects they promote benefit themselves and their donors. This brings me to my final, and most important, point.

Fifth, the greater benefits of the activities of the international development profession accrue to the donor countries, and these benefits are also largely hidden. It

is the donor countries mainly that promote the globalization agenda and the
donor countries that largely benefit from it in the end. There are numerous
benefits that donor countries receive through providing international development assistance to the developing world.[34] However, the money that flows from
donor to recipient countries such as Honduras in the form of grants and low-
interest loans does not return to donor countries directly. Although Honduras
does have a huge debt to pay back to its donor nations, this money is usually returned at a rate below inflation (i.e., the loans are "concessional"). In the traditional sense, there is little profit in promoting development. Providing ODA
costs the donor countries money; why would they choose to absorb this cost?
Contrary to the discourse of aid, it is not out of the goodness of their hearts.
There are other, direct and indirect, returns on this investment. International
development assistance amounts to a "globalization subsidy" that donor nations provide in order to advance the economic interests of their own "global
reaching" enterprises. If you want to play the globalization game (like the
United States, Germany, Japan), you need to get into the aid business.[35] ODA
gets your foot in the door. It gives you access to the markets of the developing
world. ODA primes the pump that gets the globalization engine running. In
other words, donor countries are definitely getting something out of the deal.

There are direct benefits to donor countries in the form of contracts for
their high-tech industries and jobs for their professionals. There are also indirect benefits. In particular, the international development profession can serve
to foster the economic interests of the donor countries in a number of ways.
First, it can help locate and acquire inexpensive natural resources from the developing world. Much development practice, for example, involves working in
the areas of forestry, mining, and agriculture. The globalizers can also advance
the economic interests of the donor countries by locating and creating access
to cheap labor. Another indirect economic benefit is access to markets in the
developing world. ODA often helps donor countries open up and secure markets for their goods in developing countries. For instance, the work of the
globalizers in Honduras often involves removing Honduran trade barriers to
goods from donor countries.

There are also political benefits. Although they are difficult to quantify in
terms of dollar amounts, they are nevertheless important to consider. Donor
countries may, as an example, make it easier to pursue their own political interests in the region through development aid. It would not be hard to argue,
for instance, that the ability of the U.S. military to locate a base at Soto Cano

and carry out missions in Honduras in the 1980s was, in part, due to the overwhelming amount of economic assistance the United States was providing to the Honduran government.[36]

Development assistance is thus a boon for donor countries. It is a direct boon in the form of contracts and jobs for development professionals. It is a boon to their economic interests in terms of finding natural resources, labor, and markets. It is a boon to their political interests both in the region and domestically. Although no single development project being carried out by the globalizers encompasses all of these benefits, all development projects involve some benefit to the donors. Taken as a whole, the globalization agenda ultimately enhances these benefits across the board. Donor countries stand to gain the most from the globalization project. That is why they are setting up and coordinating the international system of aid and sending the globalizers into the developing world on their behalf; they benefit. This conclusion goes against the very idea of development assistance, which posits donor countries as giving something away. Moreover, these donor benefits are largely hidden from view; recipient countries, in particular, are often unaware of them.

In sum, the development profession—a profession whose ostensible mission is to help the poorest of the poor—is allowing rich countries to more effectively exploit poor countries for their own advantage. My hope is that, by the end of this book, I will have provided enough evidence to convince readers this is exactly what is happening in the case of development assistance and the globalizers in Honduras.

CARE Worker and Child

© 1994 CARE/Staff

Part I / Who Are the Globalizers?

USAID Building, Tegucigalpa, Honduras

CHAPTER ONE

The Institutions

There are currently more than three hundred organizations in Honduras whose main purpose is to promote development in the country. Only a handful had offices in the country before 1975. The majority began their activities after 1985. Their emergence on the Honduran landscape coincides historically with what globalization scholars cite as the rise of the global system in the 1980s and 1990s.

This wide array of development organizations in Honduras constitutes a new and influential force in the local body politic. They are prominent on the local scene through their implementation of programs and policies that affect every segment of Honduran society. Like a surrogate government, they share in the mission of providing numerous public services to the Honduran citizenry. Whether in health care, education, business promotion, roads, energy, water, or food, they work hand in hand (and sometimes in conflict) with the Honduran state to carry out projects that, in effect, change the basic structures of society. As a whole, these institutions constitute a loosely knit international coalition of governance: that is, a global government, one whose role in promoting globalization in Honduras merits careful analysis.

In the following, I examine the development organizations active in Honduras and the large flows of their official development assistance (ODA). I also describe the arrangement of these institutions on the Honduran scene and their relationship with the national government. Finally, I focus on the United States Agency for International Development (USAID), perhaps the most significant organization in Honduras, as an example of the structures, operations, philosophical orientations, and projects of these institutions.

Development Assistance to Honduras

On December 14, 1960, the wealthiest nations of the world signed an agreement in which they set about to build a "world economy." Committed to the idea of promoting economic development throughout the world, these nations agreed to provide economic resources to recipient nations in the developing world to accomplish this lofty goal.[1] The Organisation for Economic Co-operation and Development (OECD, based in Paris) was born.[2] Since that time, financial flows from donor countries to developing countries throughout the world have constituted the economic fuel running the engine of development. The OECD is currently made up of twenty-two donor nations that provide ODA to the developing world.[3] According to the OECD, official development assistance is defined as: "those flows to developing countries provided by official agencies, including state and local governments which meet the following tests: a.) it is administered with the promotion of the economic development and welfare of developing countries as its main objective; and b.) it is concessional in character and conveys a grant element of at least 25 per cent."[4]

Generally speaking, ODA is money given to developing countries by official agencies and developed countries usually for the purposes of economic development and welfare. ODA given by national governments is referred to as "bilateral aid." That provided by international organizations like the World Bank (WB) or the United Nations (UN) is referred to as "multilateral aid." ODA can be in the form of either a grant, for which no repayment on the part of the recipient country is required, or a loan, which must be repaid. As stated, for a loan to qualify as ODA, it must "convey a grant element of at least 25 per cent," meaning the loan must be offered at below-market interest rates or be relatively long term. The OECD states: "Generally speaking, a loan will not convey a grant element of over 25 per cent if its maturity is less than 10 years, unless its interest rate is well below 5 per cent."[5] ODA generally does not include financial contributions from private, nongovernmental organizations (NGOs).

ODA to Honduras has grown significantly over the past thirty years. In 1970, Honduras received approximately $20 million in net ODA (fig. 2).[6] This equaled about 3 percent of the Honduran gross domestic product (GDP) for that year (fig. 3). Beginning in 1975, ODA doubled to $52 million, and the amount has grown steadily since and remains high. It rose tremendously in the eighties, increasing from about $100 million in 1980 to over $300 million in 1988. In 1990, Honduras received $448.1 million, the largest amount of ODA in its history prior to Hurricane Mitch. It represented more than 15 percent of that year's GDP. ODA remained high in the nineties, fluctuating between $300 million and $400 million a year. In 1999, the year following Hurricane Mitch, net ODA to Honduras amounted to $816 million dollars, thirty-five times what it was in 1970. For such a relatively small country of 6 million people, this amount comes to roughly $136 for every Honduran citizen (which is more than one month's income for the average person). The amount of development assistance currently entering Honduras is equivalent to about 10–12 percent of its GDP (fig. 3).

There are a number of different ways in which ODA is channeled into Honduras. Bilateral aid is disbursed through various bilateral agencies in

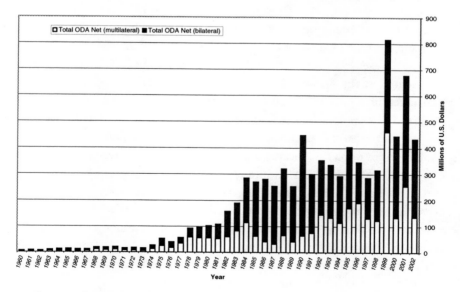

Figure 2. ODA to Honduras

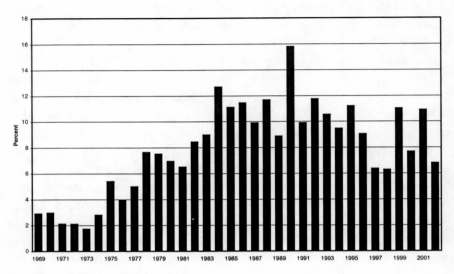

Figure 3. ODA Relative to GDP

Honduras, which means *every donor country* has offices in Tegucigalpa charged with coordinating the disbursement of funds and implementing the projects those funds support. ODA from the United States is channeled through the U.S. Agency for International Development (USAID). That from Japan comes through the Japan International Cooperation Agency (JICA). Germany has the Deutsche Gesellschaft für Technische Zusammenarbeit (GTZ), and Spain is represented by the Agencia Española de Cooperación Internacional (AECI). The larger bilateral agencies, such as the aforementioned four, have their own office buildings; other bilaterals have offices housed in their respective embassies. The offices of Sweden's International Development Cooperation Agency (ASDI), for example, are located in the Swedish embassy. (See table 1 for a list of bilateral institutions in Honduras.)

Second, multilateral aid is disbursed through various multilateral agencies. Some multilaterals have permanent in-country representatives located in permanent office buildings. This is the case, for instance, for all the UN agencies, such as the United Nations Development Programme (UNDP), United Nations Children's Fund (UNICEF), and the Food and Agriculture Organization (FAO). These UN entities are all housed in a large UN office tower near the center of Tegucigalpa. The Inter-American Development Bank (IDB) also has a perma-

Bilateral Institutions in Honduras in Order of Net ODA Amount 1969–96

Donor	Starting year	Implementing agency in Honduras
United States	pre-1969	United States Agency for International Development (USAID)*
Japan	1975	Japan International Cooperation Agency (JICA)*
Germany	pre-1969	Gesellschaft für Technische Zusammenarbeit (GTZ)*
Spain	1988	Agencia Española de Cooperación Internacional (AECI)*
Canada	1971	Canadian International Development Agency (CIDA)
The Netherlands	1973	SNV Netherlands Development Organization (SNV)
Switzerland	1976	Agencia Suiza para el Desarrollo y la Cooperación (COSUDE)*
Italy	1978	Government of Italy (Italian embassy)
France	1980	Government of France (French embassy)*
United Kingdom	1970	Department for International Development (DFID)*
Belgium	1974	Gobierno de Belgica (Belgian embassy)
Norway	1982	Gobierno de Noruega (Norwegian embassy)
Denmark	1978	Gobierno de Dinamarca (Danish embassy)
Sweden	1991	Swedish International Development Cooperation Agency (ASDI)*
Finland	1979	Finnish International Development Agency (FINNIDA)
Austria	1976	Government of Austria (Austrian embassy)
Ireland	1994	Agency for Personal Service Overseas (APSO)*
Australia	1986	Government of Australia (Australian embassy)
Republic of China	1990	Government of the Republic of China (Taiwan) (Chinese embassy)*
Venezuela		Government of Venezuela (Venezuelan embassy)
Mexico		Government of Mexico (Mexican embassy)*
Argentina		Government of Argentina (Argentine embassy)
Chile		Government of Chile (Chilean embassy)
Costa Rica		Government of Costa Rica (Costa Rican embassy)
Kuwait	1990	Government of Kuwait (Kuwaiti embassy)*
South Korea	1999	Government of the Republic of Korea (Korean embassy)

*Included in this study.

nent in-country office. Other multilateral agencies operate out of a regional office located outside Honduras and send delegations to the country in order to coordinate the implementation of their programs. Such was the case for the WB, for example, prior to 1999. With no permanent residential staff before that time, it customarily sent representatives from its headquarters in Washington, D.C., to visit with local project supervisors and Honduran government officials dealing with its projects. (Table 2 lists current multilateral institutions in Honduras.)

Most of the ODA to Honduras, whether bilateral or multilateral, is spent on programs and projects that are designed and managed by the agencies themselves, and they hire staff, rent office space, and buy vehicles and equipment for this purpose.

Third, much official development aid goes directly to existing Honduran government institutions and is utilized for their own budget expenditures. ODA constitutes a significant portion of the national government's revenue, and without it, the government would in fact not have enough income to carry

Table 2. Multilateral Institutions in Honduras

Development banks, financial organizations	
IDB*	Inter-American Development Bank
CABEI	Central American Bank for Economic Integration
WB*	World Bank Group
· IBRD	International Bank for Reconstruction and Development
· IDA	International Development Association
· ESAF	Enhanced Structural Adjustment Facility
IMF*	International Monetary Fund
IFAD	International Fund for Agricultural Development
UN organizations	
UNDP*	United Nations Development Programme
WFP*	World Food Programme
UNICEF*	United Nations Children's Fund
FAO	United Nations Food and Agriculture Organization
UNESCO	United Nations Educational, Scientific, and Cultural Organization
UNIDO	United Nations Industrial Development Organization
UNHCR	United Nations High Commissioner for Refugees
UNFPA	United Nations Population Fund
Other multilaterals	
EU*	European Union
PAHO	Pan American Health Organization
OAS	Organization of American States
NDF	Nordic Development Fund
OPEC	Organization of the Petroleum Exporting Countries

*Included in this study.

out its programs and would run a deficit. Close to 17 percent of the income used by the Honduran government comes from such *fondos externos,* or "external funds."[7] These external sources are especially significant in relation to government investment programs and projects. In 1995, for instance, 78 percent of the funds used by the national government to build roads, schools, and health centers came from bilateral or multilateral sources.[8]

During the 1990s, the task of managing this aid and coordinating its disbursement among the many institutions within the Honduran government became so large that the it created two new institutions for that sole purpose. The Secretaría Técnica y de Cooperación Internacional (SETCO) was created in 1996 to manage foreign grants to national government institutions under the purview of the Honduran presidency. And the Unidad de Apoyo Técnico (UNAT) was created to manage foreign loan assistance within the executive branch.

The creation of new government institutions represents a fourth manner of disbursement of development assistance. Another example of this in Honduras is the creation in 1993 of the Fondo Hondureño de Inversión Social (FHIS, Honduran Social Investment Fund). At the time, the WB, IMF, and IDB were concerned that the austerity measures and cutbacks—known as "structural adjustment"—they were requiring the Honduran government to undertake in order to receive further loans would have a deleterious effect on the health and education of the country's poorest citizens. To mitigate this potentially harmful consequence, the large development banks offered the government "structural adjustment mitigation loans" that were to be used to fund health, sanitation, and education projects directly targeted at the poorest segment of the population. The government created the FHIS to disburse these funds. Housed in one of the newest and largest office buildings in Tegucigalpa, the FHIS disburses millions of dollars of ODA each year for a variety of projects, such as building rural schools, latrines, and health clinics.

A final way that ODA is channeled into development activities in Honduras is through NGOs. Most bilateral and multilateral agencies use some of their official funds to support the work of local or international NGOs. For example, 26 percent of Spanish ODA distributed through its agency AECI in 1999 went to support the work of such NGOs as Architects Without Borders, Ayuda en Acción, and Farmaceuticos Mundi.[9]

Where is all this aid coming from? Many people assume that the overwhelming majority of aid to Honduras is from the United States because of the heavy U.S. involvement in the Contra war in Nicaragua and Honduras during the eighties. During this time, Honduras was often thought of as the "U.S. aircraft carrier" in Central America because of the amount of resources the U.S. military and government placed there. And in fact, ODA to Honduras did grow in the 1980s owing primarily to increased U.S. economic assistance. In 1985, for example, development assistance from the United States represented 60 percent of all aid to Honduras (fig. 4). There has since been a relative decline in U.S. aid and an increasing transnationalization of ODA to Honduras as the number of bilateral donors has increased and the amount of assistance from multilateral sources has grown. By 1995, the United States was contributing only 11 percent of Honduran net ODA (fig. 4). This is the result primarily of the increased flows coming from multilateral donors, Japan, and Europe. Between 1985 and 1995, multilateral aid to Honduras increased from 24 percent of all ODA to 43 percent. By 1999, it had reached 57 percent. Europe's contribution to Honduran development assistance between 1985 and 1995 increased fourfold, from 6.7 percent to 27 percent. In 1996, Japan became the single largest contributor to Honduran development assistance as its contribution jumped to 18 percent of overall ODA.

In addition, other bilateral donors have become more involved in Honduran development initiatives. In 1970, there were only three donor countries send-

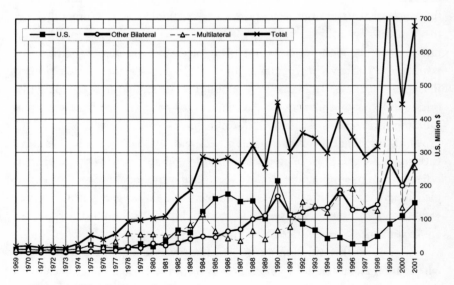

Figure 4. ODA by Source of Donor

ing foreign aid to Honduras: the United States, Great Britain, and Germany. Clearly indicative of the transnationalization of aid to Honduras, today twenty-six different countries provide ODA, including Japan, Canada, Sweden, China, Switzerland, Ireland, and Mexico.

Nongovernmental Development Aid

The ODA figures from the OECD describe only official aid flows to Honduras. There is, however, a substantial amount of development assistance coming into the country from private, nonofficial sources. The actual amount of money entering Honduras through nongovernmental development organizations is difficult to estimate since the records are private; and no one, as yet, has conducted a survey of these organizations in Honduras to determine how they acquire their financial resources. There is, in short, no available information regarding the amount or origin of the donations these organizations administer.[10]

Still, although there is very little information regarding the actual finances of development NGOs in Honduras, we do know that their number has risen dramatically over the past twenty-five to thirty years. There has been a virtual NGO boom in Honduras as the number of organizations operating there has jumped from approximately twenty in 1970 to as many as two hundred eighty in 1996 (fig. 5).

The significant increase in the number of development NGOs in Honduras is consistent with the general worldwide pattern of NGO growth in recent years.[11] The increase is the consequence of increased bilateral and multilateral official aid resources being funneled into NGO efforts. For example, USAID, the official U.S. bilateral aid agency, funds a large number of development NGOs in Honduras, and the NGO boom there is largely attributable to changes in USAID implementation strategies, which favor the subcontracting of work to local NGOs. This has earned USAID the Honduran nickname "Señora Aida."[12] Some critics of the USAID-funded NGO boom argue that NGOs in effect constitute a Trojan horse that carries out U.S. interests in the guise of popular, locally supported organizations.[13] CARE (Cooperative for Assistance and Relief Everywhere), for example, receives the majority of its funding through USAID. Catholic Relief Services (CRS), another development NGO, receives much of its funding from official sources. In some cases, the trail of money from official agencies to nongovernmental agencies becomes complicated. For

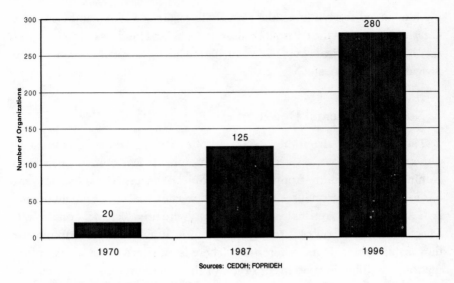

Figure 5. Number of NGOs in Honduras

instance, when I asked an employee at a local Honduran NGO where their funding came from, the reply was, "It's all from within Honduras. It comes from FOPRIDEH." What that development worker did not know was that almost all of the funding for FOPRIDEH (Foro de Organizaciones Privadas de Desarrollo de Honduras, a Honduran umbrella organization that funds a large number of local development NGOs) comes from USAID. Other sources of NGO funds include private contributions, individual donations, foundations, and Honduran government contributions.

However, USAID is not alone in promoting the trend toward increased official support of NGO activities. The WB, IDB, and the UN all have increased their support of the growing number of development NGOs in Honduras by providing institutional funding. Local NGOs are favored by these official agencies because they are seen as having greater local political legitimacy and cost-effectiveness in carrying out projects.[14] Official aid agencies thus usually cast the NGO trend in a positive light: the official development aid organizations claim that, by funding NGO efforts, they encourage local autonomy in the development process and nurture a growing civil society. Some perceive private groups as more efficient than government agencies and so believe the primary benefit to be the privatization of development work. Others believe that the main benefit of NGOs is their popular base and commitment to the grass roots.[15] My own view is that NGOs are, in the main, becoming integrated into the overall frameworks and agendas of the donor countries (G7, G22) that provide the majority of funds upon which the NGOs depend to carry out their work. In any case, the growing presence of development NGOs in Honduras remains clear. (See the list of NGOs operating in Honduras during the time of this research in table 3).

These trends are strongly related to globalization. We can make several observations in this regard. First, the significant rise in ODA to Honduras occurs during the same period—1970–90—that globalization scholars identify as the historical moment when globalization emerges as a worldwide phenomenon.[16] Second, the increase since 1970 in the number of donor countries providing aid and the growth of multilateral aid overall indicate there has been a transnationalization of ODA—what might be termed a "globalization of foreign aid" to Honduras. Third, the Honduran government itself has been transformed by this globalization process much as scholars of globalization would predict.[17] This transformation is not a "withering away of the state," which concerns some scholars; rather, it is a changing of the state apparatus to more effectively engage with the emerging global structures. Honduras must confront the new dynamics of global aid flows and, as a result, the state adapts to the new global system. In particular, it must account for and administer this foreign aid within its own institutions and invent new ones devoted to its management. Fourth, the NGO boom in Honduras coincides with the growth of international organizations and "civil society," a phenomenon that has been cited as an example of globalization in the rest of the world. Finally, the overall result of the globalization of foreign aid to Honduras is a greater number of organizations carrying out development work there; there has been an increase in the number of institutions "governing" the country.

The Hierarchy of Development Organizations in Honduras

Not all development institutions are equal in their ability and power to carry out development projects and influence local policy making. Those who administer greater amounts of ODA have more economic resources with which to carry out projects and programs. As a result, there is a hierarchy of development organizations operating in Honduras in terms of power and wealth. At the top of the hierarchy in Honduras are the IDB and USAID. The

Table 3. NGOs in Honduras (**Bold** indicates development/aid NGO; non-bold indicates environmental, business, human rights, labor, or educational NGO receiving some foreign assistance)

ACAN	CADERH*	COMUNICA*	Fundación Friedrich Ebert	MAPROMA
Acción Internacional*	**CAHDEA**	CONASEL	Fundación Friedrich Naumann	**MASTA**
ACDI	CARE*	CONCERN	Fundación Guadalupe	**Médicos sin Fronteras**
ACODE	CARITAS	CONDERH	Fundación PROLANSATE	MOPAWI
ACORDE	CAS	CONFORTEH	Fundación San Jose del Mariol	**Movimiento de Agricultura Sostenible**
ACPH	Casa Alianza*	CONPAH	Fundación Vida	OCDIH
ADAI	CAUSA	CONSEDE	FUNDEMUN*	ODECO
ADECOH	CCCH	COREDIH	FUNDHICOMUN	ODEF International
ADEROH	CCD*	COSECHA*	FUNHDEMU	OFRANEH
ADESAH	CCEDIVE	COSIBAH	FUPROCODEH	OXFAM
ADIH	CCFH	COTAF	FUTH	PADF
ADINCOH	CDH	COTEDIH	GEMAH	Pan American Health Service
ADP	CDJF	CPDECAP	GEO	Partners of the Americas
ADRA-OFASA	CDM	CRECERH	GRAPLA	PASOLAC
ADRO	CEASO	CRS*	Grupo Ecológico ABC	Plan en Honduras
ADROH	CECADESH	CSJB	**Grupo Juvenil Dion**	PREDISAN
AESMO	CECI*	CTH	**Habitat para la Humanidad en Honduras**	PRM
AHCODEH	CEDECO	CTN	HAMCHAM*	PROALMA
AHDE	CEDEN	DED	**Healing the Children***	PROCONDEMA
AHDEJUMUR	CEDOH*	DEICO	**Heifer Project***	PRODAI
AHMUC	CEHPRODED	DIA	HIBUERAS	PRODAPMA
AIEH	CEIDH	DNI-H	ICADE	PRODELCAS
Aldeas S.O.S.	CEM	ECO LAGO	IDENA	PRODEPAH*
ALDERH	CEN	ECOREDES	IDEPH	PRODERSI
ALFALIT	CENCOPH	EDUCSA	IDH	PRODIH
Alimentos para Millones	CENET	**El Arca de Honduras**	IESC	PRODIM
Alternativas*	CENFODES	**Embajada Cristiana**	IFC	**Proyecto Aldea Global**
AMAB	CEPROD	**Enersol***	IHDER	**Proyecto Hope**
America Mano a Mano	CESADE	**Escuela Agrícola Panamericana**	IHER	**Proyecto Lempira Sur**
Americares	CGT	FACACH	IHPEJ	**Proyecto Victoria**
Amigos de las Américas	CHF*	FAFH	IHS	PRR
AMINA	CID*	FAMA	IICA	RAMAH
AMITIGRA	CIDEC	FEC	IISE	RDS
ANACH	CIDICCO	FECORAH	INADES	**Red COMAL**
ANAFAE	CIPE-Consultores	FED-AMBIENTE	INASC	**Red Nacional de Alfabetización de Honduras**
ANAMUC	CIPRODEH	FEDECOH	INCADES	**Save the Children***
ANDAR*	CJP	**Feed the Children**	INDESEC	**Save the Children U.K.***
ANDI*	Club Rotario	FEHCIL	INEHSCO	SETELEC
ANEDH	CNC	FEHMUC	INHBIER	**Sociedad Médica Cristiana**
ANMPI	CNTC	FEPROEXAH	INHDECOR	**Solidarias Mujeres para el Desarrollo**
APAN	COCOCH	FEPROH	INHDEI	SOPEC
APAS	CODDEFFAGOLF	FESITRANH	Intercooperation	SPAH
APDI	CODEH	FETRIXY	INTERFOROS*	SUR SUR
APDP	CODEMUH	FHA	**International Eye Foundation**	Trocaire*
APEAM	CODIMCA	FHIA*	IRC	UNC
APRHU	COHASA	FIDE*	ITEC	UNISA
APRODIB	COHMEAI	FINCA	IVS	UTC
APRODESH	COIPRODEN	FITH	Katalysis*	Via Campesina
Arquitectos sin Fronteras	COMAPROMA	**Fondo Ganadero de Honduras**	**Los Abuelos Management Sciences for Health**	Visión Mundial*
Arte y Acción	COMICORUHL	FOPRIDEH*		VOCA
ASCONA	Comisión Alternativa no Formal	FUHRIL*		**Water for the People**
ASDANH	Comité Conservación Medio Ambiente	FUNADEH		Winrock International*
ASECOVE	Comité de Servicios de los Amigos	FUNBANHCAFE		**World Neighbors**
ASEPADE	Comité Hondureño de Mujeres por la Paz "Visitación Padilla"	FUNDAAHPROCAFE		WRH*
ASHONPLAFA*	Compañeros de las Américas	**Fundación Democracia y Desarrollo de Honduras**		
ASIDE	COMPARTIR	**Fundación Ecologista "Héctor R. Pastor Fasqualle"**		
ASJO				
ASODES				
ASONOG*				
AVANCE				
Ayuda en Acción*				
BAYAN				
BICA				
Brotherhood of Honduras				

*Included in this study.

IDB is the largest multilateral donor to Honduras, and USAID is the largest bilateral donor, historically speaking. As such, these two organizations are the most significant development organizations in Honduras.

The second tier is made up of the other most significant bilateral and multilateral donors. In the case of bilateral aid, Japan's JICA and Germany's GTZ top this tier, and in multilateral aid, the WB and the UN are the largest development institutions after the IDB.

A third tier of wealth, power, and influence comprises the largest NGOs (such as CARE, the CRS, and World Vision), the other bilateral development organizations (such as Canada's L'Agence Canadienne de Développement International, or ACDI, Sweden's ASDI, and Spain's AECI), and other multilateral organizations (such as the European Union, or EU, the Central American Bank for Economic Integration, and the Pan-American Health Organization). Although these institutions are not as prominent or influential as their larger counterparts, they nevertheless carry out important projects utilizing large amounts of money. They are thus a part of the larger global government (discussed in chapter 5) operating in conjunction with Honduran government institutions to design and carry out policies and programs at a national level.

A fourth tier is formed of the smaller bilaterals such as APSO (Ireland) and the government of South Korea that operate in the country carrying out a range of development initiatives in addition to the hundreds of local and international NGOs (big and small) and private voluntary organizations undertaking development work. Some of the smaller organizations are quite influential, such as Casa Alianza (Covenant House), which works with street children and promotes children's rights in the country. Others even smaller nonetheless perform an important role in the delivery of services that the Honduran government might otherwise provide. FUHRIL, which receives funds from various European sources to assist the disabled, is one such organization. Some NGOs concentrate their activities in a specific area. The Cooperative Housing Foundation (CHF), for example, conducts a number of housing programs throughout the country with support from various donors. Others, such as Trócaire, the Irish Catholic Development Agency, work in several areas at once. Such agencies cannot be overlooked: they have a significant number of Honduran constituents and, as we shall see, often find themselves in the middle of major public policy discussions within the elite institutions of the national government.

The Development Landscape

Another way we can see how the emergence of these institutions in Honduras coincides with the 1970–2000 globalization period is by examining what they look like and where they are located in the Honduran capital of Tegucigalpa. If we were to map out this historical transformation on the streets of the city, how would these various structures of governance appear? Tracing the global government in Honduras, figure 6 shows five things:

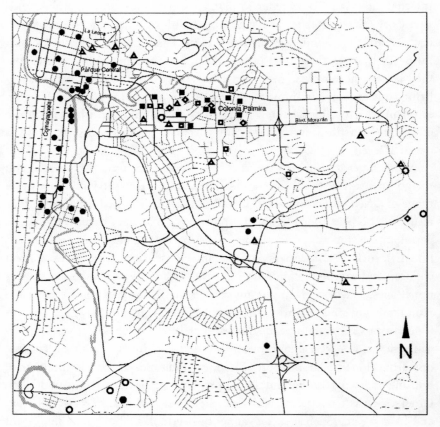

Figure 6. Geographical Location of the Globalizers in Tegucigalpa

First, the solid circles indicate the location of the original Honduran governmental institutions. These various bureaus (the Congress, the presidential offices, and the various ministries) were virtually the only institutions carrying out national policy in the country prior to 1970. They tend to be located in the older, historic center of the city, concentrated on narrow streets near the Parque Central (Central Square) and the oldest part of town called Comayagüela. Many of these buildings were built before the turn of the twentieth century and show signs of wear and tear. The shops and restaurants in this area tend to be small, family-run establishments catering to the various workers employed by the nearby government institutions. As such, their prices are more in tune with the Honduran pay scale and their facilities are relatively modest. In addition, there are thousands of street vendors who make their living on the many sidewalks and promenades located in this older part of the city. They often erect makeshift stands, tables, or shanties to display their wares.

The squares represent the different bilateral institutions operating in Honduras. As shown in table 1, many of these agencies began their work in Honduras in the seventies, with the majority becoming established in the country after 1980. Their location in Tegucigalpa coincides with the growth of the city eastward during that period.[18] The great majority of the bilaterals are found in one, relatively affluent area of town called Colonia Palmira. This neighborhood contains most of the foreign embassies (solid squares) and their foreign assistance offices located therein. The office buildings of the larger bilaterals (USAID, JICA, GTZ, CIDA, and AECI), indicated by hollow squares, are also located close to Colonia Palmira. Tegucigalpa's most upscale shops, restaurants, and hotels cluster in this part of town and cater to the wealthy Hondurans and expatriates who inhabit it. The new fast-food enterprises and luxury mall built since 1994 also tend to be situated in this part of the city.

The diamonds indicate the location of the various multilateral institutions (the IDB, WB, UN agencies, the EU) that carry out policy in Honduras. As can be seen, these multilaterals are located in the same area of the city as the bilateral institutions. The UN agencies are all housed in a large, modern office building within walking distance of the international hotels in Colonia Palmira. The offices of the EU are one block away. The IDB is several blocks east on Boulevard Morazán. The new WB offices, built in 1999, are found farther east in a large, new office building containing several banks near Tegucigalpa's newest mall and a TGIF restaurant. Walking in these areas, it is clear that the multilateral and bilateral institutions occupy the newer, wealthier parts of the city as compared to the Honduran government institutions.

This is also the case for most NGOs—corresponding to the triangles—especially the larger ones. The offices of CARE, Save the Children, CRS, and World Vision, for instance, are located in new buildings primarily in Colonia Palmira and the neighborhoods to the east, in close proximity to their bilateral and multilateral sources of financing.

Finally, the hollow circles represent those new or transformed Honduran government institutions that have emerged as a result of the aid boom of the seventies, eighties, and nineties, such as the FHIS, UNAT, and SETCO. They are situated close to their international counterparts. The offices of SETCO, for example, are located just one block away from the new WB office building.

Walking through the neighborhoods where the foreign assistance agencies are located—the neighborhoods of the globalizers—one is struck by the differences between these areas of the city and those near the older Parque Central. The streets of the former are wide and clean. The restaurants and shops are modern and air-conditioned, much like what one would find in the United States or Europe. Police officers and private guards patrol the entryways to most buildings and keep various "undesirables" away. As a result, there are virtually no street vendors or children begging for coins.

In addition, the vehicles parked outside the different agencies are most often brand-new models. This is no small thing in a developing country such as Honduras, where owning a car is a privilege enjoyed by a very small percentage of the population. The new Toyota Land Cruisers, Front Runners, and Jeep Cherokees (the most common makes among the development agencies I visited) are conspicuous on the streets of Colonia Palmira. Many display the logo of the agency they represent, although CARE decided, after a rash of auto thefts, to stop displaying their emblem on their vehicles.

In contrast with the cars of the globalizers, most Honduran government vehicles tend to be older and run-down. A spray-painted stencil of the Honduran flag and the words "Gobierno de Honduras" adorn the sides of these vehicles and often appear on top of a previous sticker revealing the car's origin: USAID or the UN. The computers used in government offices are also sometimes hand-me-downs. On a visit to the offices of the Honduran Health Ministry, I noticed USAID tags on the computers. This is no great surprise considering USAID had an office within the Ministry of Health. Other agencies—

such as the GTZ, JICA, IDB, and the FAO—were given similar privileges to establish offices within Honduran government institutions.

What this institutional geography reveals is the tremendous wealth disparity between the foreign development agencies and Honduran government institutions. This disparity, so clearly revealed by the property—buildings, office equipment, and vehicles—of these organizations, has an impact on the relative power and influence of these institutions on Honduran society.

This geography also shows that these institutions, located close to each other, tend to function together. As the following chapters will make clear, sometimes the relationships are strong and significant, and in other cases, more tenuous. In any case, public policy and political agendas are carried out in Honduras as a consequence of the interactions among these institutions and the people they employ. I wish to emphasize, however, that the hierarchy of power among the various development organizations results in most development institutions (including the NGOs) becoming incorporated into the major agendas of the dominant institutions. In terms of hierarchy, the most influential development organizations are those involved in promoting capitalist growth and neoliberal political reforms. Less influential are the organizations and NGOs working on humanitarian issues such as health or human rights. And least influential are agencies whose goal is to reform or regulate capitalism or that promote socialistic policies and political reforms. Despite these differences, the less-influential organizations often buttress and work directly with the more powerful advocates of free-market policies and, as I describe in the later chapters, actually become incorporated into the neoliberal agendas of the donor countries and often end up directly facilitating their interests over local interests. The institutional arrangement between official development agencies and NGOs, for example, illustrates this: Many powerful development institutions such as the WB and USAID have attempted to deflect criticism that their activities are heavy-handed by bringing NGOs into their practices. As a result, NGOs have become integrated into the structures of global governance and donor-country agendas.

In order to show in more detail the institutional arrangement of foreign aid in Honduras, I explore in the following one site within this development landscape: the USAID building. USAID's operation in Honduras is representative of the development profession as a whole, and, since it has been the most significant agency in terms of funding development initiatives in the country over the last thirty years, a tour of its offices will reveal the complexity of the aid business and highlight its power and influence.

Inside USAID

The USAID building is a large, five-story concrete structure located near downtown Tegucigalpa on Avenida La Paz just across from the even more imposing U.S. embassy. Every day there is a long line of Hondurans outside the embassy trying to get visas to go to the United States. The morning I visited was no exception as a crowd of roughly seventy-five Hondurans congregated in front of the massive office building. The U.S. embassy stands out among buildings in the city as one of the most modern and heavily fortified. Surrounded by a twenty-foot-high concrete wall topped with concertina wire, the embassy building sits in the middle of a compound that occupies an entire city block. The entrances are heavily guarded, and, seven stories up, security cameras are mounted on each corner of the rectangular building. The USAID building, formerly the embassy before the new one was built, is just as well protected. Black iron bars are mounted on all the building's windows—indeed, with the steel bars, chain-link fence, and barbed wire surrounding the building, the whole USAID complex resembles more a prison than an office building. Pulling open the heavy security door, I went inside.

A line of USAID employees passed their bags and briefcases through a metal detector as they entered the offices. They all had ID badges clipped to their clothes, and security guards waved each employee through from behind thick, dark-tinted, bulletproof glass. One asked me my business, and I explained I had an appointment with Greg Lamar.[19]

As I waited, I noticed some posters and plaques on the wall. One read, in Spanish, "If it's not appropriate for women, then it's not 'appropriate technology'." Anyone familiar with the development industry would understand the slogan's reference to the relatively new emphasis in development practice of placing women at the center of development initiatives—in this case, "appropriate technology" projects (an example of development "lingo" meaning the practice of using equipment and technologies well suited to the Honduran context). Another advertised a different global agenda: "Ecotourism, more than just an adventure." Also on prominent display was the insignia—an image of two hands shaking—of USAID. Two awards given in 1978 and 1990 by AID in

Washington to USAID/Honduras for "excellence in promoting development" hung just beneath it.

A young Honduran woman came through the door, introduced herself, and gave me a badge with a big black V on it. She guided me through well-furnished offices, past new cubicle dividers, new furniture, and new computers to a large office area with a mahogany reception desk where I was told to wait for Greg Lamar. I picked up a copy of the USAID newsletter *Front Lines* lying on a table. It featured pictures of well-dressed Americans (identified as USAID representatives) smiling at less well-dressed "recipients." The newsletter was filled primarily with news about USAID personnel: who was moving where, what positions were available—even an obituary.

An interview with the director of USAID in Guatemala about something called re-engineering caught my eye. Describing how USAID/Guatemala was undergoing various institutional reforms, the article mentioned that USAID is now calling the third-world beneficiaries of its projects "customers." While admitting she wasn't terribly fond of the new term, the director maintained that it would create more of a "business focus" within the organization.

Next, I picked up a glossy, color publication distributed by the FHIA, a new research center created and funded largely by USAID. Extolling the successes of the FHIA over the last several years, the brochure appeared to be a public relations tool. It described some current agricultural projects and reforms the FHIA was pursuing: fighting diseases in bananas (the Gold Finger variety, FHIA-24, was "doing quite well" and was particularly praised for its export potential); developing new strains of corn and soybeans; pursuing cocoa production; and promoting nontraditional crops (black pepper, chilies, heart of palm, cantaloupes). These were all discussed in some technical detail.

Greg Lamar, "El Técnico"

Greg walked in and apologized for being late. He explained that he got up a little late because of a big Christmas party he and his wife had attended at the house of a Honduran government minister. "There are so many Christmas parties we have to go to right now," he said, sounding slightly overwhelmed. He added he had had to straighten out a few things with his housekeeper and gardener. This small talk allowed me a glimpse into development workers' lives: gardeners, housekeepers, and parties with Honduran officials were the norm for many of the development workers I met.

As we walked to the conference room, Greg showed me a computer terminal. "See, we're now hooked in to the Internet! We have a satellite feed and this is hardwired, so we're fully connected!"[20] After seating ourselves in ergonomic chairs, I asked Greg if they used that terminal for communicating more effectively with USAID in Washington.

"No," he said, "we have our own internal e-mail system for that. That's just so we can have access to the Internet—you know, to be able to pull off information from various home pages and stuff." I mentioned I had noticed USAID had a new home page. "Oh, yeah, . . . that," he replied. "Well, there's not a whole lot there yet. It's just kind of telling people what we're working on in a very limited and glossed-over kind of way. . . . But I guess that's good. We want people to know about the good stuff we're doing."

I had visited the newly established Web sites of USAID and many other development organizations before I arrived.[21] They often presented a large amount of information regarding the organization and its projects in Honduras, and, not surprisingly, they tended to show only the good side of their activities. I knew I would have to talk with the development workers themselves to learn about what goes on behind the scenes.

Greg put a photocopied list of telephone extensions on the table. "Here are all the current employees at AID. We have about a hundred and sixty full-time employees. Twenty-five or thirty are direct hires—I guess what you would call 'foreigners' from the U.S. The rest are Honduran FSNs."

"FSNs?" I asked.

"Foreign service nationals," he clarified. "Local Honduran staff who do a lot of the basic day-to-day work of the organization: administration, phones, building maintenance, security, and so on. For them, it's a job. They clock in and out every day and get a paycheck at the end of the week."

I thought about the security guards and Greg's Honduran assistant.

Greg continued, "But they're not as involved in the actual development work. There are several Honduran local hires who are. Maybe ten or twenty *técnicos*."

Técnico, a Spanish word I had heard before in my conversations with development workers, means "technician" and refers to development workers with a specific area of expertise or professional degree such as agronomist, economist, nutritionist, or engineer. The FHIA brochure I had been looking at was most likely written by técnicos.

Greg added, "Now this list doesn't include the various consultants we hire from time to time but it should give you a sense of all the different areas we work on."

Re-engineering

Pointing to the list, Greg began to tell me how USAID worked. The U.S. government spends about one-half of 1 percent of taxpayer money on foreign assistance each year.[22] Operating under the authority of the State Department, USAID disburses most of these funds to developing countries throughout the world. In each country, aid is distributed through various projects and programs designed according to something he called strategic objectives.

Greg explained: "That's the new phrase under re-engineering. Right now we have four strategic objectives in Honduras: 'Enhance economic participation,' which should result in an increased income for the poor; 'Utilize natural resources for sustainable economic growth,' which should raise the GNP; 'Improve family health,' which is a number of issues based on various indicators; and 'Promote more responsive democratic policies,' which we measure in terms of election participation and some other things. You see, with each strategic objective, the idea is to have a specific result that we're looking for."

He elaborated, "We have four objectives and we're looking for specific results. In this case, four 'results packages.' A results package is like a set of indicators for a specific goal. So if our goal is to improve family health, we might look at infant mortality, maternal mortality, childhood disease statistics, worker illnesses, and so on. We might also look at education. So you could have a number of results packages under each strategic objective. For instance, there are three results packages under 'encouraging economic growth.' In each case, we want to see improvement as a result of our programs. If there is no improvement, then we haven't been effective and we could get our program cut."

"Under the old system," Greg continued, "they would just evaluate us in terms of if we carried out an 'action plan' or not. And that was all. So if we said we were going to build a certain number of schools, they would evaluate us on the number of schools we built. If we built what we said we were going to build, that was it! That was deemed a 'success.' Now, we're looking at results. What is the school for? Is it being used? Is it effective in terms of educational achievement? And so on. So it's much better. Who cares if the school was built if it isn't being used? With re-engineering, we're shifting away from the outcome—a school was built—to the results, which are the long-term goals. In this case, raising education levels."

Referring to the mention of re-engineering in one of the lobby brochures I'd read, I asked if it was basically a new way of evaluating development projects.

"Yes," Greg answered. "But it's much more than that. It's a whole new government system. It came in with the Clinton administration. It's based on that book *Reinventing Government* by David Osborne. . . . The idea is to make government more business-like, . . . more responsive to the people it serves. Now they're called 'clients' or 'customers,' not 'beneficiaries.' It's more of a business model. Under Clinton, all government agencies are re-engineering. They're all becoming more streamlined and efficient. But each agency does so in a different way. Here is our re-engineering strategy. . . ."

Greg brought over a large binder with more than three hundred pages. "We've been working on this for a while, and it basically lays out our strategic objectives and the results packages. Every federal agency has one of these. Even within USAID, every country develops a different strategy. In Honduras, we have the four strategic objectives I just mentioned. In India, it's different. There, population control is probably the most important objective. In each case, the goal is to match local concerns and needs with the various U.S. interests in that part of the world."

Greg was talking faster now. "So each AID office has a custom plan for that particular country. The other thing this new system does is it creates competition among the various agencies."

"How?" I asked.

Well, let's say that you're working on a population control project in India and you've been able to show a lot of success in making improvements as measured by your results package. But then you notice that AID in Honduras isn't meeting its goals in terms of population or health or whatever. Well, then you can put in a request for those funds. You can say, "Hey, those guys in Honduras aren't meeting their results package and I am, so I should get those funds." And under re-engineering, that guy in India would get those funds because he is doing a better job. He's showing results that we aren't. So we have to be much more competitive in order to hold on to our programs. If not, we can lose our funds.

"AID in Washington decides whose projects get cut and whose get funded," Greg continued. "And of course, AID Washington is accountable to the State Department and Congress and so on, . . . so they're operating under the priorities set by various groups in the U.S. government. The main point is that we have to be doing a good job. In order for our projects here in Honduras to continue, we have to show results. Otherwise, they can pull the plug. That's the bottom line."

"What is your opinion of that?" I asked.

"That's the reason I think it's such a good system. It rewards success. If we can't show that we're having some impact with our projects, then we shouldn't be allowed to continue them. That's my view, anyway. I think it's good."

The Structure of USAID

Referring to the sheet in front of us, Greg explained how the office was organized. "The director is at the top and has ultimate authority for AID/Honduras. This person answers directly to AID in Washington on a regular and sustained basis. Then there is the executive office, which handles the basic functioning of the organization: personnel, travel, communications and records, data systems, and property management."

Pointing to the "Contract Management Office," he explained, "This is Contracts over here. They deal with all the contracts out to NGOs, private businesses, . . . also consultants. A lot of our work is actually done by contractors. We'll often hire a local NGO or a private business firm to do the work for us and Contracts will write up the papers to have it done."

Asked if subcontractors carried out most of the projects, Greg responded,

Yeah. It's more efficient this way. For example, right now we have a contract with Chemonics International to work on one of our ag. policy projects. They're a private firm based in Washington that we use a lot. They're doing the day-to-day project work . . . actually promoting some new agricultural policies in the country. At AID, we're the managers. We tell them what we want and how we want it done. Then they carry it out. They're a really good group—economists mostly. . . . Chemonics is an example of a private business firm that's paid a fee to carry out a project. Sometimes it's a private firm, sometimes it's an NGO. . . . We have FUNDEMUN, which is a local Honduran NGO that we support to work on issues of municipal development. We have CADERH, an NGO that we contract to do management and worker training. You can also have individual consultants that are paid to perform a specific task.

The Money

Turning the page, he pointed to "Controller's Office." "The Controller's Office handles all the money—accounting, disbursements, project vouchers, and payroll. You want to have a good relationship with those folks because they also have FARS, which is Financial Review. They make sure all the money is going where it's supposed to and not being siphoned off into somebody's pocket."

Tapping his finger on the "Financial Analysis and Review Section (FARS)," he emphasized its importance for the organization. "We haven't had too many problems with things like that at AID. But you want to make sure you have all your numbers straight for FARS, because they really look at everything very carefully to make sure there's no funny business."

I was familiar with stories of corruption within the world of development assistance. Development organizations have millions of dollars at their disposal for projects in developing countries. I wanted to ask Greg about the problem of corruption but decided, at this first meeting, to hold my tongue; I wanted to get an overall picture of the institution before getting into a discussion of sensitive matters.

Greg went on, "Finally, we have Development Finance and Development Programming. These two divisions basically coordinate and oversee all of the projects carried out by the technical divisions. Development finance does the budgeting and programming. Development programming does the basic project design. They also do monitoring and evaluation."

I was getting lost. Greg, an insider, was trying to explain the relatively complex structure and operations of USAID in Honduras using an insider's language of jargon, euphemisms, and bureaucratic code words. I, an outsider, felt I had to translate Greg's language in order to understand his explanation. In an effort to put the pieces together, I asked, "OK, so Development Finance and Development Programming oversee the technical divisions. What are the technical divisions?"

Three Technical Divisions

Greg explained, "That's what I assume you're interested in. Those are the development projects. The technical divisions are responsible for setting up and coordinating the various development initiatives in the country. These can change over time as our strategic objectives may change. But currently, here in Honduras, we have three technical divisions: Human Resources Development; Agricultural and Natural Resources; and Municipal Development and Democracy Initiatives."

Greg indicated on the sheet the three divisions. Under each heading appeared a list of between ten to twenty-five names, divided into subcategories.

"These are the people that you probably want to meet. . . ." Greg stated. "They're the ones actually designing and carrying out the various projects and programs. These are all the técnicos."

I looked at the names. Most were Spanish surnames such as Gutiérrez, Echevarría, and Torres. There were also some Anglo-looking names: Simpson, Foster, Murphy. The name at the top of each list was fully capitalized. I assumed this indicated the head of the division. Greg, for example, who was the head of his division, was listed in all capital letters above a list of mostly Spanish surnames in a mix of capitals and lowercase. This pattern—American names in full caps above a list of Spanish surnames in upper- and lowercase—appeared to be predominant for most of the lists.

Asked if each technical division worked on a different area and if, within each division, there were various development projects, Greg responded, "Right. For example, over here in HRD [Human Resources Development] you have all the education and health projects. They're all related, in a sense, so they're grouped together. The idea is that all these projects develop the human resource base in Honduras by enhancing the education and overall health of the population. You simply must have a population that's educated and healthy. So anything having to do with improving schools, teacher training, and so on would be handled by these people in 'Education/Training.' And here, in 'Health, Population & Nutrition,' you have all the health projects: potable water, sanitation, the *bonos infantiles* project, and family planning."

The bonos infantiles (children's bonds) project, I had learned, involved offering cash rewards to poor women who visited health clinics with their newborn infants. For years, Honduras had been plagued with some of the highest infant mortality rates in Latin America. Various strategies had been tried to address the problem, but the high rates persisted. This new cash reward strategy was supposed to serve two development goals at once: first, it provided an incentive for women to bring their children to the attention of health-care providers and, second, it put much-needed financial resources in the hands of the women who actually care for the children. Institutions such as the WB had experimented with cash-reward projects as a poverty-alleviation and development strategy in many countries during the 1990s. The bonos infantiles project was a new version of this approach developed by policy makers at USAID.

Still referring to the Human Resources division, Greg continued, "These people work primarily with the Honduran government, in the Ministry of Education and Ministry of Health. You could talk with them to find out what it's like to work directly with the government. Over the years, we have developed a very good relationship with the Honduran ministries. Not all agencies can say that, but I think we can."

He added, "They work with NGOs as well. For example, this division also co-ordinates the [food aid] program, which is mostly implemented through NGOs."

Greg moved on to the Municipal Development and Democracy Initiatives division. "They do the various democratization projects: decentralization, enhancing municipal governments, legal system reforms, elections, and so on. A lot of this work is done in conjunction with Honduran NGOs. You should probably try to pay a visit to FOPRIDEH. They can get you a list of most of the NGOs we work with."

I noted down the mentioned NGO. It was becoming clear to me that USAID had close ties with the Honduran government and many Honduran NGOs and that understanding their role in Honduras required paying attention to those relationships.

"Finally," Greg went on,

we have Agricultural and Natural Resources. There are about five or six different areas in Ag./Resources, all pertaining to improving the way in which Honduras manages its agricultural base. As you probably know, Honduras's economy is heavily dependent upon agricultural products: coffee and bananas mostly, but other products as well . . . lumber, for instance, beef. Now that's part of the problem. Honduras needs to continue to develop other industries as well . . . like tourism, like the apparel assembly factories, and so on. But in the meantime, Honduras's chief exports are mostly agricultural. So we work on a number of different areas in agriculture which we hope will lead to higher economic output in these areas. This, you may remember, is strategic objective numbers one and two: increase the income of the poor, and utilize resources for sustainable economic growth. Well, how can we do that?

Greg was entering lecture mode. "We do that by addressing concerns on a variety of levels: at the community level, at the governmental level in terms of policy, and at an international level in terms of figuring out how Honduran exports fit into various markets. So what we do at AID is we try to address all of these various levels in our programs. You see?"

He was explaining the sublevels within the division.

He continued: "What we have is three areas within Ag./Resources. First, you have the ag. export division. Their focus is on expanding Honduran exports through various projects: rural credit union projects, micro-enterprise, enhancing marketing strategies, and so on. The main idea is to foster much more of a business model in the agricultural sector in order to improve efficiency and productivity. You should really talk with Art Lennox about that. He's an ag. economist who works in rural credit. . . . He can explain why the business model is so much better than co-ops in terms of economic development."

By "co-ops," Greg was referring to rural agricultural cooperatives, a farming strategy based upon communal landholdings that has existed throughout Latin America for centuries, particularly among indigenous groups. The land is maintained and utilized by the community as a whole with no (or little) individual private property. Likewise, the harvest and any surplus from the land are divided among every member of the community. Advocates of co-ops maintain that this strategy minimizes risk for any one individual farmer, guarantees a minimum living standard for the most people in the community, and fosters strong community ties. Critics argue that it is an inefficient form of subsistence living that maintains poverty and fails to adequately provide for the increasing needs of a growing, modernizing population. Greg was letting me know which side of the debate he and Art Lennox were on. I would meet Art Lennox later and he would give me an extended lecture on why agricultural projects based upon free-market principles and private property were better than those advocating collective or community property ownership. USAID was selling the idea of private enterprise pretty strongly. [23]

Proceeding to the second sublevel, the "Natural Resources and Environmental Division," Greg explained,

> This is where the issue of environmental sustainability comes in. It's no good for Honduras to exploit its natural resources if they're all gone in thirty years. And that's a real possibility. The current figures we have on deforestation indicate that, if we continue to cut down trees at the rate we are now, the forests will be gone in thirty to fifty years. So that's an important concern for this division. Here we have all the forestry projects, for instance. Honduras exports a lot of wood, and that's a good thing for economic growth. We think we could export more. What AID does is work directly with the Honduran Ministry of Natural Resources and CODHEFOR, the state forestry service, to develop forest management plans which increase wood exports while, at the same time, doing so in a sustainable fashion. We work with others as well. The Germans have done quite a bit of work in forestry over the years. So have the Canadians. We've been working together with them as well on various forestry management plans.

Listening to Greg's accounting, I imagined American representatives from USAID sitting around a table with Germans from GTZ and Canadians from

ACDI discussing national forestry policy with Hondurans from the national government. The fate of Honduran forests would be determined by this process of international cooperation. I wondered who ran such meetings, who had the greatest influence, and who was left out of the discussion.

Greg continued,

> The third area within the Ag./Resources area is "policy": the "Agricultural Policy Division." This is one area that is very exciting because of what USAID has been able to do. We have brought about some significant changes in the country that will have a tremendous impact in terms of development. For instance, we have the "Ag. Policy Project" that played a big role in the Agricultural Modernization and Development law being passed in Honduras. That's what I referred to earlier. When the Ag. Modernization law was adopted by the Honduran Congress in '92, it basically opened up the Honduran market to the rest of the world. They used to control imports with tariffs, and they used to have price controls on basic grains. All of that has changed. And that was changed mainly because of what AID did. We worked with the Honduran government: the Ministry of Economy, the Ministry of Natural Resources, and others. And what we were able to do was bring in very high quality economists and political thinkers to work with the Honduran government planners in order to reshape national policies relating to agriculture and agricultural exports. As a result of this process, the Ag. Modernization law was written and put into law. Since then, there has been a revolutionary change in terms of the way in which Honduras does business with the rest of the world. And that's a good example of some of the things we have been able to do.[24]

I was beginning to get a clearer picture of the power USAID had in Honduras.

The New Policy Environment in Honduras

"So AID was able to change Honduran law?" I ventured.

"Well, I wouldn't put it that way. That makes it sound too much like we're running things. And that's not exactly how it works. What we did was bring in high-quality people to consult with Honduran government officials who were already looking into making reforms. They wanted to know how to improve their exports. We have some experience and expertise with these kinds of things, and we were able to put up some money to help in the planning phase. Ultimately it was the Honduran Congress who made the decision to pass the

Ag. Modernization reforms into law. We were involved in the early phases. We were involved in the planning."

I began to ponder the significance of what Greg was telling me. His example was an illustration of direct influence in Honduran policy making. Although he was careful about how he put it so as not to imply direct control over the Honduran political process, Greg had just given an example of how USAID had been involved in changing the law of the land, an influence that had generated controversy in the past. For years, USAID had been viewed in Honduras as having too much sway in the country, especially during the 1970s and 1980s, when the United States was heavily involved militarily in Central America. As noted, at the time USAID was sometimes called a Trojan horse of U.S. imperialism.[25] Since then, it had been criticized for being one of the many "tools" at the disposal of the United States in carrying out U.S. policy in the region. The Honduran sensitivity on this issue was illustrated by a well-publicized newspaper poll that had taken place several months prior to my visit with Greg. One of the national newspapers had conducted a survey in which Hondurans were asked, "Who is the most influential man in Honduras?" The large majority named the U.S. ambassador, William Price, over Carlos Reina, the president of Honduras.[26]

I would not have been surprised if, owing to the controversy around U.S. involvement in the development of the laws of Honduras, Greg would have shown reluctance to discuss the subject openly; yet, he seemed quite matter-of-fact about it.

So I felt free to ask, "How significant is the influence of AID in Honduras, do you think?"

"I think quite significant. And I think it's very good. I think what we're working on in Ag. Policy, for example, is quite significant. But it is quite welcome, too. We're not imposing this on anyone. The people we interact with—the Honduran government—it's at their request."

I asked how exactly USAID works with the Honduran government.

"Well, in Ag. Policy, we interact with the Ministry of Natural Resources, like I said, with UPSA [Unidad de Planificación Sectorial Agrícola] primarily. . . . UPSA is the planning unit within the Honduran Ministry of Natural Resources. That's our main counterpart. We work with UPSA and we're supposed to be providing them with analysis and support. That's what the Chemonics contract is all about. It's meant to be a policy and analysis support project to UPSA. The project is called 'PRODEPAH': Proyecto de Desarrollo de Políticas Agrícolas en Honduras [Honduran Agricultural Policy Development Project]."

"So PRODEPAH is the project that AID funded through its contract with Chemonics," I asked, "who is supposed to then work with and provide support to the Honduran government?"

"Right," Greg confirmed, "we hired Chemonics to provide the actual economics expertise to UPSA as they were looking at agricultural reform. There are no Chemonics offices here in Honduras—just the project. They're only known here as 'PRODEPAH.'"

I thought about how confusing this might be. Did people in Honduras know that PRODEPAH was really a private Washington-based company with a contract from the U.S. government to lobby and provide advice to the Honduran government?

"How much did this agricultural policy development project cost?" I asked.

"That contract? They have about—they have an $8 million contract. In addition to that, we have another $7 million to do a variety of other things with regard to Ag. Policy."

I was amazed at what I was hearing. If I understood correctly, the U.S. government paid a U.S. contractor, Chemonics, $8 million to set up an organization called PRODEPAH in Honduras, that, among other things, would work directly with Honduran government officials to put a new law into place; to implement the Ag. Modernization law. Wishing to be sure I was following Greg's description clearly, I asked, "It seems as if AID has a lot of influence in making Honduran public policy, then. Is that true? Are you saying AID is involved in making Honduran laws?"

Although I expected Greg to again downplay USAID's influence, instead he surprised me by emphasizing its role. "Well, I would say we have quite a bit of influence, particularly with the policy projects. It's sort of our role, really, to guide the policy discussion through UPSA. UPSA is in the Ministry of Natural Resources, and so they have legislative power. They can introduce legislation in Congress. PRODEPAH will draft what they call an 'anteproyecto,' or draft legislation. It will give the draft to UPSA. Then UPSA will refine it and pass it through the minister onto Congress. Congress, of course, can change things again, but you get the idea. We're writing the original draft. We've done this in a couple of cases. So we're able to be involved that way."

"How do the Honduran agencies view your involvement? Are there ever any conflicts?" I pursued.

Again to my surprise, he answered, "Not really because we're there at their request. I would say that we're all kind of operating from the same perspective.

AID, PRODEPAH, UPSA, and the current minister of natural resources—we all see the world in the same way. We're using the same kind of market language and we all have a basic understanding of where we want to go. And for that reason, I think the relations are very good. There haven't been any notable strains."

"How do you think AID compares with other development agencies working in Honduras. Is AID more influential in this way?"

Greg responded,

Well, a number of agencies are influential in this way. I just think AID does the best job. GTZ is doing a lot of policy work with the Honduran government as well. The problem with GTZ is that they don't have a business-minded philosophy that is consistent over time. Depending on the party that is in power in Germany, GTZ will often fall back into the old socialist models of doing things. That's a big problem for the UN agencies as well. I wouldn't work for the United Nations, like the UNDP. They're too state-focused, socialistic. And we've moved away from that model for a very good reason; it doesn't work. Yet there are a number of agencies that still operate using this model. Most of them work through SECPLAN, the Honduran Ministry of Planning. In my opinion, SEC-PLAN should be abolished.

Greg's proposing the elimination of a Honduran government agency provoked me to ask why.

He explained,

SECPLAN totally ignores market principles and really muddies the waters on a lot of reforms we are trying to put through. For example, SECPLAN has some ag. programs which are throwbacks to a socialist era: subsidized credit, price controls. These were proven to be faulty ideas because they don't help: they hurt, never help. Not only that, but they totally disregard the Ag. Modernization law. The Germans come in, do their work through SECPLAN. The Japanese come in, do their work through them, the UNDP comes in and does work through them, and, in many cases, their projects violate the Ag. Modernization law. Some of these agencies are coming around. But really what you're doing is creating conflict between the minister of SECPLAN and the Ministry of Natural Resources over agricultural policy because different agencies are pursuing different ideas.

I pictured the two Honduran government ministries, each with its contingent of foreign development agencies, fighting over which agricultural policy to pursue: SECPLAN with the GTZ, JICA, and the UNDP on its side; and the Ministry of Natural Resources with USAID on its. In light of Greg's enthusiasm for his point of view, I would be surprised if USAID wasn't on the winning side.

"What about the development banks? The World Bank? The Inter-American Development Bank?" I asked. "Where do they fit into the picture?"

"They're pretty influential, too. Very big. The problem with the big banks is that they just come in, tell the Hondurans how it should be done, and then leave a lot of debt behind. They don't have the intellectual mentoring that AID does."

I asked him what other development agencies in Honduras he felt were doing a significant job.

"Well, PAHO is doing a good job in health. And UNICEF kind of plays an important role on some of the child-survival and basic-education kinds of stuff. CARE is a good organization in terms of carrying out basic development work. But in my opinion, USAID has the best overall approach. We have a model that is the most systematic and scientific when it comes to actually creating a new policy environment in Honduras. We have the intellectual focus needed to connect Honduras to what's going on in the rest of the world." As he finished, Greg sat back in his chair and looked at his watch.

I thanked Greg for his orientation to USAID in Honduras. He shook my hand and escorted me back down to the guard booth, where I handed in my visitor's pass and went out the door.

As I walked along the street toward my car, my head was swimming with the details of all Greg had told me about USAID. I envisioned the agency as a large, complex organism, one that was thriving and growing. I imagined it reaching out to other complex organisms of various names: Chemonics, the U.S. Congress, the Honduran Ministry of Natural Resources, the WB, the UN, the GTZ. Together they formed a network of mutually interdependent organisms, an international network of institutions that governed Honduras.[27] It was a network that appeared to be highly efficient in carrying out whatever it wanted to accomplish.

I wanted to understand this network. USAID was just one organization, and I had dozens more to visit. Each would have its own set of institutional arrangements, personnel type, objectives and policies, and particular relationship with the Honduran government. Yet, they were all interconnected. There were direct ties through funding and subcontracting, but there were also indirect ties via common projects or common Honduran counterparts. Greg had given me a glimpse into this network, but his was only one point of view; and,

I realized, to fully perceive the development landscape in Honduras and understand this world unto itself, I had many more people to interview.

The network of international development organizations in Honduras is not easy to identify: there is no road map or diagram illustrating how the organizations are interrelated or which does what kind of project and which has the most money. There is no publication indicating which Honduran government agencies work with, say, the GTZ and which with USAID. My goal, therefore, was to try to find the connections.

To that end, I visited and became familiar with the numerous institutions that make up this world. I spoke with representatives of the UNDP and UNICEF, who were eager to tell me about their work. I visited the offices of NGOs such as Save the Children and FOPRIDEH. I called on the CARE offices, where, despite the initial suspicion that greeted me, I was invited to observe their work and speak with their employees. I also visited the lavish offices of the two main development banks, the IDB and the WB.

In all, I observed forty-eight development institutions in Honduras: ten bilaterals, six multilaterals, and thirty-one NGOs. In addition, I made sure to examine the most influential and powerful institutions in each category: the bilaterals USAID, GTZ, and JICA; the multilaterals UNDP, UNICEF, the EU, IDB, and WB; and the NGOs CARE, CRS, and World Vision. These agencies, together with others I did not directly study, form the institutional base from which globalization takes off. They finance and house the globalizers, to whom I shall now turn.

The connections among the international development organizations started to become visible to me through my relationships with friends and neighbors working within the various institutions, and these individual globalizers, the development workers themselves, are the focus of the three chapters that follow. Their perceptions of the development institutions they worked for allowed me, an outsider, to peek behind the scenes. Part 2 then offers a picture of what I saw: the globalizers in action.

Houston International Airport

© Stockyard Photos

CHAPTER TWO

The People

We do not really know who the planners are.
—A. F. ROBERTSON, 1984

The bilateral, multilateral, and NGO development institutions that have become part of the Honduran landscape during the past thirty years play a central part in promoting various global agendas throughout the country. But institutions do not function by themselves. They are created and maintained through the individual and collective action of human beings interacting with one another.

Employees of development agencies have, however, received little scholarly attention. As Robertson's quote suggests, we do not really know who these globalizers are. This gap in the research is mainly a result of most globalization scholars employing a macrolevel perspective that takes nations, corporations, or political economies as their units of analysis. Few researchers start at the individual level in analyzing globalization. Most current scholarship on globalization simply alludes to these individuals—the "experts and advisers" who promote globalization throughout the world—without fully addressing their importance.[1]

The first thing to realize is that these individuals live in an international space; as part of their work, they must undertake regular cross-border travel.

Consequently, an airport, a familiar place, is a good place to start when looking for globalizers and for seeing how their daily lives and activities make the larger processes of globalization possible.

Houston International Airport

Continental Airlines flight 1116 to Tegucigalpa, Honduras, leaves George Bush Intercontinental Airport every morning at 9:33. Each day, approximately 124 passengers make their way to gate C-23 at the end of concourse C. There they find a Boeing 737 waiting to take them on the three-hour trip to this small Central American country 1,206 miles away. In the crowded waiting area (the flight is usually full), one sees the usual array of jet travelers: well-dressed Honduran families with children saying good bye to relatives and loved ones, weighted down with shopping bags full of electronics and other consumer goods; tourist couples wearing Patagonia shorts, Tevas, and the latest in backpack technology; businessmen, both Honduran and gringo, dressed in guayabera shirts or suits, talking on cell phones, carrying briefcases and laptop computers.

In addition to these typical travelers, various missionary groups are also common. On my most recent trip to Honduras, there were three different evangelical missions on the plane. Each consisted of ten to twenty people wearing matching T-shirts emblazoned with colorful logos and hip motifs. Although missionaries have been traveling the globe for hundreds of years, the suburban, middle class, MTV fashion sense of these predominantly teenage travelers (along with the ubiquitous digital cameras and MP3 players) was entirely twenty-first century. From their Tommy Hilfiger jeans to their hundred-dollar Oakley sunglasses, these Christian evangelical teens were heavily laden with the same products of mass consumer culture as adorns the tourists, equips the entrepreneurs, and fills the shopping bags of the well-to-do Honduran families. I began to wonder whether such groups promote this consumer culture as much as they promote evangelical Protestantism.

Speaking with one of the teenage missionaries—a boy in a bright red T-shirt—from the Baptist "Sports and Play Mission" of Tennessee, the possibility seemed likely. When I asked him where his group was going, he responded, "I'm not really sure. I can't pronounce the name. . . . It's a little village in the countryside that my church knows. It's about three hours from Tegucigalpa."

"What's your group going to do there?" I asked.

He replied, "We're going to be giving them this baseball equipment that we have. We have a baseball team in our church and our team is going to play their team. But their village is too poor to buy gloves and balls and stuff, so we're going to give them all this equipment so they can play. I've never been there. But some people in my church have. It's like our sister congregation. We support them with food and stuff. I'm mostly going because of my friends. It's going to be fun! I've never gone to another country before."

I nodded, smiling slightly as I imagined a large group of American adolescents, baseball bats and Bibles in hand, descending upon a small village in rural Honduras. I pondered the implications of such an encounter. What would the rural villagers think of the large group of American teenagers and their designer clothes and digital cameras? How would the American teenagers react to the austere living conditions they were likely to find—no electricity, perhaps, no hot showers. What would these two very different communities from two markedly different social environments do together besides read the Bible and play baseball? And why baseball? Every rural town I had ever visited in Honduras had a community soccer field—not a baseball diamond.

"How about you? What are you going to Honduras for?" the boy asked, snapping me out of my daydream.

"Me? I'm going to do research. I'm a sociologist. I'm studying the aftermath of Hurricane Mitch," I responded.

"We learned about the hurricane, too," he said. "Our church sent down food and clothing to the village after the hurricane happened."

"Do you know those guys over there?" he asked, pointing toward two tall men dressed in white T-shirts and blue jeans. "They're going for Hurricane Mitch, too," he informed me. "Something about working on the roads that were damaged."

I looked more closely at the two men. They had light hair and appeared to be American, probably in their early forties, and despite their casual dress, they had an official air about them. As with the missionaries, their T-shirts revealed—though in a more understated way—the reason for their trip: "Rebuilding after Hurricane Mitch: U.S. Civil Engineering Team" was printed in small block lettering on the back of their shirts. I noticed, too, on the front pockets the small logo of USAID (United States Agency for International Development).

There they are, I thought, development workers. I knew a few of the subjects of my research—along with the Honduran families, tourists, entrepreneurs, and missionaries—were likely to be on the plane.[2] But they're often not as easy to spot in a crowd.

Associated with one type of development project or another, these international travelers earn a living by offering their technical and professional expertise to various institutions promoting development in countries like Honduras. Their services are in high demand, especially in times of national crisis such as the one facing Honduras after Hurricane Mitch (the subject of chapter 10). From what the young missionary had told me, I surmised these two men were probably contracted by USAID to do consulting on one of the numerous road-rehabilitation projects in Honduras being funded by the U.S. government. In 1999, the U.S. Congress donated $350 million for hurricane recovery and rehabilitation assistance. Fifty million dollars went toward repairs and reconstruction of 1,250 kilometers of roads.[3] As is the case with most "aid" given by wealthy countries to poor ones, much of this assistance profits the United States in various ways; in this instance, in the form of salaries and employment opportunities for U.S. civil engineers.

"Those are the kind of people I'm studying," I confessed to the teenager.

Transmigrants in a Global Age

This airport scene illustrates a new social phenomenon.[4] Dubbed "transnationalism" by sociologists, it refers to the recent growth of "activities that require continuous cross-border travel" and is defined as "the occupations and activities that require regular and sustained social contacts over time across national borders for implementation."[5] In other words, human beings are increasingly creating and maintaining relationships with one another beyond the borders of their own countries. The Honduran families visiting relatives in the United States are maintaining a transnational network. So are the teenage missionaries whose churches send groups on a regular basis to create and maintain a global connection between sister congregations. The development professionals, however, are perhaps the clearest example of transnationalism.[6] Their work requires sustained social contact across borders and regular international travel; they are, in effect, international migrant laborers.

Most discussions of international labor migration revolve around the experiences of migrants from less-developed countries traveling across national borders to find employment (usually in low-paid, low-skilled jobs) in developed countries. As a result, we know a lot about third world immigrants who come to first world countries such as the United States in search of economic opportunities. Sociologists have recently pointed out that, in contrast to earlier periods, many of these migrant workers maintain ties with their sending communities, often returning to their country of origin after working for a period of time. This cyclical pattern of migration differs from the earlier one of immigration and permanent settlement in the host country. This new pattern of migration is known as "transmigration," and the individuals who engage in this regular cross-border travel are called "transmigrants." Specifically, they are "people who live dual lives: speaking two languages, having homes in two countries and making a living through continuous regular contact across national borders."[7]

But what about migrant workers from developed countries? The two USAID civil engineers at the Houston airport prove that they indeed exist, that there are people from the wealthy countries traveling across national borders to find job opportunities in the developing world. These migrants, however, assume a strikingly different position in the global labor pool. In contrast to the low-skilled, low-wage workers from developing countries, first world migrant workers find their opportunities abroad in high-skilled, high-wage professional employment. The international labor migration of North American, Asian, and European professionals recruited and hired to work as managers and policy consultants in developing countries at high wages is, in the context of globalization scholarship, a neglected phenomenon. As I will describe, these international professionals are attracted by a relatively better living standard, the fun and adventure of working abroad, and the ability to live out certain political ideals in their work. International development professionals thus not only play a key part in globalization, but, exemplifying transnationalism themselves, they actually embody it. They are truly transmigrants in a global age.

The Globalizers

Development workers provide a unique window onto the very processes of globalization. They are crucial to any study of globalization because they are the ones creating, enacting, promoting, and maintaining global agendas in the developing world. For this reason, a new terminology is required. I use "development worker" to refer to the people who work as employees, consultants, and volunteers for the various international development agencies mentioned in the previous chapter, but they are also something else: they are "globalizers."[8]

Globalizers are individuals employed by an international or transnational organization in order to pursue their various professional activities on a global scale under the broadly conceived mission of promoting "development." This definition has two elements. The first is institutional: a globalizer *is employed* by an official development assistance agency (multilateral or bilateral) or a development NGO. As employees of these organizations, the globalizers are active agents in promoting the agencies' agendas. The other element of the definition is ideological: globalizers *believe* in the principles of development or adhere to the goal of bringing development to "underdeveloped" regions of the world through their work.[9] In so doing they promote a multiplicity of agendas on a global scale, viewing the entire developing world as their domain.

By using the word *globalizer* instead of *development worker,* I intend to shift the frame of analysis that has customarily been used to examine these professionals. Most research has studied development workers in terms of how effective or ineffective they have been in bringing development to the recipient countries. But I argue that "bringing development" is really something else. "Development" is a euphemism for a multiplicity of agendas being promoted by donor countries to advance their own interests globally. Therefore, development workers are agents of globalization. I believe the term *globalizer* provides us with a new lens onto the world of development that exposes previously unexamined dynamics of the international development profession. It helps to illustrate more accurately what "doing development" means. In particular, it allows us to see how the international development profession is linked directly to the processes of globalization. My argument is that these individuals are the architects of globalization in the developing world. Without them, globalization (as we currently understand it) would not be happening.[10]

Globalizers in Honduras

The globalizers in Honduras are not a disparate collection of individuals living independently and interacting only within the bureaucratic confines of their work for the development agencies that employ them. Rather, I found them to be a close-knit community: an international clique of sorts concentrated in little pockets around Tegucigalpa, with tendrils extending beyond the capital to every region of the country. Made up of expatriates and their Honduran colleagues, this development crowd is prominent on the Honduran social scene. They hobnob with the president and his ministers; they consult with the elite bankers and entrepreneurs from Honduras and abroad. Their faces often appear as part of front-page news. Making things happen at the highest level, the globalizers are real movers and shakers in the country. But they can also be found in the humblest areas of Honduran society. They work alongside community leaders in the poorest urban slums and in the most remote rural areas.

In other words, it is not hard to find development workers in Honduras. Their work carries them into every social sphere. This is something I quickly learned when I traveled there in 1995 to conduct the initial research for this book. As I tried to make sense of the international development profession in the country, several questions came to mind: What were all these development workers doing in Honduras? There were so many of them, working for so many agencies, and promoting so many different projects—what business did they have there? And how did they fit into the larger picture of globalization?

To address these and other questions, I conducted in-depth interviews in Honduras with fifty professional development workers during a ten-month stay in 1996 and another twenty during a one-month visit in 2001. They varied in terms of age, experience, nationality, profession, and organizational affiliation.[11] I also undertook ethnographic observation of development workers' lives during my two stays in the country. My direct interaction with development workers during these visits included living in an apartment building and a neighborhood where many other expatriates lived, observing the workplaces where development workers I knew were employed, and participating in many social events that included large numbers of development workers. As a result, I was able to conduct many informal interviews and collect numerous stories and accounts of development worker experiences that I later recorded and analyzed. Finally, I collected hundreds of documents and newspaper accounts related to the activities of development agencies in Honduras. These interviews, experiences, and documents form the empirical basis of this book.

What my study revealed is they are part of a global network of development professionals with a highly specialized role in the global political economy. Although the professionals I met and interviewed were located in Honduras, most of them had worked in other developing countries before coming to Honduras. I chose Honduras, therefore, not as an exceptional case, rather as an exemplary case, one with compelling similarities to other aid-recipient countries. Honduras is an example of the globalization occurring throughout the developing world. Although the particular configurations of that process are unique in each nation, the process itself is more general than this or any other single case. The globally mobile experts I encountered in Honduras are found throughout the developing world because their expertise is in increasing demand.

The Export of Experts

Historian Harold Perkin has observed that expertise is a scarce resource that, currently (in the postindustrial, information age), is in growing demand: "The modern world is the world of the professional expert. Just as pre-industrial society was dominated by landlords and industrial society by capitalists, so post-industrial society is dominated by professionals . . . who control the scarce resource of expertise in all its manifold forms."[12]

Perkin argues that the professional expert has risen to prominence in Europe and the United States, and he foresees these highly educated and trained experts becoming the most powerful group in society as keepers of the knowledge required to maintain today's high-tech computer-based, information-based institutions.

We are all growing increasingly dependent upon experts. But experts are expensive, and this shift toward a postindustrial society poses a problem for the developing world: how are the poorer countries going to be able to tap into this scarce resource of expertise when they cannot afford it, when there exists such a global inequality in the economic wherewithal to produce these experts?

Like many aid-recipient countries, Honduras lacks many of the resources required to produce the full gamut of modern professional experts: doctors, lawyers, engineers, scientists, economists, agronomists. Creating such experts is expensive, and the poor countries of the world often find it a challenge to do so, especially when it comes to producing highly specialized, state-of-the-art expertise. In order to run their private and public institutions in accordance with modern standards, which increasingly entails automation, computers, and the sophisticated creation and management of data, they must do two things: (1) send their best and brightest abroad to be trained, and (2) hire outsider expertise to consult and advise local professionals when necessary. International development organizations historically have filled this second role and often facilitated the first. But in the context of globalization, these institutions have become employment opportunities for both the foreign development experts and the local Honduran professionals, trained abroad or not.

Donor countries, on the other hand, have plenty of resources for creating the range of modern professional experts. The wealthy countries have the most advanced universities and research institutions and, as a result, churn out the most highly trained doctors, lawyers, engineers, scientists, economists, and agronomists in the world. It is an expensive undertaking, but the rich countries can afford it; plus, as I shall point out, it is ultimately in their best interest to do so.

At issue here is global supply and demand. In the international division of labor, the wealthy countries have specialized in producing Perkin's professional experts. With their universities and state-of-the-art scientific research facilities, they hold a comparative advantage in the production of professional expertise and high technology. Not only do they train professionals from their own countries, but they even train professionals from around the world, as the growing number of international students in U.S. and European institutions of higher learning can attest. In sum, wealthy countries, on the supply side, are exporters of experts.

On the demand side, it can be argued that, inasmuch as developing countries (especially those receiving development assistance) lack the resources to fully train their own cadre of professional experts in all fields, there is a demand for experts in the developing world. Honduras, for instance, would find it difficult to create and maintain state-of-the-art research facilities for hydroelectric engineering, nuclear engineering, or neurosurgery that could compete with similar institutions in wealthy countries. As a result, Honduras is an importer of experts.

This is the context in which the globalizers are produced. The international development profession acts as a sort of global rent-an-expert service. Development organizations work to facilitate the export of experts to the developing world, where their technological know-how and professional skills are in demand. The conceptual frame I use to analyze the development worker experience takes as its starting point this global supply and demand of expertise, the current structure of global human resources, and the system of global inequality that exists in terms of producing and using modern professional expertise.

Development organizations have been created in the donor countries over the last thirty years to serve this export purpose. Donor countries have trained their professionals in the latest techniques and skills for building bridges, running hospitals, planning cities, writing laws, raising crops, and managing banks efficiently and effectively. In addition, they have encouraged, by various means, their professionals to take these skills abroad: Donor countries have funded and promoted university curricula that educate students about such things as third world development, health care in tropical countries, and how societies can progress from one stage of development to another.[13] They have supported international exchange programs that train globalizers-to-be in foreign languages and cross-cultural tact. Finally, donor countries have taken public resources and invested in foreign aid, which provides professionals from the donor countries with opportunities to volunteer or become employed in development organizations.

Why would donor countries invest large amounts of public and private resources in creating experts who end up plying their trade abroad? At first glance, this might appear economically irrational because donor countries are expending valuable resources on training experts for the apparent benefit of other countries. Experts are expensive: why not save themselves the large expense and simply encourage those countries to train their own?

Likely there is something the donor countries are getting out of the deal: these countries use their global advantage in technical expertise to advance their own interests in the developing world; and the development experts donor countries create advance those interests in many ways. In particular, they get to set the terms on which global capitalism expands, terms that can be tilted to the donor countries' advantage. For example, development experts may advise a country to change its laws in a way that is conducive to the interests of transnational corporations based in those countries, or they might encourage the production of a crop in demand in the developed countries. For these advantages and others, donor countries are willing to pay a high price to create these experts and ship them around the planet.

These advantages also explain the importance of the veneer of beneficence. The veneer gives the appearance that this dispatch of experts to the third world is done out of the goodness of the donor countries' hearts (even contrary to these countries' own economic self-interest—a sacrifice). But this is not the case. Donor countries use their comparative advantage in professional and technical expertise to advance their own agendas in the developing world. The veneer of beneficence makes it hard to see the benefits flowing back to donor countries, and it gives the poor countries the appearance of being beneficiaries of development assistance. But, in fact, the real beneficiaries of development aid are the donor countries.

Making Globalizers

These macrolevel benefits are most clearly revealed by an examination of the experiences of individual globalizers, for they also benefit from this global system of unequal human resources and, as a consequence, end up working for and maintaining that system, whether consciously or not. Their experiences can, therefore, illuminate the larger institutionalized practices of the donor countries that foster globalization. By looking at how donor countries "make globalizers," we can begin to see how these countries promote certain agendas globally and how that promotion advances their own interests.

In exploring the role of development experts in the processes of globalization, my examination of the individual experiences of development workers (detailed in chapters 3 and 4) is framed by four key issues: (1) the system of socialization and education that allows the globalizers to acquire technical expertise, professional experience, and a pro-globalization, prodevelopment worldview; (2) the systems of rewards that motivate individuals to become involved in promoting global agendas; (3) the social networks and resources enabling the globalizers to be effective in promoting these agendas; and (4) the ultimate benefits donor countries receive through the work of the globalizers.

Systems of socialization and education. How are globalizers created within a system of social institutions, and how do they themselves participate in the process of self-creation as a "development worker"? I start with the basic sociological premise that human subjects are constituted within social relations. Development workers do not pursue their careers in a vacuum; they encounter a common set of educational opportunities that provide them training, skills, and benefits.

First, development workers acquire professional expertise from university education. This professional socialization is similar to that needed for a career in their own countries. What makes development workers unique is that they are often exposed to a process of training and socialization in the broad field of development. They enter the overarching ideology of development through either formal education in development issues (university course work, advanced degrees in development planning, development economics, etc.) or international development work experiences (volunteering, internships, or employment with international development organizations). Development workers learn from these experiences that globalization and development are good and right. Whether their professional expertise is in medicine, engineering, labor organizing, or urban planning, they unite around the ideology of third world development. As such, the international development profession can be thought of as a metaprofession: a profession of professions made up of experts from an array of technical backgrounds united under the same discourse of bringing this expertise to developing countries in the name of development.

Second, these international training experiences accustom development workers to the idea of living and working globally; they adopt a global worldview. They understand cross-border travel and the transnational relationships formed as a result of their work as normal and good. Another distinctive feature of development workers is their attunement to the idea that engaging in transnational activities is the wave of the future and that building international networks of people and institutions should be encouraged and expanded. They are involved in the normalization of global relationships.

Third, international development workers usually learn other languages and often undergo training in cross-cultural tact and awareness. These skills are also acquired by either formal education or on-the-job experience working in an international development organization. These systems of socialization and education as a whole give the globalizers a common set of skills and beliefs and a common professional outlook.

Systems of rewards. How are globalizers (foreign or Honduran) motivated to participate in and promote a global agenda in the developing world? International development organizations provide important rewards in an effort to attract professionals to their work.

First, globalizers generally receive good salaries for their work. Although foreign globalizers make more than their Honduran counterparts, both receive attractive compensation in comparison with what they could make in nondevelopment-related employment. Foreign workers are usually paid the same as (or sometimes less than) what they would earn working in their country of origin. Foreign development workers often accentuate the sacrifice involved in earning a little bit less for their professional services in the developing world by emphasizing the hardship of development work. Nevertheless, this lower salary is often supplemented with additional "difficulty pay" many development agencies offer to motivate first world professionals to live and work in particularly poor or conflict-ridden areas of the world. Furthermore, earning a first world wage while living in a developing country is an additional bonus: many foreign development workers I spoke with mentioned that they could afford a luxurious home, gardeners, cooks, and maids and still save a considerable amount of their salary for their return home.

In addition to attractive salaries, working for a development organization often involves perks such as access to vehicles and chauffeurs, free housing, and free private education for children. Foreign development workers thus often realize a higher standard of living than they would back home. Honduran workers, for their part, are usually paid a much higher salary than what they could earn in nondevelopment-related employment in Honduras. Sometimes they are paid in foreign currencies (e.g., U.S. dollars) that are more stable than the local lempira. Nevertheless, they usually earn significantly less than their foreign counterparts, even for performing the same tasks in many cases.

In addition to these extrinsic rewards, globalizers are also motivated by a number of intrinsic benefits from development work. Many foreign development workers are attracted by the travel, fun, and sense of adventure it promises. They have the opportunity to spend their careers traveling to remote regions of the world, experiencing a wide variety of languages, cultures, and scenic locations. Others mention the importance of feeling a strong sense of purpose in their work: helping the poor in the less-developed countries is associated with contributing to a greater good. The satisfaction this gives some development workers should not be underestimated. In sum, globalizers are motivated by good salaries, perks, a sense of adventure, and a feeling of purposefulness.

Access to resources and networks. What allows the globalizers to effectively promote global agendas in the developing world? Besides the individual talents and skills acquired through their professional and intellectual formation, globalizers receive, via their affiliated institutions, both globally and locally, technological and material resources and entrée to networks of powerful interests. The more powerful the institution, the more easily the globalizers can promote their organizations' global agendas.

In the case of Honduras, the globalizers, as employees of international development organizations, have access to million-dollar budgets that are striking in the Honduran context. They not only furnish the globalizers with significant technological and material resources, but also give them the ability to hire even more personnel (both foreign and local) with which to develop and promote their specific agendas. This is often done through subcontracting to local institutions.

In addition, the globalizers' institutional positions give them access to powerful local and global interests. Development workers are connected to the transnational networks of official development aid; in particular, they are institutionally linked to key gatekeepers and levers of power within the global development apparatus, which allows them to secure (or shut off) important resources (capital and information, in particular). The globalizers can bring these powerful transnational networks to bear on the local Honduran scene in ways their Honduran counterparts often cannot.

The globalizers are also connected locally. Their institutional affiliation puts them in contact with powerful Honduran networks (in both the private and public sectors). They may even have access to Honduran officials at the highest level of government. They often interact with representatives of the most powerful local business or civic organizations. Moreover, many development agencies solidify these connections with powerful Honduran networks by hiring individuals from these networks as consultants or employees and, in that way, turning these Honduran professionals into globalizers, too.

Donor-country benefits: These three institutionalized practices that shape the globalizers' experiences—education and training, rewards, and access to powerful networks—do not benefit only the individual globalizers and the developing countries that receive their work. These practices also greatly benefit the donor countries.

The donor countries receive direct economic benefits by sending their professionals abroad. Such benefits include job opportunities for their citizens and contracts for their firms. A clear example of this is the bridge-building contracts awarded to the major donor countries in the aftermath of Hurricane Mitch (see chapter 10).

Second, the globalizers' activities grant donor countries many indirect economic and political benefits, such as access to markets, wealth, natural resources, and political power and control. An analysis of the *maquiladora* industry in Honduras and how the construction of these factories benefited first world apparel producers is a case in point (see chapters 8 and 9).

Also, the globalizers pave the way for the expansion of other donor-country agendas. In addition to their commercial agendas, donor countries promote such global scripts as environmentalism, feminism, and labor and human rights. Although they may not appear to be based on self-interest, it is usually the organizations and individuals from the developed countries that shape the scripts and define these global social movements in conjunction with donor-country priorities.

Finally, by sending globalizers out into the developing world, donor countries eventually acquire an even larger knowledge base from which to build expertise and train more development experts. The globalizers' experiences form the basis of new master's theses, dissertations, professional journal articles, and books that are then housed in donor countries' libraries and read by future development workers. These resources constitute specialized knowledge about developing countries that is increasingly monopolized by developed countries.[14] The World Bank's annual reports, for example, written by international experts and published in Washington, D.C., are used as the basis for policy making throughout the developing world. Although the production of this kind of information is not inherently problematic, it is important to be aware of who controls it. As the work of Michel Foucault reminds us, knowledge ultimately leads to the power to control and the power to exploit.[15]

The institutionalized practices of the globalizers and their benefits to donor countries form the framework for my analysis of the experiences of the development workers I interviewed in Honduras. In the two chapters that follow, I highlight the careers of two globalizers, one foreign and one Honduran. Their stories illustrate not only the similarities and differences between the careers of the typical expatriate and Honduran development professional, but also the key part that globalizers play in promoting globalization on behalf of donor countries.

Expatriate Volunteer in Intíbuca, Honduras

Photo: Amigos de las Americas

CHAPTER THREE

The Expats

La Leona

"You should definitely stay in La Leona—it's where many of the expatriates live," the e-mail read. It was a response from a Honduran man to a query I had sent to several Honduran e-mail groups in my search for a place to stay in Tegucigalpa. He told me that the apartment owner, Florencia, worked for a Honduran NGO and "preferred to rent to aid workers."

I wasn't too surprised, then, to find when I arrived that many of my neighbors were not Honduran. One, a Swiss woman, worked with Cosude, the Swiss development agency. Her boyfriend, a Spaniard, lived across the street and worked for Cooperación Española, the Spanish development agency. Next door was a Canadian woman who worked with the Canadian NGO Center of International Cooperation and Study. Down the road lived an American working for the United Nations Children's Fund (UNICEF); two Belgians and a Swede who volunteered for the Honduran NGO Fundación Hondureña de Rehabilitación e Integración del Limitado (FUHRIL, an agency that works with disabled children); a Canadian historian from Yale studying the Honduran campesino movement; and an American artist on a Fulbright. I was not only studying globalization, I was living it. This microcosm of globalization in Honduras was my entrée to the world of development.

They referred to themselves as "expats" (expatriates), and I soon discovered the moniker was more than just a convenient abbreviation: it was an identity. It expressed the kinds of experiences that a whole group of individuals were going through living and working in the developing world. True, they came from different countries and worked for different agencies, but I began to understand that they traveled in the same social circles; they were a cohesive group, a community of sorts. I began to think of them as "the development set."[1]

How does someone become a globalizer? I present the experiences of one expatriate development worker, Elaine van Royan, in some detail to highlight the common themes among development professionals and show the process of how people become globalizers and thus agents of globalization in Honduras. As I mentioned, I describe the experiences of the expats and their involvement in the promotion of globalization in the framework of systems of socialization and education; system of rewards; access to resources and powerful networks; and benefits to the donor countries.

Elaine van Royan: Water and Sanitation Civil Engineer for UNICEF

When I called Elaine to set up an interview, she suggested that, rather than doing the interview in her office, I come to her house for dinner instead. So along with my tape recorder, I took a bottle of wine I had purchased at Mas por Menos (one of a growing number of American-style supermarkets in Tegucigalpa) and headed toward Colonia Palmira, one of Tegucigalpa's wealthier neighborhoods where many development workers live.

Elaine was twenty-nine years old and a citizen of the Netherlands. This was her first time living in Honduras, where she had served three and a half months of her two-year contract as a technical adviser to UNICEF's water and sanitation program. Like most of the development workers I met, Elaine had lived in a number of developing countries prior to arriving in Honduras. She had been in Sri Lanka four months as an intern with an NGO, two years in Guyana as a junior technical assistant in a European Union (EU) development assistance program, and one year in Chile as a technical assistant.

She explained that she had always wanted to "work in development," ever since she was six or seven years old: "It was in primary school . . . we learned a lot about problems in other countries, and I thought, 'OK, that's where I want to work.' . . . What always attracted me was the social part of the work . . . that I would be able to do something worthwhile. I always felt that there was not much for me to do in my own country—it was already so developed."

During high school and college, Elaine pursued architecture, then civil engineering. "But I always had a focus on developing countries," she added. "Within architecture, I had a specialization in building for developing countries. Then when I switched to civil engineering, I followed the courses you could take in respect to development issues and became involved with a group of students called 'Civil Engineers for Developing Countries.' The university Elaine attended in the Netherlands had a history of emphasizing development issues in what she referred to as "the tropics": "My university has existed for the last one hundred seventy years and, traditionally, has a link with tropical countries . . . Indonesia, with the West Indies. And almost all the teachers in this university have worked in the tropics. As a matter of fact, part of a normal career for a civil engineer in Holland is to work abroad for a couple of years. So almost everybody has this experience. And I think for me it was quite a good preparation."

Her university gave Elaine her first experience living and working abroad, in Sri Lanka as an intern with a Dutch NGO involved in promoting rural water projects. In reply to my question of what she found significant or meaningful about her experience there, Elaine replied, "For me it was really the first time being in the tropics, being so far from my country. And trying to work there was sometimes very frustrating."

When I asked what she had found frustrating, she explained, "Well, we lived in the countryside and everything there was just so slow. But actually the main problems we had were with the professional development workers . . . with the other Dutch people there. I just found it difficult."

Most non-Honduran development workers I interviewed indicated their first experiences abroad represented profound moments in their lives, personally and professionally. Their stories often conveyed experiences of culture shock, logistical mishaps, and personal suffering or hardship. They were often the tales of relatively affluent individuals from wealthy countries witnessing firsthand the poverty in the developing world. Despite these difficulties, development workers usually viewed these first encounters in a highly positive light; it was the time when they "cut their teeth." These volunteer experiences were significant not only because they gave development workers professional, hands-on experience and skills at running particular development projects; they were also symbolically important. By volunteering, these individuals acted out the ideals of aid and assistance. Offering their time and professional expertise (however embryonic), they embodied the notion of generosity inherent in the development discourse. As a result, they came to view themselves through the veneer of beneficence described earlier. Individual development workers seemed to deal with this issue differently: some embraced it wholeheartedly, whereas others dismissed it as naive or idealistic and adopted more pragmatic or even cynical views of the development work they did.

To gain an idea of how Elaine viewed her early experience in Sri Lanka, I asked if she could describe any difficulties she had had.

"Well, I don't know . . ." she began, "actually, it was very mixed. I mean, we did a lot of nice, interesting work. We did some evaluation of existing rural water projects and how they were functioning . . . how successful they were. And now, with the experience that I have at this point, I think this was really good because I know how important it is to have a proper evaluation of the things you're doing."

She continued, "But I learned a lot about the problems of this kind of work, too. Like, as volunteers for only four months, we were probably more of a nuisance than a help. I mean, first of all, they hardly knew we were coming. This Dutch guy was there and was supposed to be our supervisor, but he wasn't very interested in cooperating with us. He felt a little bit like, 'What am I supposed to do with these two young, stubborn ladies from Holland trying to participate in this project they don't really know about?' So we were searching for another project and someone else who could supervise us. Things like that . . ."

"Also," she went on to explain,

we had living difficulties. We had to live in kind of a community center with about forty Sri Lankan people. And the first couple of weeks they put us in a corridor which had five doors and no windows. It was so terrible! It was just a hallway. So you learn about these kinds of difficulties. And what I really learned there was a little bit about myself. I mean we didn't have anything. We didn't have our own transportation, of course. And I thought, "OK, I like to live abroad. I like to work as a development worker. But on the one condition that I have some of these things. That I earn enough to rent my own place, to buy my own way of transportation, to find a place where, when I come home from the office, I can close myself off and live the life that I lead." Because you can never change into an Asian or a Latin American. You need to have the possibility to fall back into your own culture from time to time.

Her Sri Lankan experience, Elaine suggested, had given her the opportunity to come to this realization: "I think for me it was very good to make a decision early about how I want to work and how I do not want to work."

After Sri Lanka, Elaine returned to her university to get a master's degree in civil engineering (with a specialization in water and sanitation). Upon graduation, she entered a special program sponsored by the Dutch government that recruited and trained professionals interested in working in foreign assistance. The program, called the "associate expert program," was coordinated by the Dutch Ministry of Development Cooperation. Elaine explained that "it's a program for young people where the Dutch government is financing you for five or six years to work for different Dutch development projects. You work in a number of areas within international cooperation and learn where you might fit in, and the government pays your salary."

Government programs such as this one were another common experience among the development workers I interviewed. It was especially common for European development workers, like Elaine, to have been sponsored by their own government at one time or another in their careers. Usually these programs were coordinated in cooperation with developing countries that were former colonies or with which the European nations enjoyed trade relationships. The United States (through its Peace Corps program) provides a similar opportunity, but on a volunteer basis.[2] The Netherlands paid Elaine a professional, entry-level civil engineer's salary for her work in this program. Such programs serve the purpose of channeling professionals into foreign assistance work when they might otherwise pursue career opportunities in their own countries.

Elaine explained that her first job with the program—which took her to her next developing country, Guyana—was working with a delegation from the EU monitoring the implementation of programs associated with the Lomé Convention, a special treaty (signed in Lomé, capital of Togo) the EU created with many of the former colonies in Africa, the Pacific, and the Caribbean. The EU had allocated about $38 million to implement in Guyana over a five-year period various development grants and projects associated with the convention. Elaine was part of a larger delegation sent there to monitor the success of these projects.

When I asked Elaine what she had found valuable about her experience in Guyana, she responded, "As a development worker? Well, looking back I think mainly I learned about the bureaucratic part. The implementation part. Political things. I learned very much about how to make links with other organizations . . . other development work. I mean, I would say 'the game.' *I learned the game there.* How to play it, how to do it."[3]

I pressed her to elaborate what she meant by "the game."

She explained, "Well, on a lower level, I learned the basics of doing development work. As a junior assistant I had to help out with all the details of running the program. So I learned the game of contracting people, working with consultants, writing evaluations, setting up meetings, and coordinating all the various programs. All these things. I mean, it's really a game you have to learn."

She continued,

> But I think it was also more on the political level that I learned the most. Before Guyana, I had not worked with the local government on that level. And that was really the advantage of working in a small country. I mean, we had weekly meetings with the government ministers. With the Lomé treaty, we were often discussing the amount of funds to be allocated. The treaty says that the local government is supposed to decide what they are going to spend it on. The EC gives its approval, but it isn't supposed to tell the country how to spend the money. But, of course, we didn't want the money to go to certain things . . . certain types of purchases. So we were trying to influence them to make sure the money wasn't being spent for someone's own personal benefit. So this was very political. We would try to make sure the money was being spent on the right things. I was just a junior person, so I wasn't really involved. But sometimes it's good when you're in a junior position because you don't have to speak, you can just observe—observe and see what's the game.

Elaine's description illustrates how professional development workers must learn to negotiate the complex networks of institutions surrounding most development projects. The development "game," as she refers to it, involves becoming proficient at managing the interpersonal and institutional relationships forged among donor agencies, subcontractors, local government agencies, and their officials. Development workers learn how to bridge the large transnational entities they work for (in this case, the EU) and the local political-economic scene (the other development agencies operating in Guyana and the Guyanese government). They must set up meetings, negotiate, draw up contracts, formulate plans, and so on—all the while remaining sensitive to the politics (globally and locally) such negotiations entail. According to Elaine, this is not a skill that can be taught in school but is something one has to learn through direct, on-the-job experience.

Elaine's story also makes clear that the "game" includes learning who is in charge. Under the Lomé treaty, the local Guyanese government was given control over how development funds were to be spent. But, as her account makes apparent, the development agencies can effectively manipulate the process to ensure that the "right things" are done with the money. Elaine interprets this as a way of preventing corruption, but much of the "very political" work globalizers do involves meeting with and lobbying local government officials to give priority to the agendas of the development agencies. The rules of the game indicate those giving the money have the greatest say in how it is spent. These often subtle dynamics of power—what I refer to as "garnering consent"—are explored further in the second part of the book.

Elaine spent two years in Guyana. Under the Dutch government's associate expert program, after two years in one place development workers are assigned to a different posting. Elaine was posted to Chile, this time to work with one of the UN programs. Whereas Elaine described her experience with the EU in Guyana as a positive and productive one, her stint in Chile was a disaster.

According to Elaine, the problems started her first day when she was told by her new boss that he didn't have anything for her to do. She explained, "He told me that he had applied for me to be hired but that it would be a while before he had something specific for me to do. He said, 'Just try to find something for yourself to do in the meantime.' So for two months I was paid for doing nothing. Absolutely nothing."

She laughed as she recalled the experience: "Everyone in that office started late. We used to start officially at nine, but I would come in at a quarter to ten. Then we would all go down to the canteen, take a coffee. We wouldn't do anything until 10:30 or 11:00, at which point it was almost time for lunch. It was ridiculous. This was the most ridiculous office you can imagine."

Describing her frustration at the time, she continued, "I was mad because . . . I mean, I don't come to a country just to do nothing! And I didn't like the whole complacent atmosphere in the office. I like to work. But everyone was telling me to be quiet. 'Don't complain, just accept it and sit there.'"

Within her first two weeks on the job, Elaine faxed the Netherlands asking to be transferred. After several months of back-and-forth, she was transferred to another UN unit in Chile. "But," Elaine declared, "the other unit was even worse."

"How so?" I asked, "I mean, your impression of the UN must have been kind of bleak at this point."

"It was!" Elaine exclaimed, her initial outrage rising as she spoke.

They were making things up for me to do. It was the most ridiculous thing. This was the most ridiculous institute within the UN that you can imagine. I don't understand why any country is spending money on this total bullshit. People doing studies on studies without any social relevance . . . or economic relevance, or anything! People just sit in their office and think, "Oh, I'm now going to study this or that." . . . Then you work three years on it and you write your report or an article, and that's it. It's a total waste of money. I don't mind when people do studies where there is some kind of demand for the information. But these studies are so general, without any details, that nobody can ever use them in the field. It's a waste, . . . a total waste of money.

Many of the globalizers I interviewed confessed they were aware of the bureaucratic waste often characterizing development agencies. Although waste is commonly associated with bureaucratic organizations, it is often overlooked in the case of development organizations because of the veneer of beneficence that shields development workers and their institutions from criticism.

Ultimately, Elaine chose to leave this situation and convinced her Dutch sponsors to transfer her to another position outside Chile. When I asked Elaine if, given her negative experience with the UN organization in Chile, she had any concerns about transferring to UNICEF in Honduras, she replied, "Well, after Chile I really did have concerns. And I considered changing organizations to go work for an NGO or something."

"Are there any organizations that you wouldn't work for?" I asked.

"I wouldn't work for a development organization who has missionary work as one of its main objectives. I also probably wouldn't want to work for some of the big development banks like the World Bank or the Inter-American Development Bank. I'd have to work too much with economists . . . dictating all sorts of economic policy for the country. I hate economists."

I asked her why.

"They think they know everything about the world. How it works. They think everything turns around money. . . . But there are some things that are more important . . . things that have a social impact as well as an economic impact. And to me, development isn't just economics. Personally, I think the social part is more important."

I asked Elaine to explain this distinction between the work of economists and the social part of development work in terms of her work as a water and sanitation engineer—did she have a specific example?

The social impact means . . . I mean, when you go to these purely urban areas in Tegucigalpa, it's so hilly! People have to walk five hundred meters uphill! And these ladies walk uphill and come back, children too . . . especially children, with buckets on their heads. And they do this every day ten times. I mean, have you ever tried to walk uphill to collect water? Or can you imagine a seven-year-old child . . . who has only eaten two tortillas for breakfast? Can you imagine what a gigantic impact this has on the people? Every morning, seven days a week they are busy collecting water. Children have to stay out of school because they have to help their mothers with fetching water. Supplying water there has a gigantic social impact! An economist might say, "Oh, but these people might not be able to pay for this water system if we put it there. It might not be economically sustainable." They will want to charge a fair market price for the water. I say, 'We have to find another way.' I don't care if the market doesn't quite work. I don't care if they view our projects as effectively a government subsidy. I think water is essential for everybody . . . every human being. On that social level it has a gigantic impact.

Providing running water to every human being is the global agenda Elaine is employed to promote. She also personally believes that water is a universal human right, and her role as a development worker is advancing that belief on a global scale. Although important to UNICEF as an organization and to Elaine as a professional, this agenda is not ranked at the top of the hierarchy of globalization agendas. She points to the stark contrast between her view of water provision as a social need and that of the economists, who may often frame water as a free-market commodity, and her hostility toward the economists' worldview indirectly reveals that the economists occupy a dominant position within development institutions, and that some development agendas are more powerful than others. It is clear from other examples in this chapter that Elaine's organization is powerful in the developing world, but it is important to note that she views herself as the underdog in this case. Her criticism of the economists suggests that global agendas supported by free market logic are hegemonic while hers are subordinate in the development industry at large.

I asked Elaine if her ideological commitment to working on social issues was the main reason she took the job with UNICEF in Honduras. She replied, "Yeah, things like that are important to me . . . but I have to say also I was in a luxurious position of receiving a nice job offer. When you receive a fax from Dutch cooperation saying, 'OK, you can start, with a nice salary, we financed two years for you,' it's difficult to say no. But I do think UNICEF is one of the most interesting UN organizations."

When I asked her why, she explained that UNICEF had a much better reputation than other UN organizations. In part, she attributes this to UNICEF raising much of its own funds from selling postcards and other merchandise, making it less dependent upon contributions from donor countries.

In addition, Elaine liked UNICEF's clear mission: "I think the main thing is that it is one of the few UN organizations that really has a message. It really has something to do . . . a clear task that is indisputable in almost all the world."

I asked what she thought that task was.

"Working for children. Working for children's rights. Working for families and trying to improve their situation. I mean there are only a few people in the world who would fight against that, no?"

Elaine proceeded to tell me more about her current work with UNICEF in Honduras. She was hired, she explained, as the director of the agency's Water and Sanitation Program. Its main focus was to provide running water primarily to urban communities. The program originated in 1987 in coordination with SANAA, the Honduran national water authority. The idea was that communities wishing to have a water system installed in their neighborhood but could not afford to pay the normal cost for the installation could apply for UNICEF's assistance.

Elaine emphasized that one of the strengths of the program is that the community itself must initiate the process: "The good thing about our project is that everything starts up through community participation. The community or representatives of the community go to SANAA and apply for the program. They say, 'OK, we want to be a beneficiary of the UNICEF program.'"

Once approved for the program, communities are normally asked to provide the labor (to dig the trenches and lay the pipes) and some locally available materials (such as sand and bricks). UNICEF provides the concrete, pipes, and other technology that is often imported from abroad (such as pumps). SANAA engineers usually design the project in coordination with UNICEF engineers and with economic support from UNICEF.

Although UNICEF pays for some of the more expensive design work and technology associated with putting in a water system, Elaine was quick to point out that it is not a giveaway. She explained, "The good thing about this program is that it's not for free. They get it as a kind of a loan. We look at how much the community can truly afford and present them with a 'revolving fund' schedule. The people pay something every month, and this money is put into a bank account. Part of it is used to run the offices of the 'conjunta de agua'— the water board for their community—and part of it goes to pay off the loan they've received for the construction of the project. In some cases, we subsidize quite a bit. In other cases, the community pays for almost all of the costs eventually. In some cases, the funds generated by the initial project allowed the community to extend the public standpipes (which had to be shared) so they could all have in-house connections. That was a very successful case."

Elaine added that, although urban water supply projects were the main focus of UNICEF's water and sanitation program, it was in the process of setting up a similar program for rural communities. It was also doing more in the area of sanitation, such as constructing sewage systems and latrines in these same communities.

Hoping to find out more about what Elaine actually did in her position, I asked, "In terms of your day-to-day work in the office, what kinds of things keep you busy? What specific tasks occupy your time?"

Well . . . I suppose I'm ultimately the one responsible for just making sure things run smoothly, . . . trying to coordinate with our counterparts . . . with SANAA, making sure all the construction things go smoothly. That's one thing. But also, I think a very important task is to try to set up some new programs. We're trying to set up some new models and trying to expand our activities. And I think in that respect, at the initial stage of a project, I have gathered quite a bit of experience over the years and can help with that. My colleague is a Honduran engineer and he knows the local situation very well. I know the international situation. I know what works internationally and what doesn't work internationally. Because I've seen some things in Chile or in Sri Lanka or in Guyana. And I think, "Why can't we try to do this too?" Or "No, I've seen that this won't work . . . perhaps we should do something else."

Elaine's statement revealed her perception that the roles of foreign and Honduran development workers differed; the international development worker, in this case, seemed to have the ultimate say regarding what would work and what wouldn't.

Elaine paused for a moment before continuing, "Now if you were to ask me about my day today, however, I was doing something different. Today I was busy setting up a big national seminar on health education. We're going to be sponsoring it and people will be coming from outside Honduras to contribute to the conference. Another thing is that there are always a lot of people . . . other donors . . . other agencies, coming in to meet with you or ask you for information."

"So you interact pretty regularly with other development agencies?"

"Definitely. That's a big part of the job. Sometimes people just want to learn about what we're doing . . . so we'll make a field visit to check out some of the projects we've been working on. We have to meet with donors . . . meet with evaluators. Like Sweden . . . the water project is financed by the Swedish government. Then others come because they want to work with us on something. For example, the people from Japanese Cooperation come and say they also want to do something on water and sanitation. Then we might start working on a deal with them."

"The Japanese government wants to become a donor for this project?" I asked.

"Not exactly, they want to emulate our project and offer a similar one on their own. I mean, they are interested in financing SANAA's urban water projects, but they want to do them through their own agency. They have a lot more money than UNICEF and so they are taking over part of the program in order to expand it more broadly. But we were there to develop the model, and now they're like, 'OK, we see this is successful in Tegucigalpa,' and they take much of it over because they have much more funds than we have. But it makes me feel good because they are expanding upon our model."

Elaine's position clearly gave her access to powerful networks on the Honduran scene, and her regular coordination, as part of her job, with numerous international development organizations as well as the local SANAA put Elaine and UNICEF in a good position to successfully advance their political project, exemplified in this case by the Japanese adoption of the UNICEF water system model.[4]

"How about your performance?" I asked. "Who is evaluating you?"

Elaine responded, "Well, officially—according to my contract—I am under a six-month probationary period. After six months, they normally write an evaluation report on your performance and then renew your contract. But in my case, since I am financed through my own government, it doesn't cost UNICEF anything. It would be very strange for them to say, 'OK, we don't like this lady, please send her back to Holland.' I would have to do something really bad for that to happen."

Most UNICEF workers, she explained, are paid from UNICEF general funds, and so her position is somewhat exceptional in this regard. Curious if this created any problems of accountability, I asked, "So what does that mean in terms of who you feel accountable to? Do you feel more accountable to UNICEF in Honduras or to Dutch Cooperation, who is paying your salary?"

"Well, I don't know exactly. I suppose it is both. I mean, I am working really for both organizations. I am kind of in the middle. Also, because much of our financing is through donors, like Sweden . . . and these donors do evaluations, I suppose I feel like I have to meet certain expectations from them."

"How about Honduras? Is your work, or the work of UNICEF, evaluated by Hondurans?" I asked.

She seemed a little confused by my question, "The Honduran government or . . . Honduran staff? I mean the majority of my colleagues are Hondurans."

"I mean," I clarified, "for UNICEF working in Honduras. Do either the government or the citizens have input into the UNICEF process? How is UNICEF accountable to them?"

"Actually, I don't know exactly. Now the government has a five-year plan, a 'master plan,' which is sort of an agreement between UNICEF and the Honduran government. But what I feel is a little strange within UNICEF is that they don't really have a legal agreement. What I've seen in other organizations is that you sign a contract. The government has its obligations and you have yours. But UNICEF doesn't do it that way here. What happens is that the government comes to us and says, 'OK, we want this and this and this,' and UNICEF says yes or no. But after that, there isn't really any evaluation."

Elaine's confusion regarding accountability was a common theme in the interviews. The confusion may stem from globalizers being situated in a position where they are accountable to multiple institutions simultaneously: donor countries, development agencies, the recipient government, and the direct beneficiaries of the project. Although Elaine (and many globalizers) felt accountable to all these groups, in reality there was little accountability to the local institutions. Elaine felt primarily responsible to the Dutch government, which paid her salary (though even this accountability seemed remote to her). There did not seem to be a mechanism in place for the Hondurans whom she serves to evaluate her work in a way that would affect her employment.

"Do you consider your job to be well paid?" I asked.

"Yes. I mean, it's the worst paid job I've had so far in development work, but it's still very good pay," she answered.

"How much do you make, if you don't mind my asking?"

"Uh . . . about four thousand dollars a month," she replied. This was a pretty typical salary for the foreign development workers I interviewed.

Asked if this were comparable to what her Honduran colleagues made, she answered, "Well, no. It's about the same, but I have some allowances for renting a house, some travel. . . . I get one ticket to Holland in two years, which is not too much. I think the Hondurans here make about two thousand or twenty-five hundred dollars. That sounds like a lot less, but I am in a lucky situation that my colleagues have good salaries—especially for Honduran standards."

I had discovered from other interviews that the issue of salary disparities between Honduran professional workers and their foreign counterparts was a touchy subject. Foreign development workers were usually paid in dollars and often according to what they could earn professionally in their country of origin. On top of that, they often received bonuses such as rent-free apartments, housing allowances (as did Elaine), tuition for their children to attend top-notch private schools in town, and free use of vehicles. Honduran employees of international development organizations such as UNICEF, on the other hand, were paid in lempiras, and their salaries were determined by the local Honduran labor market. As a result, they were often much lower than the pay of their foreign counterparts doing the same job—usually less than half. Some Honduran development professionals made only 10 percent of what their foreign counterparts earned. These benefits and perks are part of the system of rewards meant to attract foreign professionals to development work in a country such as Honduras and give them a comfortable life there.

Wondering how Elaine viewed this issue, I asked, "How do you deal with the issue of earning a first-world professional salary in a country like Honduras where the average income is so low comparatively?"

"Well, like I said before, I am in a good situation because most of my colleagues earn a good wage. But actually, I never tell anybody how much I earn. And I don't tell them that I save most of the money I earn. I don't talk about it. Of course, we live in a luxurious house and we have a very comfortable life here . . . but I've learned to live with it."

I pushed a little further, "You say you don't talk about it with your colleagues. Why is that?"

Elaine sighed, and after a pause, responded,

Because I've learned that it's better not to talk about it. They can't understand everything about the situation. They can't compare it with what I would have earned in Holland, which, by the way, would have been an enormous salary compared to what I make here. Also, if we were in Holland, we would have a lot of tax benefits, we would have bought our own house; we would have paid many years on the house loan. There are many things that they wouldn't understand. Plus, they are making good salaries at UNICEF. Our Honduran engineers make much more than the government employees. They make about two thousand dollars—a SANAA engineer only earns about three hundred dollars a month.

"Wow—what do you think about that?"

Well, of course this is a problem. When I see professional engineers who are very qualified people that earn only three hundred dollars a month . . . I'm surprised. Mostly, I'm surprised they're still working for that. But, are they the fools or am I the fool? And then maybe I don't know the whole situation. I have learned through the years that these government employees possibly have only three hundred dollars from SANAA, but they have their own *finca* [farm], they have inherited three houses from their parents, and they rent two out to foreigners, where they make another fifteen hundred dollars a month. I mean, not to defend myself but . . . but some people easily have three houses. I don't know how it is in the States, but in Holland, you don't generally find people who have three houses. So sometimes you can't judge.

The expatriates had many justifications for the wage gap between themselves and their Honduran coworkers. Some, like Elaine, emphasized the amount of money they would be making if they worked in their own country. Others pointed to the unique difficulties involved with working and living abroad, for which they felt they should be compensated. It is important to recognize that these explanations are not simply generated by individual development workers but are embedded in the institutions for which they work. The worker categories (e.g., expatriate or in-country) and pay scales are organized according to an understanding that international development workers are more valuable than local counterparts. For most of the foreign globalizers I interviewed, the compensation they received for their work was a nonissue. Not that they are unaware they are at the high end of the pay scale, or oblivious of the disparity being a sensitive issue with their Honduran colleagues; expatriate globalizers simply take their privileged status for granted. As I will show in the next chapter, this is certainly not the case for the Honduran development workers.

I asked Elaine to talk a little bit about her experience living in Honduras as a foreigner. She said she sometimes felt, as "blond and white," conspicuous and out of place, and that even though she was "kind of used to being different," she didn't particularly like it. But, she stated, as a woman and an engineer, she felt gender issues outweighed other differences: "I'm a woman in a man's job, and I think that gives me more problems over the years than being a foreigner. Engineers are just used to working with men and not with women."

When I asked her how she dealt with this issue, she replied, "I just make sure they're aware that I know what I'm doing as an engineer. As long as they see that I'm a professional, that I'm serious, that I have expertise . . . then it's not usually a problem. As a matter of fact, I've found that it's easier here than in my own country."

"It's easier in Honduras?" I asked.

Elaine clarified, "Yeah. I think it's easier because you're a foreigner and you're sent here to be kind of an expert, and so I have more clout than I would normally have as a woman in Holland. Men here are just not used to women knowing these technical things. So I think it kind of surprises them that I know what I'm talking about when it comes to engineering."

I found it interesting that Elaine's status as "foreign expert" trumped her lack of status as a woman in Honduras, and although she may be aware of the privileges of being male in the field of engineering, she seemed less aware of the unearned privileges she enjoys as an expatriate engineer in the context of Hondurans.

As the interview drew to a close, I asked Elaine why she felt someone in the Netherlands should fund development projects such as hers. She replied, "First of all, I think because you have to. I mean, you have to help people that don't have as much as you have. I think it's a duty of somebody in a developed country where everybody has a good standard of living to support the people here who don't have enough."

Although some development professionals I interviewed emphasized the benefits to donor countries of providing development assistance (such as, in the case of the United States, expanded markets and curtailed immigration), Elaine's response was typical, underscoring the idea of "helping."

When I asked her if she felt this assistance was bringing about development in countries such as Honduras, however, her attitude turned from positive to pessimistic in the blink of an eye. "I suppose development is occurring in Honduras," she explained, "I mean, could you imagine what it would be like without development organizations like UNICEF? But to be honest, I don't think Honduras will ever change." Elaine burst into laughter.

Taken aback, I asked, "Really, why?"

"I just think that culturally, the people don't believe in it. They're kind of fatalistic and they just don't think Honduras will ever develop. I don't know. It just seems like they're not really a people. It's not really a country. They don't have a kind of country spirit, like 'yeah, we can do this.' But I don't know. If I actually knew the answer, then I could become rich." She laughed again.

I laughed, too. But I was put off by Elaine's patronizing view of Hondurans. Many foreign globalizers, I found, tended to blame Honduras for its problems. They claimed either that Honduran culture was inferior or that Honduras was too dependent on foreign aid and expertise. I thought it ironic that professionals trained in development nonetheless explained the ongoing problems facing Hondurans in terms of a culture of poverty. Even more alarming was hearing from someone whose mission is to promote social change that such change in Honduras was impossible. Although the globalizers are familiar with the realities of exploitation in Honduras, they rarely cite this exploitation as the root cause of its underdevelopment, and they certainly rarely see themselves as a part of the problem.

As a final question, I asked, "Where do you see yourself five years from now?"

"After my stint here is over, the plan is to go back to Holland and stay there for a couple of years—maybe five or ten years. And then I will go back again working overseas."

Elaine seemed to see development work not as a one-time or temporary experience but as a career. She was clearly aware that there were future opportunities for her overseas in other countries where her technical expertise would be highly rewarded. Many of the expatriates I interviewed explained that their employment with one development organization gave them access to many other lucrative global jobs they could pursue. In this age of globalization, international development work thus appears to be a promising profession, and globalizers will continue to be in high demand.

Becoming a Globalizer

Elaine's career experience is unique, but it illustrates common trends among foreign development workers. As in Elaine's case, there is usually an early interest on the part of future development workers in other parts of the world. Lola, for example, a development worker from Belgium, claimed her interest stemmed from watching TV documentaries about the third world. Steve, from the United States, said that growing up with his family in a number of developing countries sparked his early interest in development.

This early interest is often followed by a life-altering or eye-opening experience of seeing poverty in the developing world for the first time. Many of these first encounters occurred while serving as a volunteer for a church organization or development NGO working on the problems of "alleviating poverty." Whether with the Peace Corps (*the* eye-opening experience for most USAID workers I interviewed) or some other type of volunteer experience, most of the foreign development workers I interviewed had an experience that broadened their worldview and took them far beyond the social environments where they had grown up.

These early experiences usually left the globalizers wanting more. A common theme in the interviews was how these formative experiences motivated them to seek even more profound experiences abroad. Elaine's decision after her time in Sri Lanka to continue her development studies and participate in a government internship program guaranteeing her overseas work is a typical example.

And although many expressed a commitment to alleviating poverty, some development workers I spoke with mentioned the desire to travel, to have a job that would allow them to see and experience different places and cultures throughout their working lives. Willis, an NGO volunteer from Sweden, for example, said, "I do this work because I think it's fun. You learn about other people, learn a new language. I like to travel most of all. When I worked in West Africa, I bought a car and we traveled all over West Africa. So for me it was just really satisfying."

Most development workers reported finding "being abroad" or "working overseas" very appealing. Linda, an NGO employee from Belgium, admitted she "romanticized third world countries" early on and felt she had an "adventurous" career. Others, like Wes, a USAID employee, emphasized the rugged individualism that working in developing countries requires: "You know, you're out there on your own, adapting to new environments, getting your hands dirty—making things happen. After that first experience, you get all fired up. You always want to be on the move, doing something different. You get hooked."

This sense of adventure overseas development work afforded was something everyone mentioned, and, for many, this aspect of an international development career was the draw behind its pursuit as a long-term goal.

Systems of Socialization and Training

Once an initial interest had formed, development workers from first world countries found many opportunities available to them. The system of education and socialization in developed countries made it possible for them to become globalizers. Elaine's international studies curriculum at her university and five-year Dutch-government sponsorship as a development worker represents a pattern followed by most development workers. Jill, a nutritionist from the United States, for example, studied development at a university and received a prestigious fellowship from the East-West Center in Hawaii (a U.S. government program) to conduct a field study in Asia as part of her graduate degree training. She later got a grant from the Harvard Institute for International Development to write a book on nutrition in Asia. In both cases, her academic pursuits dovetailed with her professional work opportunities. Most development workers reported having at least one educational or governmental resource at their disposal early in their careers that gave them credentials or opened opportunities to work for professional development organizations down the road.

Once established in a career in a developing country, many interviewees reported finding it difficult to explain their work to family and friends back home. "My family thinks I'm nuts," said Nancy, an NGO employee from the United States. "They can't understand why I would subject myself to such hardship, why I wouldn't want a 'nice job' closer to home." Frank, from Austria, told me his family has a hard time conceptualizing what he does as a UN consultant. "They can't seem to get the picture in their heads of what my work here in Honduras is like. They think I'm handing out bread to starving refugees or giving polio vaccine to babies. When I tell them I work in a nice air-conditioned office meeting government ministers, they act disappointed—like it's not what they thought I should be doing."

As development workers negotiate their relationships with family and friends back home, many come to realize the difficulties associated with living what many reported to be the "dual lives" inherent in international development work. Many spoke of the difficulty of moving between two or more cultural spaces. "You're kind of a misfit," Art, an economist from the United States, relayed, "You don't fit in back home because no one really understands what you do. And you can never fully fit in with the country you're working in because you'll always be a foreigner. When you're here, there are things you miss about being in the States. But when you go home and everyone is talking about their cars or their lawn mowers or whatever, you think, 'God, this place is even crazier than I remember. I need to go back to Honduras.'"

Each development worker seemed to have a unique way of dealing with this transmigrant status. Some, like Elaine, worked several years abroad, then returned to their home country to work for several years before going abroad again. Others went back and forth more frequently, maintaining two or more residences. To cope with the back and forth, Art said, "I just shift gears, mentally. Plane touches down and, 'all right, now I'm gonna deal with lawn mowers and parking lots.'"

This continual transitioning from one place to another often brings with it a shift in how development workers view themselves. Although many development workers reported having a very clear sense of themselves as citizens of one nation alone (their nation of origin), some I interviewed spoke of an international identity they deemed significant. Michael, for example, a U.S. citizen, told me, "I feel more tied to a human identity . . . an international identity. I don't consider myself openly 'American.' And with the Hondurans and Europeans I hang out with here, I try to accentuate my international view more than I would claim my American identity." Luther, from Denmark, had a similar outlook: "I view myself much more as a citizen of the world. I mean, I have a Danish passport, but I subscribe much more to the idea that our nationality is not as important as our humanity." This way of looking at the world and themselves beyond local or national allegiances sets development workers apart from their colleagues in their home countries.

System of Rewards and Privileges

Many globalizers talked about (and even accentuated or exaggerated) the extent to which their work required them to "rough it" or make sacrifices. In this way, they perpetuated the veneer of beneficence that defines them as selfless do-gooders. But the fact remains they are extremely well paid and receive a variety of nonmonetary perks and benefits for the work they do. Foreign globalizers might not earn as much as they could back home, but the salary is often comparable, and moreover, earning a first world salary in Honduras allows the expatriates to experience a way of life far more luxurious than what they could have in their own country. Lewis, an American employee of an NGO, put it this way: "I'll tell you, people working in foreign aid are living *really*, really well here. I mean, look at me. I'm making a relatively low salary [around thirty thousand dollars], but I can afford hired help—cooking, keeping the yard, cleaning the house. And who can say that it isn't really, really nice? It's great. I can't imagine how nice it must be for someone making seventy thousand dollars a year here. It would be complete luxury!" "Complete luxury" was a phrase I often heard from the expatriate development workers I interviewed; indeed, many said they "lived like kings."

That foreign development workers in Honduras are so highly rewarded leads to three observations. First, their technical and professional expertise is in great demand in developing countries. The high remuneration seems to lend support to those who argue that, in a postindustrial era, experts with specialized knowledge find growing economic opportunities.[5]

Second, the rewards and privileges of the international development profession accrue to international over Honduran workers; that is, there is a wage gap within development agencies. This gap can be explained in part by the concentration of professional expertise in the donor countries. The wealthy countries can afford to provide experts with the most advanced skills to do development work, and, as a result, these experts may be worth the higher cost. It is essential to note, however, that the very practice of maintaining a two-tiered pay scale within development agencies—high pay for expatriates, lower pay and staff positions for in-country hires—ensures that expatriate professionals will continue to occupy the most powerful positions in these organizations. There is in effect a global inequality being perpetuated *within* these transnational development agencies. As long as Honduran professionals are not paid on equal terms with their expatriate coworkers, there is little hope they will have an opportunity to participate as equal partners in the processes of globalization. Globalization is thus driven by the interests of the powerful countries and the institutions they have created to promote development. We are left with the sobering observation that the development institutions themselves may actually do more to contribute to global inequality than to mitigate it. The perspectives of Honduran development workers explored in the next chapter make this point even clearer.

Finally, as beneficiaries of this system of rewards, the expatriate development workers are less likely to demand radical changes in the system and more likely to maintain the status quo. When a particular globalization project comes under attack or criticism, it is the globalizers—the beneficiaries of the system—who are likely to come to its defense. They have a vested stake in promoting these global agendas, not only because they have an ideological commitment to development, but also because they benefit on an individual level from the institutionalized system of rewards. In other words, they stand to lose their career opportunities—and nice houses, maids, and the adventures of international work and travel—should the legitimacy of their work come into question.

Access to Resources and Networks

In addition to the high salaries and benefits they receive, globalizers move in elite social circles. They have access to top business executives, government ministers, the president, and directors of international development agencies. Their interaction with these powerful social elites in Honduras occurs formally as a part of their work responsibilities (as officials within the development organizations that employ them) and also informally: they attend parties with important Honduran government officials and hobnob with them on weekends.[6]

This formal and informal access gave them more social status and prestige than they would enjoy in their own countries and allowed them influence over major policy decisions for Honduras. John, a director of a medium-sized NGO who frequently worked with the president and other powerful people in Honduras, said, "Somebody told me that the dumbest thing I could do is go back to the United States, where I would be just another speck of dust just like everybody else." Many expatriate globalizers I spoke with were made to feel they were "somebody" in Honduras. Such special access made the expatriate workers effective promoters of their development agencies' agendas, and, indeed, taking into account the development workers' access to these networks is one of the best ways to understand the power donor countries exercise in Honduras.[7]

Benefits to Donor Countries

In conclusion, besides the many benefits to individual expatriate development workers, a large-scale accumulation of expertise is pouring into the wealthy donor countries. This expertise takes the form of data, statistics, development agency reports, theses and dissertations, articles in academic journals, and books housed in donor country libraries, as well as insider knowledge about political and legal processes in developing countries. The result is that donor countries may know more about developing countries than the developing countries themselves. Under the guise of helping developing countries create their own experts, professional knowledge and expertise become further concentrated in the developed countries: the individuals and countries already rich in expertise are becoming richer.

Waterworks Project, San Pedro Sula, Honduras
Photo: David Mangurian/IDB

CHAPTER FOUR

The Locals

Honduran Globalizers: Cooperation or Cooptation?

Most development workers in Honduras are not foreigners; they are Honduran. Whether the United States Agency for International Development (USAID), the United Nations Children's Fund (UNICEF), Save the Children, or the Inter-American Development Bank (IDB), international development agencies operating in the country employ Hondurans for the majority of their staff positions. Development organizations refer to them as "foreign service nationals" or "in-country hires" and use a different pay scale to determine their salary, one that, according to the development agencies, is in line with local labor market conditions.[1] These local hires include both support staff and professional development workers, or "globalizers."

Honduran globalizers are locally hired employees of development agencies who are making a professional career promoting global agendas within their own country. Through their education or professional experience, they have become connected to the activities of the international development profession. The process of becoming a globalizer is different for Hondurans compared to foreigners. Unlike foreign development workers such as Elaine who decide to practice their professions abroad in the service of development for the world's poorer countries, Honduran development workers make the decision to work with the internationals in their own country; they choose implicitly to participate in the globalization agenda.

Some would view this decision as an instance of cooperation. Honduran globalizers may often be in full agreement with the stipulations of foreign aid and view them as a means of pursuing a particular local agenda. As they see it, by cooperating with a global agenda, Honduran professionals can boost the resources devoted to their particular local concern. Others might argue the decision is an example of cooptation in which Honduran professionals are enlisted to serve global concerns (or the concerns of certain donor countries) over local concerns. This would be the case, for instance, if Honduran professionals were taken away from locally initiated political projects to work on externally initiated political projects. I would argue that both processes—cooperation and cooptation—are important to consider while examining Honduran development workers' experiences vis-à-vis the power of the international institutions for which they work.[2]

The story of Julia Navarro, a Honduran employee of the international NGO Cooperative for Assistance and Relief Everywhere (CARE), is representative of these experiences. Her job is to help administer food aid on behalf of USAID. Her story illustrates many of the issues Honduran development workers face as they become involved in the work of the international development agencies. Similar to the framework used to analyze the experiences of foreign development workers, I will focus on four central questions in looking at the experiences of Honduran development workers. First, what is the system of education and training for Honduran globalizers? Second, how does the system of rewards and privileges within the international development profession affect Honduran employees? Third, how does working on behalf of the global agendas of the development agencies grant Honduran professionals access to powerful networks? And finally, how does hiring local professionals serve the interests of donor countries as they advance their globalization agendas in Honduras?

Julia Navarro: Food Health Manager for CARE

I sat on a worn Naugahyde sofa in the lobby of the CARE building waiting for my 8:00 A.M. meeting with Julia Navarro, the food security program manager for CARE. I looked at the posters of smiling children on the walls around me. One pictured a child standing in a tin bucket being given a bath, his mother pouring a pitcher of water over his soapy head; another showed a child playing with a ball on a straw mat; in another, a girl lifted a glass of milk toward the photographer.

I noted the offices were neat and modern. There were computers on most of the desks, air conditioners in the windows, and new, ergonomic chairs behind each desk. But the facilities seemed more run-down than those at UNICEF or USAID, and I realized, when I saw USAID stickers on some of the computers, that perhaps much of the equipment was hand-me-downs.

I had been encouraged to contact Julia Navarro by Berta Alvarez, a USAID employee I had interviewed several months before. Berta was a Honduran foreign service national monitoring USAID's PL-480 Title II food aid program, the U.S. "food for peace" program devoted to sending food to developing countries. She was, in effect, one of Julia's bosses: Julia had to write reports and hold frequent meetings with Berta (and Berta's superiors at USAID) accounting for how CARE was utilizing USAID's funds and whether it was doing so in accordance with USAID guidelines.

I found it interesting that two Honduran nationals were managing—albeit under the supervision of American coworkers—what amounted to a U.S. government program in Honduras. I wondered how they had come to participate in this American-driven program. Was it a process of cooptation, or cooperation? How did they reconcile this program with Honduran interests? And in what ways, if any, did they try to shape the U.S. program to more effectively address those interests?

Julia arrived with a cup of coffee in one hand and a briefcase in the other. Dressed professionally in a dark blue business suit, she welcomed me into her office with a wide smile and an enthusiastic handshake. She was energetic and punctuated her rapid speech with frequent laughter as we talked. She gave the impression of enjoying what she did for a living and the people with whom she worked.

Julia had never really planned on working for a development organization, she told me, but she had always wanted to do something to help her country. "Ever since I was very young, I think I was sensitive to the social problems we have in Honduras," she said. [3]

Recalling her years growing up in a middle-class environment in the midst of poverty, she said, "We lived near one of the United Brands banana plantations when I was a child. It was one of the big transnational fruit companies, and we had a nice house in the neighborhood where their managers lived. And I always used to compare where we lived with what I saw as I looked where the others lived . . . the campesinos who worked the banana fields. I always wondered why there was such difference."

Julia's description reveals an important characteristic many Honduran globalizers had in common: their middle- or upper-class position. Almost all of the Honduran development professionals I interviewed reported coming from a relatively affluent background. Many of them had studied abroad or attended private schools. Most were college educated (placing them among the top 1 percent most educated in Honduras).[4] In addition, many of them came from families with significant political or business connections. If not members of the Honduran upper class (made up of the small number of families who own and control the majority of the country's wealth), they were certainly in the next highest tier.[5]

The differences Julia noticed between the wealthy and the poor in her own country became even more apparent to her when she moved to the United States. At the age of thirteen, Julia was sent there by her parents for high school. "My parents educated me under the North American system," she explained. "It was a very significant experience because I was able to see another way of life and had to become a part of that way of life. . . . So when I came back to Honduras to attend the university, it was . . . a shock to me because suddenly I could see all of the differences between Honduras and the United States. I returned with a . . . kind of . . . transcultured mentality" (*mentalidad transculturizada*).

Like Julia, many Hondurans I interviewed had studied abroad. Eleven of the sixteen Honduran development workers in my sample earned at least one degree at a foreign university. Cecilia, for example, completed her undergraduate training in special education in Venezuela. Paula earned her college degree in the United States. Isela received her master's degree in public health and community development in Colombia. Armando got his M.B.A. in Italy, and Florencia studied social work at a Mexican university. Hondurans going abroad to get an education to bring back to Honduras represents an important contrast with foreign development workers receiving an education in their own countries and taking it to the underdeveloped areas of the world. In both cases, of course, the source of the professional training and expertise applied in Honduras lies beyond its borders.[6]

Study abroad provides Honduran development workers a cross-cultural awareness similar to that of their expatriate counterparts. Their experiences and awareness give the Hondurans a certain amount of social and cultural capital necessary for their work with the expats. They often learn English or other languages, for example, an essential skill for Honduran development workers because their work with international development organizations often requires them to read or write non-Spanish documents and communicate with expats whose Spanish language skills are poor. Such language ability proves to be a tremendous asset for the Honduran development workers. In addition, Honduran development workers who have studied abroad tend to value the cosmopolitan, international worldview such an experience can encourage. A "transcultured mentality" like Julia's is useful when working for an institution that operates transnationally. This dual identity she shares with her expatriate counterparts may make her seem more successful in their eyes, more cosmopolitan—more like them. *cynical*

Although Julia's parents wanted her to remain in the United States for her university studies, Julia felt strongly about returning to Honduras for her remaining education. She explained, "At the age of eighteen, I decided I needed to be in my own country and study the problems here. I struggled with my parents to let me come back to Honduras to study for my university degree. They wanted me to stay there. But for me, I felt a lot of shame that I didn't know more about my own country and its problems. So I decided to study social work at the university here."

Attending university in the early seventies, Julia mentioned there was "a lot of student activism at the time. There were many student organizations that looked into the problems of our government and the larger economic and socio-political issues. There were some that were more radical, like the Socialist Student Front, and others that were more affiliated with the traditional political parties. But everything was very politicized. And that's how I became involved in social work, because it was considered a very politically progressive career."

Like the expats I interviewed, Honduran development workers often expressed a personal dedication to a career devoted to working on "progressive social issues" such as poverty. However, whereas expatriate development workers tended to view the entire developing world as their mission ("it doesn't matter whether it's Honduras or Sri Lanka, I'm working on poverty"), local Honduran development workers expressed a concern for their own country.

Julia's fieldwork in the poor urban barrios of Tegucigalpa and the impoverished rural areas of Honduras during her university training was a profound
experience that opened her eyes to the poverty problems she had wondered
about as a child. "It was," she said, "the first time I really became aware of what
the reality is for most of our people in Honduras. I had the opportunity to
work in the poorest urban areas, and I spent a year in the countryside doing
my practicum. It was like I was in the Peace Corps: working with the people,
becoming involved in the campesino movement. I helped do an assessment of
a workers' cooperative there. I became really involved. It was marvelous. I
enjoyed it so much. And I learned so much about my country."

The Peace Corps analogy was a recurring theme in many of my interviews.
Julia saw her opportunity (as someone from the middle class) to experience
poverty firsthand as comparable to the experiences of her U.S. coworkers. This
equation suggests how common a frame of reference the Peace Corps is
among development workers, but it might also be a way for Julia to put herself on a par with her expatriate colleagues; it marks her as having a similar
class background and comparable job qualifications. Having lived and worked
in poor communities, she knows about the aid recipients in the same way
foreigners do.

Interested in finding out Julia's level of comfort there as someone from a
middle-class background, I asked if the work was difficult for her. However,
Julia interpreted my question as being about the political climate in the country at the time.

"It wasn't difficult," she said, "because there was a lot of campesino organizing at the time. It was in the late seventies during the reformist administration of Osvaldo López Arellano. He had proposed land reform on behalf of
campesino groups and, therefore, there was a space for those of us who were
social workers to support these groups. It was a good time to be working as an
activist."

Julia's words again express her dedication to the progressive social issues that
are the bread and butter of development agencies. What is also interesting in
her case, however, is that work on such agendas often came under attack from
repressive Honduran political regimes. In the context of such political repression, development work is perhaps viewed as the only legitimate space within
which political activism can occur. This is a key point to keep in mind with
regard to the issue of cooptation versus cooperation. In the face of political
repression, Honduran professionals may see the globalizers as allies in advanc-

ing their own interests as critics of the Honduran government. Indeed, several Honduran development workers I interviewed indicated they preferred working with the international development organizations in Honduras because they saw them as an alternative to what they believed to be a repressive Honduran state. Obviously, this demonstrates a voluntary cooperation with the global agendas of the international agencies rather than cooptation.

Julia's graduation from the university coincided with a less repressive era in Honduras. Her first job opportunity came from the Honduran government. She accepted the government post because, she explained, it was the "best option" at the time. She took up her new duties as a social worker for the National Junta of Social Welfare, headed by the country's first lady. She soon discovered, however, that she did not much like the work. "I spent two years doing case work in Tegucigalpa," she said, "but I did not feel very satisfied."

"Why not?" I asked.

"Because it was very palliative, very conservative," she responded.

> The whole approach was to treat the individuals in poverty as if they were the problem, that they were responsible for their own destitution and that they should be thankful that the government was helping them. If you suggested changes or if you said that you thought the problems in these poor neighborhoods extended beyond the individual poor people, they would call you a communist and say that it wasn't your job to worry about unemployment or community development. It was a complete contradiction to me, so I didn't last there very long. I left the government work and went back to school to get my master's degree in social work—"Social Work and Latin American Development" is the title.

Julia's study of "development" as a part of her master's degree course work is significant as yet another experience of training and socialization that puts her on common ground with her foreign coworkers.

After earning her master's degree, she returned to government, training volunteers from poor communities to be "health promoters" in their neighborhoods. When I asked her about this government program and how it began, she explained that it was a development project designed by an international development organization: "It was called the 'National Plan of Infant Survival,'" she said, "It was paid for by funds from UNICEF."

Although a government employee, Julia's salary was covered by funds from UNICEF. She stated she felt this particular government job was a valuable experience that enabled her to later pursue her career in development. During this time, Julia took advantage of many training opportunities offered to Ministry of Health employees by various international development organizations. She said,

> We worked directly with the rural health workers . . . the volunteers. And so the work was very satisfying because the fruits of what we accomplished were easy to see. We were able to install a health monitoring system at the local level . . . in terms of epidemiological information . . . throughout the whole southern region. We worked in 154 communities in all. I learned a lot! Even now I say that my "real school" was the Ministry of Public Health. I learned more there than I did studying for my master's! We had many training sessions. . . . They were conducted by the World Health Organization or the United Nations, in general, and so it was a great experience in terms of professional training. I learned about management plans and all sorts of important things . . . things that were more up-to-date, like "local participation" and "decentralization." I also learned how to work more closely with the World Health Organization and the United Nations.

Julia's government job provided her opportunities to directly interact with development agencies and to receive the professional training from these same organizations—in this case, UNICEF and the World Health Organization (WHO)—necessary to become a development worker. Her experiences and training under both the Ministry of Health and UNICEF were similar to those of many Honduran globalizers I interviewed. Isela, for instance, worked with the Ministry of Health and, as part of her job, was required to attend training sessions with USAID. Cecilia received UNICEF training as an employee of the National Council of Social Welfare. For many Honduran development professionals, a government post is thus often a stepping-stone into the development field.

When I asked Julia why she left her position with the Ministry of Public Health, she explained,

> Well, that's an interesting story. I was in the Public Health Ministry, and my boss told me about a project that CARE was working on. It was called "Enhancement Two," and it was financed with funds from the Title II [food aid] program of the United States government. So he asked me if I would like to serve as the official liaison to this project. I would be the "government counterpart," you see? So I accepted this position as liaison and then I worked with

them . . . in this project of CARE's. We were working on something practically equal to what we were doing already in the Health Ministry, which was trying to improve the social participation of the volunteers in these areas. And so I was working with CARE as an official government liaison for . . . five months, and that's when CARE stole me!

Julia's case is not unusual. Honduran development workers often leave their posts in government—or some other national organization—in order to work for an international development agency. Cecilia, for example, mentioned above, left her job with the National Council of Social Welfare in order to take a position with the UN. Oscar moved from the government Social Welfare Council to take a job as a social worker in a private NGO. Marisela went from her position at a Honduran hospital to work as a doctor for a private, foreign NGO. And Armando, who had been working for the government, took a job with an international development bank.

Why do Honduran development workers leave their posts as government officials or employees of various Honduran organizations? For many the decision was based on the higher salaries international agencies offer. As Oscar told me in an interview, "There is a lot of desertion from government posts because the salaries are so low. Why work for the government when you can earn twice or even three times as much working for the foreign agencies?"

Florencia, a former employee of a large Honduran NGO, said she would never take a government position, because of the low salaries: "I thought about working with the government, but the salaries are so low. They simply don't have the resources. At times they don't even have paper and pencils. I have a friend who has to bring office supplies with her to work because they don't have any."

When I asked Julia if it was the higher salary that attracted her to the job at CARE, she claimed that her principal reason for leaving the government had much more to do with career opportunities than with monetary gain. "The salary was higher," she explained, "but that wasn't really the reason. I was getting paid slightly more but it was only about twenty dollars a month more. No, for me it had much more to do with the professional opportunities. I felt like there wasn't really a future for me in the government . . . not many opportunities. What attracted me was the ability to be working on new plans, new project goals, and, from a professional perspective, to be able to work on larger projects and perhaps have more of an influence."

"More of an influence—how is that?" I asked, wondering how CARE could have more influence in Honduras than the Honduran government.

She responded, "Well, that is the advantage of a private organization such as CARE. It has greater capacity to execute projects than the government. In terms of money, in terms of people, and, especially in terms of avoiding the political conflicts. At least for me it seemed that the management of these projects was less political and that you could get things done more effectively. You could accomplish in reality what you set out to do on paper. So I said to myself, 'Here is an opportunity to put into practice everything I know about public health without having to constantly fight with everybody about how to do it.' So I definitely saw CARE as being more effective than the government."

This belief that private development organizations are more effective than the government in accomplishing goals was echoed by other Honduran development workers. Observing that development agencies often influence the government itself through their work, Oscar, for example, maintained that "the international organizations can influence things more because they actually shape the way the government operates. Through their economic assistance, they influence the direction the government takes with regard to public policy."

This belief that international development agencies affords Honduran professionals access to institutions they consider more powerful than their own governmental organizations was shared by many, though not all, of the development workers I interviewed. The significance of this perception should not be underestimated. I believe these Honduran professionals, who are well connected to the ruling establishment and have an intimate, insider's knowledge of both the international development organizations and the Honduran government, are privy to a certain truth about the power dynamics in their country that is crucial to our analysis here: the external development agencies have greater resources and are often more influential in shaping Honduran politics than the national government.

Aware of this influence, Honduran development professionals consciously choose to work for the agendas of the globalizers. They see their work as more significant in the context of international development agencies because it can have a greater impact upon the society they wish to change. Although they may view the agendas of development organizations as consistent with their own, they are nonetheless becoming incorporated into institutions whose policies and priorities arise ultimately in accordance with donor-country interests. As in Julia's case, Honduran professionals are lured away from Honduran institutions carrying out ostensibly Honduran agendas. The opportunities Honduran professionals perceive for themselves in international agencies for more money and influence results in an *internal brain drain* of some of Honduras's best and brightest.

I asked Julia to tell me more about her current work responsibilities at CARE. Essentially, she told me, she coordinated and oversaw the dispersal of eight thousand metric tons of food a year that came through CARE from the U.S. government's PL-480 Title II food program. "The overall focus of CARE's program," she explained, "is promoting what we call 'human development,' and the fundamental objective of the program is to achieve what we define as 'livelihood security' among the poorest communities in the country."

I asked what she meant by "livelihood security."

She explained, " 'Livelihood security' is one of the ways we assess the development status of the communities we work with. It refers to the ease with which a family is able to provide for their basic needs . . . the extent to which these basic needs are readily available in their immediate social context. A community with greater livelihood security will be able to sustain itself through economic hard times like a drought. A community with less livelihood security will be more vulnerable to famine, disease, and other maladies in the event of an economic downturn."[7]

Julia went on to explain that in order to achieve "livelihood security" among the poorest communities in the country, CARE divides its efforts into three central missions. The first, "emergency relief," entails responding to food shortages and other crises such as drought or floods that can lead to food scarcity. CARE employees respond by delivering food wherever it is needed. The second is the "protection of food security," an ongoing project targeting vulnerable areas of the country for special programs designed to maintain and improve the level of food production in those areas. Third, CARE has a "development component" that seeks to enhance the ability of poor communities to provide for their own needs. The latter two programs are intended to lessen future need for the first.

"How does the disbursal of Title II food from the United States fit into each of these agendas?" I asked.

"Well," Julia answered,

obviously, if we have a drought or a famine, the food goes directly to the affected areas. But usually, we use the PL-480 food in conjunction with our other projects . . . such as health . . . through "food for work." We will provide a family ration of food for individuals in communities who participate in all sorts of development projects. We often work with other organizations in this regard, USAID, CRS, World Vision, United Nations. They receive food for working on putting in water systems, for example, or building a road into their community, or helping to improve the infrastructure of their local market. We even do this in times of crisis. So in June, for example, there was a drought and we provided food aid to affected families in exchange for their help to improve their health clinic. So we were able to attack two problems at the same time: giving food to people who need it while improving local infrastructure.

"So, from your point of view, how does this fit into the overall mission of CARE? What are your principal goals?" I asked.

She replied, "If our work in food security protection and development are successful, then in the long term, emergency food aid won't be needed in the future. The goal is to make sure that all communities in Honduras have access to minimum food needs at all times, not just the wealthy communities."

She continued, "I suppose it is important to know that we have a 'basic needs' focus to our program. That is to say that we view our role as to offset the negative effects of neoliberal structural adjustment policies. Many agencies view these policies as necessary for economic development and the creation of wealth in Honduras, but structural adjustment can have a devastating effect on the most vulnerable communities, the poor communities. So our focus is to work on programs which target these vulnerable communities in order to maintain a basic level of food security."

Julia's elucidation of her role and that of her organization bring up some important issues in the context of globalization. "Structural adjustment policies" are policies created in the 1980s by the International Monetary Fund (IMF) and the WB in order to more effectively manage the economic affairs of developing countries that were in debt to international lenders. These policies entailed many neoliberal economic reforms, including privatization of government businesses and the lowering of protective trade barriers. Most significantly, perhaps, structural adjustment required the national governments of developing countries to tighten their belts. Countries such as Honduras wishing to borrow money from the WB or the IDB had to demonstrate to the IMF that they were making cutbacks in government services. Most of these cutbacks occurred in the social sector: health, education, and social welfare programs. This led to a serious problem for Honduras and most other aid-recipient countries: the poorest of the poor were devastated by these cutbacks. As a result, the international development apparatus devised "structural adjustment mitigation" programs aimed at ameliorating these harmful effects. Both donor countries and recipient nations were concerned that if the poor suffered too much because of structural adjustment, it could lead to civil unrest and political destabilization. Some sort of social welfare was required, therefore, to prevent such a crisis, and the development agencies were encouraged to step up their social programs.

In Julia's case, her organization was being contracted by USAID to provide social welfare (in the form of food aid) to the very Hondurans the government was being told (by the IMF) to no longer assist. Although Julia may have viewed her work as an alternative to (or even in opposition to) the notorious structural adjustment policies that have received so much criticism throughout the developing world, most sociological accounts of structural adjustment mitigation programs such as CARE's in Honduras would maintain that her work serves more of a Band-Aid function: by providing modest relief to communities harmed by neoliberal reform, Julia's work at CARE actually reduces the social costs of such reforms, mutes the criticism they have provoked, and ultimately enhances the likelihood such reforms will continue. Hence, Julia's work at CARE does not present a challenge to globalization; it is part of the larger globalization agenda.

"So you are responsible for all of these projects?" I asked.

Well, I supervise these particular projects. The director of CARE is the one responsible for them, I suppose. I currently have three submanagers who handle the logistics. One of them handles the actual disbursing of food. The others help me with the other "livelihood security" projects we have going. For instance, there is the HOGASA program, which is a project designed to extend community health services to these very poor communities. We work with the Ministry of Public Health on that one. Then we have EXTENSA, which is an agroforestry project designed to promote new high-value crops in these communities so that they will have more disposable income in the home—what we call "household resilience." This project also has a conservation component, which is the promotion of better stoves that don't use as much firewood. Each project has its own submanager who reports to me. And then I report to the office manager and the director. Finally, we have the PODER project, which is a broader, policy-based project which is designed to train government officials about the importance of food security. This is another interinstitutional project. We work with the UN, Save the Children, Catholic Relief Services, and others on that one.

Asking if her work with these other development organizations was frequent, she responded, "Yes. It seems that much of my time is spent in meetings with members of our various partners. Usually, it goes pretty well, although it is difficult at times because there are so many organizations and there is often a lot of jealousy," she said.

"Why is that?" I asked.

"Sometimes it has to do with turf conflicts," she explained, "many organizations working in the same area. I think that some of the organizations are just not as large as CARE and so they view us as some sort of monster that comes in and tries to get its way. But for the most part, we have good relationships with the other development agencies. . . . We also have government counterparts: the Ministry of Natural Resources, Public Health, and so on."

Julia's comments revealed her awareness that she had access to a powerful network of international development agencies and Honduran government organizations; she understood how it operates and the need to be sensitive to its subtle power dynamics in performing her work. The conflicts Julia pointed to often emerge, as I will explore later, when different organizations seek to advance their particular agendas.

When I asked Julia if there were development organizations she wouldn't work for, she replied, "Well, I wouldn't work for the United Nations organizations. I feel there is too much bureaucracy there. When I worked with UNICEF, it was very difficult to accomplish certain things. The management style there is very top-down. Also, I prefer a little less formal work situation. I prefer a place where I can go into my boss's office and tell him exactly what I think . . . a place that is more 'straightforward.' CARE is like that."

Julia used the English word *straightforward* in her explanation. I asked her what she meant by "too much bureaucracy."

She said, "I just think that there are some agencies that are more organized. They have greater accountability. . . . I can only speak for myself, and it's not only that I love CARE and that I work for CARE, but I have had experiences working with other institutions, and, as I mentioned, my work constantly involves ties with all of these other development agencies. But I really feel that

CARE is one of the best development institutions in the country, especially if you look at it from the perspective of administrative costs."

"How so?" I inquired.

"If you do an analysis of our program, you will find that 32 percent of our budget goes to administration. That includes salaries, benefits, and everything else required to run the administrative offices. The rest goes to the recipients . . . the recipient communities. That's significant! Because if you look at other institutions . . . the government, for example, or the United Nations . . . you would find very different figures. And I know this because I have a confidential source. They pay millions and millions of dollars just to pay foreign experts—their salaries, their houses, their vacations, and so on."

When I asked if she thought their administrative costs were much higher than that 32 percent, she responded, "Well, I don't know exactly because I don't have access to those exact figures. But in my experience, I would say yes, there is a lot of waste. I'm not going to say that CARE doesn't have high costs, because it does. But we are constantly working to improve our cost-effectiveness. And I think if you compare CARE with the United Nations in that regard, you would find much less bureaucracy here."

Seeking an insight into how Honduran development workers view the issue of expatriate development professionals, I next asked, "What is your view of hiring foreign experts? Is it worth the cost?"

"I think it depends on the quality," Julia stated. "If I am paying for something that is worth it, then I don't mind. But I've got to see that it's worth it. We have cases where people are earning five or six times what I make. I don't think that's fair. But you can't really fight it. I've brought the issue up and, you know, they have their reasons: their contract is made in the United States, they have expenses in the United States. I understand that. And I've had some excellent working relationships with international personnel, some of them. I think it depends on the professionalism of the person."

"How do you assess that? When are the high salaries worth it, in your opinion?" I asked.

Julia responded,

For example, I have had to make a choice between hiring a local and an international. And so I know that many times the international person has capabilities and knowledge to come here and do something that we can't do ourselves. It is not because we're less intelligent or something. Perhaps we just haven't had the experience, you know, . . . of going to a University of Arizona where there is a special program on soil erosion. I had to make this choice, and someone here told me that there are Honduran experts who work on this problem at Zamorano [the local agricultural university], but I said, "Look, we're going to bring this person in from the University of Arizona. They have better contacts in Washington, they've done fund-raising there, they've put together conferences. They're simply better qualified." That's what I look for—I don't care if the person is Honduran or not.

Julia explained she had had to hire a consultant to put together recommendations regarding an agricultural project addressing soil erosion in a community in southern Honduras. Her decision to hire an expert from the United States was met by the view of some of her colleagues that a Honduran was capable of doing the job.

She continued, "This national/international issue always comes up. I was asked, 'Don't you think there is someone locally who can do this job, someone who can do it for less money?' And I said, 'This is the best person for the job. They have the professional expertise that we need.' 'But are you going to pay that much?' and I said, 'That is what quality costs.' That is simply the reality. So you shouldn't look at someone as North American or Japanese, you should look at them for their professional and intellectual capability."

"So it's worth the cost," I said.

"At *times* it's worth the cost," she clarified. "I mean, of course the United States is a highly developed country and there are many people there who are the best in the world at what they do. But we have resources here as well. And that's the important thing to keep in mind. Often someone here can do a *better* job than a foreigner—because they have more local experience and understand the local context. I can't tell you how many times, in my position, I have had to train a foreigner how to do *their* job. And this is something that the foreign experts don't realize. We often have to teach them how to do things even when they think they are teaching us."

Julia's observation reminded me of my interview with another Honduran development worker, Marcos, who had worked over the years as an agronomist for numerous aid agencies. He had received many job contracts to carry out evaluations or write reports on particular agricultural development projects in the country that usually required him to work in collaboration with foreign consultants. He told me that, though he felt his foreign counterparts always had good intentions, he was often upset by their lack of due regard for his position as a professional—all the while depending on him for most of the information they needed to carry out their work. He complained,

A lot of times . . . not every time . . . but often enough that I prefer not to take these jobs anymore, they would view me as their "assistant." It used to piss me off! Nowhere in the contract did it say I was an "assistant." I had the same degree as they did, I had the same job title. But that is how I was treated. I would drive them to the project site. We would look at the fields or the crop in question, and they would interview *me* about what was going on. I would share with them my professional assessments, and they would write them down. Later we would sit down and write the report, and it became clear that they didn't know a thing and I would end up having to write the majority of the report. But they acted like they were the ones in charge and that I was their assistant. Maybe it's because they had flown down from Washington or Berlin or wherever. Maybe it was because they were the ones who got to present the findings to the higher-ups. I don't know. But it would piss me off because they would get a higher consultancy fee than I would. I felt like they were stealing from me. Not only were they stealing my expertise in agriculture—what I know about erosion prevention or how a particular hybrid crop grows under particular conditions—they were stealing my local knowledge and claiming it for their own.[8]

I asked Julia if this sort of discrepancy bothered her.
She answered,

No, I don't feel bad about it. I feel like that's just the way it is. I am fulfilling my role within the world of development, not just in my country, but in the world as a whole, because this person that I am teaching to understand the problems of Honduras may one day go to another Latin American country and be a little more effective in their job. Or maybe they'll go to Africa and then they can compare what they learned in Honduras with the situation there. I think this type of exchange is necessary. There should be a dialogue where we all learn—not just the developing countries, but the foreign experts, too. We can all exchange ideas and experiences. There should be this worldwide exchange. Globalization demands it. We should all have an international viewpoint.

Probing a bit further, I asked, "But isn't it difficult to have these exchanges when there is such a large difference in terms of the salaries?"

Julia laughed, "Of course it is! And the problem is that most organizations don't even discuss this matter. Most Honduran employees of development organizations don't even know about the high salaries of the foreigners. It's not discussed. Also, most of the employee manuals are written in English, so how would the Honduran employees be able to find out? There is very little transparency."

Although it is apparent Julia views the wage gap between Honduran and expatriate development workers less critically than, say, Marcos, she, like most Honduran development workers, believes it should be addressed. But, as Julia's statement reveals, few development agencies—or their foreign staff members—were asking how the gap might appear from the Honduran point of view. Recall my interview with Elaine, who said that her high salary is something she has "learned it is better not to discuss" with her Honduran coworkers. Elaine was obviously concerned her Honduran colleagues might be upset if they knew what she makes as a development worker. And of course, as Julia's remarks suggest, Honduran development workers *are* concerned. Every Honduran development worker I interviewed stated that this was a problem that should be addressed. The problem, as they saw it, has several important aspects.

First, they felt that local Honduran expertise was undervalued within development institutions, and that local knowledge "came cheap" compared to expertise and knowledge regarding transnational networks; second, Honduran development professionals felt exploited by their foreign counterparts, who used the local knowledge of the Honduran workers to enhance their professional merit and advance their own careers; third, because development agencies were under the control of donor countries, development workers from those countries created for themselves preferential conditions in terms of salaries, perks, and other benefits; fourth, since development workers from recipient countries are peripheral to this process, they have little power to negotiate for better benefits for themselves; and fifth, even when they are allowed to negotiate their salary, they are held to the market standards of Honduras, not the world as a whole. Although they believe they deserve remuneration based on the value they bring to the international organizations, they are reminded they are earning more than they could elsewhere in Honduras.

It is important to understand that, despite the dissatisfaction with this inequality, Honduran development workers recognized the higher level of expertise possessed by many of their foreign colleagues. They agreed that development workers from abroad should be paid higher salaries when their technical skills or professional training demanded it. Consequently, acknowledging the fundamental dilemma of the global market of professional expertise, most Honduran development workers viewed the wage-gap issue with some degree of ambivalence. They know there *are* Honduran experts who are getting less than they deserve for their work, but they also recognize that, overall, there is a higher level of expertise abroad. As a result, Honduran development workers feel ill-equipped to argue for higher salaries. Most stated that it was an issue that had yet to be fully brought to light, in large part because of the reluctance on all sides to talk about it.

When I asked Julia if she considered her job to be well paid, she replied, "I just received a promotion, and I am making 19,300 lempiras a month [about U.S.$1,600]. In addition, I have good insurance and a pension. But I could make more money working abroad. As a consultant in another country, I could make maybe three times what I make here. But I'm convinced that what I do here I wouldn't be able to do elsewhere. That is to say, I probably wouldn't be able to work at such a high level in another country. Other developing countries don't want a Honduran consultant, they would rather have a German or an American. So working as a consultant wouldn't allow me the opportunity to participate in making the important decisions."[9]

Julia's assessment discloses the more limited access of Honduran development workers relative to first world professionals to jobs in other countries: Honduran development workers cannot enter international posts as easily. They are thus not international globalizers but local globalizers, valued for their local expertise and less so for their professional or technical skills. The international development agencies tap their recognizably superior knowledge of the local situation as they pursue their global agendas. As Julia's conclusion suggests, Honduran expertise and specific knowledge remain peripheral. Some globalizers, it would seem, are better than others: the expatriates are more highly valued and vested with greater authority in the international development profession than the local globalizers.

As we came to the end of the interview, I asked Julia why she felt donor countries should fund development projects in countries such as Honduras. Questioning the implication of my query, she countered, "Well, I don't think it's an issue of *should*—they *do* . . . and that's a different matter."

She continued, "International aid doesn't exist because donor countries feel motivated by some sort of obligation. They give aid because they want to. The reason they do this is because of global conditions and international politics that have nothing to do with Honduras. In part, it used to be over the struggle between superpowers. Now, it's more about imposing certain macroeconomic policies on developing countries. Even though an organization says they are advocating development, and I would include the Honduran government here, really it's about putting in place certain policies that the wealthy countries would like to see in place.

"So I don't say donor countries *should* give aid, they just do," she added. "Maybe they should and maybe they shouldn't. I think there are times when development institutions create more chaos than development in Honduras." There was a long pause. Julia's demeanor had changed, and her words had a more critical edge to them.

"How so?" I prodded.

"Because," she explained,

> there are so many of them and there is no one to coordinate it all. Do you know how many different agencies have their little project going on here or there? They come in and they have complete freedom to enter into communities and carry out health projects, or give inoculations, or build houses—or schools or latrines. Who is going to say no? And I'm not just talking about the official agencies—the Americans or the Germans or the Japanese—but the private ones, too, the NGOs. And I think we have started to realize that having all of these agencies each carrying out their own project, each with their own agendas and ideological points of view, may not always be a good thing. It can also undermine the local government's ability to carry out its own plans and projects. Or even overwhelm the local government who is trying to figure out what *it* should be doing in the midst of all this foreign aid.

I asked if she could give me a specific example.

> Well, I can just tell you that this is a big concern. As a matter of fact, we just had a meeting last week at SECPLAN [the Honduran government planning bureau] about this problem. [I have a close relative who] works in SECPLAN, and I agree when they say that we need to create some sort of agency in order to coordinate foreign aid. HACIENDA [in the Treasury department] typically has done this, but they just keep track of the financing; they don't monitor the programs themselves. We need the ability to reject certain types of aid—to say yes to certain programs, yes, this aid is consistent with the development goals we have as Hondurans. But we also need to reject some of these projects, because they are not consistent perhaps with what we should be striving for.

From her unique vantage point as a development worker and a citizen of Honduras, Julia was in a position to view the development process as both an insider and an outside critic.[10]

She continued, "I think there are simply some projects that we should be able to reject. You shouldn't be able to come here and bring used clothing from the United States and say you're going to sell it, and that this is a great development project. I'm serious! We've had to deal with containers of used clothes that someone has donated and said, 'Here, this is for Honduras.' We should be able to reject as well as accept aid. But we don't have that ability. That is the main problem facing Honduras, in my opinion."

Her use of "we" underscored that she was speaking as a Honduran now. It also expressed that she viewed her own position (despite working for an aid agency) as somewhat apart from the countries giving aid to Honduras. Her displeasure in the control donor countries wield over the development is also apparent in her remarks.

I asked what she thought needed to be done to address the problem, and she replied, "Well, I would say that money is not the problem. The money is here, the aid is here. The thing that needs to happen is that we need to reorient what is done with the money and create coordination among the various agencies that are working on development under the authority of Hondurans. It would be good if we had more control and more ability to reject the projects that aren't productive."

Julia explained that, although the government had a national plan guiding development decisions, during the past twenty years, so many different organizations had moved into the country, that it had become difficult to coordinate all the aid: "In the nineties, there was a proliferation of private development organizations and NGOs. Anyone could go to the Ministry of Exterior Relations and set up a development agency and collect funds and start carrying out projects. The government was happy to receive the economic assistance, but this is no way to make public policy. This is no way to run a country."

"So now," she continued,

SECPLAN and other Honduran government offices say they want to regain some control over the process, regain some order. That's what the meeting last week was about. But when we want to coordinate, the foreign agencies often do not want to. Do you know why? Because they would rather have chaos than be told that their projects might not be needed. If the Honduran government were to say, "You know what? Maybe we just want the Japanese to do the health-care projects, because they are doing the best work. And you other organizations should stop your health-care projects and let the Japanese work in the communities where you used to work." Those organizations would become angry at the Japanese. They become jealous. They think their project is the best, and why should they have to stop? It becomes a big debate, and the NGOs that aren't doing as well in the eyes of the Honduran government leave the table and say, "Well, we're going to do our project anyway. We think it's needed."

"Why," I asked, "wouldn't a development organization want to follow the wishes of the Honduran government?"

"Because they have their own ideas about what the country needs, and they want to continue to expand their own work, not cut back. If they cut back, how are they going to justify their existence? A lot of agencies want to blow wind on their own windmills. They just want to ensure that they're growing— maintaining their offices, buying computers, buying vehicles, writing reports, and bringing in new people to coordinate new projects. They don't want to cease to exist. But it never reaches that point, because the government doesn't want to turn away the money that comes in from these organizations. So they never ask an agency to follow a coordinated plan. The government would rather let the chaos continue than cut off the money."

"Poverty generates a lot of money," Julia declared, laughing again. "It sounds ridiculous, but it's true. Poverty is a cash cow. It can generate a lot of money. Organizations can raise a lot of money saying they're going to fight poverty. The question that we have to ask ourselves in Honduras is, Do we want all of these groups coming down and implementing all of these projects all around the country? Sometimes maybe we do. But maybe we want some control over the process."

Her reference to "we" again meant not only "we at CARE" but "we Hondurans." Clearly, Julia is aware that international development agencies have more power than Honduran institutions and that these agencies benefit the donor countries. Her depiction of poverty as a cash cow and reference to the reluctance of the development agencies and the Honduran government, despite the chaos, to pull back on certain projects neatly pinpoint the problems associated with donor control over major political projects in the country.

Julia's position as a Honduran working on behalf of a foreign development agency was a difficult one. She was caught between the interests of the donor countries paying her salary and setting the priorities of her work and the interests of her own country. Thus, simultaneous to carrying out her duties as an employee of CARE, she had taken upon herself expressing her belief that development assistance from donor countries be placed more firmly under local control.

Wondering how she viewed this issue in relation to her position with CARE, I asked, "Doesn't CARE fall into this same problem?"

"Well, yes and no," she vacillated. "Because this is something we are trying to work on and improve upon. I can't speak about CARE in the past, but since I have been here, I have seen how CARE has moved a long way to trying to work in accordance with the local government and what they want. Basically, we won't begin work in a particular community unless we are asked to. It's a decision of the local government, not CARE."

She explained,

For instance, with this HOGASA project, the local communities would have to come to us and ask to participate in the program. In one case, a mayor from a small town had decided to enter his community into our program, but the UN's World Food Programme was already working there, and when the WFP found out that they were trying to get CARE money, they threw a fit! They said, "What is CARE doing working on health-care issues in this community? We are already working there!" And they threatened to leave. They said they would withdraw their support if the mayor accepted CARE's help. They were really angry that the community had made this decision. So we proposed that we work with WFP in a partnership in the community. It was a little difficult; WFP viewed our program as a threat to theirs. But we were able to coordinate with them in a way in which both organizations could support the community.

"But why did the World Food Programme view CARE as a threat?" I asked.

"Because it was their turf and there is a different ideology, a different style of work between the two organizations. CARE requires certain accounting practices, they [the WFP] don't have any controls. But I think it was a matter of competence, you know. I think it might have had to do with the director of the program, who felt that we were a threat. Perhaps we had a better sense of the problems in this community. Maybe someone who isn't Honduran doesn't have the same sense of the community as we do. It could be many reasons. I don't want to go into it in too much detail. The important thing is that the community wanted us there. They could see we had a quality program. Maybe that's threatening to other organizations."

She continued,

> That's the important issue to me. That we're providing a quality service. I mean,
> I think that's the way the world is going, and I imagine that development agen-
> cies are no different. Whoever has the most advanced program is going to get the
> clients—whoever is the sharpest. The communities are going to decide. . . . I
> think we're heading to a moment within development where the clients are
> going to look up at all these various agencies, and they are going to choose the
> one that they think is best. They're going to say, "No, I think we should go with
> WFP," or, "I think we should go with CARE because they have the best program
> for what we need." And I think this is a good thing because, even though it might
> be difficult for some organizations, competition is a good thing. It's the wave of
> the future. May the best organization win.

Julia's belief CARE was better able to serve a community than the World
Food Programme failed to acknowledge that certain development organizations have greater resources than others and so are higher on the resulting
hierarchy. As I mentioned in chapter 1, UN organizations occupy the second
tier in the hierarchy of international agencies in Honduras. USAID and the
development banks are in a higher tier and give more aid to Honduras. Consequently, CARE may benefit from its close ties to USAID, and so, whereas
Julia views competition between development organizations as a good thing
and the community's pick of the CARE program over that of the UN as just,
she is also supporting the hegemony of the more powerful international development organizations and their agendas.

When I asked Julia what she would like to do with her career in the future,
she explained, "All my life I've dreamed about setting up and being the director for a training center in the area of development, but something different
from what already exists. What I'd like to do is subcontract with development
organizations in order to carry out their training programs. They would pay
me for these trainings, and I would be in charge of the design and carry it out
for them. That's my idea."

Julia's plan to set up her own NGO is based on her belief that she would
have greater control and, perhaps, even a higher salary for herself. She saw this
plan as a move up the career ladder. Unlike expatriate development workers,
who usually believe they have the most to gain from continuing to work within
the development agencies, Julia saw the promise of her career future outside
her development organization. Ironically, such a move would likely place her

lower on the development apparatus food chain than she is at CARE. As a sub-contractor working on behalf of development agencies, she would have less authority and so less control over the activities of development organizations than she enjoys in her current position as a manager of numerous projects under CARE.

Julia's vision of her future, in which she is essentially removing herself from the powerful positions within the development profession, represents a telling implication about the continuing power of foreign aid in Honduras. It was interesting to me, for instance, that she did not consider moving up the career ladder within CARE. Could this be, I wondered, a reflection of a glass ceiling within international organizations, one through which the "locals" are rarely allowed to pass? Julia's career goal was markedly different in this regard from that of her expatriate coworkers, who often mentioned becoming more in-volved with "higher management" and "policy making" inside the interna-tional organizations for which they worked. Whereas expatriate workers often sought to work "back at headquarters" in Washington, D.C., or Rome, this was not usually the case for Honduran development workers like Julia. None of those I interviewed believed they would one day rise in the ranks of the inter-national agencies they worked for to become managers or policy makers on a global scale. Access to these positions, it seems, is in the hands of development professionals from the donor countries.[11] If the experiences of Julia and the other Honduran development workers I interviewed are typical of profes-sionals from other developing countries, clearly then, local experts are largely peripheral to the main agendas of international development agencies.

Honduran Cooptation and Cooperation with Globalization Agendas

So what is the role of Honduran development professionals in promoting globalization? The common image of international development work often leaves the local professionals out of the picture: Hondurans are supposed to be the recipients of aid, not among those who disburse it. But, as Julia's ac-count demonstrates, local development professionals have a critical role in the aid process. In addition to their labor, Honduran globalizers provide local knowledge, access to Honduran networks, and legitimacy to the external aid agencies employing them. It would be difficult to imagine institutions such as CARE, USAID, or the WFP operating in Honduras without them. Hondurans, for their part, choose to work for the transnationals because they offer attractive salaries, career opportunities, and, most significantly perhaps, access to institutional resources that surpass what these Honduran professionals could find working in Honduran institutions.

Moreover, by working for international development agencies, Honduran globalizers are advancing the same global agendas as their expatriate colleagues. But they play a different part: whereas foreign development workers are employed for their technical expertise first and foremost, Honduran development workers are hired for their local knowledge and local political connections. Having generally a subordinate role, they are usually paid less. Yet, most local development workers are striving to improve their professional status vis-à-vis foreign development workers. In addition, they are attempting to exert greater local control over the development assistance process. The Honduran globalizers I interviewed thus were negotiating a very different set of circumstances in their careers as development professionals from those of the expats.

Benefits to Donor Countries

As I pointed out in the previous chapter, expatriate development workers bring their particular expertise, and they also facilitate donor control of the development aid process. But what is the purpose of having Hondurans become globalizers, too? How is their participation essential to maintaining the globalization agenda in Honduras?

My conclusion is they give the foreign aid agencies an in. It would be difficult for the development agencies to implement their projects without access to (and intimate knowledge of) the local community. And this is where the Honduran development workers play an important part. International development agencies hire Honduran development workers to gain local cooperation while never relinquishing control. They also gain the local knowledge of Honduran professionals, which is crucial to the advancement of global agendas in the country.

This local knowledge consists of several distinct, interrelated parts. First, Honduran professionals have *local technical knowledge* (e.g., regarding agricultural conditions). This local expertise often places Honduran agronomists, economists, engineers above or on a par with their expatriate counterparts because the expatriate expert is dependent upon the local expert for understanding "how things are done here" and how the professional expertise is best applied in the local context. Second, the Honduran globalizers have *institutional knowledge*—their connections to government insiders and familiarity with local institutions and customs. This institutional knowledge is crucial for foreign agencies to have at their disposal when forging relationships with the Honduran government. As in Julia's case, many Honduran globalizers have worked as government counterparts for a development project. By hiring former government employees, who are thus already members of powerful networks, international agencies instantly acquire the social capital of these local professionals. This institutional knowledge also includes Honduran globalizers' knowledge of nongovernmental institutions and networks, such as civic and business organizations.

Third, hiring a Honduran to work for them in promoting global agendas gives development agencies *legitimacy*. When a Honduran worker goes out into the countryside to meet with community leaders in connection with a development project or makes a presentation before a group of business associates as a representative of an international development organization, that person is, in effect, turning a global agenda into a local one. The development agency becomes represented—embodied even—as Honduran. This is crucial for foreign organizations carrying out political projects within the borders of a sovereign nation: the more local participants you can get to cooperate in what is a donor country agenda, the more legitimate that agenda will appear in the local context.

Finally, Honduran development workers provide the international development apparatus a cheaper source of labor. It would be very expensive to staff your entire administration in Honduras with foreigners. Therefore, international agencies send expatriate workers to Honduras to occupy only the most important posts; Hondurans, who work for less while providing the aforementioned benefits, are taken on to fill the remaining positions.

Consequences for Honduras

This arrangement has consequences for Honduran professionals and for Honduras as a whole. In terms of benefits to local professionals, as mentioned, they get better salaries. Second, they often receive technical training and professional experience from the international development organizations that might not otherwise be available in Honduras. By participating in the seminars and on-the-job training offered by the more technologically sophisticated international organizations (in particular, by the expatriate professional experts who come to the country to "transfer" their knowledge to the Hondurans), Honduran globalizers can increase their professional capacities and skills. This benefit of "knowledge transfer" to the developing world is highly touted by the development agencies and, portrayed as it usually is as an act of generosity on the part of donor countries, becomes a part of the veneer of beneficence.

A third benefit to Honduran professionals is the ability, by virtue of participating in the global agendas of the international development community, to advance a local political agenda. Honduran human rights advocates, for example, found it very difficult in the 1980s to carry out their work to improve the human rights conditions in Honduras. However, through the support of such international NGOs as the Washington Office on Latin America, Human Rights Watch, and Amnesty International, they were better able to challenge the Honduran state apparatus in advancing their concerns.[12] Connection to a global agenda thus furthers the realization of a local agenda.

But, working for international development agencies has its costs, too. Many Honduran professionals reported that, with their relatively lower salaries, they felt exploited by the international development agencies. Their expertise and local knowledge was undervalued. This sense of exploitation was exacerbated by their frequently occupying subordinate positions within the organizational hierarchy. Some resented their non-Honduran bosses, especially if they perceived them to be less knowledgeable than themselves regarding the problems Honduras faced. Although most Honduran globalizers claimed these costs were minimal, and that they found ways to cope with their subordinate status, I believe their misgivings reflect a significant cost imposed by the international development profession on local professionals in developing countries. The disparity allows for the continuing disempowerment of these professionals and the reification of the donor-recipient status hierarchy.

The local development workers are aware of the glass ceiling in international organizations. Honduran professionals know they will never be the in-country director of USAID or CARE. Such positions are reserved for expatriates. They also know their opportunities to work for these agencies are largely limited to Honduras. No one I interviewed expressed aspirations to move up the ladder within these agencies to become a regional director or a higher-level manager back at headquarters in, say, Washington, D.C., or Berlin. This awareness reinforces the dynamics of dependency and inferiority that the development agencies themselves claim to be working to change. It also demonstrates that the agendas of the donor countries, not Honduras, are preeminent.

There is an expression common among development workers regarding what development means: "If you give a man a fish, he will eat for a day. But if you teach a man to fish, he will eat for a lifetime." The intended implication is knowledge is a greater gift than charity; it precludes the need for charity.

The problem, as Julia and other Honduran globalizers see it, is that the foreign development professionals always want to be the teachers. "When do we become the teachers, too?" Honduran development workers seem to ask. Their subordinate role under the glass ceiling and the resulting disempowerment they feel within the very institutions claiming to be trying to empower them represents an important cost to Honduran professionals.

This sense of exploitation and subordination is usually kept hidden in most development organizations. As the interviews with both Elaine and Julia revealed, it is viewed as a volatile issue. It is not often discussed between Hondurans and their foreign coworkers. Honduran workers might allude to it, but they do not want to risk losing their relatively advantageous positions. On an individual level at least, Honduran professionals thus seem to believe the benefits outweigh the costs. But the costs are there, and many Honduran development workers admitted to sometimes passive-aggressive means they took to compensate for the inequality they experienced in the workplace.[13]

Another hidden cost is that many Honduran institutions lose their professionals to the global agencies. The internal brain drain of the best and brightest Honduran professionals to the international development organizations certainly affects local institutions and their ability to build up their human resource capacity. This cost is difficult to determine, especially since development agencies claim to be building up local capacity and, once it is built, that they will leave. But what if they do not leave? What damage might the international development agencies be inflicting upon Honduran society by skimming the professional cream off the top for their own purposes? Might this not leave Honduran institutions at a greater disadvantage vis-à-vis the international institutions down the road?

The likelihood that this system will change in the future is slight. As has become clear, workers in the international development profession enjoy many privileges. It seems unlikely that Elaine in the last chapter or even Julia in this chapter would want to dismantle a system that benefits them. The system of rewards encourages the globalizers, whether expatriate or local, to want to maintain their positions. The opportunities development work offers keep them in it. They will write new grants, apply for new jobs, create a new NGO, and so on. The individual globalizers feed the growth and expansion of development work. It is a self-perpetuating system that well rewards its individual participants and is, therefore, likely to grow larger, not smaller, in the future.

Within this growing system, we can also expect the transnational to supersede the local. The marginalization of Honduran professionals and their local knowledge to the periphery of the international development apparatus bodes ill for local agendas that may run counter to the globalizing agendas of the donor countries. Only local agendas linking into the global ones are going to succeed, and only Honduran institutions giving their consent to globalization are likely to prosper.

So Who Are the Globalizers?

The globalizers in Honduras are the people and institutions that make up the international development profession. Behind the veneer of beneficence of development work appear the hundreds of institutions promoting various projects in Honduras on behalf of the donor nations. In addition, there are thousands of professionals in the employ of these institutions carrying out these projects. The individual globalizers are highly rewarded professionals who do their work in large part because of the intrinsic and extrinsic rewards these jobs provide. Both the institutions and people are the actors in the globalization process in Honduras, the agents of globalization.

Moreover, these agencies and their workers exist in a particular configuration of power: a hierarchy. Some personnel—the expats—are more powerful and receive greater privileges than others—the Hondurans. And some institutions have more resources, and so greater power, than others. Elaine mentioned how her work for UNICEF pales in comparison with the work of the economists at the WB. Julia referred to the greater influence of CARE over the WFP. Although these power differentials do not necessarily prevent any one development organization from carrying out its projects, they can lead to conflict between these global institutions in the Honduran setting. They also create the conditions under which these agencies seek to coordinate their activities with each other. As I shall describe in the next half of the book, this donor coordination is an increasingly important dimension of the global governance these institutions carry out in the developing world.

Part II / The Globalizers in Action

International Donor's Meeting, Stockholm, Sweden

Photo: Hans Pettersson

CHAPTER FIVE

Global Governance

"What *are* the experts up to?"   — ARUNDHATI ROY

Besides knowing who the globalizers are, we need to understand the globalizers in action, to look at the specific ways in which they carry out their global agendas in Honduras. Although the focus here is on Honduras, many countries in the developing world confront a similar process. For example, in her book *Power Politics,* Arundhati Roy writes about the development experts who are responsible for the highly controversial Narmada dam project in India. She claims that the activities of the international development banks, NGOs (nongovernmental organizations), and the donor nations have largely gone unnoticed by the media, much to the detriment of the Indian citizens who have been negatively affected by the project. She argues that the development planners are not held accountable for their actions because no one really knows or understands what they are doing. In particular, she believes that if we in the donor countries really understood what was occurring in the developing world—what the World Bank (WB) and other large development organizations were doing—we would be more likely to put a stop to it.

What are the experts up to in Honduras? The development agencies themselves claim to be carrying out development "projects" or "initiatives." Although these terms make their activities in Honduras seem temporary, they are not; they are ongoing. These agencies do not come and go, entering the country to carry out a project and then leaving (perhaps to return later, perhaps not). Most have entered the country to set up permanent (or at least long-term) residence.[1] Some are big and powerful, and others are small. Although their activities may be conceived of as projects, they are also political agendas. Even though these agendas are usually carried out with the approval of the Honduran government (the legitimate agent of national political projects), the official development organizations and NGOs are playing power politics. They are involved in governing.

In this chapter, I describe what I mean by "global governance." I define what global power and global governance entail and, by placing the activities of international development agencies in Honduras in the context of what globalization scholars call the "globalization project" and the "transnational state" (TNS), I specify how these activities exemplify power and governance as opposed to assistance. In particular, I examine the mechanisms of global governance these agencies use. By providing a model of the emerging global state and illustrating where the international development organizations are situated within that model, I intend to make clear the structures of global governance operating not only in Honduras but throughout the developing world.

Global Power definitions

Sociologists define power as "the capacity to produce, or contribute to, outcomes—to make a difference in the world."[2] They emphasize the social nature of power and that, most often, this ability to "make a difference" occurs through social relationships among human agents acting in institutional settings. How power operates in society is the subject of an entire subdiscipline in sociology, yet few theorists of power have examined how it operates on a global scale. Using these sociological debates regarding power as a framework, let us consider four of its central features.

First, power involves *intervention.* Anthony Giddens's definition of power as "the capacity to intervene in a given set of events so as to in some way alter them" makes this point most clearly.[3] In this sense, power is predicated upon acting—upon inserting oneself (or one's institution) into the social or political arena.

Second, power is often built upon *surveillance.* This understanding of power comes most directly from the work of Michel Foucault. According to

Foucault, power entails the invention of "social mechanisms to 'discipline' individuals, shaping their discourse, their desires, indeed their very 'subjectivity.' "[4] This ability to "discipline" others, according to Foucault, hinges upon surveillance, the direct and indirect monitoring of the subjects of power. "In discipline," Foucault writes, "it is the subjects who have to be seen. Their visibility assures the hold of the power that is exercised over them."[5] Surveillance, he emphasizes, is "a way of seeing" that is more than simply the act of observing; it is observing as an exercise of power and as a product of power relations. Those in positions of power utilize, in surveillance, their "gaze" (their worldview) to place their subjects under scrutiny. Surveillance involves decisions regarding what to look at, how to view it, and the ability to mold our understanding of social reality through this act of "seeing." Most importantly, surveillance is functional to the apparatus of power. The subject of the gaze becomes known to those in power, and those in power, through this knowledge, are able to more effectively put the subject under their control. In contrast, those without power are often unable to subject those in power to surveillance because the power holders shield their activities. According to Foucault, knowledge (through surveillance) and power go hand in hand. This model of power/knowledge is often implicit in other scholars' views of power. Such is the case of Harold Perkin (cited earlier), for example, who, although he does not draw upon Foucault in his analysis of modern professionals in the world today, nevertheless argues that the "power of the modern professional" is based upon their access to technical expertise, information, and knowledge.[6]

A third theme in theories of power is the notion of *agenda setting*, which assumes that the exercise of power is based on some degree of intentionality. Bertrand Russell, for instance, defines power as "the production of intended effects," and Max Weber as "the ability to carry out one's will."[7] Sometimes the idea of agenda setting is framed in terms of "goals," as in Talcott Parsons's definition of power as "the capacity of social systems to achieve collectively binding goals."[8] All of these definitions emphasize the extent to which power is intentional action, the act of agenda setting. This emphasis is important for understanding power and how it is exercised through the drawing up of plans and blueprints for action. It is also important, however, to keep in mind that the exercise of power—the carrying out of plans—can have unintended consequences. It is useful, in these cases, to examine how those in power have "the ability to secure advantage for themselves" even in those events.[9]

Finally, power entails *garnering the consent* of the subordinate group. According to Outhwaite and Bottomore, the key question here is: "What distinguishes power relationships?" Are they ridden with conflict and characterized by the powerful group exerting coercion over others in order to force compliance with their goals? Or are they characterized by cooperation and interdependence?[10] Sociological theories of power have tended to emphasize the negative sense.[11] Weber, for instance, defines power primarily as domination, as securing compliance through violence or authority.[12] Theories drawing upon the work of Karl Marx emphasize "the capacity of one class to realize its interests in opposition to other classes."[13] This capacity includes control over the mechanisms of coercion (such as the state apparatus and the police) as well as the ideological systems of meaning (hegemony). Yet power as domination is not the only view. Hannah Arendt, for instance, defined power as "the human ability to act in concert," and maintained that "power belongs to a group and remains in existence only as long as the group holds together."[14] This cooperative notion of social power is also seen in the work of Robert Dahl, who examines power as the social process of "decision making" in which elites typically dominate a nevertheless open "participant political culture" in which various groups participate.[15] Outhwaite and Bottomore suggest that there is room for "a more comprehensive view" of power that stresses "both the need of the powerful to enlist cooperation and form coalitions *and* their need to avert or overcome opposition."[16] This more comprehensive view of power is what I have in mind in using the phrase "garnering consent."

All of these elements of power—insertion, surveillance, agenda setting, and garnering consent—are equally significant as they bear upon the "ability to make a difference in the world." Each is discussed in relation to the globalizers in the following chapters, but first it is necessary to take this definition of power to the global level. What does power look like on a transnational scale?

Global Governance

Many scholars have attempted a theoretical understanding of global power. All have drawn upon the various theoretical traditions briefly referred to in the preceding. My analysis borrows primarily from the world-system and world-polity perspectives in sociology. Most pertinent is the work of William I. Robinson, who utilizes a Marxian interpretation of state power to develop a model of global politics he refers to as "the transnational state apparatus." Although my theory of global power adds some important elements missing from Robinson's framework—in particular, the Foucauldian emphasis on knowledge systems and surveillance and the cooperative elements of power that can shape global political relations—I consider Robinson's frame to be the best articulation of global power relations to date and, therefore, I use it as a central point of departure for my interpretation of the globalizers in Honduras.[17]

According to Robinson's model, what we think of as the state is a historically contingent entity. Nation-states (or "national states," as Robinson prefers) arose as "particular embodiments of the constellations of social groups and classes that developed within the system of nation states in earlier epochs of capitalism."[18] But these relations between classes and groups have now "outgrown" the nation-state, even as its original institutions persist.

Classes and groups have outgrown the national state because of economic globalization. Economic globalization, in Robinson's view, is a "new stage . . . of world capitalism" and is the result of a "profound restructuring of world capitalism that began in the 1970s . . . the near culmination of the centuries long process of the spread of capitalist production relations around the world and its displacement of all pre-capitalist relations."[19]

Robinson makes a distinction between what he calls "a world economy" (pre-1970s) and "a global economy" (the current post-1970s system). A world economy entailed national circuits of accumulation that were linked to each other through commodity exchange and capital flows in an integrated international market. A global economy, on the other hand, arises as globalization breaks down borders between nations and integrates the national circuits into a global circuit of accumulation.

Such a new economic system, he argues, compels us to reconsider the politics of the nation-state. "The political reorganization of world capitalism has lagged behind its economic reorganization," he maintains, but we can see the emergence of a new transnational state.[20] I disagree with Robinson that the TNS has lagged behind economic globalization. In fact, economic globalization may be contingent upon political globalization. I illustrate in the chapters that follow, for example, how economic globalization (such as the emergence of offshore assembly factories in Honduras) was actually *preceded* by political decisions and policies put in place by the globalizers. Nevertheless, Robinson's model of the TNS is a highly effective tool for explaining the nature of global governance in Honduras. It also elucidates the broader global structure of international development assistance throughout the developing world.

In defining the TNS, Robinson writes, "It is a particular constellation of class forces and relations bound up with capitalist globalization and the rise of a transnational capitalist class embodied in a diverse set of political institutions . . . an emerging network that comprises transformed and externally-integrated national states *together with* the supranational economic and political forums that have not yet acquired any centralized form."[21]

Robinson argues that the emergence of the TNS is a dynamic, unfolding process, but it *is* observable. Its emergence is characterized by two things: first, we can observe "the reorganization of the state in each nation," and, second, we can study "the simultaneous rise of truly supranational economic and political institutions." These processes are not mutually exclusive; rather, they go hand in hand.[22] In other words, the state does not wither away as a result of globalization but becomes "transformed with respect to its functions"; it becomes a "functional component of the larger transnational state." The function of the nation-state shifts from the formulation of national policies to the administration of global agendas "formulated through supranational institutions." These supranational institutions are gradually supplanting national institutions in policy development and in the management and administration of the global economy. Such institutions, according to Robinson, consist of: "economic forums" such as the International Monetary Fund, WB, and the World Trade Organization; "political forums" such as the Group of Seven nations, the Group of Twenty-two, the United Nations, Organisation for Economic Co-operation and Development, and the European Union; and "regional trade groups" such as the North American Free Trade Agreement and Asia-Pacific Economic Cooperation (fig. 7).[23] To this list I would add "international development organizations" such as the bilateral aid agencies (USAID, United States Agency for International Development; GTZ, Deutsche Gesellschaft für Technische Zusammenarbeit; JICA, Japan International Cooperation Agency, etc.), since they, too, are institutional arrangements that operate politically at a truly transnational level.

These two processes—the transformation of the nation-state and the increasing prevalence of transnational institutions—are, as I will show, observable phenomena in Honduras. It is important to keep in mind that the two components, the national state and transnational political institutions, function in tandem to make up the TNS; as will be seen, there is cooperation between international development organizations and the Honduran national government.

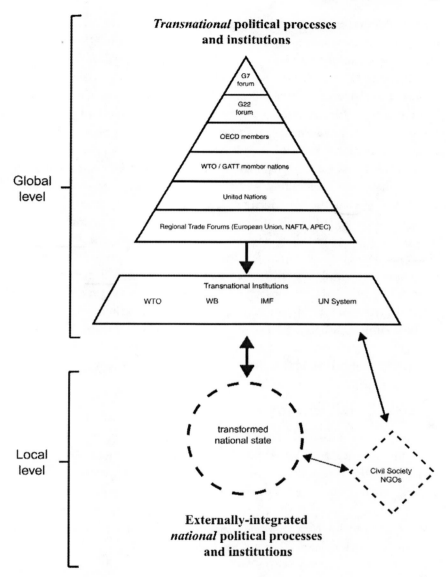

Figure 7. Robinson's Model of the Transnational State Apparatus

So who works in the TNS? Robinson argues that "transnational functionaries" and their transnationalized "counterparts" at the national level staff the "transformed national states."[24] I have termed these two sets of agents "expat" and "Honduran" globalizers, respectively. Together, these globalizers form a "transnational state cadre" that acts as the "midwife of capitalist globalization."[25]

In the end, Robinson argues, peripheral societies such as Honduras become transformed by, and eventually participate in the activities of, the TNS. They change from nation-states to "neo-liberal states" functioning as part of the larger TNS. These transformed neoliberal states perform three essential services—what I have been calling "global agendas"—in the interest of economic globalization: First, they provide the basic infrastructure necessary for global economic activity. They build and maintain air and sea ports, communication networks, roads and bridges, energy and educational systems. Second, they adopt fiscal and monetary policies that ensure macroeconomic stability, foreign investment, and export-oriented economic growth. Third, they provide social order and stability through coercive and consensual mechanisms of social control (what Robinson calls "democracy and development"). According to Robinson, "when the transnational elite speaks of 'governance,' it is referring to these functions and the capacity to fulfill them."[26] These are the three central global agendas that the globalizers are advancing in Honduras.

[margin note: 3 key "neo-liberal state" functions]

Global Governance in Honduras

Analyzing the broad array of development projects going on in Honduras, it is difficult to find areas where the globalizers are not involved. They are into everything—from coordinating women's sewing cooperatives in the remote rural towns of Olancho to designing macroeconomic stability programs for the Honduran Central Bank; all fall under the globalizers' domain.[27] Using Robinson's model as a frame, we can see how this extremely broad range of development activities reflects the three key global agendas pursued by the TNS: infrastructure, neoliberal reform, and social welfare.

Regarding the first, the globalizers in Honduras engage in a large number of development initiatives targeted at building infrastructure. The WB, USAID, and JICA have built and maintained the seaports at Puerto Cortes; developed proposals for a new airport in Tegucigalpa; installed satellite dishes and telecommunication cables; built electricity-generating facilities and transmission lines; and constructed thousands of kilometers of roads and bridges.

The infrastructural attention has reached as far as even the garbage trucks in Tegucigalpa, which were donated by a bilateral aid agency as part of an "urban sanitation" development project. Curious residents of the capital city might be pleased to know that the garbage trucks that pick up their weekly rubbish have a Japanese flag painted on their doors because the matter of "garbage and sanitation" is governed through the cooperation between JICA and the Honduran Ministry of Water and Sanitation, SANAA. Tegucigalpa's residents might also be interested to know the Japanese are also involved in the redesign of Tegucigalpa's roadways, the design for the new airport, and the installation of a new water treatment plant.

The second main activity of the TNS, fostering broad economic policies that promote macroeconomic stability, foreign investment, and export-oriented economic growth, is also easily observed in the globalizers' activities in Honduras. In its official planning documents, the WB refers to this global agenda as "trade and investment promotion." USAID calls it "reviving and accelerating economic growth." Other agencies (such as the GTZ or the United Nations Development Programme), no matter their name for it, promote the same agenda. When development workers talk about "economic development," in reality they are referring to this agenda. In Honduras, these projects focus especially on its largest economic sector: agriculture. The globalizers are deeply involved in banana and coffee projects (Honduras's main export crops); but they are also promoting the "diversification" of Honduran agricultural products. They support growing "winter vegetables"[28] such as asparagus and onions; cantaloupes, exotic vegetables and fruits;[29] as well as shrimp, beef, fish, and swine.[30] In addition, each of these products requires the development of various technologies—which become a part of development agencies' agendas—such as erosion prevention, fertilizer and pesticide application, the development of sustainable agricultural practices, irrigation, land terracing, and the transportation, distribution, processing, and marketing of agricultural products.[31]

Agriculture may be the largest economic sector in which the globalizers are involved, but it is not the only one; they also work in what are broadly defined as "natural resources," such as logging and forestry projects and mining. Indeed, wood products, silver, gold, and other ores are becoming major Honduran exports as a result of the globalizers' activities. In addition, industrial activities such as offshore manufacturing are promoted as part of the global agenda of export-oriented economic growth.

The globalizers also work on economic growth at the highest levels of banking and finance. Numerous development agencies are involved in macro-economic policy development with both the private and public sectors. USAID carried out a project training Honduran bankers in agricultural subsidy issues. The Central American Bank for Economic Integration, in conjunction with Harvard University, undertook a project designed to promote private enterprise, the privatization of infrastructure, strengthening the financial sector, and market regulation. The project aimed to train entrepreneurs, bankers, and government officials on these issues. In addition, the WB, as a part of its "foreign investment advisory service" promoting direct foreign investment, established a project for preparing a "diagnosis of the business environment" in order to "assist the government to improve the investment climate" by promoting "tourism, forestry, and maquila [activities]."[32]

Honduran government reform is another agenda under the broader "economic promotion" platform. There are many development agency projects devoted to improving governance, state modernization, institution building, and decentralization in the national government. Some of the globalizers' projects have directly targeted the legal system. The elimination of "fito-sanitary" import certificates; the creation of juvenile prisons; the modernization of land-titling procedures; the promotion of children's and women's legal protections; and the training of Honduran judges in legal practices more consistent with the U.S. legal system are some of the reforms that have resulted in part from these projects. Even the Honduran military and police force have received training and equipment from international development organizations and bilateral donors.

In relation to the third global agenda, social welfare, the globalizers engage in a wide range of activities under the broad rubrics of "poverty reduction," "social development," and "social safety nets." Their projects include health, education, housing, and other social welfare programs. In the area of health, they fund and coordinate health projects with the Ministry of Health: immunizations, AIDS prevention, infant health, family planning, and broad public health campaigns related to various diseases and concerns. The globalizers even deliver such key health services as aid to the disabled, dental and eye exams, and oral rehydration therapy. There is not one area of health care taken care of solely by Honduran governmental authorities; health in Honduras is managed through global governance.

In 1995, for example, the Honduran government hired the Japanese development organization JICA to conduct an investigation of their national health-care system and formulate a master health-care plan for the country based on the results. This represents a striking case of the government turning over to a foreign development agency the important matter of the national policy on health care.

In response to Arundhati Roy's question at the beginning of the chapter as to what the planners are doing, the answer is clear. A better question might be, What *aren't* they doing? They are working on every policy issue in Honduras. They are also, in each case, applying a global agenda for the ostensible purpose of bringing about development for Honduras. The globalizers, it must be concluded, are involved in governing Honduran society. The larger agencies, the WB, USAID, and the Inter-American Development Bank, for example, work in every social sector. Others—like CARE—occupy a niche within this system. The Spanish work more in water and sanitation; the Germans, in forestry. Still others, such as Fundación Hondureña de Rehabilitación e Integración del Limitado, an NGO devoted to helping the disabled, or ENERSOL, which installs solar-power generators in rural areas, have a highly specialized role. Whatever the scope of their activities, Honduras is de facto governed by the globalizers and their Honduran counterparts.

Taken together, all of the "governing" that gets done by the international development organizations becomes significant in a small country of only six million people. There are hundreds of agencies from around the globe carrying out development activities in Honduras, each working with the government and with one another; they can be viewed as a *global consortium* conducting governance in Honduras. This consortium of institutions and people are in the country neither to solely build up the national government (even as they often call their work "nation building") nor to tear it down; they tear down some national institutions and build up others. They do not want to completely take over by replacing national institutions with their own, but neither do they want those national institutions to have complete control over the globalization process. Instead, they work to *transform* the Honduran government into a part of the structures of global governance. In this way, development organizations are responsible for bringing about a metamorphosis of the public space in the developing world. As catalysts of governmental transformation, they facilitate the process through which the Honduran national government becomes integrated into the transnational processes created by the donor countries in order to govern globally. The agencies and experts, both foreign and Honduran, are thus changing the national government of Honduras into something new: a global government, or a global state (fig. 8).

Mechanisms of Power

To understand the globalizers' involvement in governance, it is necessary to clarify the mechanisms of power they have at their disposal. I briefly discuss below how each of the four mechanisms of power—insertion, surveillance, agenda setting, and garnering consent—relates to the activities of the global-izers in Honduras. I then use these four mechanisms as a framework in my analysis of the three case studies presented in the chapters to follow: El Cajón, the *maquiladoras,* and the reconstruction after Hurricane Mitch.

Insertion: Intervening in Local Politics

International institutions intervene in the local Honduran political process. This intervention can be called the *insertion phase,* the phase in which an international organization gains entrée to the local political process or inserts itself into the local policy debates. Insertion takes place in one of two ways: either the development organization is invited by a local institution to partici-pate in an initiative, or, through its own efforts, it inserts itself into the local po-litical process. In the case of an invitation, the development agency has already achieved some degree of consent from local interests. Frequently, the distinc-tion between the two means of insertion is difficult to determine. There are cases in which the Honduran government, for instance, is approached by an ex-ternal agency requesting it be asked to become involved. Therefore, even though the government is technically inviting the agency to participate in a particular policy concern, the invitation is in effect the result of the agency's self-insertion.

Surveillance: The Governor's Gaze

Once the external agency is involved, next comes the *surveillance phase.* During this phase, the globalizers conduct monitoring, research, and evalua-tion in order to gather information regarding the problem and to develop plans of action. These activities often take place in conjunction with local agencies and in accordance with the development organization's general as well as more specific objectives and agendas. The ability of development organizations to subject Honduras to their "gaze" reveals the nature of their powerful position in Honduran society.

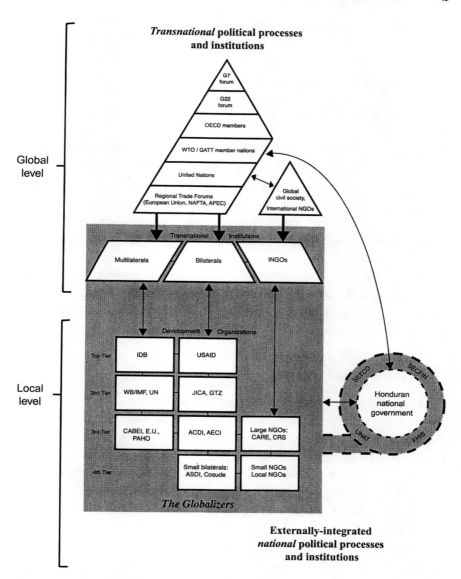

Figure 8. The Global Government in Honduras

I use the terms "surveillance" and "governor's gaze" in reference to the vantage point from which the development agencies view public policy in Honduras because of their implication that this observation is done for a purpose, to achieve a particular end. The terms also imply a power disparity between the observers and the observed. The relationship is a top-down one, with the development workers looking down on the societies they are assisting from their elevated positions in the social hierarchy and making policy decisions, designing programs, and generally planning for those down below. They look at macrolevel problems and implement solutions far from where they live and work, thus relatively free from having to live with the results. If Honduran, they are unlikely to live in the same neighborhoods as the aid recipients. And if they are expatriate development workers, they have usually left the country long before the consequences of their decisions are fully felt and understood.

Surveillance gives the globalizers information and knowledge they can use in developing their plans of action and in garnering consent should their plans face the need of persuasion or justification. I turn now to these latter two mechanisms of power.

Agenda Setting: Creating a Multiplicity of Blueprints for Running the Country

Effective governance requires not only information about the conditions of the country and its problems; concrete plans and mission statements regarding how they will act in relation to the conditions they observe and the problems they seek to address are also needed. The development organizations I visited in Honduras all had blueprints setting out the various planned initiatives and their rationale. Reading their official reports, mission statements, and master plans is a good way to see how development institutions view their particular mission.

Often when asking international development planners to explain their mission, I was referred to official institutional documents for answers. I was told by one such official, for example, that if I wanted to see the big picture of what his organization was doing in Honduras, I should read their "Long-Range Strategic Plan." The hundred-page document outlined his organization's objectives and projects for the next five years. It contained background information on Honduras and its "development status," including "basic indicators of poverty" and "Honduran trends." It identified key "priority areas for intervention" and specified what the organization's "niche" was within these priorities. Finally, it outlined various "program changes," "new project initiatives," and "funding projections" for 1995–2000, along with "benchmarks" for ascertaining the success or failure of such initiatives down the road.[33]

There are other such blueprints: The WB has its "Country Assistance Strategy"; USAID had a "Strategic Country Objectives: Annual Report"; CARE and UNICEF produced "Long Range Strategic Plans." Regardless of the name, every agency possessed formalized plans for their activities in Honduras. These reports outlined courses of action and usually argued the particular suitability of the institution in an area of development and its comparative advantage or institutional niche in Honduras relative to others. Nevertheless, all situate their activities in the context of governing the country as a whole.

Garnering Consent

Putting a plan into action requires *garnering consent* from local institutions. Sometimes these local agencies have their own concerns and agendas that conflict with those of the globalizers. In these situations, external agencies must promote their plans and encourage their acceptance through various means, such as providing financial assistance, engaging in public relations campaigns, lobbying, or by conducting trainings, workshops, and coordination meetings.

Ultimately, this is where much of the globalizers' power and influence resides, and the international development agencies spend a lot of time and money on "creating influence" and getting the "locals on board" with their agendas. The most common strategy for garnering consent is adopting a policy whereby the development agency acts *only* if approached by a local institution. Such a policy stipulates that Hondurans must first define a goal or project and bring it to the attention of the donor community. The globalizers are thus assured that the local institutions doing the asking are also implicitly giving their consent for external intervention. Often (though not always) this consent is given in a legal agreement. Such agreements create the illusion the Hondurans are in control. It is an illusion in the light of the realities of the broader context in which the decision is made to pursue a particular plan of action. Honduran institutions bring their plans and requests for assistance to international organizations with already established global agendas. Therefore, requests for assistance that coincide with these global agendas are likely to be funded and pursued through development projects, whereas requests

A "we know best" approach
by people w/ agendas.

in conflict with these global agendas are likely to be turned down, or more often, ignored. In other words, by making Honduran institutions draft formal requests or plans for international development assistance, the globalizers are requiring the Hondurans to learn which global agendas are considered realistic and which are out of fashion or unrealistic. Hondurans, for the most part, are aware of this dance they must do and usually craft their proposals so as to correspond with what the globalizers want. The globalizers thus bring about compliance with their agendas through their positive decisions regarding global agendas they wish to emphasize and through negative decisions concerning global agendas that do not appear in their blueprints.

The Consequences of Globalizer Power and the Repeating Cycle of Governance

Having garnered local consent, the plan is carried out and the development project is implemented—and the globalizers "make a difference in the world." This ability to permanently alter Honduran reality is the ultimate measuring rod for the globalizers' power in Honduras, and I examine its consequences in the following chapters. Worth emphasizing, however, is that the globalizer's work does not end with a project's implementation. Once a development project is concluded, it, too, becomes subject to the governor's gaze; it must be evaluated and studied in the light of ongoing global agendas. In other words, the cycle begins again as the globalizers insert themselves into new questions, new problems, and new agendas to be implemented. The globalizers create plans of action and garner consent for these new concerns. Although this process is sometimes chronological, the phases are more often overlapping and cyclical in nature; they are built into the operative structure of the international development institutions themselves.

El Cajón Dam

CHAPTER SIX

Building Dams

The El Cajón dam is a monument—literally and figuratively—to an out-moded concept of development. This concept views development as a top-down process led by technocratic and political elites whose primary task is to replicate the social and economic conditions of the wealthy countries in poorer countries (like Honduras) primarily through the transfer of technology.

— ANTHROPOLOGIST WILLIAM LOKER, 1998

El Cajón

As I leaned against the concrete railing and looked over the edge of the dam, I held my breath. Seven hundred feet below churned the turquoise water of the Humuya River. I was standing on El Cajón, the eighth highest dam in the world. Nine feet higher than Hoover Dam in the United States, it is perhaps even more impressive because of its state-of-the-art, high-tech design. The dam's concrete wall has a concave shape, like a membrane under pressure, and so anyone standing on top of the dam is positioned out over the canyon as the wall of the dam curves away beneath their feet. Looking at this curved wall from above gives one a strong sensation of vertigo.

Near the bottom of the dam's wall, I noticed four jets of water shooting out of the rock cliff into the river.

"Those must be from the turbines," I said, pointing at the four outlets.

"Yes," my guide explained, "the powerhouse is down there. That is where they are supposed to be making all the electricity. But as you know they have had many problems."

I had come to visit the dam because of the controversy surrounding these problems at El Cajón. The hydroelectric complex was built in 1985, but by 1994 it was not producing as much electricity as its design had promised. As a result, the entire country of Honduras was experiencing major energy shortages. During the dry season in 1994, for instance, these shortages became so severe that the government had to impose energy rationing throughout the country. The blackouts, many lasting up to ten hours at a time, had become a black eye for the government, especially its electrical utility company, ENEE (Empresa Nacional de Energía Eléctrica), which owned the dam. They were accused of mismanaging the hydroelectric facility and not taking the measures needed to ensure its successful operation. The government's defense was that it simply had not rained enough over a two-year period to fill the reservoir adequately. Whatever the reasons, El Cajón was widely perceived to be the cause of the country's energy problems.

It was not supposed to be this way. El Cajón was born as a development project designed to "provide, at the least cost, generating capability adequate to serve the . . . growing demand in Honduras."[1] Developing countries need electricity to pursue industrial and technological development, and El Cajón was designed to produce enough electrical power for the Honduran energy grid so that it would have enough left over to export to neighboring countries for profit. Its four turbines were supposed to produce 300 megawatts of power, representing 70 percent of Honduras's electricity demand. Before El Cajón, the country's single largest electricity-generating facility was the Rio Lindo Dam, which produced 84 megawatts. The Inter-American Development Bank (IDB) and the World Bank (WB) had come up with the El Cajón design as "the best solution" to Honduras's future energy needs.[2]

It was the largest single development project in Honduras's history. The dam cost over $800 million to build. Subsequent repairs put the final tally closer to $1 billion. The debt incurred by the Honduran public to meet this cost represented 40 percent of its total foreign debt at the time. Some Honduran groups had expressed concern that El Cajón was too big, that it might be better to build several small dams instead. They argued that investing so much money in a single dam would be like putting all your eggs in one basket. In the face of these concerns, the government and the international development banks emphasized the promise of El Cajón: It was the best means for quickly building up the Honduran energy infrastructure; moreover, they insisted, citizens' concerns were unfounded. The dam would be state-of-the-art.

Its international consultants and engineers called it "the best of its time" and believed it would provide maximum hydropower to the country for at least fifty years.[3] This prediction proved to be overly optimistic. As I stood on the crest of the dam that day in 1996, El Cajón was operating at only 60 percent of its electricity-generating capacity. It was only eleven years old. It had failed at nine.

As I crossed to the other side of the walkway and looked into the vast reservoir of water behind the dam, it was easy to see the problem. The reservoir was only two-thirds full. The water level was one hundred feet lower than it was supposed to be. To the right, near the dam, was a large concrete structure with a cylindrical tower (the "spillway vortex tower," I later learned) rising above it. It was at least one hundred feet tall.

"That is supposed to be underwater," my guide informed me. "The water level is pretty low right now. They don't really know what the problem is."

The tower was completely dry; it was hard to even imagine water covering it. The water level would have to rise another twenty feet just to touch its base. And the level in 1996 was much better than two years prior, when it reached a historic low, some two hundred feet below its intended capacity. The water level was so low at that time it barely reached the dam's power-generating intakes; the plant almost had to be shut down entirely. This was the cause of the 1994 energy crisis. The newspapers offered various explanations for why the reservoir was so empty: drought, watershed mismanagement, deforestation, dam mismanagement, and leaks beneath the dam had all been reported as possible causes. But no one seemed to know for certain.

As I stood there on the parapet looking over the depleted reservoir, thinking about the turbines below operating at only two-thirds capacity, I was confronted by a jarring juxtaposition: here was a state-of-the-art piece of technology designed and constructed by the best engineers on the planet—and it didn't work. What had gone wrong?

Development Banks and the Global Agenda of Infrastructure

Building dams poses unique difficulties for the developing world. In the first place, developing countries often lack the economic wherewithal to build such high-cost pieces of technology. In the case of Honduras, for example, the cost of El Cajón amounted to more than 50 percent of its total yearly economic output and four times its total central government revenues for one year.[4] In comparison, a similar project in the United States would represent only a tiny fraction of its annual national production or government expenditures.

Second, the specialized engineering expertise and sophisticated equipment required to build such high-tech projects are often scarce in developing countries. Although Honduras has engineers trained in various fields, it does not have a dam-building industry in which its engineers could gain direct experience in concrete dam design, hydroelectric turbine manufacturing, or electrical generator construction. These engineering technologies require highly specialized training, much more specialized than what is available in Honduras. In addition, these tasks can be undertaken only by unusually sophisticated research and technology firms with huge capital investments, and there are perhaps only ten to twenty firms in the entire world engaged in hydroelectric dam construction. One turbine for a hydroelectric dam, for example, requires metallurgical, structural, hydraulic, and thermal engineering expertise and costs approximately $5 or $6 million to build.[5] Developing countries look to the industrialized countries for such advanced technologies. Engineers, too, must be imported from abroad.

Enter the globalizers. They serve as liaisons in the transfer of know-how and technologies from the donor countries to the developing world. In the case of hydroelectric dam construction, the engineering expertise and high-tech equipment have been distributed to the developing world principally through the big development banks: most commonly in Latin America, the WB and IDB.

The WB started as an institution designed to finance European reconstruction after World War II. Once Europe was back on its feet, it turned to "development" as a way to continue its lending. The majority of early WB loans to developing countries went to building dams.[6] During the past fifty years, the WB alone has provided financing and technical assistance in ninety-three different developing countries for the construction of 604 large dams.[7] Approximately 40 percent of all dams built in developing countries have received WB funding. Currently it lends an average of $1 billion a year on large dams, and these loans return benefits to its member countries.

Other international development banks such as the IDB, the Asian Development Bank, the African Development Bank, the Caribbean Development Bank, and the Central American Bank for Economic Integration (CABEI) have also financed a significant amount of dam building and often work directly in conjunction with the WB, from which they often take their policy cues.

Dam building has been a preferred activity of all the development banks. One reason is these institutions prefer not to give small loans. It is easier and more efficient in terms of meeting their goals to approve a few large loans than to spend administrative resources on many small ones.[8] This is especially so vis-à-vis the pressure to lend, a well-documented phenomenon in the international development banks. This pressure originated in the 1960s as leaders of the WB realized that if its lending failed to grow, it would be receiving more money from developing countries in loan repayments than it was giving in the form of new loans—what are called "net negative transfers." As a solution to this problem, then president of the WB Robert McNamara suggested the WB become more integrally involved in the promotion of development projects throughout the developing world. During the 1970s and 1980s (the time when the El Cajón project was approved), consequently, virtually every project that came before the WB was approved, often despite environmental or feasibility concerns. According to a report by former WB vice president Willi Wapenhans, WB staff were so concerned with securing loan approvals for their projects that they would often downplay the risks associated with large dam projects and actively oppose any suggestion that a project not be approved because of environmental or social costs. The Wapenhans report referred to this dynamic as an "approval culture."[9]

The consequences of this approval culture are now widely known to have created problems. In recent years, nongovernmental organizations (NGOs) have become increasingly active in opposing large dam projects funded by the WB and other development banks.[10] Many of these organizations have raised environmental concerns. The harmful effects of large dams on the environment are now well understood,[11] but, as these NGOs have pointed out, for much of the WB's history (and certainly during the period 1970–85 period, when the El Cajón project was approved), there was virtually no environmental oversight. The WB did have an environmental appraisal department at the time of the El Cajón project, but it was grossly understaffed and operated principally as a rubber stamp on projects that had already been approved.[12] As a result, according to the environmental NGO the International Rivers Network, "most [dam project] reports concluded that [the dam] would have 'no significant environmental' impact."[13]

Many NGOs have opposed the WB's involvement in dam projects also because of its failure to adequately address the needs of people displaced by dams. Although WB policy dictates that a resettlement plan be included in

[handwritten margin note: Mass person displacement and a source of urban-migration]

dam projects, its own internal studies have found that half of its dam projects had no resettlement plan. The WB failed in many cases to take these issues fully into account because of the pressure to lend.[14]

Perhaps some of this pressure to approve projects came from powerful interests in the donor countries themselves. Besides the WB's internal dynamics that may obstruct its staff's ability to evaluate potential projects objectively, there is the authority of the donor countries. Much of the WB's lending activity is directly related to financing contracts for donor-country industries. In the case of hydroelectric power projects, the international development banks have operated in tandem with the multibillion dollar global dam-building industry. This industry is dominated by German, Swiss, Japanese, and U.S. engineering and heavy industrial firms such as Siemens and Toshiba. WB loans to developing countries for the purpose of building dams usually end up returning to the donor countries in the form of lucrative contracts for the companies based there. According to the WB's own internal audit of dam-related loans to developing countries worldwide, "in 1993, 58% of Bank project funds went to businesses located outside the borrowing country. Most (78%) of that amount was paid to contractors in the industrialized North."[15] In other words, international development banks provide what amounts to a global government subsidy to the world's largest dam builders, which are located mainly in donor countries whose governments finance those development bank activities in the first place. As in the case of El Cajón, this relationship is often rather direct. The specific donor countries most involved in the development project are typically the countries where the major contractors for the project are headquartered.

[handwritten margin note: Lots of First-world expertise required]

Despite the benefits donor countries receive from financing the international dam-building industry, erecting dams has certain risks that make it an inherently *political* process. First, dams mean that a vital public resource, a river, will be impounded. People both upstream and downstream will be affected. Above the dam, the rich agricultural zones that typically exist along the valley bottom will be flooded, and if the flooding is significant, as it was with the formation of the El Cajón reservoir, the many people living in these zones and dependent upon them for their livelihood will have to be relocated. Their political consent is therefore vital for the successful construction of a dam. The political agreement of people downstream is also important since the river on which they may depend for their livelihood (for irrigation, fishing, tourism, etc.) will be diverted to new purposes; the amount of water flowing down the river will be regulated by dam authorities. These authorities

[handwritten margin note: Major Environmental Consequences]

must have political legitimacy because they will be held accountable for any problems the dam may cause the people living both upstream and downstream.

Impounding a river entails, too, the exploitation of an important natural resource: the large area of land serving as the river's watershed. The decision to exploit thousands of square kilometers of land for the purpose of generating electricity (again, as was the case for El Cajón) has local, national, and international consequences. A dam fundamentally alters an ecosystem, for example. Fish and other aquatic wildlife dependent on the ability to migrate through the river may become endangered; flora and fauna living on the valley floor could suffer a similar fate once it is flooded. White-water rapids, which provide important ecological functions, may be reduced to a trickle. The question of who has the right to dam a river and cause such dramatic environmental consequences is a political one. And the legal authority to do such a thing typically involves some sort of state apparatus that is expected to take into account the various interests and consequences related to such an activity. Any review of the long human experience of building dams throughout the world makes clear that such decisions are usually left to some sort of governmental structure.[16]

Furthermore, dams are expensive. Most are built using the pooled resources of public revenue. Government taxes, bonds, or loans are the typical manner of financing the high costs of dam construction. In part, this is because market mechanisms may not provide enough incentive for private entrepreneurs to invest in their construction: start-up costs are very high and the potential for making a profit is low and long term. It also has to do with the economic benefits of a dam, inasmuch as they depend on the utilization of a public resource, being defined usually as a public good. The electricity generated by a hydroelectric dam, for instance, or the water provided for irrigation, or flood protection—all are typically viewed as something that should be made available to everyone and not just a privileged few.[17] Because dams typically rely on public financing, they generally require broad political support.

In sum, building dams poses political, financial, and technical risks and challenges. Nevertheless, dams are frequently seen as offering potentially high economic returns and are attractive means to provide energy infrastructure. Such is the agenda advanced by the globalizers. They argue that dams are a cost-effective way of providing the electricity developing countries need to develop. And, as mentioned, the donor countries are mindful of the significant economic benefits the dam builders in their countries stand to win. How this

NO ACCOUNTABILITY TO POPULACE BY GLOBALIZERS!

global agenda figured in the story of El Cajón Dam in Honduras offers an important insight into the international political processes of dam building in other countries as well.

Insertion of the Globalizers into ENEE's Local Agenda

In 1957, the Honduran government, under the leadership of the newly elected president, Ramón Villeda Morales, created the National Electrical Energy Company (Empresa Nacional de Energía Eléctrica, ENEE). As part of a national plan to generate more electricity for the future, ENEE launched an inquiry into the possibility of building hydroelectric dams to supplement the thermoelectric (diesel) plants that it had been using up to that point. ENEE hired the Harza Engineering Firm of Chicago to survey and identify possible locations for future dams. The study identified a water basin in the north-central mountains where two of Honduras's largest rivers (the Suyapa and Humuya) meet as one of the most promising options.[18]

By 1960, ENEE had made arrangements with the WB, the IDB, and the United States Agency for International Development (USAID) for financing various electrical power projects in the country, including power transmission and distribution lines, more diesel plants, and several relatively small hydroelectric dams. In conjunction with these externally financed projects, ENEE developed a Honduran hydro potential master plan in 1965 identifying hydroelectric power as an optimal solution to the country's previous dependency on imported petroleum for its energy needs. This master plan laid out a time line for upgrading the Honduran electrical grid, calling for new generating facilities and, most importantly, expert contractors to conduct more precise prefeasibility studies regarding the hydroelectric dam projects being considered.

In 1967, the Motor Columbus Consulting Engineers of Baden, Switzerland, won the contract to conduct feasibility studies for all of the potential basins. The studies examined the specific hydrological and geological conditions at the potential dam sites and whether the conditions would allow for the cost-effective construction of hydroelectric power plants. In addition to collecting rainfall and other important hydrological data in the watersheds under study, ENEE asked the Motor Columbus engineers to carry out a comparative study of the Humuya River site relative to other potential sites. It was identified as the best choice in terms of maximum power-generating potential at the lowest construction cost. ENEE therefore contracted Motor Columbus to design the dam.[19]

It must be kept in mind that by the late 1960s, early 1970s, the transnational political arrangement I have been referring to as "global governance" was already in place. Honduran government officials at ENEE were already working with officials from the international development banks and the foreign engineering consultants that would be responsible for the construction of El Cajón Dam. The administration of the project was clear from the outset: First, the development banks were given top authority in terms of overall project management. They would work directly with national personnel from ENEE and their board of directors, made up of other Honduran government officials (from the Ministries of Public Works and Natural Resources and Planning). This management group would facilitate overall project financing and coordination. Second, the construction group was put under the authority of the chief contractor, Motor Columbus. This group would be made up of Honduran personnel advised by foreign experts and be in charge of coordinating the multiple engineering services, project design, and construction.[20] In addition, because of the significant technical, contractual, and administrative aspects of the project, a special independent consultants' group was set up to oversee all aspects of the project. This group was made up of "five renowned experts who have technical abilities and professional experiences that place them among the most qualified in the world in regard to projects of this nature."[21] These experts were to meet every three months at the project site to "evaluate its progress, discuss relevant technical issues, review the planning and quality of work, study alternatives and solutions should any problem arise, and give their recommendations such that the great effort that the nation is putting forth in constructing the work bears optimal fruit for the good of the country."[22] With the WB and the IDB given top authority, the Swiss engineering firm Motor Columbus in charge of project design and planning, and prestigious foreign experts making up the independent consulting team, the El Cajón project was firmly in the hands of the globalizers and their Honduran counterparts.

Surveillance: Feasibility Studies for El Cajón

As a first important task in the dam project, geotechnical, thermodynamic, mechanical, structural, and hydraulic engineers were hired to perform diagnostic studies providing key data for the dam's construction. Motor Columbus coordinated and conducted most of these feasibility studies, for which it would receive approximately $14 million between 1967 and 1975, financed by the WB and CABEI.[23] These studies included geological and geotechnical observations of the seismic activity, water table characteristics, and properties of the riverbed.[24] They revealed that the geological formation of the El Cajón valley is mostly impermeable volcanic rock, perfect for containing the planned reservoir of 5.7 billion cubic meters of water. It was noted, however, that near the actual dam site, the Humuya River had eroded the volcanic rock, exposing a number of limestone fissures through which water could seep and cause not only water loss but also enormous uplift pressure under the dam that would cause severe damage. These fissures had to be plugged, and the engineers proposed drilling hundreds of holes into the sides of the valley near the dam and injecting them with forty thousand cubic tons of cement grout. The resulting grout curtain would seal off the entire basin around the dam and prevent any leakage through the limestone.

Accurate hydrological data (average rainfall in the catchment area) was crucial to the dam's designers, and this posed an immediate problem: Normally, to build a dam of this size, engineers would need rainfall data for at least fifty years (preferably one hundred) in order to accurately predict the maximum (flood) and minimum (drought) levels of inflow to the dam reservoir. However, no such data existed for the El Cajón watershed. Motor Columbus began recording rainfall in 1967 and continued through 1978; they then extrapolated from these figures to arrive at estimates. Fortunately for the engineers, a hurricane (Fifi) struck Honduras in 1974, which gave them a fairly good idea of a maximum rain event. With only eleven years of real data, however, the engineers were forced to use estimates in the dam's design that, as will become evident, turned out to be wrong.[25]

In addition to the technical studies, Motor Columbus was assigned the task of assessing the ecological, environmental, and resettlement aspects of the project. Environmental assessments were rare in the 1960s and 1970s. Few environmental policies were in place in the WB at the time of the dam's approval.[26] Perhaps because of this fact, Motor Columbus was not required to conduct any systematic wildlife inventories or the sorts of environmental assessments currently used to evaluate the environmental consequences of large dams. There was, for example, no biodiversity study to assess whether species of fish would be adversely affected or whether the broader genetic diversity of the basin would decline as a result of the project. There was also no study on how building the dam might impair water quality downstream. Nor did the El Cajón designers examine the issue of deforestation in the region and whether it might affect dam performance. Motor Columbus did evaluate river sedimentation, finding that "sedimentation has no significant impact on project economy."[27]

On the issue of resettlement, it concluded that the dam would have negative effects on the population living in and around the reservoir area. Motor Columbus determined the project would have to compensate for loss of land and houses and provide alternatives to displaced families.[28] Twelve potential relocation sites were evaluated in terms of suitability. In 1976, at the time of the resettlement study, neither the WB nor the IDB had any specific policy guidelines regarding the resettlement of dam-affected populations.[29] Such cases were dealt with on an individual basis. In the case of El Cajón, the project management group developed a resettlement program designed to cover "resettlement and compensation of the approximately 2,000 families affected by the project, including provision of means to maintain or enhance their standard of living."[30]

To "establish the precise number of people living in the El Cajón basin," the group contracted the Honduran Instituto Nacional Agrario (INA, National Agrarian Institute) to design and conduct a census of the area.[31] Completed in 1979, the study estimated that 1,848 people (six hundred families) would be displaced by the dam and 313 houses would be flooded.[32] The INA and Motor Columbus concluded that the project should offer $12,500 per family for "relocation costs."[33]

The WB arranged to have anthropologist Thomas Schorr—an expert consultant from the Pan American Health Organization (PAHO)—"help ENEE and the INA" plan the resettlement.[34] They designed an elaborate resettlement plan that included monetary compensation for displaced families, job training programs, and other social assistance to the affected population. The programs were placed under the responsibility of ENEE and the government of Honduras, and, according to anthropologists who subsequently studied the resettlement program, most of these benefits never materialized.[35]

There was one feasibility study in particular more important than all the others: the assessment of whether the project would be cost-effective. Using a five hundred thousand dollar loan from the IDB, ENEE and Motor Columbus hired EBASCO Incorporated, an independent consulting firm from New York

City, to conduct a detailed "system optimization study" comparing the costs and benefits of building El Cajón with those of alternatives.[36] These alternatives included building smaller dams first and postponing El Cajón until later; thermal plants first, then El Cajón; or thermal plants alone.[37] The study concluded that the "completion of El Cajón (with about 300 MW) in the mid-1980s was found to be less costly than all others." The economic benefits from the efficient production of electricity and its sale in a market that was expected to grow 10–11 percent a year, it was decided, far outweighed the project's cost. Furthermore, these benefits were calculated to be greater than those any other power-generating scheme would produce. In sum, El Cajón was going to make ENEE a lot of money. This conclusion, more than any other, was instrumental in the project going forward. One report, typical of the confidence the bank had in the economic projections, enthusiastically concluded that "the project has been chosen on an economically sound basis."[38] A report from the WB's president, Robert McNamara, states that "studies by . . . consultants have shown that the El Cajón project would be the least-cost solution for Honduras."[39]

The optimism[40] of these economic projections was based on two factors.[41] First, the world oil crisis of the mid-1970s made hydroelectric energy seem particularly attractive. Producing its electricity using diesel-powered thermal generators, Honduras was importing all of its petroleum from abroad, and hydroelectric energy was thus seen as a way to reduce its oil dependency.[42] EBASCO's cost-efficiency calculations were in fact based upon projected rising oil prices that, however, eventually failed to fully materialize. Second, there were other initiatives by the development banks to create an interconnected Central American power grid, and El Cajón would provide electricity to a broader Central American market (particularly to Nicaragua, which was already connected to Honduras through an earlier IDB loan).[43] Although the economists calculated that the benefits of El Cajón would be significantly large even if Honduras did not export electricity to its neighbors,[44] the ability to do so was seen as a major additional economic benefit of the project and is often cited as such in both WB and ENEE project documents.[45]

Because of the importance of the economic considerations in deciding whether the project should be given the green light, EBASCO's forecasts and feasibility conclusions were independently examined and updated by a Canadian firm, Montreal Engineering Company (MONENCO), as well as by Motor Columbus. MONENCO and Motor Columbus agreed with EBASCO's conclusions.

According to a subsequent evaluation of the EBASCO study conducted by the WB's own Operations Evaluation Department in 1989, however, the econometric tools used to assess the cost-effectiveness of El Cajón were *highly flawed*. The evaluation concluded that the economic studies left "much to be desired" and had led to "calamitous results."[46] In particular, EBASCO failed to consider several important economic risks: First, it did not "test sensitivity to market development," meaning it did not give cost-benefit estimates in the event the electricity market *failed* to develop as predicted. This "was a lapse not easily rationalized today . . . it seems simply to have been overlooked."[47] Second, EBASCO's forecasts did not take into account risks associated with future devaluation of the Honduran lempira, despite its devaluation vis-à-vis the foreign currencies making up the El Cajón project loans being an original concern.[48] Were the lempira to fall significantly, the economic gains from generating electricity would be far outweighed by the higher costs of servicing the debt denominated in foreign currencies. Again, this is something that EBASCO's economists missed.[49]

There were other economic factors that none of the globalizers considered. For instance, EBASCO's computer programs forecast economic costs and benefits of the dam only in terms of ENEE's bottom line. What about other Honduran institutions or groups? The foreign economists who evaluated the project did not take into account, for example, the broader costs of lost agricultural production. The lost access to the rich valley soil by Honduran farmers and corresponding decline in agricultural output demanded an evaluation of whether the net power benefits and increased revenue to ENEE would compensate for these losses, but this analysis, too, was neglected.[50]

The result was a skewed economic analysis that, even the WB admits, painted a rosy picture of the economic benefits Honduras could expect from building the dam.[51] The economic justification for the project neglected not only the predictable possibility of market failure but also the negative economic consequences suffered by people living in the El Cajón valley. Yet, as I shall point out, this "flawed analytic technique" would be used to justify the project when the globalizers had to sell El Cajón to its Honduran critics.[52]

There are two ways of interpreting the economic feasibility study and the importance placed upon its results by the international lenders and consultants who were designing El Cajón. The flaws of the report were either unintended error or they were intentionally overlooked in order to present a best case scenario for a project both Honduran government officials and the representatives from the international banks wanted to go forward. In the case of the former, blame would be placed upon the expert consultants at EBASCO and the WB for making the mistake of not undertaking standard risk assessments and for drawing conclusions that were "contrary to intuition, common sense, and experience."[53] If, however, they were deliberately overlooked, the blame—unshifted from EBASCO consultants and WB analysts—and its implications would be much more serious. It would be a case of malfeasance—of corruption—in which powerful interests manipulated the results of a supposedly independent study in order to advance a project that was worth millions. Although it is doubtful it could ever be ascertained which is the case, the WB's own assessment certainly leaves room for either conclusion:

> This was a lapse not easily rationalized today. Testing the sensitivity of results to market development is a standard *sine qua non* in electric power analysis. It seems simply to have been overlooked.... The experience of El Cajón raises the unpleasant question of whether or not the analytic technique was substituted for judgement. Curiously, there seems to have been no discussion of these issues by the Bank's watchdog group, Central Projects staff, or by anyone on the Loan Committee.[54]

Since no one knew at the time the economic analysis was flawed, such concerns were not in the minds of El Cajón's designers. There are no details in ENEE's official version of the project proposal, for example, regarding the economic feasibility study or the calculations and data on which it was based. It simply stated that Motor Columbus had "conducted a feasibility study ... demonstrating the advantages of El Cajón as the real and best choice." From ENEE's point of view, the estimated $35 million a year in petroleum savings meant that the project would pay for itself in about twenty years' time. The ENEE report cites these petroleum savings as *the* economic justification for the dam.[55] This is part of the power that the globalizers have: everyone must rely on their expert analysis of data they have created through their own surveillance.

Setting the Agenda: Final Design of the Dam

After a decade of feasibility studies conducted by an array of international consultants from various fields of professional expertise, ranging from engineering to economics to anthropology, Motor Columbus and ENEE had enough data and expert analysis to proceed with their final design. Motor Columbus was retained by ENEE and the government for the final engineering and design of the dam and to supervise construction and testing. For these services, Motor Columbus received $55.3 million, provided through a 1975 loan from CABEI.[56] The company was also assigned the task of coordinating project procurement, which meant it facilitated the international competitive bidding process determining which dam-construction companies would receive the estimated $300–$400 million in equipment and construction contracts.

Nicholas J. Schnitter, executive vice president of Motor Columbus, was the chief civil engineer in charge of coordinating the dam project from Baden. In Honduras, Dr. Harald Kreuzer, head of the dams department at Motor Columbus, served as the resident chief engineer in charge of coordinating the specialized designs for various elements of El Cajón. His counterpart at ENEE, A. Diaz Arriviallaga, was the in-country El Cajón project director and, under Kreuzer, was responsible for the supervision and construction of the project. The final dam blueprints were the result of the coordinated efforts of dozens of engineers, foreign and Honduran, working for numerous agencies.[57] Among them were ENEE geologists Ramon Guifarro and Jorge Flores, who worked along with Italian engineer M. Gerodetti on the grout curtain design, and D. Schulthess of Zurich, Switzerland, who designed the vortex spillway tower.[58] Many of these engineers published articles in professional engineering journals in the United States and Europe detailing their engineering activities in conjunction with the project.[59]

The final design was ambitious. The proposed dam spanned the 1,253-foot-wide canyon using an "elegant doubly curved maximum cantilever" variable-radius parabolic arch design "based on membrane theory."[60] According to UC Berkeley professor emeritus Jerome Raphael, one of the independent consultants advising ENEE and Motor Columbus, the El Cajón dam represented "a half-century's progress in concrete arch dams."[61] The designers installed a high-volume spillway and decided to raise the crest of the dam higher than originally planned to maximize the dam's flood-control potential. The resulting concrete wall was 741 feet tall, making it the highest concrete dam in the Western Hemisphere and the eighth highest dam in the world.[62] The design called for two stages of construction for the dam's underground powerhouse. The first stage, to be completed upon initial dam construction, would entail the installation of four Francis turbines, each producing 75 megawatts of electricity daily, for a total of 300 megawatts. A second stage called for four more turbines, for a daily total of 600 megawatts, to be added at an unspecified future date. According to ENEE, "the dam's generation of 600 MW will provide enough electrical energy to satisfy the power demand of the entire Honduran population for the next twenty years."[63]

Garnering Consent

Lending to a Military Government

By the time of El Cajón's final design, the Honduran government was, in many ways, already on board with the project. The government's consent had been garnered as early as 1965, when ENEE hired Motor Columbus to undertake its feasibility studies. At the time, Honduras was under the military rule of Colonel Osvaldo López Arellano. López remained in power throughout the period of surveillance and planning, and by the time the El Cajón project was ready to be signed and approved, the government was in full support.[64] In 1975, López was ousted by a military coup, and the new head of the armed forces, Alberto Melgar Castro, gave approval for the final design phase. Although Castro was subsequently overthrown by a military junta, the WB-led project was never in jeopardy. In fact, most of the project loans from the WB and the IDB were signed between 1978 and 1981, the period during which an unelected group of generals from the armed forces ran the country. There is no indication in WB project documents that lending hundreds of millions of dollars to a country under military rule was a concern.[65] This unconcern seems consistent with the findings of the International Rivers Network, an international NGO that has examined WB loans for large dams to military governments throughout the world; it concluded, "Neither these governments nor the Bank ever had to prove that building the dams would be in the public interest."[66]

Between November 1978 and June 1979, the Honduran government and representatives from the WB, the IDB, and other international development organizations completed the final negotiations for the El Cajón power project. The loan agreement (Loan 1805-HO) was signed with the WB on March 27, 1980.[67] ENEE was the borrower, but the Republic of Honduras guaranteed the loan. The WB loan of $125 million was only one part of the total $774 million "bank group package." The IDB provided another $185 million in loans, the CABEI lent $31 million, and the Organization of the Petroleum Exporting Countries provided $7.5 million. Most of these loans were given on concessional "official development" terms. For example, most of the IDB loan was repayable in twenty-five years at 1 percent interest. Others were not, however. The CABEI loan, for instance, was a commercial loan to be repaid in fifteen years at 8.75 percent interest. Consequently, the "concessional element" was not significant enough for the El Cajón financing to fit the definition of a development loan. Because of the commercial rates of many of the loans, Honduras would have to repay the El Cajón project costs at close to market rates, which would earn the donor countries even greater benefits than if the loans had been given on more concessional terms.

In addition to the multilateral lenders, the project had seven significant bilateral donors providing grants and loans to finance the dam's construction: Japan, Switzerland, Canada, Germany, Italy, the United Kingdom, and Venezuela. Of interest in terms of my analysis is that these primarily European donors are, across the board, the same countries in which the major contractors hired to construct the dam are based. This is the result of the project procurement rules, which required firms bidding for dam-related contracts to secure credit and financing from their own governments and commercial banks as a condition for consideration. The very donors providing the so-called economic assistance to Honduras for the dam are thus the same countries to which that money would return in the form of lucrative construction contracts for large corporations based in those countries. For example, Japan provided $33 million in official development assistance (ODA) and $11 million in commercial credit from the Japanese Exim Bank. In return, Ishikawa Heavy Industries won the contract for the $12 million hydraulic steel tubing that would carry the water from the dam's intakes to the powerhouse. Switzerland gave $8.4 million in ODA and $24.1 million in loans in conjunction with the participation of five Swiss firms in the building of El Cajón: Motor Columbus, with its $55 million worth of engineering design contracts; Ateliers de VEVEY, which supplied the $12 million Francis turbines; Brown Bovey, which provided the $3.6 million powerhouse control equipment; Losinger, contracted to undertake dam construction; and Swissboring, which worked on the grout curtain. Canada offered $26 million through its Canadian International Development

Agency, and the services of four Canadian firms—MARKHAM, ASEA Inc., Canadian Wire, and MONENCO—were engaged to build the electric substations. Germany was the next largest donor, giving $14 million of mixed ODA and credit toward the $15 million purchase of four generators and accessories from the German firm ABG Telefunken. The German construction firm Züblin was also selected as part of the dam construction consortium. Italian commercial banks lent $16.1 million, with participation from five Italian contractors: Impregilo (dam construction), Rodio, Cimentazioni e Sondaggi (grout curtain), Astaldi, and Codelfa (powerhouse). The United Kingdom contributed $10 million through its Commonwealth Development Corporation; Colcrete of London was contracted for "foundation treatment." And finally, Venezuela, through its Venezuelan Investment Fund, provided $33.8 million in commercial credit[68] and a Venezuelan firm, SVECA, was hired to install $9.3 million worth of high-voltage transmission lines.[69]

This $774 million dam project was to become the most expensive civil engineering undertaking ever in Honduras (even to this day). In all, 74 percent of the total project cost came in the form of an external loan or donation. The remaining 26 percent ($200 million) was provided by the Honduran government through its public works budget and the future ENEE revenues the dam was expected to generate. Nevertheless, this single project doubled the country's external debt[70] and absorbed 40 percent of internal public revenues for 1980–85.[71] Considering the "major financial undertaking" required by the project, even WB president Robert McNamara offered a word of caution: "Because of the large size of the project in the context of the Honduran economy, special precautions have been taken to reduce the risk of substantial cost overruns and to secure financing on appropriate terms."[72]

Quelling Civic Protest

> "The negotiations stage of the project cycle is seen by many borrowers as a largely *coercive* exercise designed to 'impose' the Bank's philosophy and to validate the findings of its promotional approach to appraisal." (World Bank Wapenhans report, 1992, cited in IRN, p. 14; *emphasis* in original)

The enormous cost of the dam caused concern among many Honduran engineers and public policy makers. Organizations such as the Honduran Society of Civil Engineers (Colegio de Ingeneiros Mecánicos y Eléctricos de Honduras, CIMEQH) and the Honduran Forestry Commission (Comisionado

Hondureño Forestal) began to openly criticize the plan as "too risky" and "a gamble." Even ENEE's employee union (Sindicato de Trabajadores de ENEE) opposed the WB plan on the grounds that it was "too big."[73] All of these organizations expressed concerns regarding the project design and argued that it would be more beneficial (and less risky) for Honduras to build a number of smaller, regional dams first. Miguel, a Honduran civil engineer I interviewed who was involved with the debates surrounding the dam explained it this way:

> At the time, there were a lot of protests in Honduras. The forestry commission was worried about deforestation in the basin. The indigenous populations living in the area did not want to get flooded. There was even a protest in CIMEQH. I remember there were a lot of meetings and conferences where people debated the logic of this project. It was a big deal, and a lot of money was about to be tied up in this one dam. What if something would go wrong? Some of the protest was irrational—like people who thought the dam would crack and flood the valley. But some of the protest was very sane. A number of engineers from the El Cajón project itself even had some criticisms. They even came up with an alternative plan to build five smaller dams all around the country rather than one huge one. Many of us thought this was a good idea because it was a little scary putting all of your investment into one solitary dam. Plus, we knew very little about hydroelectric dams, and we figured that if you are going to make mistakes, it is better to make them on small things rather than big, expensive things. You have to walk before you can run. Of course, now we know it would have been better because nobody even imagined then that El Cajón would dry up.

WB documents make it clear that ENEE and the WB were aware of the protests to which Miguel referred; they nonetheless bluntly state that these "dissident voices" were ignored at the time of the project's approval. The tone of one WB report clearly expresses that the concerns were regarded with disdain by WB staff, who referred to the objections as "unsolicited screeds" and "obloquys":

> The Bank's files contain two unsolicited screeds by Honduran engineers . . . F. L. Paret, 1974 and Francisco Garcia G., 1979. Garcia appears to have written to both the President of the IDB and the Bank's Regional Vice President. Parts of these obliquys [sic] are quite poetic . . . [These Honduran engineers] were adamantly

opposed to El Cajón on the grounds of its high cost, potential for endangering the downstream population in the event of a failure of the dam, and above all, diverting scarce resources from other development needs. Such complaints are not unusual, and the Bank's refusal to be drawn into a debate was the correct stance.[74]

The patronizing tone of this official statement is perplexing; its dismissiveness implies the bank had no responsibility whatsoever to reply to the concerns of Honduran citizens' groups opposed to the plan, and the very grounds on which El Cajón was being criticized by these groups did in fact turn out to be valid. Indeed, the same report later concludes that these "dissidents" were right.[75] They could be ignored, however, since they were not part of the national or international power elite making the decision.

Dr. Becky Myton, a U.S.-trained Honduran ecologist, was at the time an adviser to the minister of environment. In 1982, she served on a commission reviewing the plan for El Cajón. She stated, "The consensus was that we shouldn't build such a big dam there and that a stricter watershed management plan was necessary, but we were overruled in both cases by the [international banks] and local economic interests."[76]

Myton's recollection is consistent with others' interpretations of the WB decision to go ahead with El Cajón's construction. Anthropologist William Loker, who has studied the people living in the reservoir area that were affected by the dam project, concludes in his analysis of El Cajón's failure that,

> The El Cajón dam failed . . . because [its] . . . top-down approach cut out most Hondurans from the decision-making process regarding the financial, technical, and social risks associated with the construction of such a grandiose project. . . . Greater public participation . . . may have raised questions about the scope, scale, and technical feasibility of the project. Alternative strategies, such as a series of smaller dams (now viewed as a better alternative by some World Bank personnel in light of the current dam's difficulties), might have been seriously considered.[77]

It should be recalled that the various loan agreements with the WB and the IDB to build El Cajón were signed by Honduras's military rulers. The authoritarian tendencies of these regimes likely meshed well with the top-down approach of the international development banks. In this case, then, the global-izers did not really need to garner public consent; they could just as easily squelch or ignore it, and it appears this may have been the case. Miguel recalls the final decision to go forward with the dam as follows:

> The military government had made up its mind and manipulated the process. They quelled the protests. They wouldn't listen to any alternative plan. They already had their project design. An implementation team had already been put together by the international development agencies. They had their plan and they were ready to go. And, of course, all the foreign representatives of the consulting firms and the Inter-American Development Bank here in Teguci-galpa . . . all the foreign diplomats . . . were here. By now, they were very com-mitted to the idea and felt it had to go forward. They put a lot of pressure on the government to accept the project. At whatever the cost, it had to be done.

Miguel's belief the political decision to go forward with the project had been made by the Honduran government in concert with representatives from the IDB and their foreign consultants is correct, as an examination of the WB project documents confirms. In particular, the WB's 1989 evaluation of the project describes the "*ambiente* [mood] which prevailed at the time El Cajón was being advanced as the next logical and economically attractive investment in power-generating facilities."[78] The use of the passive voice in this bureau-cratic document makes it difficult to determine who was responsible for El Cajón "being advanced" in this fashion. The only actors present were the WB, ENEE, the Honduran government, and consultants. It can thus be safely as-sumed these negotiations took place among the original project management group to the exclusion of the broader Honduran citizenry. As mentioned, this management group was made up of representatives of the international de-velopment banks, ENEE, and its board of directors. It will also be recalled that the development banks were given "top authority" within this group. It is therefore clear that in the WB's attempted reconstruction in its evaluation report of the decision to build El Cajón, the *ambiente* it refers to is "the mood" of this group. The report states: "Although it is difficult to reconstruct the *ambiente* which prevailed at the time . . . it does seem clear two major factors were present: first, an understandable concern in Honduras with the cost of, and security aspects of, relying upon foreign oil for electric power production, at a time when oil prices were high and suppliers uncertain; and, second, no other program for electricity production had been studied in depth and brought to a state of readiness."[79]

The report goes on to describe how the EBASCO economic feasibility study was *the* "economic analysis leading to the justification of El Cajón."[80] In other words, the decision to build El Cajón was made in the context of fear about rising oil prices (which never materialized) and based on a study premised on those rising oil prices that failed to consider the risks if oil prices should fall; and it failed to fully explore potential alternatives because no alternatives had been studied in depth. The decision amounted to the following: We are going to build El Cajón because our (optimistic? flawed?) studies show that it is the least-cost solution compared to hypothetical alternatives that have not been studied in much depth because we have mostly been focusing on El Cajón as the solution.

WB president Robert McNamara confirms the decision was made in this fashion in his 1980 report. Although McNamara may have had no way of knowing the flaws of the EBASCO study (could he have known?), it is clear that the study was used as the justification for the project. He stated:

> Before deciding on El Cajón, ENEE evaluated several hydro-thermal alternative programs which could supply to the Honduran market. . . . A study by consultants showed that after installing some additional thermal units, the completion of the El Cajón project as early as 1985—the earliest possible year—would enable ENEE to meet, at least cost, the growing main system demand for electric energy. The study also determined the most economical pattern of system expansion . . . interconnecting with [Nicaragua]. The result indicated that El Cajón's construction would be the least cost alternative for the interconnected system expansion, as well as for ENEE alone, and that El Cajón should be built as soon as possible. For these reasons, the Government has assigned highest priority to the project within its energy development program.[81]

Despite the obvious green light from the WB and the government of Honduras to go ahead with the project, WB documents reveal there were major concerns regarding the various risks inherent in the project perhaps requiring that some consent be garnered. In particular, the WB representatives were concerned about the project's "lumpiness," referring to the project's huge cost relative to the size of the Honduran economy. The WB's project appraisal put it simply: "Undertaking a hydroelectric project of the size of El Cajón involves a substantial financial risk for Honduras. Such projects are subject to considerable uncertainties."[82]

McNamara states, for example, that "because of the lumpiness of the El Cajón project costs, it is projected that ENEE's financial structure would deteriorate somewhat . . . during the project period." Yet he quickly emphasizes that this should not be a concern because of the revenues El Cajón would quickly generate: "However, . . . when the project [comes] into operation, this trend would reverse and ENEE's financial situation would improve substantially."[83]

McNamara's optimism that El Cajón would produce revenue for ENEE notwithstanding, the WB encouraged ENEE to take various precautions and assured it that it would help it overcome any difficulties. In order to minimize the risks from project lumpiness, the WB insisted ENEE hire an outside consulting firm, Jacobs Associates Construction Engineers (a U.S. company), to carefully review project costs in order to safeguard against overruns.[84] In addition, the WB provided a loan for ENEE to hire a "specialized insurance consultant," Sedgwick, Forbes (British), to "determine the best suitable insurance coverage for the Project."[85] These measures not only likely served to garner the consent of ENEE officials but also provided further benefits to the donor countries in the form of contracts to private consulting firms.

The WB itself also took some specific steps to mitigate risk and garner consent. First, "the Bank mounted a strenuous effort to arrange financing on concessional terms."[86] By financing the dam at below-commercial rates, they believed, its debt-servicing costs would be kept to a minimum.[87] Second, they asked an expert (again, from one of the donor countries) whether the project should go forward. Their evaluation report states,

Clearly preoccupied by the size of El Cajón—in terms of electric power markets and in terms of large capital requirements in the country—the Bank engaged a consultant experienced in addressing just such issues, Arnold Harberger (USA). The consensus of his and the engineering studies was that, although the risks inherent in undertaking so large a project were substantial, the rewards of success would be great and, "on balance," it should be built.[88]

The bank also set about emphasizing the gains of the dam, highlighting such benefits as flood control and irrigation. It stated, "recognizing the tenuous nature of the Project's economic justification, the Bank investigated the possibilities of *invoking benefits* attributable to flood control and irrigation en-hancement."[89] The WB's accent on the positive aspects of El Cajón fits well within the broader pattern in the development profession of stressing the benefits while downplaying the risks.

The Dam Is Built

In the end, of course, the globalizers went ahead and built the dam. The list of contractors, consultants, and financiers of the project is indicative of the truly global nature of large-scale development projects in the world today. The dam was constructed by two international consortiums assembled by the WB, the IDB, Motor Columbus, and ENEE. The first, Concorcio El Cajón (CECLA), was responsible for building the actual arch dam wall as well as the 330-square-mile cement grout curtain designed to make the reservoir area impermeable. CECLA was made up of three contractors: Impregilo of Milan, Italy, Losinger of Berne, Switzerland, and Züblin of Stuttgart, Germany. The second consortium was Concorcio Internacional El Cajón. Responsible for constructing the underground power plant, it was made up of Astaldi of Rome, Italy, Codelfa of Milan, and Motor Columbus of Baden, Switzerland (through its Panama branch). The four Francis turbines were manufactured in Switzerland; the high-pressure steel hydraulic tubing was from Japan; the generators were from Germany; the transmission lines from Canada; and computer training was undertaken by a Venezuelan consulting company.[90] It is evident that, although Honduran engineers and construction workers were employed in the construction of the project, its planning, design, and supervision were carried out by foreign engineering firms.

The dam's construction required building roads to the remote mountain site and accommodations for the hundreds of workers needed for the project. A new cement mill was set up near the dam site to mine the rich pozzolan rock in the area and mix it with cement from Portland, Oregon, for the 1.5 million cubic meters of concrete required for the dam wall.[91]

The globalizers built the dam in five years, completing it ahead of schedule. In July 1984, an inaugural ceremony marked the opening of the El Cajón hydroelectric complex. The ceremony was dedicated to the memory of the twenty-five Honduran workers who lost their lives during the dam's construction. During the ceremony, the gates of the river diversion tunnel were closed and the basin began to fill with water.

What remained to be dealt with, however, were arrangements for resettling the valley's occupants. The relocation efforts were, in a word, a disaster. The task had been relegated to ENEE and government authorities, who were following a program based on the Pan American Health Organization's preconstruction feasibility study. According to this plan, which characterized the massive undertaking of relocating approximately six hundred families as "social engineering," the objective of the resettlement scheme was to "maintain or improve the living standards of those involuntarily displaced by the dam."[92] This entailed finding a resettlement zone, providing cash payments for lost property, and health benefits.

Although the WB loan required that this plan be in place when El Cajón was approved and that the Honduran government allocate funds to cover the estimated relocation cost of $12,500 per family, the international development organizations themselves played no part in the supervision of this relocation effort, nor did they provide any funds. ENEE and the Honduran government could have used the help. According to William Loker's investigation of the resettlement, the relocation efforts on the part of the government agencies "failed." Most of the people living in the reservoir impact zone, in fact, had not even moved when the waters began rising in 1984. After examining ENEE records on the resettlement effort, Loker found that only one hundred of the six hundred families living in the immediate reservoir zone had left the region. Forty-seven families were relocated in an "organized fashion" and resettled in an area called Bajo Aguán, a location PAHO had singled out as "least desirable."[93] Fifty-three families, whose status was never discovered, left the area entirely. The remaining five hundred families "elected to receive cash indemnification and stay in the zone."[94] They simply moved their belongings up the hillsides and continued their subsistence farming on the lesser-quality soil there. Loker claims that not only did these families have their prime agricultural land flooded but also the cash they received from the government, in the vast majority of cases, consisted of "token sums" amounting to "little or nothing." This occurred because more than 75 percent of the ENEE funds spent on cash payments went to a small handful of landowners (most of whom did not even live in the area) who could demonstrate clear legal title to reservoir zone lands.[95]

The people living in the region were much worse off than before. A survey conducted by Loker found that 75 percent of respondents claimed that they received "no benefits" from the dam.[96] They suffered, in addition, an increased rate of malaria and illness and "reduced access" to land adequate for farming. As a result, the average daily wage for people in the zone had *declined* because of the project.[97] Writing that the dam "caused deprivation over and above what would have been experienced in the same population in the absence of the project," Loker concludes, "In the case of the El Cajón project, the Government of Honduras recognized its obligations to local people, but for various reasons—most directly having to do with the power of the state and the poverty and lack of power of those affected—it failed to provide fair compensation. This neglect was so pervasive and resulted in such harm to the local population that it did indeed constitute a violation of their basic human rights."[98]

But while the people living in the El Cajón basin were being flooded off their lands, the engineers at ENEE and the foreign consultants were heralding the dam's completion as a success story. The international engineers from Italy, Switzerland, Honduras, and the United States who helped design the dam published their technical designs in international engineering journals and presented papers at conferences. The articles described the El Cajón project as "a milestone," "a significant achievement," and "the best of its time." They also extolled the virtues of the dam design ("elegant," "state-of-the-art") and elaborated upon the technological breakthroughs resulting from its construction.[99]

Between 1984 and 1986, the El Cajón valley filled and formed a new lake on the Honduran landscape. By 1986, there was enough pressure in the pipes to begin running the turbines and generating electric power. ENEE described the process in poetic detail: "The eternal water of the Humuya River which feeds the turbines is captured by way of four intakes located at 198.5 meters above sea level and channeled by pipeline . . . [to the] . . . power station below, where it turns the turbines at high pressure. Once the water has provided its valuable service to the country by generating electrical energy for the benefit of all Hondurans, it is returned to the river."[100]

All the while ENEE was beginning to generate electricity and the international engineers were basking in praise and recognition for their technical achievements, the dam suffered the first of its difficulties. In 1986, one of the turbines was damaged by debris and had to be sent to Switzerland for expensive repairs. In operation for less than a year, the power plant was already running on only three turbines.

Later that year, the dam engineers discovered another problem. As the reservoir filled, the tremendous weight of the water caused cracks in the cement grout curtain. Concerned about the growing cracks, ENEE called the Swiss team of engineers from Motor Columbus who had supervised the dam's construction back to Honduras to inspect the problem. The engineers were alarmed to discover a major leak near the intake filters. The water was beginning to erode pockets of clay in the limestone under the dam. In addition to the leak, there was pressure building under the concrete curtain, a problem demanding immediate attention. ENEE and the Swiss team of engineers testified before the Honduran congress in late 1986 that a $70 million emergency repair was needed. The congress approved the repair (thus adding $70 million onto the original IDB loan for the dam), and an Italian concrete firm, S. A. Cimentazioni e Sondaggi, was hired to apply a high-pressure injection of concrete to plug the leak. As a safeguard should the plug fail, the Swiss engineers also assisted ENEE in installing a drain hole that would allow some of the leaking water to escape into the river downstream and thus eliminate a dangerous buildup of pressure. The drain hole connected the leaky area to the underground powerhouse, where the water could be collected, monitored, and pumped back into the river. A large sump area was excavated at one end of the powerhouse to gather this leaking water and pump it outside. By 1990, the $72 million repair job was complete; the dam would have a slight leak, but at least it was no longer in danger.[101]

Despite its initial problems, the El Cajón dam was lauded in the Honduran press as a magnificent achievement. It was portrayed above all as promising the means for Honduras to achieve economic development; the dam would produce the hydroelectric energy the country needed for industrialization and modernization in the years to come. The hope the dam represented was clearly expressed in the decision by the National Congress in February 1992 to name the dam after Honduras's greatest national hero, General Francisco Morazán.[102] Under Morazán's leadership, the Central American states formed, in the wake of the collapse of the Spanish empire, a federation lasting from 1824 to 1838. He is revered as the father of Honduras as well as a symbol of the dream of Central American unity. Honoring the bicentennial of his birth, a ceremony was held at the dam site in which the newly elected president of Honduras, Rafael Callejas, officially unveiled the plaque changing the dam's name from El Cajón to Complejo Hidroelectrico General Francisco Morazán. In attendance were government and military officials, ENEE representatives, and foreign diplomats.[103] The significance of the project's completion in the eyes of Honduran government officials was evident in the grand declarations of national pride and accomplishment in the speeches marking the event. As ENEE director Federico Brevé Travieso put it,

> It is something for which all Hondurans should be proud. . . . Therefore there should be no doubt that it deserves this great name. It is clear, ladies and gentlemen, that this hydroelectric complex, which represents the most important man-made structure ever produced by Hondurans in this century—perhaps throughout our history—carries the name of the most illustrious national hero this land has ever produced: Francisco Morazán. This power plant . . . will radiate energy throughout the Central American isthmus bringing with it prosperity and progress, unity and harmony. It is therefore an indisputable living sign of Morazán's dream and of the creative spirit of all Central Americans. It is a source of pride for the present and a source of inspiration for the immense tasks ahead. It serves to remind all Hondurans that an energy policy with foresight is the only way to defeat . . . underdevelopment.[104]

President Callejas echoed the deep national pride expressed at the ceremony:

> In this work is reflected all of Central America. Our energy will be sold to Panama, Costa Rica, Nicaragua, and we are already interconnected with El Salvador. Here to this dam arrives the fluid necessary to give energy and life to all these peoples whenever it is needed. For this reason it is so significant. It is an extraordinary work built with the strength and the sacrifice of the Honduran people, and with great result. The veins that interconnect Central America today and tomorrow will forever contain the lifeblood of the waters-turned-to-energy that originate in the country that gave birth to General Francisco Morazán. This concrete bulk is an example of his character, his strength, his vision and his commitment.[105]

But the president also knew about the difficulties the dam was experiencing at that very moment. Even after the initial problems were solved, the dam was still producing only about 250 megawatts a day, far less than the expected 300 megawatts. Callejas's predecessor, President José Azcona Hoyo, was warned by ENEE in 1988 that the dam might not be capable of providing enough energy to meet the expected national demand, and ENEE therefore advised Azcona to put back into operation a number of diesel-fired generators, which had been sitting dormant since El Cajón became operational. Azcona refused and publicly complained to ENEE that it was "ridiculous" to start the thermal generators again after so much had been spent to build El Cajón. And at the time, since ENEE had more energy than it could sell to the Honduran market and neighboring countries such as Nicaragua were not buying it, there appeared to be no need for the thermal plants.[106] ENEE then suggested that the generators be put in mothballs in case of future need. The cost of maintaining the generators, however, was high, and the Honduran government consequently sought another WB loan to keep the generators functional. But the WB and the IDB advised against the plan and refused the loan, a decision that would soon prove to be very costly.

Honduran Geologist Jorge Flores and IDB Engineer Rolando Yon-Siu atop El Cajón after it was repaired.

Photo: David Mangurian/IDB

CHAPTER SEVEN

Fixing Dams

This was not a natural disaster. This was the result of human mistakes.
— MIGUEL, HONDURAN ENGINEER,
INTERVIEWED BY AUTHOR

The Origins of the 1994 Energy Crisis

In June 1992, just four months following the ceremony marking the renaming of El Cajón after the Honduran hero Morazán, a group of engineers from the Honduran Society of Civil Engineers (Colegio de Ingeneiros Mecánicos y Eléctricos de Honduras, CIMEQH) announced to the press that they had discovered a "serious energy shortage" that would result in "inevitable energy rationing" within one year.[1] One of the engineers, Rául Flores Guillén, was the former general manager of the Honduran National Electrical Energy Company (Empresa Nacional de Energía Eléctrica, ENEE) who had been fired for insisting that the crisis be addressed. He was one of several ENEE engineers who had expressed concern regarding the possible energy shortage and were fired as a result.[2]

Perhaps to show the potential problem was being swept under the rug—or his disgruntlement with the administration that had fired him—Flores Guillén called a press conference to announce that the energy problem was because of El Cajón. At the press conference, he stated that, following the drought in 1991, the dam had been "overexploited" in 1992, which would result in insufficient water in the dam to provide full energy generation in 1993 and 1994. Flores Guillén noted, "Not even a Hurricane Fifi–like flood this winter can bring enough water to prevent an energy shortage next year."[3]

The water level in the dam at the time was 27.5 meters below the optimal operation level (285 meters above sea level—m.a.s.l.) and was declining at a rate of 10–15 cm a day. President Callejas was aware of the problem, but, like his predecessor, he avoided addressing the issue because of the possible negative political implications arising if he was perceived to have mismanaged the dam. Callejas refused to invite foreign experts to Honduras to inspect the dam in 1992.[4] In the same year, his administration allocated public funds for refurbishing and restarting the old diesel generators, but many of them were rusted and in ruin. Although ENEE suggested overhauling the generators, Callejas considered the cost to be too great; leaving the final decision to repair the generators to his successor, who would come into office in 1994, Callejas made what one Honduran journalist called a "political indecision."[5]

President Carlos Roberto Reina entered office during another dry winter. The drought of 1993–94 triggered alarm among ENEE engineers and the Honduran government that there would soon be an energy shortage.[6] Owing to the low water level, El Cajón was producing at only 75 percent capacity, and this downward trend would mean fewer and fewer megawatts of electricity.

By early February 1994, the demand for electricity had exceeded its supply. ENEE began to initiate temporary power outages to make up the difference.[7] That spring, ENEE officials were called before the Honduran congress to justify the rationing and request permission to increase electricity tariffs.[8]

Already facing a $15 million deficit because the expected revenue from El Cajón never materialized, ENEE became the target of much public criticism in response to these power shutoffs. Business owners, newspaper editors, and government officials blamed ENEE for poor management. Not only were people without electricity when they needed it, but turning the power off and on again resulted in dangerous power surges that damaged household appliances across the country. Readers were advised in newspaper articles to protect their electric equipment by unplugging it. "Televisions are the most easily damaged appliances," one article reported, quoting an electronics repairman who claimed he had received, in just a week's time, over one hundred short-circuited televisions to fix: "ENEE's to blame," he stated.[9] On the same page as this article a photograph shows a barbershop with a sign in its window reading: "Closed. Thanks to ENEE."[10]

Responding to the criticism, ENEE held a press conference, at which it made the chilling announcement: "Now the rationing of energy is a matter of hours; very soon it might be in terms of days."[11] Aware that the dam would be minimally operative sometime during the coming summer, ENEE's leadership forecast for Honduras a serious energy crisis as it faced a major reduction in the supply of electricity. Frantically searching for more power, ENEE also began an investigation into the causes of the problem. It was at this point the globalizers reentered the story.

Continued Insertion: The Globalizers' Role as Monitors and Advisers

Of course, the globalizers had never really ceased being involved with the maintenance of El Cajón. They were involved on an as needed basis, advising ENEE managers and engineers whenever problems arose. During the repair of the grout curtain in 1987, the "independent consulting group" recommended "close monitoring" of the curtain repair. They also suggested a series of studies on other potential problems relating to dam performance. Of particular concern was the sedimentation behind the dam, which seemed to be occurring at a rate faster than anticipated and a possible threat to the dam's viability.

Following the group's recommendation, ENEE and the Inter-American Development Bank (IDB) signed a loan agreement to undertake a watershed assessment study with the government's Forestry Commission (Comisionado Hondureño Forestal, CODHEFOR). Conducted in the late 1980s and released in 1990, the study concluded that the deforestation rate within the El Cajón catchment area was much higher than the dam designers had accounted for. This deforestation meant two things: less rainfall and greater sedimentation. Forest loss meant less water was retained by the hillside vegetation when it rained, which led to higher rates of water runoff into the rivers and streams and, subsequently, lower rates of evaporation from the hillside vegetation and so less rainfall in the watershed area. The greater runoff resulted in a much higher silt content and sedimentation rate than originally calculated by the dam designers. Not only is the loss of topsoil itself a serious ecological problem, but the accumulated silt and sediment in the reservoir raises the reservoir floor and diminishes the dam's functioning. Ultimately, the higher rate of sedimentation could affect the dam's ability to generate electricity. In short, the ever diminishing amount of water provided by the annual rainy season and the faster rate of sedimentation were causing the reservoir to run shallow.[12]

The findings from this surveillance by the globalizers led the IDB to propose a $20.4 million "emergency loan" to reforest and protect the El Cajón watershed. Although this proposal was eventually approved by the government in 1996, it arrived too late to mitigate the energy crisis of 1994, and, ultimately, it could address only part of the problem.

On April 6, 1994, ENEE announced plans to purchase 80 megawatts a day from neighboring countries. It also disclosed it was considering purchasing new 50-megawatt diesel generators to help cope with the problem.[13] Although ENEE was aware of two causes of the El Cajón problem, only one was publicly acknowledged at the time. The official explanation of the problem (given by ENEE and the Honduran government) was that the drought Honduras had suffered two summers in a row had simply depleted the reservoir. Mother Nature was to blame, and the country was desperately in need of rain. Unbeknownst to the Honduran public at the time, however, there was another serious problem at the dam that had nothing to do with the elements and everything to do with the globalizers. El Cajón had a severe leak.

Re-insertion: Globalizers to the Rescue

On April 19, 1994, ENEE brought in four international consultants to examine El Cajón. Newspapers reported the consultants were from the World Bank (WB) and were "experts on hydroelectric dam problems." However, the press was able to gather little information regarding the true nature of the visit and its findings. The only fact mentioned in connection with the consultants' visit was in an article reporting that the consultants were being paid $500 an hour to inspect the dam. The article followed a press conference given by the Congressional Emergency Energy Commission's vice president, Jack Arévalo, who announced the visit in an effort to demonstrate what the government was doing to try to solve the El Cajón problem. When a reporter asked Arévalo (who accompanied the consultants to the dam) if he thought the expensive consultants were worth it, he responded, "Son sabios. Por eso pagamos tanto." (They are wise. That's why we pay them so much.) Explaining further why he believed the foreign consultants were necessary, Arévalo stated, "These technicians are specialists who participated in the design of the dam. . . . They know every inch of El Cajón . . . as well as its faults. One of their decisions could be worth 20 or 30 million lempiras to us. So it's worth it because they are extremely qualified."[14]

Arévalo would not comment on whether the consultants found any problems with the dam. When reporters pressed him on the question of whether the dam was malfunctioning or in need of repair, he responded, "The dam is fine. It doesn't work well because of a lack of water."[15]

The somewhat ludicrous nature of this comment was lampooned by editorial newspaper cartoonist Sergio Chiuz several days later. In the cartoon (fig. 9), a well-dressed gringo is walking off with a huge sack of money. His briefcase reads "Foreign 'Genius'" and he declares, "El Cajón doesn't work well because of a lack of water." Upon hearing the gringo's self-evident assessment, Chiuz's poor, sad character (who regularly appears in his cartoons representing the average Honduran citizen) comments, "If these guys are 'geniuses,' then I'm an astronaut!"

What exactly was happening with El Cajón at the time was never revealed in the Honduran press. Throughout the entire 1994 energy crisis, no one knew the dam had major leaks. The rumors of a big leak were quickly downplayed by ENEE and government officials. An ENEE technician at El Cajón, Manuel

Figure 9. Cartoon, by Sergio Chiuz. *El Periódico*, April 22, 1994.

Cañada, told the press "there are leaks, about 500 liters per second, but this is not alarming."[16] One of the WB consultants, Giovanni Lombardi, called the leaks "small" and "insignificant."[17]

The seriousness of the leakage was a secret known only to engineers working at the dam site, President Carlos Reina, government officials from ENEE such as Arévalo and Cañada, and the WB consultants who visited the dam in 1994 and helped solve the problem thereafter. In other words, only the globalizers and their local counterparts had access to this knowledge.

Surveillance: Inspecting the Dam, April 1994

The $500-an-hour consultants were part of El Cajón's independent consulting group, and most were involved in the initial dam design and construction: Andrew Merritt, U.S. engineering geologist, Giovanni Lombardi, Italian grouting expert, and Peter Lupold, an engineer who worked on the grouting repair.[18] William Large, an IDB consultant who accompanied the engineering experts in April 1994, reported that the visit was an "emergency mission." In an article that appeared three years later in an IDB newsletter, Large reported that they were called to Honduras by ENEE to see how the IDB could "help save the project it had originally financed."[19]

According to this article, when Large and the other engineers entered the powerhouse at the dam on April 19, 1994, they saw "water . . . leaking everywhere. Without a doubt, it looked like the powerhouse would flood." The 1987 emergency repair to plug the leak in the grout curtain had, it turned out, not been successful. The diversion channel that was originally created to vent water pressure from under the dam and guide leaking water into a sump area in the powerhouse was now flooding the entire powerhouse. A torrent of water was pouring in at a rate of 1,600 liters per second. Moreover, it was cloudy with clay, which indicated the fissures and leaks under the dam were getting larger, despite repeated attempts to plug them.[20]

Worse still, the sump pumps responsible for pumping the accumulating water outside were barely able to keep up. If the water in the sump area rose above the level of the floor where the turbines and generators sat, the whole powerhouse would be permanently and irreparably damaged. As the IDB article explained, if the "powerhouse turbines flooded, the hydroelectric plant would have become an enormously expensive white elephant, literally leaving the country in the dark, crippling business and the economy." El Cajón would become "a \$775 million pile of rubble."[21]

On April 24 of that year, a power surge short-circuited the pump and it stopped working. The water in the sump area began to rise rapidly. The engineers in the powerhouse attempted to start the emergency generators, but they would not start. As the water rose near the level of the powerhouse floor, workers scrambled to figure out how to pump the water out before it damaged the turbines. Jorge Flores, the chief geologist for El Cajón and one of the workers there that day, recalls, "It was tense. The water nearly reached the floor level." The pumps finally started up, preventing a disaster.[22]

Garnering Consent

Fixing the Leak

The globalizers involved in fixing the leaky dam hardly needed to garner the consent of the Honduran government to go ahead with the repair; they already had it. ENEE had requested WB assistance as early as 1993 to initiate a repair of the growing leak under the dam. The government thus offered its approval for any repair project that could save the dam. The development banks, for their part, were clearly concerned that the leak could jeopardize one of their most significant development projects. The global management team for El Cajón, made up of ENEE officials, international development bank consultants, and foreign engineering experts leapt into action once again.

The WB approved a \$12 million loan in 1993 to finance a "rescue operation." The details of this repair work appeared much later in an engineering journal in a piece published by the engineers who had conducted it.[23] The article described the nature of the leak, the repair, and the international array of experts who completed it once the agenda was set. First, the independent consulting group—made up of engineers Dr. Giovanni Lombardi (Switzerland), Dr. Andrew Merritt (United States), and Dr. F. Gallavresi (Italy)—"improvised a new grout curtain design" expanding and reinforcing the original, failing grout curtains. Harald Kreuzer, originally the chief engineer for Motor Columbus and now a member of a Swiss private consulting firm, Colenco Power Consulting, served as engineer in charge of the project. The actual grouting works were done by CONRODIO, a consortium of Italian, Spanish, and Swiss firms. In addition, ENEE engineers Ramon Guifarro and Jorge Flores served as Honduran project director and chief geologist, respectively.[24]

Lombardi, Merritt, and Gallavresi had two main concerns. First, they assessed the water leakage "to be high."[25] That the leak was characterized as high at the time reveals that the ENEE officials and foreign consultants were not completely truthful with the Honduran public in 1994 when they characterized it to the press as "insignificant" and "small." The article also specifically mentioned that the potential "risk of flooding the power plant" from the leak was a primary concern.[26] This stands in stark contrast to the public characterization of the leak as "not alarming."

Identifying seven probable "leakage pathways," the experts closely monitored the four most significant among them. The total leakage rate for just these four pathways was 1,650 liters per second—much higher than the publicly claimed "500 liters per second." It is likely that this rate was at least partially responsible for the low reservoir level since the total water inflow rate to the reservoir during the dry months was only 17,000 liters per second, much of which was used to run the turbines.[27] The repair team therefore set an objective to "reduce the leakage rate to 250 liters per second, a value close to the initial leakage."[28] Perhaps the engineers had determined that the low reservoir level was related to the leak and that fixing it was crucial to the dam's ability to hold enough water to run the turbines in the future.[29]

The second main concern was the structural stability of the dam itself. The water seepage was causing tremendous uplift pressure on the concrete dam wall. Should the limestone fissures under the dam become any more porous, the dam's foundation would be in jeopardy. Consequently, a second objective was to "lower the uplift pressure . . . to the stipulated contractual value."[30]

The problem was the grout curtain. In 1993, the repair team regrouted the basin; but, by the beginning of 1994, it was clear this strategy was not solving the problem. CONRODIO, the European company hired to do the job, tried different combinations of cement, sand, and gravel grout to fill the leaks, but every time the grout was pumped into the leaky fissures, it simply ran right through and ended up in the powerhouse sump area.

By April 1994, the team had run out of WB money and the leak was as bad as ever. That is when "the IDB came to the rescue."[31] Along with a new $32 million loan to Honduras to help deal with the energy crisis (including the purchase of new thermal generators), the IDB provided an "emergency loan" of $5.14 million specifically for the El Cajón leak. The article described how the engineers arrived at a solution:

> Geologists and engineers decided they needed to inject larger objects that would stick inside the fissures and karsts and prevent the grouting from passing through before hardening. But there was no well-sorted, round gravel of this size anywhere nearby. Honduran geologist Jorge Flores then came up with a bizarre idea: plastic balls sold for toys were just the right size and could be filled with concrete. So his staff went to every store and market in the region and bought balls by the hundreds. It was a crazy idea, but it began to work. . . . Next they tried balls made of wood, and that worked even better. Altogether, the engineers injected 8,650 plastic and wooden balls into the hundreds of karstic flow holes they had drilled into.[32]

The toy balls reduced the leakage rate significantly. The engineers also injected twenty-five thousand rolled-up polypropylene feed sacks into the holes, followed by the grout mixture. In the end, the combination of feed sacks, grout, and toy balls plugged the leak (fig. 10). The leakage at the dam was reduced from sixteen hundred liters per second to less than one hundred liters per second: the dam had been saved. The article ends with a quote from an IDB engineer: "What we learned at El Cajón may someday save a dam somewhere else in the world."[33]

Quelling Social Unrest

Because the dam repair was largely kept from public view during the energy crisis of 1994, it had little to do with the social unrest that was growing as the El Cajón reservoir continued to decline. Unaware of such concerns as "uplift pressure" and "leakage rates," Hondurans only knew that El Cajón was half empty and, as a result, their electricity kept going off. No amount of repairs could instantly refill the reservoir and solve the problem of the empty dam; it would take the rainy season to do that, but the question was: would the rainy season arrive before the dam had to be shut down entirely.

Two days after the WB consultants left the country, President Reina declared a national emergency. Newspaper headlines announced in huge type: "President Declares Emergency"; "Dam Will Fail in Two Months"; "Rationing to Increase."[34] On the same day, the Honduran congress authorized ENEE to do whatever necessary to avoid a complete shutdown of El Cajón.[35]

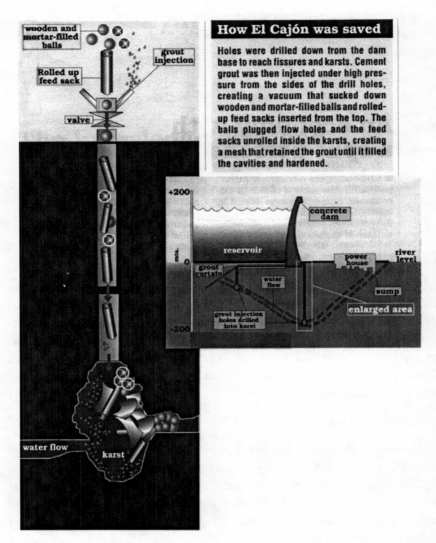

Figure 10. How the Dam Was Saved
Graph: Cecelia Jacobson/IDB

Several days later, ENEE announced its new plan: everyone in the country would have their power turned off for five hours each day. Following a rotational scheme, power in certain segments of the country would be shut off from 7 A.M. to noon; in others, from noon to 5 P.M.; and in still others, from 5 P.M. to 10 P.M.[36] The country was in a self-declared state of crisis.

In conjunction with the consultants' visit, the Honduran government set up an Emergency Energy Commission made up of officials from ENEE and the El Cajón project management team (including the international agencies that were integrally involved at this point), Honduran congressional representatives, and representatives from the Honduran private sector (in particular, the Honduran Council of Private Enterprise (Consejo Hondureño de la Empresa Privada, COHEP). This international ad hoc committee was charged with "finding solutions to the energy crisis facing the country."[37]

A number of solutions came out of the initial meetings of this commission. The IDB announced the approval of a $10.5 million loan to build an 80 megawatt diesel-fired power plant; in addition, the Mexican government agreed to donate four diesel plants.[38] Entrepreneurs from the Honduran private sector also promised to look into producing their own electricity.[39]

In May 1994, ENEE announced that it would permanently cut off all major debtors. Many electricity customers had stopped paying their bills to protest what they believed to be ENEE incompetence. Some of these customers were large businesses that owed ENEE millions of lempiras. Between 1992 and 1994, electric power rates had increased by 90 percent, and many in the business community were feeling "swindled."[40] ENEE lashed back by blaming President Reina for the crisis, claiming, "there were things he could have done to avoid the problem."[41] President Reina, in turn, blamed his predecessor, Rafael Callejas, saying, "we have discovered that they intentionally let water out of the dam in 1990."[42]

By the end of May, El Cajón's water level had fallen to 231 m.a.s.l. Newspaper headlines reported, "El Cajón in Agony."[43] ENEE engineers stated that "not even a flood will save El Cajón"[44] and announced more rationing: no electricity for the entire country between the hours of midnight and 4 A.M.[45] Businesses, many of which had turned to the late night hours for production, claimed they were losing $20 million lempiras a day as a result of the energy crisis; many purchased their own diesel generators to keep their operations going.[46]

As June and July 1994 rolled around, Hondurans everywhere were literally praying for rain. Senator Fonseca, in a public speech before the media, asked "for all the Honduran people to pray to the Virgin Mary that she fill El Cajón."[47] Prayers for rain became included in the weekly masses at many churches throughout the country. Even the ENEE director, Jorge Valle, declared, "We need a miracle. El Cajón will be paralyzed if it doesn't rain in 15 days."[48] Valle's announcement triggered a national countdown. Newspapers and television reports kept close tabs on the falling water level at El Cajón: "9 Meters to Chaos!"; "Dam Is at 227!"; "6 More Meters and Dam Shuts Down!"[49] Reporting that gas-powered generators had been sold out across the country and that propane stoves and kerosene lanterns were the norm, the newspapers portrayed Hondurans as a "People in Darkness."[50]

Behind the scenes, ENEE officials were investigating every possible solution short of a miracle. Apart from secretly trying to fix the leak and working around the clock to get the newly arrived Mexican power plants up and running (which was going much slower than expected), ENEE explored the possibility of cloud seeding. On June 27, 1994, the headlines of the San Pedro Sula newspaper announced, "The North Americans Begin Bombarding the Clouds." ENEE had hired a U.S. company to seed clouds above the El Cajón watershed at a cost of $60,000 a day. Using its airplanes and on-board Doppler radar to locate cloud formations, the American team began to dust the clouds with a solution of silver iodide and salt in the hopes of generating some rain.[51] Two days later, it did rain. But it only slowed the daily loss of water from twenty centimeters to ten centimeters. By the end of June, the water level of the dam had dropped to 225 m.a.s.l., just five meters higher than the point at which El Cajón would be shut down. Gilberto Ramos, another ENEE engineer, reported to the press the dangers of running the dam at this low, "supercritical" water level: "225 is really the minimum level at which we can operate the dam safely. Once the water falls below 225, there is not sufficient pressure in the tubes, and the turbines start to have problems: there is increased operating temperatures and the low pressure can cause vibrations which can cause damage, . . . It is not really that safe to operate the dam below 225."[52]

According to Ramos, the dam would be shut down in twelve days. Across the country, Hondurans began preparing for the worst. Newspaper articles encouraged readers to stock up on candles, canned goods, and other items to prepare for the "big blackout." A full shutdown of El Cajón would mean that Honduras would lose the 130 megawatts that it was still struggling to produce each day; the remaining power plants in the country could fulfill only half of the daily electricity demand. ENEE prepared for this eventuality by announcing at the end of June that daily rationing would be extended, first to ten hours a day, then twelve hours. Factories, churches, government buildings, restaurants, stores, discotheques, museums, art galleries, and cinemas all tried to figure out how to operate in the absence of electric power.[53] Newspapers reported that the nation's economy was grinding to a standstill, and businesses predicted that their losses would run into the millions of dollars. But things would get much worse if El Cajón shut down.

On July 1, 1994, a newspaper disclosed that "an anonymous engineer at El Cajón reported that one of the turbines at the dam stopped momentarily today but resumed operation shortly thereafter." The water level at the dam had fallen to 225.05 m.a.s.l.; ENEE refused to confirm the report and declared "there is no problem at El Cajón."[54]

The next day, one of the turbines stopped turning. "Turbine Number One, PARALYZED!" ran the headline in *El Periódico*.[55] An ENEE spokesperson revealed that the pressure in the tubes was not sufficient to turn all four turbines. There was also a buildup of algae and other debris in the pipes, and this debris may have damaged the paralyzed turbine. Nevertheless, the ENEE representative denied that any of the three remaining turbines was experiencing any vibrations.[56]

On July 22, 1994, the director of ENEE, Jorge Valle, resigned. Congressional leaders had been calling for his resignation, and Valle finally "gave in to the pressure."[57] Another director was appointed, Jerónimo Sandoval Sorto, who promised to resolve the energy crisis within ninety days. The water level at El Cajón at the time was 223.5 m.a.s.l. and declining.

On August 10, newspapers reported that a twenty-two-year-old, 15 megawatt diesel-powered plant was being refurbished by ENEE workers at a cost of $3.5 million. It would be another two weeks before the plant could begin to produce power. On August 11, another turbine at El Cajón seized up. At 222.85 m.a.s.l., the water had dipped to its lowest point in the history of the dam, and, as a result, there was no longer enough pressure to safely turn the turbines. With only two turbines operating, the power plant was producing a mere 96 megawatts. ENEE officials determined that the water was still running out too fast and the pressure was too low to continue running the two turbines and decided to shut down a third. The water level had to be kept above 220 meters at all costs.

With only one turbine running and El Cajón on the verge of a complete shutdown, it finally began to rain. The strong winter rain everyone in Honduras had been waiting for had arrived, and by late August, the water in the dam began to rise. For the time being, the crisis had been averted.

The Aftermath: Consequences of the 1994
Energy Crisis for Honduras

Four months later, on December 14, 1994, ENEE finally discontinued its highly unpopular electricity rationing. One newspaper headline read: "Today They Give Us Back *La Luz*" (*luz* means both "electrical power" and "light").[58] A picture of a button-pushing ceremony accompanied the story and showed a smiling President Reina pressing a button on a control panel and thus activating all national circuits as other important dignitaries stood nearby smiling and applauding. Included at the ceremony were many of the same international dignitaries present at the El Cajón naming ceremony six years earlier. The assembled forum was a reflection of the coalition of global governance that had built and fixed El Cajón. Besides President Reina, the director of ENEE was there, as were cabinet ministers and congressional representatives. There were also a number of invited guests present at the ceremony so the president could "express gratitude to those who were most responsible for helping the country emerge from the crisis." These guests included Honduran business leaders, the president of COHEP, and officials from the National Industry Association. Also in attendance were representatives of the three major development banks, the IDB, WB, and the Central American Bank for Economic Integration; the ambassadors from Mexico, China, the United States, and the Netherlands were also present.[59] The assembled forum was a microcosm of the coalition of global governance that had built and repaired El Cajón.

The energy crisis was officially over, but in the following months Hondurans would learn about the economic toll it had taken on the country: The business sector reported an estimated $120–$150 million in losses in 1994.[60] Economists estimated that construction costs had risen by as much as 850 percent for some materials. ENEE claimed that it was as much as $90 million in debt. To top it all off, the national economy had experienced *negative* economic growth. The gross national product (GNP) in 1994 was 1.5 percent less than in 1993. For a country with a population increase of almost 3 percent a year and whose economy had been growing rapidly prior to 1994 (between 3.3 percent and 6.2 percent in the previous three years), a −1.5 percent growth in the GNP was considered a major economic setback. In GNP terms, 1994 was a year of "negative development."[61]

These were enormous economic consequences for such a poor country. El Cajón's reservoir remained depleted until 1998, when Hurricane Mitch hit.

Even after the 1994 repair of the leak, El Cajón never produced at its maximum of 300 megawatts a day. This was mainly because of ENEE's decision to run the plant on only two or three turbines based on their calculations regarding "reasonable rainfall expectations" in the deforested El Cajón watershed. In 1996, in an effort to avoid any future replay of the 1994 energy crisis, ENEE set out a long-term plan to permanently operate the hydroelectric plant at only 75 percent capacity for the "foreseeable future." Of course, the plan to install four additional turbines for an expanded output of 600 megawatts has been abandoned indefinitely.

To make up for the energy deficit resulting from its decision, ENEE permanently installed the three Mexican diesel plants. It also signed a $700 million contract (roughly the amount of the original El Cajón loan) with a private U.S. electric company (American Power International Development Corporation) to provide another 75 megawatts of power a day for the next fifteen years. As a result, ENEE concluded that it was more dependent upon petroleum (oil imports rose by 22 percent after the El Cajón fiasco) and foreign companies to meet the Honduran demand for electricity than it had been before. The money for this came from yet another IDB loan. The more problems El Cajón experienced, it seemed, the more money the globalizers could lend.

The emergency repairs to the dam only added to Honduras's overwhelming foreign debt. The cost of repairs to El Cajón amounted to $41.4 million: $24.2 million for "civil works" and $17.2 million for "drilling and grouting."[62] To pay this bill, due mostly to the European private contractors CONRODIO and Colenco that undertook the repairs, ENEE finalized its IDB emergency loan in the amount of $36.8 million.[63] The loan was for "priority works at Francisco Morazán dam."

In 1996, Honduras's total external public debt was about $3.1 billion. According to the WB, this equaled around 135 percent of yearly exports and more than 300 percent of the country's annual government revenues. It is estimated that almost one-third of this current debt is related to the loans associated with El Cajón. Although such staggering debt recently qualified Honduras for debt relief under the WB's Heavily Indebted Poor Countries initiative, the fact that Hondurans are still paying for a faulty dam was not taken into consideration by the WB when it awarded Honduras the debt-relief package.

In addition, facilitated by the globalizers at the international development banks, Honduras's private sector has taken on a much larger role. In 1995, three private power plants began operating in the country: ELCOSA, Lufusa, and Emce. By September 1996, these three companies were selling their energy to ENEE as it was cheaper than what four of ENEE's most inefficient thermal plants were producing; ENEE later shut down the four plants.

Power, Blame, and the Leaky Dam

What precisely were the causes of the 1994 Honduran energy crisis and the problems at El Cajón? At first glance it appears to be an engineering problem. Not only was the original dam design flawed in terms of the watershed's expected rainfall and capacity, but the unforeseen, severe leak in the dam's grout curtain required a sophisticated, ingenious, and expensive engineering solution. So perhaps the foreign engineers and international development banks supporting them are to blame for the catastrophe. Should they shoulder the burden for the mistakes that were made?

Public policy scholars Jonathan Fox and L. David Brown define accountability as "the process of holding actors responsible for actions."[64] The central questions for this discussion are: to what extent were the actors involved in the construction of El Cajón held responsible for their actions? And to what extent is Honduras able to hold those actors accountable for their actions? As I will demonstrate below, the international development agencies involved in the construction of El Cajón were not held responsible in any way for the problems caused by the dam despite their major role throughout the story.

Examining the social context and political process in the case of the El Cajón fiasco, it is clear that the international development agencies played a major part. The WB and IDB in particular were centrally involved. They were part of researching potential sites for the dam and choosing its final location. It is likely that they actively promoted the El Cajón project in favor of such alternatives as building several smaller dams. They coordinated the Honduran government's efforts to hire foreign contractors—"the best in the world"—for the dam's design and construction. They helped finance the dam, contributing part of the $700 million loan package to Honduras's military government. They were of course also key players in helping to solve El Cajón's problems. In particular, they were the "specialists" called in to consult with ENEE engineers about repairing the leak, and they "came to the rescue" with emergency loans to the government for the regrouting and purchase of supplemental energy sources.

The other globalizers in this story were the foreign engineering firms contracted by the international banks and ENEE to design and construct the project.[65] Despite the possible negligence on the part of these firms in the dam's design and construction, no inquiry has been made as to whether these contractors deserve any of the blame for the El Cajón leak or if they should bear any of the burden for its consequences. In fact, this story ends with the international experts hired to build the dam being well paid for their work and earning a degree of notoriety from their articles about the "valuable lessons learned" published in prestigious international journals.

Honduran institutions involved in the El Cajón project did not fare as well as their foreign partners. ENEE, for example, faced serious economic problems as a result of the dam's troubles. It also suffered severe criticism from the broader Honduran society. Furthermore, because of the policies it was forced to adopt during the energy crisis, its legitimacy as a public institution in Honduras has been questioned and its reputation damaged.

The Honduran government, too, appears to be worse off after the El Cajón fiasco. Not only is Honduras once again dependent upon petroleum products for energy production, but the government must pay about $15 million in debt service each year for every $100 million it borrowed to build the dam. This economic burden ultimately falls on the country's citizens, who must pay (through taxes or diminished state services) for the leaky dam. In development terms, the only possible conclusion is that one of the poorest, most heavily indebted countries in the Americas had the misfortune of being the recipient of a development project that, in the end, made it poorer and more deeply indebted.

The supposed benefactors in this project, the development institutions and international development professionals offering their help, suffered no great losses despite the likelihood that they made mistakes. Apart from the brief gibe in the press questioning the $500 an hour salaries that foreign experts earned, the IDB and WB were not subjected to public criticism or scrutiny. Indeed, they were the heroes who "came to the rescue," bringing money in a time of need. But do international development organizations and the contractors they hire with development funds share *some* of the blame and responsibility for what occurred? And if so, should they bear some of the costs of the mistakes they made?

Miguel, a civil engineer in San Pedro Sula who had participated in some of the early El Cajón protests, had, since then, collected hundreds of newpaper articles on the El Cajón debacle. Wishing to understand how the project could have turned out so poorly, I asked Miguel what had gone wrong, how a project that promised to supply enough energy to the entire country for twenty years could have failed so utterly in fewer than ten.

Miguel responded, "It was a swindle. Without a doubt, El Cajón was a rip-off. We paid for it, but the dam did not result in the benefits outlined in the original planning documents."

Asking Miguel who he thought was responsible, he replied, "The ones who are directly responsible for the crisis are the [Honduran] government authorities. . . . But some of the blame must also be on the people who gave them the loans. Why? Because they have experts and they have more information than we do. And they are supposed to have academic training that is superior to ours. So they should have seen that some of these things weren't going to work so well."

What do we get for all this exclusive "foreign expertise"?

"Like what?" I asked, "How could they have known?"

"Well, there are a number of things. First of all, the design was insufficient. A dam this size requires at least two hundred years of hydrometric and hydrological information. It needs accurate data on rainfall, river discharges, temperature—everything! You need this data to figure out a 'minimum volume' and 'maximum volume' that will be relatively accurate. But they only started collecting data in 1958 and then up until 1963. Then they started again in 1970 to 1980. That's only fifteen years of data over a twenty-two-year period! They would never build a dam this size in the United States or Europe with such poor information. Never! So they should not have recommended such a large project."

Miguel is not the only observer who believed that poor technical information may have resulted in a flawed dam design for El Cajón. Members of ENEE and CODHEFOR became aware of the watershed problems in El Cajón soon after it began operating in 1985. The siltation and water discharge rates were much higher than the dam designers had predicted, and they urged that a watershed management plan be designed. They turned to WB and IDB specialists to figure out what to do about the deforestation. The IDB responded with a new development project. In November 1993, it approved a $20.4 million watershed management loan, which it expanded in 1996 to include $80 million more of IDB development loans. The 1996 "El Cajón watershed management program" also incorporated financing from the United States Agency for International Development, which offered $20 million more in loans. The program was implemented through a cooperative effort of Honduran government agencies, official development institutions, and numerous nongovernmental development organizations, and it included such development aspects as soil conservation projects, forestry management, reforestation, terracing projects, and training campesinos in agricultural practices. In sum, the deforestation problem at El Cajón became a new task for the globalizers.

Other observers of El Cajón have echoed Miguel's conclusion that the international agencies should bear some of the responsibility. In his discussion of the problems related to the resettlement, William Loker wrote:

> Clearly, the national government and its institutions responsible for approving and implementing the project bear primary responsibility, as do international institutions such as the Inter-American Development Bank and the World Bank, which financed the construction of the dam. . . . The national and international agencies involved in the El Cajón project have a duty to redress the violations of rights that have occurred. The Honduran government and the international institutions involved in the construction of the El Cajón project should share the cost of restoring subsistence rights of those affected.[66]

In the end, Loker blames the resettlement failure on the power disparity between the globalizers and the Honduran citizens affected by their projects. He observed: "lack of participation by local populations doomed the relocation . . . effort to failure. . . . The relative power of the two parties involved—the government, engineers, and international consultants on one hand and the local campesinos on the other—explains the failure."[67] As his statement reveals, there is a serious problem in the way global governance operates. As a political arrangement, the global apparatus of development lacks mechanisms for popular participation in highly technical development initiatives such as El Cajón.

And this raises an even more important question: What is the ability of developing countries or their citizens to seek redress when a development project goes sour? There seems to be no mechanism in the structures of international development assistance for developing countries to "get their money back" if a project they have paid for fails. Not only do development projects not come with "money back guarantees," but such a notion goes against the whole discourse of the development profession, which characterizes these projects as gifts, aid, grants, and assistance. As stated previously, this discourse of aid obscures the fact that most development projects bring with them high costs that must be borne by the recipient countries. As debt-burdened Honduras well illustrates, just because a WB or IDB development loan is offered at below-market interest rates does not mean it need not be paid back; most of Honduras's debt is connected to "development assistance" projects. Obviously I am not suggesting Honduras should be able to avoid repaying such loans; rather, my point is that the mechanisms by which development loans are given offer little power to a country such as Honduras to set the terms of the initiation, receipt, and repayment of these loans.[68] Honduran political leaders have little ability to define these terms in such a way as to create guarantees for the work done.

b/c of making a country ask the country signs away rights to sign

Most public works projects in developed countries such as the United States, in contrast, *do* allow for some local control of the terms of the project. If a community in the United States, say, were to raise funds for a large project such as a dam, it would define the terms under which such a project were carried out. When the citizens of the city of Milwaukee, Wisconsin, for example, invested public funds into a deep-tunnel sewer project, one of the conditions was that the contractors who took the job had to be fully bonded and insured in the event of a failure to complete the project successfully. When the project did fail in 1998, the city sued the contractors and recuperated the millions of dollars of public funds that otherwise would have been lost. The contractors responsible for the failure were forced to pay the costs of the failed project and went out of business as a result. The citizens of Milwaukee did not have to bear the burden of the mistakes made by the contractors. In the United States, then, clearly there are mechanisms available to local citizens by which to hold contractors accountable for their mistakes in public works projects.[69]

In the case of El Cajón, however, it would appear the citizens of Honduras have no such mechanism available to them. The international consultants who built the dam were contracted through both the international development banks (mainly the IDB and WB) and the Honduran government. The development banks brokered the deal and were participants in the contract because a military government was in power at the time. The IDB and WB participation assured the contractors they would be paid. Because of the composite participation of the Honduran government and the international lending agencies, any breach of contract suit brought against the contractors based on design flaws, negligence, or faulty construction would have to be brought by both the government and the lending agencies, and the development banks

The people neither wanted nor controlled the dam or its construction.

would be extremely reluctant to do so. The spreading of responsibility among so many different actors would make it difficult to assign blame to any one unit in a lawsuit.

Furthermore, it is unclear in what court such a breach of contract case would be heard. In our globalizing world, there are a number of international courts where such cases might be pursued (e.g., the International Court of Justice in the Hague and the World Trade Organization's trade dispute court). However, to my knowledge, no such case has ever been put forth by a third world country seeking compensation for a failed development project.

[margin note: (b/c the 政府 doesn't want to lose political points, or go to ct against such a powerful org -- since ostensibly it asked for it.]

In addition, in securing the IDB and WB loans for the El Cajón dam, the Honduran government signed its own contract with these agencies. Consequently, any action the government wished to take in pursuit of compensation for the economic damage caused by the El Cajón fiasco would have to be against the IDB and the WB as well. Although there have been cases of developing countries withholding payments or threatening to default on loans to these banks, such cases have typically resulted in either failure or a renegotiation of the debt in question. This is of course because defaulting or refusing to repay a loan to these banks results in severe IMF sanctions that effectively shut off any source of international credit for the developing country choosing this course of action. In other words, because Honduras must remain in good standing with the IMF to secure international credit, it has no leverage with which to challenge the banks on the loan for the El Cajón project. No country has, in fact, ever sued the WB or IDB because of a faulty project design. Even the most infamous WB projects the bank itself has acknowledged as "mistakes" have been paid for by the unfortunate recipient countries (e.g., the Polonoreste project in Brazil).[70,71]

[margin note: All balls in WB's court.]

According to Miguel, the errors made by the dam's designers arose in relation to one important problem: there was no local political process allowing Honduran citizens and private organizations to participate in the decision. The international organizations thus share some of the blame, Miguel believes, for failing to elicit more public participation in this important decision:

[margin note: Top-down, heirchical decision and no local input.]

> These big decisions shouldn't be left up to only the politicians and the lending agencies. There should be public participation from citizens' groups and private businesses. But there was none of that. There were no citizens' advisory boards like you have in the United States or Spain. Of course the military government at the time wasn't interested in getting the citizens' input, but that doesn't mean

the international organizations couldn't consult the citizens' advice. They weren't even interested in that. They just wanted to put another development project into action without really considering the potentially serious consequences. Perhaps they wanted the contracts for the European construction companies. Perhaps they just wanted to make the loans . . . I don't know. I just know that they pushed the project through despite the protests.

Miguel has characterized the consequences of El Cajón as a "bitter experience," and, as a civil engineer, he expressed amazement that the foreign engineers, supposedly "the best in the world," could have made such egregious errors in the dam's design and construction: "All of these foreign experts should realize the human consequences of their actions and their decisions. We are a small country and we don't have a lot of resources. Therefore, we can't make too many mistakes. A mistake like El Cajón is going to hurt us for years to come . . . and it was supposed to help. . . . If they made some of the mistakes, they should take some of the responsibility."

Miguel lamented that his taxes would go toward paying off the debt from the loans for the dam. He showed me a newspaper article reporting that, as of 1996, the interest on the El Cajón loan was $15 million a year. When I asked Miguel if he believed Honduras should have to pay back the loan, he replied, "Oh, yes. We have to pay the loan back. You can't accept a loan and offer to repay it and then go back on your word . . . regardless of whether you're just an individual or a nation. No matter how hard it is, you have to repay it."

Assuming Miguel would argue the loan should be forgiven because the IDB and other development banks had made mistakes in their recommendations and so carried some of the responsibility for the economic consequences of those mistakes, I was puzzled by his answer. In an effort to clarify his position, he explained:

I am not trying to place all the blame on the international development organizations. To put all the blame on the foreigners is to say that we don't have any of the responsibility. We are also to blame. The international agencies came here because we asked them to. We accepted their advice. We could have just as well rejected it. And we didn't. So they are not totally to blame. The gringos do what we let them do to us. They will swindle us if we let them. But at the same time, I also believe that development organizations are supposed to be different. They should know that we are in a difficult situation. It is like a bartender giving alcohol to a drunkard. He knows very well that it is not good for the alcoholic . . . that those drinks are not going to help his problem. But if the alcoholic insists on drinking, there is nothing the bartender can do but fill his glass. Why? Because the bartender wants to sell the booze. That is the same thing that international development banks are doing to us in Honduras. Yes, we are a big part of the problem—we can't turn down the drink. But so are they. They keep filling up the glass. It's a destructive relationship . . . and it's usually not the bartender but the drunk who gets hurt in the end.

Miguel's description of the potentially destructive relationship between international development banks and Honduras raises some difficult questions regarding development assistance and accountability. His characterization of development banks as the bartender and Honduras as the drunkard implies a relationship not only harmful but also exploitative to the drunkard since the barman profits from the alcoholic's dependency.

His analogy points to one of the primary concerns of this book: namely, how agents of globalization use their power and authority in their work in Honduras for their (and donor-country) benefit and at Honduran expense. The El Cajón power project of 1980 and its consequences clearly illustrate this process. I shall therefore conclude the story of El Cajón with a return to the five propositions that have guided my analysis.

First, it seems clear that the agendas of the donor countries won out over local agendas in the El Cajón case. The case highlights some of the fundamental contradictions and flaws in the current "new world order" of globalization in need of serious examination. We live in a world in which wealthy countries have set up the rules of the game. As stated previously, the wealthiest countries—the Group of Seven nations in particular—have created and largely control powerful institutions such as the WB, which during the past thirty years have been carrying out a "globalization project" promoting the ideology of free-market capitalism and neoliberal economic policy throughout the developing world as the solution to poverty and underdevelopment. The globalization project declares that the peripheral societies must become integrated into the global capitalist marketplace and, using the logic of comparative advantage, must develop an export-oriented economy and attract foreign direct investment from transnational capital.[72] In order to attract such investment and pursue exports, there are certain infrastructural requirements that must be met such as the provision of inexpensive energy. Because developing countries often have difficulty raising the public revenues for such expensive infrastructural projects, the wealthy countries offer official development assistance to promote participation by the developing countries in the globalization project. The developing countries are then able to put into place the energy infrastructure deemed necessary for foreign investment.

Not only did the El Cajón dam project emerge directly from the particular globalization worldview of the WB and IDB expert consultants overseeing its design and construction, but, furthermore, this agenda prevailed over all other potential agendas in the Honduran sociopolitical sphere. Ignoring Honduras's best interests while imposing a flawed top-down development project was the outcome. The WB has admitted in its own reports and evaluations that the project was pushed through despite Honduran popular criticism. Although the WB later regretted the decision and ultimately agreed with Honduran critics that El Cajón was in fact "too big," the acknowledgment came too late: El Cajón was already built; the globalizers' agenda had irremediably subdued all others.

Second, the local agenda of ENEE succeeded because it was tied to the global agendas of the WB, IDB, and others. ENEE's power and authority were strengthened vis-à-vis other Honduran institutions (e.g., CIMEQH and campesino groups in the El Cajón region) because of its involvement in the El Cajón project. A government monopoly under the control of the military rulers in Honduras at the time of the loan, ENEE enhanced its ability to earn greater revenues through the generation and sale of electrical power to the Honduran market and beyond. This ENEE benefit was treated as superior to all other concerns in the economic feasibility analysis conducted by the foreign consulting firm EBASCO, which examined the economic costs and benefits of El Cajón only as they related to ENEE's bottom line. Had the campesinos farming the rich soil of the El Cajón valley had access to a multimillion dollar loan for their own economic feasibility study in order to demonstrate their economic losses resulting from the flooding of these lands, and had they been able to use this study to garner another multimillion dollar loan to improve their agricultural generation and sale to the Honduran market or beyond, perhaps they might have been able to pose a greater political challenge to the El Cajón developers and avoided relocation. In reality, though, only ENEE had access to the globalizers' mechanisms of surveillance and planning, and only ENEE's benefits as a local institution were calculated. As a result, ENEE's plan for the vast El Cajón basin was the one adopted, despite resistance from the campesino groups and others.

Third, El Cajón has given Honduras some benefits—highly touted by the globalizers at ENEE and the international development banks. Indeed, the dam did work for a while and continues to generate electrical power (albeit less than planned). It has also provided flood control, which, as will be seen in chapter 10 on Hurricane Mitch, is significant in economic and human terms.

Fourth, Honduras has nonetheless suffered major costs and social harm because of the El Cajón project. In the main, these costs were downplayed, hidden, or blatantly distorted by the globalizers during the project's promotion. They were likewise hidden or downplayed during the 1994 energy crisis. It seems safe to conclude the dam was a disaster in many regards. None of the promotion for the project in 1980 mentioned the devastating energy crisis and resulting negative GNP growth as potential risks in building El Cajón; yet, these were precisely the outcomes of the project. In addition, Honduran society was forced to bear the costs for the globalizers' mistakes. The country was consequently burdened with not only the nearly $1 billion price tag for the dam but also the over $40 million in additional repairs and $200 million in lost business and economic production arising from the dam's 1994 failure. William Loker's statement regarding the people forced by El Cajón to relocate eloquently captures the project's impact on all Honduran society: "The El Cajón project worsened the plight of an already poor people. The negligence of those who planned and constructed the project drove many from poverty to misery."[73]

Finally, El Cajón illustrates how, in the end, the donor countries are the beneficiaries of globalization. Whereas Honduras paid $800 million for a faulty dam, the donor countries benefited from the purchase in the form of lucrative dam-building contracts, repair contracts, and research opportunities. These same countries continue to benefit as Honduras pays off the loans, with interest, for the dam. El Cajón thus represents another example of how the institutions of global governance (i.e., the international development profession[74]) are set up in such a way that the interests of the developing countries, the alleged beneficiaries of the assistance, are actually overshadowed by the interests of the wealthy nations giving the assistance and making up the rules by which it flows into developing countries. The benefit of hydroelectric power the dam promised Honduras was realized for a number of years. But the Swiss, Italian, Canadian, and German firms that each received multimillion dollar accounts through El Cajón can be considered major beneficiaries of the WB's development efforts in Honduras. Their relative gains appear even greater in the light of the dam's flaws. Even the dam's failure was a boon to these foreign consultants, who received new million-dollar deals and were portrayed as heroes who had come to Honduras's rescue.

In the final analysis, it is important not to lose sight of the economic benefits that went from the El Cajón development project to the planners, technicians, engineers, and bankers in the developed world. Overlooking this important fact obscures the reality that international development assistance is not aid; it is not generosity or beneficence that gets expensive hydroelectric projects built in poor countries that cannot afford such technologically sophisticated megaprojects. It is self-interest. And, in the case of El Cajón, not only did the international development institutions realize greater benefits, they were also free from picking up the costs resulting from the dam's failure, costs borne exclusively by an impoverished Honduras.

Industrial Processing Zone (Zona Industrial de Procesamiento, ZIP), Honduras

CHAPTER EIGHT

Making *Maquiladoras*

Chances are, if you look in your closet, you will find an item of clothing with the label "Made in Honduras" on it.[1] This T-shirt, pair of pants, or skirt was produced in a Honduran *maquiladora* (manufacturing plant). Maquiladoras are factories that employ Honduran workers to manufacture products for foreign companies. Honduran maquiladoras produce apparel for more than two hundred foreign clothing manufacturers. They also (albeit to a lesser extent) make electronic goods, furniture, and other products.

Reading the names on these articles of clothing of such well-known transnational corporations (TNCs) as Hanes, Liz Claiborne, Polo, Tommy Hilfiger, and Gap, most people might assume the TNCs built these maquiladoras. And in fact, most scholars who have studied maquiladoras in developing countries view their emergence as a direct result of these large corporations introducing or setting up the plants in developing countries in order to move their production to where labor is cheap.[2]

But this is too simplistic. For although the TNCs may be the ultimate users and beneficiaries of maquiladoras, typically they do not build them on their own, and they did not build them in Honduras. This is not hard to understand.

Entrepreneurs and executives working for large corporations in the donor countries often know little about the developing world. They do not normally speak a foreign language and may not have business connections in the countries where, because of low labor costs, the maquiladoras would be built. Even if they wanted to take advantage of cheap labor in developing countries, they are not likely to know how to go about it. In addition, the amount of time and resources required to build a factory (in a country that, it might turn out, does not allow foreigners to build there); hire workers (who may not have the skills needed for the job); and ship materials back and forth across borders (perhaps demanding duties and tariffs be paid) with trucks and ships (that may not be affordable) are factors that may make moving offshore difficult, risky, or even impossible.

For whichever of these and other reasons, TNCs did not build the maquiladoras in Honduras. The globalizers did. International development workers promoted, built, and supported maquiladoras in Honduras, and, by doing so, paved the way for manufacturers from wealthy countries to set up shop in Honduras—worry free.

Here, then, is another example of international development professionals leaping into action in pursuit of a particular global agenda—in this case, the construction of low-skilled manufacturing facilities offering cheap labor to foreign companies based in the donor countries. This goal can be achieved only through a complex sociopolitical process in which corporations, citizens, workers' organizations, local government agencies, and public planners negotiate terms and legal agreements.[3] The globalizers are at the center of this process.

Offshore Assembly: Background

The subject of offshore assembly factories is familiar to students of globalization and most anyone who follows current events. Essentially, "offshore assembly" (also known as "coproduction" or "production sharing") refers to large manufacturing firms moving their production facilities from areas of the globe where costs are high to those where they are low in order to maximize profits. The costs under consideration are usually labor costs, but corporations also take into account taxes, tariffs, the regulatory environment, and transportation costs. The word *offshore* reveals the corporations' viewpoint: production customarily carried out at home is moved overseas, out of the country—offshore.

Offshore assembly has its origins in the early 1960s but became an increasingly common practice in the 1980s and 1990s.[4] During this period, most manufacturing companies explored the option of offshore assembly and many made the decision to move some, if not most, of their production overseas. Labor costs have featured prominently in these decisions. All along the U.S. border with Mexico, for instance, there are many assembly plants manufacturing commodities previously "Made in the U.S.A." These plants arose quickly first in such Mexican border cities as Ciudad Juarez and Tijuana, located directly across the border from El Paso, Texas, and San Diego, California, respectively. At first, these border factories engaged primarily in "assembly work." That is, Mexican plants import duty-free components manufactured in the United States, assemble them, and then export the finished product back across the border. Usually, they perform the most labor-intensive step in the manufacturing process. For example, in the production of blue jeans, American companies such as Guess and Levi's ship precut pieces of denim (these so-called components are usually produced and cut in U.S. textile mills) to Mexican assembly plants, where the labor-intensive sewing is done by Mexican workers. The sewn jeans are then shipped back to the United States (at low cost owing to the geographical proximity), where they might go through another step in the manufacturing process (e.g., stone-washing, which is done using capital-intensive machines).[5]

This type of work became known as "assembly work" because Mexican workers were engaged in only one step of the manufacturing process. A clothing label marked "Assembled in Mexico from U.S. Components" reflects this reality. Factories set up along the U.S.-Mexico border specifically to carry out this assembly work have become known as "assembly plants," "offshore assembly sites," "export processing zones," or, according to the Spanish word for "assembly plants," "maquiladoras" (sometimes shortened to "maquilas").

How did these assembly zones come about? Who created the legal conditions permitting products to be imported and exported from these zones duty-free? It is, I discovered in Honduras, more complicated than the TNCs simply deciding to operate overseas. TNCs in fact have an indirect (perhaps secondary) role in the process. The real builders of maquilas in Honduras were members of the international development profession, working primarily through the United States Agency for International Development (USAID).

The Global Agenda: Creating Maquiladoras in Honduras

For an examination of the role of USAID in creating and promoting the maquiladora industry in Honduras, it is important to first consider the larger global agendas at work. At its most basic level, the advancement of offshore assembly zones in Honduras is directly related to trade liberalization and the donor countries' interest in promoting free-market reforms throughout the developing world.[6] USAID's promotion of maquiladoras in Honduras was part of a much larger global agenda designed to advance U.S. interests in Latin America by encouraging, in particular, free-market reforms in various enterprises to foster free trade and exports to the U.S. market for the benefit of both U.S. companies and Latin American producers. Such reforms, it was argued, were in the long-term interest of the United States since they would benefit the U.S. economy and reduce immigration from Latin America because of the expanded economic opportunities such reforms would create in the recipient countries. Free-trade zones were a small part of this larger agenda, which included many other neoliberal reforms in all sectors of the economy (e.g., finance and agriculture).

In the early 1980s, U.S. foreign policy took a dramatic shift in favor of establishing free-trade zones in the third world. Foreign development assistance took center stage in this policy shift. Under the Reagan administration, the U.S. government instituted a new policy framework known as "Trade Not Aid," according to which U.S. foreign assistance, which previously had gone primarily to developing country governments, would be directed more toward the private sector in those countries. A cornerstone of this new policy was the $1.3 billion Caribbean Basin Initiative (CBI), a project designed to create a free-trade area between various Caribbean countries and the United States.

The CBI gave countries in Central America and the Caribbean the green light to export products to the United States at reduced or eliminated tariff rates. It was designed to encourage the developing countries in Central America, in particular, to enhance their exports to the vast U.S. marketplace. Many of these countries, such as Haiti and Honduras, were among the poorest in the hemisphere. In addition to opening up the U.S. market to Caribbean basin exporters, the CBI also significantly increased U.S. development assistance to those countries.[7] The aid was directed at private-sector initiatives such as promoting small business and expanding agricultural exports.

USAID became a major instrument for carrying out the free-trade reforms highlighted in the CBI. According to USAID strategy papers from that time, in fact, promoting the private sector became USAID's key mandate. It was already working on private enterprise when the CBI was passed. In 1982, the agency created its own Bureau of Private Enterprise (BPE), designed to "stimulate development by helping to strengthen private enterprise in the third world, especially small- and medium-sized businesses which serve as engines for self-propelling growth."[8]

Export processing zones were the brainchild of this bureau. The bureau funded pilot programs in Thailand, Jamaica, Peru, and Kenya. Its original plan included "expanding these private enterprise initiatives across the world . . . to all countries in which there was an AID mission." Central American and Caribbean basin countries were among the first test cases, starting in Costa Rica, Panama, and Haiti, followed by El Salvador, Guatemala, and Honduras.[9]

At the time, the U.S. government articulated three main reasons for supporting such initiatives. First, the United States was concerned about political stability in Central America and believed advancing private enterprise would garner support for U.S. policy in the region. Second, the U.S. government thought such programs could help curtail Latin American immigration to the United States by providing jobs and better economic opportunities in the countries from which migrants were flowing. Third and perhaps most significant was the conviction such projects would ultimately benefit U.S. businesses and their employees.

U.S. congressional testimony on Congress's agreement to fund the initiative echoes these three reasons. When asked why U.S. citizens should support spending taxpayer money on a particular private-enterprise low-interest loan program in Haiti, USAID's Elise DuPont responded, "The answer to that is very simple. . . . we are not providing a loan to the businessman in Haiti. A private bank in Haiti is giving the loan. We are simply using the guarantee authority that we have [through the BPE's fund] to help encourage the bank to provide [the loan]." She was quickly corrected by Congressman Dan Mica of Florida, who said, "I thought you were going to say that if we had some stability in Haiti we might not have some of the immigration problems that we have had in south Florida, and that 8 out of 10 jobs in America created in the last 10 years are due to international investment and trade, and 3 out of 5 acres of all agricultural products produced are for export. That is what I thought you were going to say." To which Ms. DuPont responded, "You said it very well and I accept your words [Laughter]."[10] In other words, it was quite clear to congressional representatives that such initiatives abroad were intended to curtail immigration and create jobs for American businesses.

Reducing Latin American immigration and creating American jobs were the central interests in this case. By taking advantage of the foreign investment opportunities created by these U.S. government programs, U.S. businesses were poised to be the biggest beneficiaries. For example, when the BPE and Trade and Development Program (TDP) initiatives were being created and the approval for their funding was under debate in the U.S. Congress, one of the congressmen on the Subcommittee on International Economic Policy and Trade asked the TDP director, Christian R. Holmes, about the project's expected benefits to U.S. industries. The congressman, again Mica of Florida, asked, "To give some scope to the program, how many firms—are we talking about four or five multinationals who are using all your money, or are we talking about a large number? How many states are involved?"[11]

Mr. Holmes responded, "I would say that we have dealt with as many as 25 contractors, and once again they are primarily engineering, procurement, construction firms, A&E firms. These firms range everywhere from Bechtel to Fluor to firms like Burns & Roe. We try to avoid a situation where we are dealing too much with any one firm as *we see the program as an opportunity to help many firms get involved overseas*" (emphasis added).

Mr. Holmes continued:

What is going to happen in terms of *business given to U.S. firms and who is going to get a piece of the project?* We analyzed [one project . . . a Jamaican coal power generation project] in terms of what business U.S. firms would really receive if the power plant were constructed because, you see, what is really not so important is who gets the feasibility study, although it is important to that firm, particularly if they get follow-on contracts, but what is really important is $100 million in exports going to Jamaica should they actually build this power facility, and the subsequent impact on the U.S. economy. Understand that this is a hypothetical situation because we do not know yet if the plant will be built. But I could give you the names of some of the firms that would possibly be in the running to sell goods and services. I could do it for the record. (emphasis added)

Congressman Mica, apparently already privy to the information Mr. Holmes was presenting, then asked, "Did you project, for instance, on one project $100 million and one firm will then subcontract to 40 firms and provide employment? Is there anything that goes that far?"

Mr. Holmes responded, "Only in a couple of projects have we gone all the way down to the level of employment. On one project we are doing, a feasibility study in the Philippines for the cost of $150,000 on their overall telecommunications network—there will be $1.7 billion in procurements in that project, we believe."

"Billion?" Mr. Mica asked, wanting to make sure he had heard correctly.

"Billion," Mr. Holmes confirmed, "We believe the Filipinos will find the exchange to finance that; $1 billion of that project could conceivably come from the United States. And we went after the project and [assisted] a U.S. firm to get into it, because we want the U.S. firm to advise, candidly, the Filipinos where they can find the best equipment, and that is not going to be in Germany or Japan. It will be right here in the States."

Mr. Holmes added, "We have taken our analysis down to the point that we know that Stromberg-Carlson, which is a big Florida firm, stands a chance to pick up approximately $100 million in contracts should the scenario eventuate along the lines we are talking about."

Making explicit the common set of interests alluded to in Mr. Holmes's statement, Mr. Mica asked wryly, "Is it a coincidence that you mention Florida, California and Washington [the other states that had congressmen present]?"

Amid laughter in the subcommittee chamber, Mr. Holmes replied, "Not at all."[12]

Congress eventually approved funding for both the TDP and USAID's new BPE.

This episode demonstrates the perception among congressional representatives of U.S. foreign affairs as an opportunity to promote free-market projects in the interest of U.S. firms. This is the sort of principal donor-country interest that would play a pivotal part in the promotion of free-trade zones in Honduras. As a result of U.S. political support for development initiatives abroad that the U.S. Congress clearly linked to billions of dollars worth of contracts for U.S. firms, all U.S. foreign aid channeled through USAID became available to support free-market reforms. Any prior restrictions on the use of development assistance for private enterprise endeavors were removed. According to one USAID policy paper cited in a 1993 article that appeared in the *Multinational Monitor*, "There are no restrictions on types of funds or modes of assistance applicable to the pursuit of private enterprise objectives. ESF (Economic Support Funds), DA (Development Assistance), and PL480 (Food for Peace) loans or grants are all appropriate ways to support private enterprise development."[13] This shift in USAID policy later became known as "AID's Private Enterprise Initiative."[14]

In 1983, as part of this new initiative, USAID contracted the private consulting firm Sabre, Inc. to analyze the successes of free zones throughout the world. The report, entitled "Free Zones in Developing Countries: Expanding Opportunities," examined free-trade zones in five different countries and made recommendations for promoting them elsewhere. The recommendations included the importance of designing legal reforms to reduce tariffs and taxes on exporters; the need for institutions that could give training in free-market reforms to key entrepreneurs and government officials in developing countries; the need for coalitions of business organizations dedicated to advancing their goals; and the importance of providing financial incentives and start-up funds for all these endeavors.[15]

In 1984, USAID conducted and published another study, "A Guidebook on Free Zones," which set guidelines and objectives for building free-trade zones in Central America. It presented building free-trade zones as an especially attractive way to get developing countries to adopt the neoliberal economic reforms international development agencies such as USAID, the International Monetary Fund, and the World Bank were promoting. "Free zones," the guidebook suggested, "represent an excellent 'proving ground' for liberalizing reforms before extending them on a nationwide basis."[16]

At an institutional level, USAID had, by this time, adopted the policy of promoting the expansion of free-trade zones wherever they carried out development projects.[17] Consequently, USAID began actively pitching the maquila industry throughout Central America and the Caribbean. In Guatemala, for example, USAID was able to change the relevant laws in the country for the benefit of potential investors in offshore assembly.[18] Kurt Petersen, who has studied the history of the maquila in Guatemala, concluded: "The underlying cause for the remarkable explosion of the maquila industry has been the highly influential and supportive United States Agency for International Development (AID), . . . with indispensable financial support and technical expertise, AID has judiciously directed the rise of the Guatemalan maquila industry."[19]

In reference to USAID's managing to change Guatemala's legal code so that free zones could operate in the country, Petersen points out that USAID development workers not only met with and lobbied high-level Guatemalan officials, but they even drafted the actual legislation that was the basis for the legal changes. Petersen attributes much of USAID's success in Guatemala to its ability to gather information on what foreign companies (particularly from the United States) would require in a potential processing site. This of course brings to mind the mechanisms of surveillance and monitoring international development organizations have at their disposal. USAID officials put together reports for the Guatemalan government and business sector outlining these requirements, which Petersen summed up as: "no taxes, no duties, no unions." USAID carried out similar programs in El Salvador, Costa Rica, and the Dominican Republic.[20]

Insertion into Honduras

How did USAID become involved in establishing maquiladoras in Honduras? There are two parts to the story. First, the Honduran business community (and the Honduran government to some extent) wanted help in building these zones and invited USAID to become involved in their own efforts. Second, as mentioned, USAID itself had been looking at promoting export processing zones during the 1980s. In effect, USAID both inserted itself and was invited to participate by powerful Honduran interests.

The idea for a maquila industry in Honduras was not a new one when USAID became involved in the mid-1980s. The growth of the maquiladora industry along the U.S. border in Mexico was well under way, and many Latin American countries had begun to explore the possibility of attracting foreign investment through similar offshore assembly zones. The Honduran government itself had tried to get a maquila industrial sector going in 1977 by setting up several government-run "free zones."[21] It was unable, however, to attract a significant number of foreign investors, possibly because Honduran law still required foreign processing companies to pay some duties on their imports and exports, as well as property taxes.[22] As of 1984, there was only one maquila zone in the entire country, with some fourteen companies utilizing its facilities.[23]

Although USAID applauded the Honduran government's efforts to set up free-trade zones, it considered the government to be overly reliant on an import-substitution model of development and reluctant to fully adopt free-market, export-oriented reforms. Between 1982 and 1984, it began holding regular meetings with Honduran business organizations that shared USAID's view that free-market reforms and export promotion needed to become a greater priority for the Honduran political establishment. It met with CONADI,[24] a local business coalition, as well as with other groups such as the National Association of Honduran Exporters (ANEXHON), the National Association of

Industrialists (ANDI), the Honduran Management Association (GEMAH), and the Honduran-American Chamber of Commerce (HAMCHAM) to discuss the possibility of local investors becoming directly involved in an entirely new development project: *privately* owned free zones with no Honduran government oversight or taxes.[25]

This idea appealed also to foreign investors. U.S. apparel manufacturers in particular had been involved with USAID's BPE and expressed an interest in being able to do "coproduction" business in developing countries; they had even been invited by the BPE to participate in a "series of private sector reconnaissance teams [visiting] target countries."[26] These reconnaissance teams were coordinated by USAID and consisted of various U.S. business-promotion institutions such as the World Trade Institute, the International Executive Service Corps (IESC), the American Management Association (AMA), the Caribbean/Central American Action Group, and the chambers of commerce "from different localities."[27] Perhaps as a result of these visits, USAID encouraged the four Honduran business coalitions (ANDI, ANEXHON, GEMAH, and HAMCHAM), each of which was already receiving USAID support,[28] to form the Foundation for Research and Business Development (known by its Spanish acronym FIDE). The foundation was "conceived to serve as the technical support arm"[29] of these Honduran business coalitions and given the objective to "stimulate non-traditional industrial exports by providing technical services to companies with an export capability."[30] FIDE was, in other words, intended to be a funnel into which USAID (or any other funding agency, for that matter) could pour resources for the promotion of export processing zones.[31]

The timing is important here. FIDE was founded in February 1984, received its legal charter in May, and was given its first USAID start-up grant of approximately $300,000 in June to cover its "costs of installation, organization, and operations during its first year." On June 30, according to USAID documents, FIDE "first opened its offices." And by August of that year, FIDE was listed on the official loan/grant agreement between the government of Honduras and USAID as the recipient of a $4.1 million grant to cover its "activities over the five-year implementation period" of the USAID export promotion project. In other words, in less than a year FIDE went from nothing to the principal institution responsible for the multimillion dollar project promoting the Honduran maquiladora industry. As detailed below, although FIDE was technically independent from USAID and characterized as a Honduran institution, it would become the main organization through which USAID inserted itself into the maquiladora-building business throughout Honduran society.

Surveillance and Planning in Honduras

The various "private sector reconnaissance visits" also led USAID to sponsor a series of studies and economic analyses for assessing the feasibility of projects fostering nontraditional exports: agricultural projects (cacao, melons, onions, and Persian limes), mining and forestry projects, and (most pertinent to the discussion in this chapter) labor-intensive manufacturing industry projects. In May 1984, USAID hired independent consulting firms such as Arthur D. Little International and International Parks, Inc. to provide analyses on "Promoting New Exports of Manufactures from Honduras" and the "Policy Framework for Export Development in Honduras." Price Waterhouse was engaged to conduct an "Assessment of Export Services and Financing Needs in Honduras" in June of that year, and in July, Manchester Associates received a grant to conduct a study on "Promoting Investment in Non-Traditional Honduran Export Industries."[32] The aim of these studies was the development of a feasible plan for creating export processing zones in Honduras. The overall conclusion of this surveillance was that export processing zones were not only feasible but likely to be highly profitable as well, earning potential investors a "windfall." Investors would, the studies declared, likely "double their income" in a matter of five years. As a result of these studies, USAID began to draft a "project paper" of what would become its maquiladora promotion project—what it called its "Export Development and Services" project. The economic analyses undertaken as of mid-1984 assured the agency the project "is considered financially viable."[33]

Setting the Agenda: Project 5220207

From all this surveillance and monitoring (and the recommendations of the reports constituting this surveillance), USAID drafted a plan of action, project 5220207, the 1984 "Export Development and Services" project. USAID conceived this as a "project to promote nontraditional exports in Honduras. The Government of Honduras (GOH) will use public and private channels to implement the project, which will reform the GOH's export policy and upgrade its export promotion capability, and expand related financial services."[34] The proposed plan entailed three central initiatives: (1) change the laws of the country; (2) support new institutions to attract foreign investors to the assembly zones; and (3) provide financial services, capital, and access to credit to potential investors through a $10 million "Export Trust Fund."

With regard to the first initiative, the Export Development and Services project plan was clear: change Honduran law. Even the language of the plan made it plain that USAID would be involved in the creation of new Honduran legislation: "Key legislation to be developed and passed under the project will: increase export incentives, extend free zone status to industrial parks; eliminate costly bonding requirements; and streamline permit procedures via a one-stop center for all government approvals."[35] In other words, USAID, in conjunction with the government of Honduras, was going to create optimal legal conditions for the construction and utilization of offshore assembly plants for the benefit of the private sector. Earmarked for this initiative was $1.4 million, which would cover among other things "observation trips" by Honduran government officials to export processing zones in Mexico and the Dominican Republic; "training programs" for government officials who would design and promote the new legislation; and "expert services" from three "export policy advisers" conducting these trainings. The experts would work directly in the Honduran Ministry of Economy, Ministry of Finance, and Customs Office for a fee of $12,500 a month.[36]

The second initiative of the ambitious USAID project provided $9.2 million for the start-up and training of other, mostly Honduran, globalizers, who would in turn promote the Honduran maquiladoras abroad. This phase of the project involved training "export promoters" who would work in both the Honduran government and the private sector. According to project documents, the plan stipulated that, "The GOH will train at least 24 overseas representatives in export promotion, as well as two trade officials to staff a New York–based Investment Promotion Office." In addition, "private sector contacts will be developed through annual seminars with FIDE. . . . Start-up, development and market-related services will be provided to manufacturing exporters by FIDE. . . . FIDE will also organize a furniture and wood producer's council, establish industrial park management companies to attract labor-intensive operations to the parks in Tegucigalpa and San Pedro Sula, and provide a wide range of other export development services."[37] FIDE received $4.7 million for the first five years of the project and, as I discuss below, was to become a major figure in the story of the Honduran maquila industry.

Third, by making available "discount loans" to potential exporters, the USAID project made it even easier for potential business interests to set up offshore assembly plants in Honduras. This new $10.2 million system of "financial services" involved the government's Central Bank of Honduras as well as a consortium of private banks. The project was designed so that,

> Financial services available through private institutions will be expanded by: creating a $10 million (AID-funded) Export Trust Fund in the Central Bank of Honduras to make foreign exchange accessible to exporters and granting the private, five-bank Industrial and Agricultural Finance Company access to the Fund; establishing a local-currency Agricultural Industry Fund to provide discount loans to low-collateral exporters for project assisted activities.[38]

USAID was in effect offering low-interest loans to any potential investors. The project also provided $200,000 to train Honduran bankers who would be involved in managing the new fund and to support "a program to ensure Honduran banks of payment by overseas importers." USAID was thus creating mechanisms whereby the new international business arrangements and contracts forged from these new enterprises would be guaranteed by a special U.S. government–established fund.

The plan also stated that "the project will require extensive technology transfer primarily from U.S. businesspersons"[39] to meet its goal of providing "technical assistance in investment promotion, product development, export marketing, and improved production methods."[40] What this meant was the USAID project was going to be a boon to U.S. private contractors who would be hired, as development workers, to come to Honduras for large fees to train personnel in Honduran institutions. One such U.S. firm is the IESC, which is made up of mainly retired U.S. business volunteers and has conducted over ten thousand training assignments for USAID since 1965. A volunteer I interviewed in Honduras was earning $100,000 a year as a consultant's fee from USAID to conduct such training. In 1984, the BPE devoted $7.4 million to such "technology transfer" programs. In fact, USAID's Export Development and Services project in Honduras allocated over $2 million to the IESC alone. Over the course of the project, many other private U.S. consulting firms received large contracts; Price Waterhouse, for example, was paid $200,000 for a feasibility study, and Nathan Associates, Inc. took in $87,000 for a FIDE evaluation. It is noteworthy that, by law, many of these contracts had to be awarded to American firms.[41]

Such kickbacks were built into the project, and it is important to realize how much of the benefits of this "aid" package to Honduras were designed to go directly back to the donor country. The gains to the development experts facilitating the project, the globalizers themselves, in particular are worthy of some scrutiny. Of the approximately $23 million provided by the United States in the project's budget, about $8.2 million (or 35 percent of the funds) was ear-marked for the salaries of the thirty to thirty-five professionals hired to carry out the project. USAID "project management" alone would require four new positions in the USAID headquarters in Tegucigalpa, amounting to $1.1 million in salaries for the five-year period. Most of these jobs were to be filled by U.S. government employees or U.S. independent contractors, and all of the positions required a high degree of technical expertise. As a result, the salaries were all relatively high for the time (especially by Honduran standards), ranging from $50,000 to $140,000 per year.[42] The project guaranteed that the globalizers working on the project would "live like kings" for the duration of their employment in Honduras.

There were benefits slated for the Honduran "counterparts" in the project, too. These local globalizers would receive $8.1 million (in salaries, equipment, travel expenses, and other amenities) from the Honduran government and private sector in association with the project. USAID would provide an additional $1.6 million to the one hundred "participants" in the project—Honduran FIDE employees and twenty-four "official overseas representatives"—for trips, trainings, conferences, equipment, and salaries. Some of these individuals became the Honduran promoters of the maquiladora industry in places such as New Orleans, Miami, New York City, and Taipei.

The project plan was later expanded, in 1989, to "include funds for the construction of new export processing zones." Administered by FIDE, these funds totaled another $9.7 million and were provided to both local and foreign investors. In particular, the funds could be used "to permit debt restructuring and the infusion of capital for firms that demonstrate a significant export potential, but are currently hindered by their debt structure."[43] This would become a great benefit especially to many local Honduran businesses that could use the funds to get out of debt and set up new maquiladora plants, which they would in turn lease to the manufacturing firms they were told in USAID- and

FIDE-sponsored workshops, conferences, and trainings, would be flocking to the country to take advantage of its new facilities and cheap labor.

In 1991, Nathan Associates was contracted to conduct a regional study evaluating the Honduran program in addition to the other export-promotion programs in the Caribbean. USAID also paid for a macroeconomic study that year by the International Finance Corporation to assess "the foreign direct investment (FDI) environment in Honduras." The findings would prove valuable as USAID began promoting foreign investment in the export processing zones and garnering local consent for these zones in Honduras.

Garnering Consent

Once the plan was in place, USAID did the work of garnering consent to get important Honduran constituencies on board. On August 31, 1984, the government of Honduras signed a "Project Agreement between the Republic of Honduras and the United States of America for Export Development and Services." And with the signatures of the Honduran Central Bank president Gonzalo Carías Pineda, the minister of economy Miguel Orellana Maldonado, minister of the treasury Manuel Fontecha Ferrari, and the USAID mission director Anthony Cauterucci in place, USAID's project plans became a matter of law. In all, the project amounted to $31.6 million, $8.1 of which was to be provided by Honduras ($2.5 million from the government, $5.6 from the private sector). But USAID's disbursement of its $23.5 million in official development assistance had an interesting condition. The initial disbursement consisted of a $450,000 grant (for "start-up costs") and a $9.5 million *loan*.[44] The project agreement stipulated that the United States would give an additional $7 million grant and $6.5 million loan on the condition the project was completed successfully. In other words, if the government of Honduras did not change its laws and implement the reforms laid out by the project within five years, it would not receive the remaining $13.5 million.[45]

Of greater significance, however, was the U.S. Congress's tying of overall Honduran economic aid to the Honduran government's acceptance of the project. According to a General Accounting Office (GAO) report published in 1993, the U.S. government approved an additional $178 million in much-needed Economic Support Fund (ESF) assistance.[46] ESF is money the U.S. government offers to developing countries struggling with balance-of-payments difficulties (usually owing to heavy foreign debt). The U.S. government told Honduran government officials they would receive the $178 million in ESF funds in 1990 and 1991 *if* they adequately implemented the free-market reforms included in USAID's 1984 export development project.[47] These funds were a pretty big carrot, one that garnered the consent of the many Honduran government leaders who stood to benefit personally from the trips, trainings, and salaries of the project anyway. According to the GAO report, "disbursement of these [ESF] funds was conditioned on the Honduran government's making progress on [neoliberal reforms]." The report added that USAID was operating in Honduras in a fashion similar to other international development organizations: "the AID policy reform agenda has been similar to that of other donors, including multinational financial institutions, and has often been pursued in concert with them."[48]

The agreement created a transnational arrangement in which USAID, the Honduran government, and the private sector would institutionally join forces to advance a global agenda. The agreement precluded USAID's ever having to lobby Honduran government officials about the merits of economic policy reform in favor of building free-trade zones. It stipulated that "key legislation" would be "developed" through the coordinated efforts of USAID personnel and Honduran government officials. USAID would never have to win the Honduran congress over to its belief that these export processing zones would help the Honduran economy. The agreement required that such legislative reform be passed. And USAID certainly would never have to conduct a plebiscite with the citizens of Honduras to see if there was popular support for the idea of creating dozens of large industrial parks throughout the country. There is no mention in the agreement that the broader citizenry of Honduras would be involved in any way (except as "beneficiaries"). The agreement thus put in place the rules and procedures through which the Honduran maquiladora industry would be born. Within this new transnational space created by the Export Development and Services agreement, the globalizers, local and foreign, would build the export processing zones in Honduras.

Local Political Consent: The 1987 Export Processing Zone Law

After the agreement was signed, one of the first initiatives of the project was to change Honduran law. USAID officials and consultants worked directly with Honduran government ministers and officials to draft an "export processing zone law" for the country. The law declared that any private local developer could build an industrial park anywhere in the country and declare it an export processing zone. They could then lease the space to foreign investors and manufacturers to conduct their operations without tariffs or duties. Thus, any foreign enterprise investing in space within one of these industrial parks could import raw materials and semifinished products without duties, and they were likewise able to reexport finished goods without any tariffs. There would be no local property taxes due and their profits were similarly exempt from taxation. The law also included such incentives as the duty-free import of machinery or equipment needed for operations; 100 percent exemption from import, export, local sales, excise, and profit taxes; unrestricted withdrawal of profits and capital; the right to hold dollar-denominated accounts in Honduran banks; and, to streamline customs formalities, access to special customs offices located in each industrial park. The law was thus aimed to maximize the attractiveness to foreign companies of setting up offshore plants in Honduras.

The question arises as to who did the actual writing of this legislation. Did the Honduran government write it with the advice and support of USAID employees, or did USAID write it? My interviews with numerous USAID workers in Honduras show USAID was likely the primary author of the law. One former USAID worker I spoke with informally, for example, told me, "You know the ZIPs [Zonas Industrial de Procesamiento—"export processing zones"]? Well, that was AID. We basically wrote up the laws that made those ZIPs legal."

Greg Lamar, a USAID employee (introduced in chap. 1) who worked on various policy reform issues that included drafting legislation, explained more clearly how this works:

> Our role, really, [is] to guide the policy discussion through [the Honduran ministries]. The ministries have legislative power. They can introduce legislation in congress. [USAID through its subcontractor] will draft what they call an "anteproyecto," or draft legislation. They will then give the draft to [the relevant ministry]. Then [the ministry] will refine it and pass it through the minister onto congress. Congress, of course, can change things again, but you get the idea. We're writing the original draft. We've done this in a couple of cases.

The claims of the two USAID employees that USAID wrote the original draft of the export processing zone law coupled with the explicit statement by the

U.S. Congress, in approving the USAID project, that such legislation would be developed and passed makes it reasonable to conclude that USAID was the originator of this new Honduran law.[49] The ability of a foreign development agency to participate in the drafting of Honduran law supports the argument that such development agencies are participating in the Honduran political process at the highest level. What is important in this case is that drafting legislation is used as a mechanism of garnering local consent for what is a global agenda. Getting a Honduran ministry to present a USAID-drafted piece of legislation to the Honduran legislature ensures the government of Honduras gives consent to the USAID project. In 1987, the Honduran congress passed La Ley de las Zonas Industriales de Procesamiento para Exportaciones (Industrial Zone Export Processing Law) and made it official Honduran law; the USAID agenda thus acquired formal local political approval.

Consent from the Local Business Elite: Honduran Business and FIDE

USAID also garnered Honduran consent for its global agenda by working closely with Honduran investors and businesspeople (again, by providing technical experts and money for seminars, conferences, forums, etc.) who themselves would invest in (and actually build) a number of export processing zones. As stated previously, USAID collaborated with Honduran business groups such as ANEXHON, ANDI, COHEP, GEMAH, and HAMCHAM, all of which became centrally involved in the promotion of the nascent Honduran maquila industry.

More significant in this regard, however, was the work of the new export promotion institution FIDE. As I mentioned previously, FIDE was created in 1984 when USAID brought together these Honduran business groups to form an organization whose sole purpose was promoting the maquila industry. These business organizations had close institutional and personal links. FIDE's president, Mr. Richard Zablah, was also president of ANEXHON, vice president of COHEP, and a board member of several of the other organizations. He also owned several companies. Mr. Leonel Bendeck was a FIDE board member and also vice president (and past president) of ANDI; he also served as president of the Advisory Council on Human Resources Development (CADERH).[50] CADERH figured prominently in the growth of the export processing zones as it won many USAID contracts providing workforce training to maquiladora workers and managers.[51]

FIDE depended almost entirely on USAID financing for its first ten years or so, receiving $8 million between 1984 and 1992 to carry out its work.[52] Its mission was to attract local and foreign investors to build more export processing zones, and perhaps more important, to encourage foreign companies to use the newly created facilities in their manufacturing process. USAID hired local professionals to work for FIDE, and in so doing, was able to garner the consent of local businesspeople, who, as employees and supporters of FIDE, became committed to the goal of investment promotion.

To carry out its primary task of attracting foreign manufacturers and investors to Honduras's industrial parks, FIDE placed ads (sometimes whole inserts) in international business periodicals—*Latin Finance, Business Week,* the *Wall Street Journal,* and in such popular trade magazines as the apparel industry's *Bobbin*—promoting Honduras as "an excellent offshore manufacturing site": "Would you like to reduce your labor costs? Honduras offers: Competitive wages (roughly twenty-nine cents an hour), an abundant and productive workforce, excellent port installations, low taxes. Honduras! A country committed to progress."[53]

Potential investors were encouraged in these ads (fig. 11) to call FIDE for more information. FIDE was thus responsible for not only advertising and promoting the export processing zones through the international media but also offering consulting services to potential investors. The phone numbers in the ads connected potential investors either directly with the FIDE office in Tegucigalpa or its U.S. office in Miami (whose name was the Industrial Development Group—Honduras). Both offices promised to send, free of charge, a packet of information regarding foreign investment in Honduras. The packet included a pamphlet entitled "Honduras: For Profitable Investment and Gracious Living," which told potential investors that "a look at Honduras may be well worth your while."[54]

The packet also contained an updated printout of investment information; in answer to the question, Why Honduras as an offshore manufacturing site? it listed: "best port facilities in Central America; proximity to the U.S.A.; permanent tax holiday; and ample availability of highly productive labor at competitive labor rates ($0.53/hr. including benefits)." The packet also had: a detailed "cost analysis of an export oriented assembly operation in Honduras," listing all the costs and responsibilities of an actual textile operation; a copy of the "Honduran Investment Law"; a large color map of the country indicating the locations of all of the new export processing zones; and a personal letter

Figure 11. FIDE Ads Promoting ZIPs

inviting the potential investor to visit Honduras. FIDE would take visiting companies through the entire process of setting up shop in one of the newly built, modern industrial parks. Referring to itself as "your one-stop office for investment,"[55] FIDE outlined its services as follows:

> Available to assist foreign companies seeking to develop investment and sourcing programs in Honduras. Your One-Stop Office for Investment:
>
> - Prepares detailed itineraries, tailored to the businessman's individual requirements, and coordinates visits to Honduras.
> - Accompanies investors on site visits to specific manufacturing facilities, industrial parks and free zones.
> - Schedules meetings with government, banking and international officials.
> - Contacts local suppliers, sub-contractors and joint venture partners.
> - Arranges appointments with lawyers, consultants and related support-service entities.
> - Provides industry/sectoral profiles, current data on transportation facilities and schedules, wage rates, incentives and legislation, economic indicators, production cost figures, and other statistical data.

- Identifies buildings and sites for rental or purchase.
- Provides follow-up assistance and full support to establish successful operations in Honduras.
- Provides assistance with immigration procedures, housing, school and other accommodations.[56]

With substantial funding from USAID, FIDE was able to coordinate the visits of hundreds of potential investors to Honduras, walking them through each step of the offshore manufacturing process. Without the globalization efforts of USAID and the related activities of FIDE, it is unlikely the offshore assembly zones in Honduras would have attracted foreign firms. Once again, it was the activities of the globalizers that facilitated economic globalization in Honduras as export processing zones (known locally by their Spanish acronym, ZIPs) began to dot the countryside.

FIDE's role as a liaison and promoter was likely a key element in the tremendous growth the zones experienced in the years following FIDE's inception. This conclusion is supported by the results of evaluations conducted by USAID examining FIDE's performance. One such evaluation (carried out in 1994 by a U.S. contractor, Nathan Associates) concluded that "FIDE had become a highly competent professional institution with influence in Honduras well beyond its small size." The assessment also stated that about one-third of the growth in export processing zones in Honduras was directly attributable to FIDE's activities. It also noted that FIDE had achieved economic self-sufficiency and had "met its economic targets" by creating $390 million in direct export sales and $195 million in new investments for the country. Furthermore, FIDE was given credit for creating thirty-five thousand new jobs for Honduran maquiladora workers, which, according to the evaluation, had resulted in "alleviating poverty."[57]

Consequences of USAID's Export Development and Services Project

The coordinated efforts of USAID, FIDE, and the Honduran government resulted in one of the most significant economic changes in Honduran history: the transformation of Honduras into a major offshore assembly site. To understand more concretely how this came about, let us look at the example of one company—Global Fashions—a Korean-owned subcontractor

operating a textile and garment assembly plant in the Choloma export processing zone (ZIP Choloma) on the north coast of Honduras near the port city
of Puerto Cortés.

Dong Bang, a Korean TNC looking to move its garment and textile facilities out of Korea (with the encouragement of the Korean government, which
works closely with the country's major multinationals, or *chaebols,* as they are
called) created Global Fashions in coordination with local Honduran investors, foreign investors, FIDE (using USAID funds), and the Honduran government.[58] FIDE encouraged companies such as Dong Bang to set up Honduran subsidiaries to operate in the Honduran industrial parks and export
goods primarily to the U.S. market. Dong Bang set up a number of subsidiaries,
giving them names such as "Trans Pacific Garments" and "Global Fashions."[59]
These subsidiaries became subcontractors for major garment retailers in the
United States such as Wal-Mart and J. C. Penney. According to Moises Reyes,
a promotions manager for FIDE in Honduras, it was relatively easy to encourage Korean textile producers to locate in Honduras. He explained, "An American company may come here two or three times before they decide to make a
move. But a Korean comes, and he's ready right away."[60]

In 1990, with the help of FIDE staff, Global Fashions selected an empty lot
in the Choloma industrial park. By 1991, it was employing over five hundred
workers—mostly women—who were making bright sundresses, skirts, and
blouses—already tagged with $8.95 bar code labels—for Wal-Mart to the tune
of $2 million in sales for just that year. These women were paid approximately
$4 a day, saving Global Fashions about one-third what it would have paid
Korean workers (and about 10¢ an hour more than the Honduran minimum
wage of 30¢ an hour).[61]

Dozens more companies, with FIDE's assistance, followed Global Fashions'
successful lead, including: Hanes (1990), True Form (1990), Kellwood (1992),
Wrangler (1992), Olga (1992), Sara Lee (1992), Fruit of the Loom (1993), and
Polo (1993).[62]

The number of export processing zones grew dramatically. By 1994, there
were eleven industrial parks spread throughout the country providing assembly factories for more than 175 different companies (foreign and local).[63] Of
these, 84 were Honduran, 37 were U.S.-owned, 34 were Korean-owned, and the
remaining came from Taiwan, Singapore, Hong Kong, Pakistan, and Macau.
By 2003, the number of zones grew to twenty-four, and the number of companies operating in them exceeded 250.[64]

The number of Honduran workers employed in the export processing zones had, by 1990, gone above 9,000.[65] That number jumped to 49,477 in 1994 and to over 100,000 by 1998.[66] According to the Honduran government, during the period 1990–94, the maquila industry contributed $288.2 million to the Honduran balance of payments, which represented much-needed foreign capital for the heavily indebted country. Likewise, the zones were providing Honduran workers with paychecks. The average monthly earning for one of the roughly 50,000 workers employed in the export processing zones was $100.[67]

The creation and growth of the maquila industry has had a fundamental impact on Honduran reality. The future of the industrial zones and whether they are truly beneficial overall to Hondurans is the source of much debate. On the one hand, the ZIP factories employ tens of thousands of Honduran workers at relatively good wages. Proponents argue that these are job opportunities that would otherwise not be available. For this reason, supporters argue, the zones are a great help to the Honduran economy because they provide a significant source of income for workers who, in turn, are better able to contribute to the local marketplace. On the other hand, critics of the maquila industry argue that the export processing zones are simply exploiting the cheap labor of Honduran workers, who are willing to work for below-subsistence wages only because of the dire economic conditions present in the country in general (and in the predominantly rural areas where the zones are built in particular). These critics believe the ZIPs will actually harm the Honduran economy in the long run because the foreign companies using the labor of Honduran workers are not required to pay local taxes that could provide for the social costs of educating workers and keeping them healthy. As I discuss in the next chapter, the critics became even more vocal as evidence began to appear that the ZIP factories were employing child labor and violating workers' rights, such as the right to assemble, the right to bargain collectively, and the right to decent working conditions.

What is inarguable is that this historic change in the Honduran economy (and its society more broadly) would not have taken place without the involvement of several important development agencies, USAID in particular. Honduran government institutions and business *did* play a key part in the creation and evolution of the export processing zones, but USAID, a foreign development agency, held the primary role. According to Jesús Canahuati, vice president of the new Honduran Manufacturers Association, 95 percent of

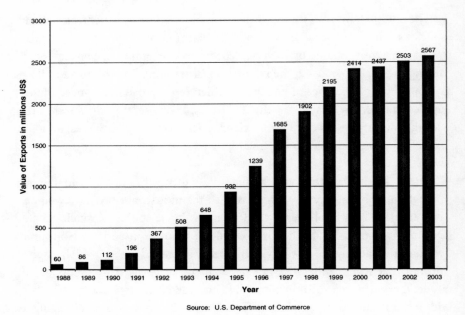

Source: U.S. Department of Commerce

Figure 12. Honduran apparel exports to the United States

the apparel plants in Honduras were built after 1989.[68] In 1988, the value of Honduran apparel exports to the United States totaled approximately $60 million. That number jumped dramatically to over $630 million by 1994 and to $2.5 billion by 2002, making Honduras the third largest apparel exporter in the world (after China and Mexico) to the United States.[69] (See fig. 12.)

But this "success" of the apparel industry set in motion a new set of problems and issues that the globalizers would be called upon to address and into which they would re-insert themselves. By the early 1990s, the Honduran sweatshop scandal had erupted on the global political scene. This scandal, the subject of the next chapter, was to have huge repercussions in the United States and Honduras and would fundamentally alter the role of the globalizers in Honduras from that point onward.

Worker protest at a Honduran *Maquiladora*, February 1996

CHAPTER NINE

Legitimating *Maquiladoras*

The Sweatshop Scandal

As soon as the *maquiladoras* were built and began manufacturing, Honduran workers in these export processing zones raised concerns that both foreign and local industries were disobeying Honduran and international labor laws. Local labor unions such as the Federation of Unions of National Workers of Honduras (FESITRANH, one of three rival union groups in Honduras) began demanding better working conditions. They claimed in particular that they were not allowed to organize workers in the new industrial parks and that workers who spoke with union organizers were routinely fired. FESITRANH blamed FIDE (Foundation for Investment and Development of Exports) for "not telling investors that there are labor rights and labor laws in Honduras—including the right to form unions."[1] They also claimed (accurately) that none of the FIDE promotional materials or ads mentioned the right of Honduran workers to form unions and engage in collective bargaining, and as a result, many new apparel subcontractors were actively discouraging unions in their plants. By 1995, only 14 percent of maquila workers were unionized.[2]

Worker protests at maquila factories throughout the country highlighted the unions' claims. In some cases, workers engaged in work stoppages; in others, they went on strike. In several cases, they took over the plant. Between 1992 and 1994, there were seven major work stoppages, two strikes, and eight factory takeovers involving between four hundred and five thousand workers.[3] In one instance in 1996, between four thousand and five thousand workers rioted at the Galaxy Industries plant in ZIP Choloma, holding a security guard hostage for two days, vandalizing the central offices, and lighting nearby automobiles on fire to protest the working conditions and demand the right to form a union.[4]

FESITRANH and the other unions invited foreign labor organizations such as the United Nations' International Labor Organization (ILO) and the National Labor Committee (NLC, a U.S.-based nongovernmental organization) to examine the Honduran maquiladora industry. A 1992 investigation by the Honduran Human Rights Commission (Comisionado de Derechos Humanos de Honduras, or CODEH; supported by foreign funds)[5] of the alleged labor abuses found extensive problems: child labor, forced overtime, limited bathroom breaks, locked fire exits, termination of workers advocating unions and pregnant workers.[6]

Some local Honduran entrepreneurs tried to distance themselves from the growing tumult. The Honduran Manufacturers Association (AHM), for instance, blamed the problem on the Korean-owned maquilas. "They need to work on their cultural problems," said the vice president of the AHM, Jesús Canahuati. In response, Paul Kim, president of Global Fashions, admitted that his company did engage in "compulsory overtime" but that it was part of a "tough love" managerial approach.[7]

In response to the growing criticism, FIDE defended its policies in the Honduran press by claiming that the alleged labor abuses were rare, isolated cases and emphasizing the overall economic gains to the country as a result of the growing apparel production industries.[8] Other development agencies such as the Inter-American Development Bank (IDB) also began holding press conferences in an attempt to ward off criticism of the Honduran maquiladora industry. IDB president Ramón Hernández Alcerro suggested that the export processing zones open their doors to the Honduran Ministry of Labor for monthly inspections so everyone would be assured they were complying with the law. The IDB was particularly concerned that the growing controversy would drive investors away. In response, union leader Claudio Villa Franca criticized the Honduran Labor Ministry for being in cahoots with FIDE, the

Honduran maquila owners, and the foreign investors. He proposed instead a "U.S. commission be brought to Honduras to see what is really going on. We don't trust FIDE or the Ministry of Labor. We only trust CODEH."[9]

The Honduran business community, on the other hand, did not view the activities of CODEH and Honduran labor organizations in a favorable light. In fact, it criticized CODEH for receiving foreign funding and attacked Honduran labor organizations as being manipulated by "foreign agitators" who ultimately wanted to shut down the Honduran maquila industry. The Honduran Chamber of Commerce even accused CODEH and the Honduran unions of being unpatriotic in their criticisms of labor conditions in the maquiladoras.

It is important to consider the political dynamics operating here in the context of global governance. The Honduran Chamber of Commerce (which was one of the founding members of FIDE and had worked closely with USAID in the creation of the maquilas in the first place) and the Honduran NGO CODEH (which was working closely with foreign human rights NGOs, particularly from the United States and Spain), were *both* trying to advance their local political agendas by linking into global agendas. What is interesting is how Honduran businesses used these foreign ties as a political strategy aimed at discrediting their political opponents in Honduras. The same criticism was never publicly leveled against the business interests that had received millions of dollars in external support.[10] It is also notable that both local agendas—advancing Honduran industry on the one hand and promoting Honduran labor unions on the other—found success by linking to the global agendas of USAID's export promotion project in the former case and to international labor and human rights organizations in the latter.

Insertion: The NLC Gets Involved

CODEH approached the U.S.-based NLC to conduct further investigations. Their findings were reported in various media outlets such as the *Guardian* in London. Scrutiny by local and international labor and human rights organizations of what was going on in the export processing zones revealed many labor abuses.[11] NLC director Charles Kernaghan claimed his organization, which had been investigating the free-trade zones throughout Central America, had found numerous examples of child labor, forced overtime, unsafe working conditions, and union busting. It had also discovered USAID's initial role in providing economic assistance to Honduras for the creation of these zones.

In 1992, Kernaghan took the NLC's investigation results to the executives at CBS's *Sixty Minutes*. The show's cohost, Ed Bradley, produced a story exposing USAID's involvement in encouraging U.S. businesses to relocate to Central America. Bradley's perspective, as conveyed in the episode, was that U.S. taxpayer money was being used to subsidize the relocation of U.S. companies to Central America. American workers were, in effect, paying taxes contributing to their loss of jobs to overseas workers.

The episode aired on September 27, 1992, and included hidden-camera footage of a visit to Honduras by Kernaghan and *Sixty Minutes* executives posing as a fictitious Miami-based company called New Age Textiles. New Age Textiles had contacted FIDE through the phone number in one of the aforementioned ads and had been invited to Honduras for a FIDE-guided tour. Was it right, Bradley questioned, for the fictitious executives to be ushered around potential factory sites by FIDE at U.S. taxpayer expense?[12]

The most damaging footage for FIDE and USAID was when the undercover executives asked the FIDE representative about potential labor problems. There on hidden camera, the FIDE representative told New Age Textiles that FIDE could "take care of" any labor problems they might have. According to Bradley, the FIDE official told the company "that workers who want to join unions can be fired on the spot and their names placed on black lists." FIDE promised, "[you will] never have to deal with a union." The exposé even contained footage of a USAID employee in El Salvador stating: "There are certain names that we know that you will probably not want to hire," clearly implying USAID in El Salvador also kept a blacklist.[13]

Three days after CBS aired the *Sixty Minutes* story, Senator Patrick Leahy of Vermont introduced an ad hoc amendment to the 1992 Foreign Aid Appropriations law curtailing USAID funding in support of the maquiladora industry in Honduras. The bill had already been approved by all the appropriate committees and by the House of Representatives and would have continued USAID funding of FIDE in Honduras, but Senator Leahy and twelve other senators who introduced the last-minute amendment decided that USAID had to be "flatly banned" from engaging in development activities that "would result in the relocation of U.S. operations abroad with a loss of American jobs." Senator Leahy stated, "The amendment we are offering to this bill deals with the problem raised by this program [*Sixty Minutes*]. . . . What I saw was outrageous and must be immediately stopped."[14]

The amendment became known as "Section 599" and set new conditions on all U.S. assistance abroad.[15] In particular, it stated that no funds appropriated under the Foreign Assistance Act could be used for: (1) any program that would encourage a business located in the United States to relocate outside the United States; (2) assistance to a foreign country for the purpose of establishing any export processing zone in which the laws of that country do not apply; and (3) assistance to any project that contributes to the violation of workers' rights as defined under recognized international law.

Congress also required that the General Accounting Office (GAO) launch an investigation into the maquila promotion activities of USAID to see if the allegations raised by the *Sixty Minutes* episode were correct. Although the GAO study concluded USAID projects in Central America were not ultimately responsible for decisions by U.S. companies to relocate to those areas, USAID would never again work directly to promote export processing zones.[16]

Milton, a USAID worker in Honduras whom I interviewed, explained it this way: "Yeah, we used to work on the ZIPs [Zonas Industrial de Procesamiento— export processing zones] at one time. But then *Sixty Minutes* or somebody came down and did a big exposé and said that AID was involved in keeping unions out and forcing the workers to work long hours. . . . So all kinds of shit hit the fan and . . . basically we were told that we can't do that anymore."

Milton was upset about the congressional decision that forbade USAID from continuing to provide economic support to FIDE and promoting the export processing zones in Honduras generally. I asked Milton why he felt U.S. support for the zones should have continued. He responded,

Because it's good for Honduras and it's good for the U.S. That's the part that people don't understand. These companies aren't going offshore because they want to steal jobs from Americans. It's because they can't get the work done in America . . . and if they did, then people would have to pay $130 for a shirt. Nobody could afford to make textiles and sell shirts in the United States for what the U.S. consumer wants to pay. Would you be willing to pay $130 for a shirt just because it's made in the U.S.? So what does the U.S. worker want? Do they want to work for low wages in textile mills sewing shirts together all day long so they can go to the store and buy one for $130? No, people in the U.S. don't want to work under those harsh conditions anymore. . . . Or does he want to go to Wal-Mart and buy it for $19? That's what people don't understand. They also don't understand that by paying Hondurans decent wages, the Hondurans can afford to buy some of the consumer goods that are produced by American companies. And they will be less likely to want to migrate to the U.S. They'll want to stay here. So it's good for Honduras and it's good for the U.S. businesses. But people don't understand that . . . and they tell us that we can't work on that because that's "evil." So, yeah, [the congressional decision is] frustrating for me.

Milton criticized not only the U.S. Congress for falling "for . . . these political concerns" and cutting off funding promoting the export processing zones but also the international labor rights groups and *Sixty Minutes* for "meddling in the political affairs of Honduras" and obstructing funding that, he believed, was helping the Honduran economy. "Ignorance" on the part of the anti-maquiladora organizations, he felt, was to blame:

> They have no idea how much they might be harming the very people they claim to be helping. They're ignorant. I mean . . . I think the ZIPs will be OK and will continue to grow, I think they're well under way and can continue under their own power. But this could be a big setback. People don't realize how significant this project was. For example, I work on a project for shipping winter vegetables to the United States. Which is good . . . people in the States probably enjoy getting cantaloupes and asparagus the whole year round and so the Congress has no problem supporting these projects . . . growing winter vegetables in Honduras, but it will not answer economic development *here* in Honduras. It's going to be a rather limited benefit. I mean, there will be maybe three or four thousand Honduran farmers growing this stuff. And these farmers will have maybe another five thousand employees helping them. That's about eight thousand workers . . . and these projects may take five or six years to fully develop. Well, this *one* ZIP project—one project!—employed about thirty-five thousand workers and hired people who are in the worst conditions of all, . . . you know, the very lowest, most disadvantaged sector of people—and pays them better than my farmers will. And each of those ZIPs developed in about six months. So what's better?

This USAID employee's perspective is important to my discussion not because of its strong pro-maquiladora position but because of the concern it expresses that U.S. policy makers are making decisions that have a significant impact on Honduras even though they may not be the best-informed people making the decisions. This particular example of the U.S. Congress's ban on USAID funding of export processing zones clearly demonstrates the global nature of development work in Honduras: the ability of an independent NGO, operating in concert with Honduran labor advocacy groups, to influence—via *Sixty Minutes*—the U.S. Congress and, in turn, the decision to force USAID to stop its promotion of maquilas in Honduras indicates the complex web of international relationships that global governance entails.

Global Governance Starts All Over Again

The growing controversy surrounding the Honduran maquiladora indus-try started the cycle of transnational engagement in the local Honduran polit-ical process all over again. The year 1992 marked the end of one phase of global governance, what I call the "making maquiladoras" phase, and the beginning of a new one, "legitimating the maquiladoras." In this new phase, the global-izers again drew on their mechanisms of power—insertion, surveillance, agenda setting, and garnering consent—in addressing the increasing concern over the problems of child labor and exploitation in the maquiladora indus-try. The growing criticism and attention on the problems associated with what the globalizers had built—the offshore assembly plants, or "sweatshops" as they were called in the mainstream media—provided, in other words, yet an-other opportunity for those very same globalizers to come to the rescue and solve the problems they were largely responsible for creating. Of interest is that in the turmoil around the Honduran sweatshop issue, it is the transnational actors (international development and human rights NGOs in particular) who have the central role. Honduran groups and citizens play a major part as well, but all the time they do so on a transnational political stage.

The collaboration between international development and human rights NGOs and transnational corporations (TNCs) to answer the political con-cerns in the donor countries is yet another tale of how global agendas tend to win out over local agendas and how local agendas succeed only as far as they are able to connect to the activities of the globalizers. The globalizers' primary concern in this case was legitimating Honduran export processing zones in the face of mounting criticisms that these maquiladoras were sweatshops. Al-though the process of global governance follows, I believe, a trajectory similar to that in the creation of the Honduran export processing zones—insertion, surveillance, and garnering consent—in this second story, USAID is no longer the principal agent of globalization; rather, international human rights, labor rights, and children's rights organizations are the main agents of globalization. Scholars of globalization often posit these international NGOs as being "antiglobalization" or "critics of globalization" inasmuch as these organiza-tions participate in global protests and activities in direct opposition to the neoliberal agendas of transnational organizations such as the World Bank, the World Trade Organization, and USAID.[17] I contend, however, that although they are often critical of the neoliberal agenda, ultimately these organizations are also participating in global governance in that they are promoting agendas largely based upon the experiences of donor countries and seek to advance these agendas in the recipient countries.

Insertion and Surveillance: The NLC Gets Fully Involved

By 1992—when USAID support for the project was curtailed—the maquiladora industry had taken on a life of its own. All the institutions created since 1984 to promote the industry, including FIDE, were growing.[18] USAID's forced withdrawal from the project, therefore, made no difference.[19] Export processing zones continued to be built and foreign companies went on moving into Honduras to utilize them. As a result, the concern in the Honduran and international media about labor conditions in the maquiladoras also persisted.

This was mainly owing to the actions by one organization in particular, Charles Kernaghan's NLC, to keep the media focused on the sweatshop issue. The NLC, a New York–based NGO with a staff of three and a yearly budget of $240,000, worked closely with Central American human rights and labor organizations such as CODEH in Honduras. Kernaghan claimed that the NLC's aim was to bring the negative consequences of offshore assembly "to the world's attention."[20] More than any other international organization, the NLC inserted itself into the public imagination by engaging in media-savvy attacks on prominent spokespersons of well-known name brands.

Kernaghan's political strategy was in part the result of his success in changing U.S. law as a result of the *Sixty Minutes* exposé in 1992. In a 1996 interview, he said that the *Sixty Minutes* episode was the first time the media had paid attention to the labor abuse he and others had been trying to expose:

> We thought of the angle of U.S. tax dollars because we realized this was a home run—in the 1992 election. We had researched all of this USAID stuff—we knew how much this organization had spent in U.S. tax dollars to lure companies out of the United States. Then we went to *Sixty Minutes*. So our first real entry into this was at a massively high level—the story was shown on *Sixty Minutes* and, from what we heard from the Clinton campaign, this became one of the primary issues of the country according to their polls. It ended up on the Donahue show, *Nightline*, a hundred newspapers. The *Sixty Minutes* experience taught us a great deal. You have to find a hook for human rights work or it isn't going anywhere in the media.[21]

After the *Sixty Minutes* airing, Kernaghan turned his attention to the issue of child labor in Central America. Using the research of CODEH (which during 1992 and 1993 conducted interviews with 927 maquiladora workers), he discovered that well-known corporations such as Liz Claiborne were utilizing child labor in the production of their clothing. CODEH's research documented that approximately 13 percent of maquiladora workers in Honduras were children between the ages of twelve and fifteen. Children as young as fourteen could work legally in Honduras provided they worked no more than thirty hours a week and had parental permission. Surveillance by CODEH had shown that many children working in the factories were under fourteen. In addition, those less than sixteen years old (the age at which they could become full-time employees) typically worked much longer than thirty hours a week. The NLC had compiled a list of prominent American apparel producers known to be importing clothing produced by these child workers. Kernaghan's list of 153 U.S. companies included among others Levi Strauss, J. Crew, K-Mart, Liz Claiborne, Oshkosh B'Gosh, Van Heusen, Sara Lee, True Form, and Wrangler. The information Kernaghan needed to launch a media campaign against these companies and instigate a global political controversy came, it should be noted, from the monitoring and surveillance of their subcontractors operating in the industrial parks.

The political turmoil started quietly. Kernaghan's list raised serious questions regarding the extent to which U.S. apparel producers were benefiting from exploitation of child labor. The allegations prompted Ohio senator Howard Metzenbaum, chairman of the U.S. Senate Subcommittee on Labor, to open a special hearing in September 1994 on "Child Labor and the New Global Marketplace: Reaping Profits at the Expense of Children?"[22] The first witness to testify in the hearings was Lesly Margoth Rodríguez Solorzano, a garment worker from San Pedro Sula, Honduras, who was brought before the committee at Kernaghan's expense. Through an interpreter, the fifteen-year-old told her story to the U.S. senators of how she dropped out of school to work in the garment factory: "My name is Lesly Margoth Rodríguez. . . . I began working in a maquila factory when I was 13. I worked for a Korean company called Galaxy Industries which is in the Galaxy Industrial Park. There are many girls who are my age, and some are 13, like I was when I started. . . . I left school after the 5th grade so I could go to work to help my mother."[23]

Lesly recounted her daily experiences working in the Galaxy Industrial Park. Her typical shift lasted from 7:30 in the morning until 9:00 or 10:00 at night, with only one half-hour break for lunch. She and her coworkers were allowed two short bathroom breaks. In order to make the weekly production quota, she often worked more than eighty hours a week. In return, she received 188 lempiras per week (approximately $21.36 at the time). She explained how many employees took sewing home with them in order to keep up with the quota: "Some of the girls are forced to take work home with them since they cannot meet the quota the company demands. About 70 or 80 girls do this. Sometimes they work to one a.m., and they do not get paid for the work they do at home."

Lesly talked about the respiratory problems many workers suffered because of the lint and dust in the air. Despite such work-related problems, the company offered no health benefits nor paid sick days. She also described the arbitrary punishment and regular sexual harassment she and her fellow workers often had to endure: "The managers are always screaming at us to go faster, go faster. Sometimes they hit the girls on the head or in the back. If they say we have made a mistake, the supervisor throws the sweater in our faces and yells that we are dogs. The managers like to touch the girls; they grab your buttocks or your breasts. Some of the girls believe that if you let them touch you, you will get a little extra pay at the end of the week."

Finally, she described how difficult it was for her and her coworkers to form a union. "When they found out we were organizing," she explained, "they fired over 35 girls and threatened the rest of us." Six hundred workers at Lesly's plant eventually went on strike, and the company agreed to build a cafeteria and pay health benefits. Lesly believed, however, that much more needed to be done: "Here in the United States, I am told that the Liz Claiborne sweaters I make cost $90. I earn 38¢ an hour. . . . I wish that the people in the United States knew what pain these sweaters cost us."

Thanking Lesly for her "great courage" in coming from Honduras "to testify before a U.S. Senate committee," Senator Metzenbaum held up a Liz Claiborne sweater that a member of his staff had purchased for $60 at Macy's. He asked Lesly if she had ever seen the sweater before. She responded that she had and even remembered that the "piece rate [was] 300 per person . . . we produced 70,000 of them." She told the senators they had had to work overtime to complete the order but had not been paid any overtime, to which Senator Metzenbaum responded, "That is incredible. That is absolutely incredible." Galaxy Industries sent a letter to Metzenbaum denying the allegations.[24]

Needless to say, having a prominent U.S. senator hold up your company's product in front of television cameras in the context of Dickensian tales of child labor exploitation was not something executives at Liz Claiborne wished to see.[25] In response to the hearings, Liz Claiborne immediately canceled its contract with Galaxy Industries and stated it would look into the issue. This and other well-known apparel producers in the industry were concerned they might be facing a public relations disaster.[26]

Kernaghan continued his campaign. With CODEH and other NGOs (e.g., the Clean Clothing Campaign and UNITE), Kernaghan launched accusations that other companies were producing apparel in Central America in violation of local or international labor laws. The clothing giant Gap Inc. was the next to be exposed by this small group of labor rights NGOs. In early 1996, a series of articles appeared in the *Telegraph* (London) reporting that Gap was violating international labor laws as well as its own "Code of Conduct," which stated that "under no circumstances may a person under the age of fourteen be allowed to work in a factory that produces Gap Inc. goods." The articles claimed Gap's contractors in Honduras, the Cheil and Mi Kwang factories— both located in Continental Industrial Park, one of the new, sparkling export processing zones in the northern part of Honduras near San Pedro Sula—employed a large number of girls under the age of fourteen in its manufacturing of Gap shorts and polo shirts.[27] The reports contained interviews with girls as young as twelve, who told reporters they were working thirteen-hour days at a wage of roughly twenty-seven U.S. cents an hour. Gap representatives responded, "We are very concerned about these allegations and are looking into them right now. What has been described are clearly violations."[28] The articles noted Gap's image as a politically progressive and ethically responsible company was in jeopardy.

Then, in April 1996, Kernaghan told the Democratic Policy Committee (a House policy guidance group) that illegal child labor was being used to make the Kathie Lee Gifford Collection line of clothing sold by Wal-Mart.[29] On a visit to the plant run by Global Fashions, the Korean-owned subcontractor operating in the Choloma export processing zone (discussed in the previous chapter), Kernaghan and CODEH had discovered more than a hundred children between the ages of twelve and fifteen working thirteen-hour shifts, five days a week, and nine-hour shifts on Saturdays. After the hearing, Gifford's attorney released a press statement claiming she had been unaware of the problem. According to Gifford, Wal-Mart informed her that her clothing was no longer produced in the Choloma plant in question. "Kathie Lee Gifford formed her clothing line to benefit children [proceeds went to a children's charity] and would never condone, tolerate or accept the exploitation of children," read the statement.[30]

Although Wal-Mart and Gifford stated the problem had been resolved, Kernaghan complained that Wal-Mart had simply ended its relationship with Global Fashions rather than work to improve the conditions in its plant. Later, in June 1996, he testified before Congress that the move had only made matters worse since it could result in a loss of jobs for Honduran workers. "There are huge problems there, but we do not think the companies should leave. . . . We are not interested in taking jobs away from Honduras."[31]

A media frenzy followed. Editorials and magazine articles chastised Gifford for her greed and hypocrisy and accused her of benefiting from the sweat and toil of children. The accusations became even more pointed when Wal-Mart acknowledged it had sent an unannounced inspector to Global Fashions' plant, confirming everything the NGOs had asserted.[32] Kernaghan's claims were in fact accurate: Gifford's clothing had been manufactured using Honduran child labor.

Perhaps in an effort to recover her public image, Gifford agreed to testify before Congress; during her testimony she tearfully admitted before the television cameras and news reporters present that, unbeknownst to her, her clothing had been produced in factories where underage girls worked in violation of Honduran labor laws. She claimed "it was nothing less than an assault on my very soul when a witness before Congress suggested that I was using the sweat of children [to produce the Gifford line of clothing]."[33] She also claimed that "in that very instant" that she became aware of the problem, she made a personal commitment to do what she could to call attention to "the sweatshop problem."[34]

Gifford's testimony took place in part out of an agreement she made with Kernaghan and the other labor advocacy groups, as well as one of the underage girls from the Honduran factory. Accompanied by her lawyers and public relations advisers, Gifford had asked the fifteen-year-old garment worker, Wendy Díaz, what it was like working in the factory. Díaz explained she was an orphan and had started working in the Global Fashions factory at age thirteen; she earned thirty-one cents an hour and had experienced numerous labor abuses, including forced overtime, sexual harassment, unsafe conditions, and reprimands for showing interest in a union. Apologizing to Díaz, Gifford reportedly responded, "I did not know this was happening. I did not know what was going on. I am sorry and I want to give you my word that this will never happen again. I want to work with you, and I want to work with other people that you work with to clean up these factories. If I cannot, I am getting out of the industry." Díaz told Gifford she did not want to see the plant closed down, rather she wanted Wal-Mart to return the work to her plant but with better conditions and independent monitoring inside the plant. Gifford promised Díaz she would encourage Wal-Mart to restart its production of her clothing line in Honduras, but only after the labor conditions there were improved.[35]

Kernaghan (now widely known in the media as "the man who made Kathie Lee cry")[36] highlighted the significance of this meeting during his congressional testimony: "This is what she told us, and then she went on to Wal-Mart and said to Wal-Mart, 'I want you to return to Honduras. I want my clothing line back in that factory, but I want that factory cleaned up, and I want independent human rights monitors to have access to the factory. I want to pay the workers a living wage,' something incredible for Mrs. Gifford to say." Kernaghan added, "I think that Mrs. Gifford's statement, for example about the independent monitoring, was very brave. She has taken on . . . the biggest retailer in the world. It will be very interesting to see what Wal-Mart does."[37]

Throughout the summer of 1996, largely in response to the Gifford brouhaha, the U.S. Congress reopened its discussion on child labor begun in 1994. As stated, Kernaghan, Díaz, and Gifford all testified. Congress also invited Jesús Canahuati, vice president of the Honduran Manufacturers Association, to address its concerns that labor-law violation was widespread in the Honduran maquiladoras. Canahuati, who was also a developer of numerous industrial parks and had a reputation for having some of the best working conditions in his factories, appeared unprepared for the grilling he was about to face.

Speaking on behalf of all 170 apparel plants operating in Honduras's export processing zones, Canahuati was the sole witness to testify in rebuttal to the child labor allegations. He was also the only representative of any official Honduran organization; no Honduran government officials, for instance, were invited to participate in the proceedings. In his presentation, he argued that the "new apparel assembly industry in Honduras . . . has grown into a shining success story of which we are proud."[38] He emphasized the seventy thousand jobs created and the $200 million annual contribution to the Honduran economy. He discussed the labor laws in Honduras, which he argued were among "the most advanced in Latin America," and enumerated the various worker benefits required by law, including twelve paid holidays a year.

Regarding child labor, Canahuati stated, "to our knowledge, there are no minors under the age of fourteen years old working in Honduran assembly plants. Of course, there may be cases where falsified documents were presented in order to obtain employment." He emphasized the "modern, comfortable, and well-equipped" plants, many of which featured a medical clinic and free health care to the workers' children. He stated that many plants also provided free breakfasts, subsidized lunches, and even day care facilities for their workers. "No person is paid less than the mandatory minimum wage," he said, adding, "we take all allegations of misconduct seriously and are working to investigate and punish anyone involved in abusive or incorrect actions. In fact, since 1992, the government has taken action to expel from Honduras foreigners who were found to be violating workers' or minors' rights." He presented a pile of government documents picturing seven Korean businessmen who had been deported for violating Honduran labor laws. Canahuati concluded by announcing that the Honduran Manufacturers Association was setting up a mediation committee to investigate worker grievances, and he invited "all members of [the U.S.] Congress and their staff to visit our assembly plants."[39]

Skeptical of Mr. Canahuati's testimony, Virginia representative James Moran said there was a clear "disconnect" between what Canahuati was saying and all the other testimony they had heard so far, in particular that of Wendy Díaz. Canahuati responded that Ms. Díaz's case was currently being investigated by the Honduran government and that no answers were as yet available. Mr. Moran responded,

> But this information has been available for quite some time. I don't know how much time it takes to send somebody out to look at the situation in this assembly plant and to come back with the information. I have to conclude, sir, that that is a dodge. You have had a lot of time to check out this plant. You are dealing with a major trade relationship with the United States. This has been as visible an issue as any issue affecting Honduras. The Ambassador is aware. Your entire Embassy is aware. I suspect your government is aware. It seems to me that you ought to give a more credible answer to this committee as to what you are going to do about the situation.[40]

Attempting to respond to the congressman's blunt demand for answers, Canahuati replied, "We will have them pretty soon, I guess."
Moran shot back,

> You guess pretty soon. That is not an acceptable response. . . . The problem is, and I think that you are representing the problem, we have laws on the books in

Latin America, in Asia, in Africa. Countries say "look what we have. . . . [But] [t]hat doesn't mean bananas when it comes to what is the reality of the workplace. The problem is that there is no enforcement. . . . I think that is the problem we have across the board here. The governments say one thing and allow people to do another. That is why we need some type of certification with an international monitoring capability that would have some credibility.

Asserting that the governments in "these countries" are often "complicit" with the "people who are violating the law," Moran cited examples of "payoffs to the police" in "countries like India and Pakistan and a lot of others."[41]

Honduran Governance in an International Setting

What kind of politics was taking place here? Why were Honduran businesspeople and workers testifying before U.S. politicians about Honduran labor laws and working conditions? This story of the Honduran sweatshop scandal and its political repercussions is another example of the transnational nature of governance in Honduras. The entire debate regarding sweatshops in Honduras occurred, it should be noted, within an international social space. Although the U.S. media and congressional hearings occupied the center of this international social space (an important example of the donor countries' tendency to set the terms for global agendas), Honduran interests and constituents were also active participants in the process. In addition, the repercussions of the debate extended to Europe, Asia, and all of Central America.

The globalizers were at the center of the controversy. In fact, it was the globalizers—in this case the ILO and international NGOs such as Kernaghan's NLC and UNITE, working in coordination with local Honduran globalizers such as CODEH—who inserted themselves directly into the process by conducting surveillance of the factories, gathering information regarding child labor, and, then, using this information to back their political strategy of exposing the companies (primarily in donor countries) benefiting from the maquiladoras. Furthermore, it seems clear from the evidence that these international organizations were at the center of the subsequent negotiations between various political entities and the policies created to resolve the problem. The NLC and CODEH were perhaps the most significant agents in this process: first, by conducting the research that became the basis for the child labor allegations; second, by facilitating the interaction between Honduran labor groups and U.S. companies; and third, by serving as a political liaison for the U.S. Congress, which used the NGOs both as key witnesses in the hearings and the means for bringing additional witnesses to the proceedings from other developing countries (Honduras was not the only country being investigated).

The actions of these new globalizers represented a different, even competing, global agenda in relation to the one responsible for the creation of the export processing zones in the first place. Whereas USAID had been involved in promoting the zones, CODEH and the NLC were regulating (and perhaps even threatening) the zones. Although these two global agendas are at odds with one another, the process of global governance in the two cases is similar, and, I believe, both groups of international organizations are acting as agents of globalization in Honduras.

Illustrating the conflicting interests between the two groups, several development workers at USAID I spoke with were critical of the labor activists. When I asked Art, one of the USAID employees I interviewed, about the child labor issue, he like Milton, expressed his anger:

Look, there's a lot of people in the U.S. right now who are feeling really good about themselves because they're saying that they're saving the children or whatever . . . and that they put a stop to all the bad things going on in Honduras. We saw a lady on the TV the other day who said that her clothes were made in sweatshops in Honduras and so she said, "We stopped all that." Well, there *aren't* any sweatshops in Honduras making clothes for anybody. And there is no "child labor." "Child" is sort of a relative phrase anyway, . . . Sixteen years old in Honduras is generally not a child anymore. Most of these people come from rural areas where, from the time that they were about five years old, they were working out in either their parents' fields or somebody else's field, and no one was around complaining about the problem of "child labor" out on these farms. So now they're working in factories. Sure, it's hard work but it's nothing like the backbreaking labor of the farm—five in the morning to eight at night. These people work eight hours sewing clothes in very nice, clean environments. They're learning to use state-of-the-art machines, getting training . . . and they're getting paid twice as much as those people on the farm do. Twice as much as the minimum wage of Honduras. That's why Hondurans are lining up for these jobs! They're good jobs! So they are *not* in conditions of slave labor. But up in the U.S. everyone is all worried and complaining. And so they take one of these young girls from the ZIPs and they take them up to the States and they dress them in little children's clothes and put them in pigtails and they say, [imitating them in a sarcastic tone] "Oh . . . they made me work. I couldn't go to the bathroom."

Art stated his belief that the export processing zone factories are ultimately beneficial for Honduras and that the international organizations "meddling" in the child labor issue were "ignorant" of the damage they might be causing to the nascent Honduran industrial sector. He claimed the labor advocacy groups were "throwing the baby out with the bathwater." Art's views were not, however, shared by all other development workers at USAID, particularly those involved in labor issues.[42] Development workers from other organizations such as UNICEF (United Nations Children's Fund) were also supportive of the work of CODEH and the NLC to end the child labor practices in the maquiladoras. Thus, assuming all international organizations advancing globalization in Honduras agree with one another on this issue would be erroneous. The different global agendas operate in a dynamic relationship with one another, sometimes in sync, other times at loggerheads, and this is just what might be expected in politics, especially transnational politics. Nevertheless, both the critics and advocates in the international development profession of maquiladoras are up to the same thing. Both sets of globalizers seek to remake Honduras according to their own global agendas, which in turn reflect the standards of the donor countries. Although the political differences in this case are clear, ultimately this is a single, coherent story: the imposition of U.S. (or international) standards on other countries, which then sets into motion a cycle of global intervention and global governance.

Legitimating the Honduran Maquiladoras

The 1994 and 1996 U.S. congressional hearings on child labor resulted in some significant political changes that would have an impact in Honduras. In 1994, Congress required the U.S. Department of Labor to conduct a study on the problem of child labor in the United States and abroad. One of the recommendations of the two-volume report (entitled "By the Sweat and Toil of Children") was that the United States promote programs abroad to "protect children from abusive situations in the international economy" and "further the consensus in the global community that the economic exploitation of children is simply unacceptable." A recommended goal was to "look closely at the international financial institutions such as the World Bank and at how they might combat the exploitation of children."[43] In other words, the very globalizers who contributed to the use of child labor in the new industrial settings of the global economy were now being put forward as capable of solving the problems they had had a hand in causing.

This idea that international development organizations could be used as a tool to combat the child labor problem in other countries won popular approval among the participants in the congressional hearings, especially in the sense these organizations would be capable of "independent monitoring." Independent monitoring (what I might call "surveillance") was widely hailed as *the* political solution to the problem of child labor abroad. The assumption was third world governments were either too corrupt or too poor to adequately protect their own workers (the underfunded and understaffed Honduran Ministry of Labor was even cited as an example). Independent religious, human rights, or labor groups, as neutral organizations without any bias for the factory owners, were therefore seen as reliable investigators of alleged labor abuses and reporters on what was going on inside the offshore assembly factories.

Congressman Moran, as referred to earlier, concluded his statements urging the companies alleged to have committed labor abuses be subject to "independent inspections and monitoring" and that the U.S. government support the monitoring. This is, of course, what Charles Kernaghan, the NLC, CODEH, and the Honduran unions had been advocating all along. Other international labor groups agreed. A representative from the labor union AFL-CIO, Harry Kamberis, recommended that the U.S. government "support UNICEF and the ILO programs" devoted to combating child labor, though with the warning "these programs must be carefully monitored to ensure they do not become local government smoke screens." The AFL-CIO also recommended Congress continue funding the National Endowment for Democracy and USAID, which "have enabled [one of AFL-CIO's international organizations] and other American NGO's to address child labor issues."[44] (Harry Kamberis was apparently not present in 1992 when USAID was criticized for supporting the export processing zones in the first place.) California congressman George Miller argued that independent monitoring by international organizations was the "best solution" to what he called "a system of deniability" manufacturers had created for themselves in coproduction and offshore assembly.[45]

What all this meant in a nutshell was the United States would provide aid to developing countries to address the child labor problem: once again, the adopted solution to the problems related to the provision of past aid was providing more aid.

On July 12, 1996, the U.S. Congress introduced House Resolution 3812, "The International Child Labor Elimination Act." The bill had three provisions: it prohibited foreign aid to countries that do not recognize child labor laws; it proscribed USAID or the World Bank from lending to businesses or projects using child labor; and, third, it allocated $50 million to the ILO for its "International Program on the Elimination of Child Labor." Clearly, in the view of Congress, funding the globalizers' agenda to fight child labor was the appropriate solution to the sweatshop problem.

Some TNCs agreed with this view. Liz Claiborne, for example, had initially pulled its operations out of Honduras following the testimony of the underage Lesly Rodríguez. But with the help of the NLC, Liz Claiborne reestablished its coproduction arrangement with a Honduran maquiladora and agreed to submit to independent monitoring from Honduran and international human rights and labor NGOs.[46]

With its public image similarly at stake, Gap contacted several Washington, D.C., organizations such as Washington Office on Latin America, an NGO concerned with human rights work in Latin America. Gap executives were given a list of names of people to talk to in Honduras for information and advice. The list included several Hondurans working in the Labor Ministry and CODEH, as well as some U.S. development workers.

In the spring of 1996, a small group of Gap executives journeyed to Tegucigalpa from their headquarters in San Francisco to see if they could arrange independent monitoring. Gap had decided "independent human rights monitors and observers" were the answer to their problem and were determined to find out for themselves exactly what was going on in the assembly factories producing Gap clothing.[47] Their visit was low profile, and neither the local nor international press reported that Gap executives were in Honduras.

I was in Honduras at the time of this visit and became interested in the issue when an acquaintance of mine was approached by Gap for advice. A U.S. national working for an international development agency in the area of labor issues and thus familiar with the export processing zones, she did not consider herself an expert on what was happening at these factories and was surprised Gap executives wished to have her views on the issue. Gap executives had been given her name as a contact person, but she thought more Honduran workers should have been consulted: "They didn't really ask any of the workers what should be done. They mostly just met with all these government and international types," she told me.[48]

Gap representatives met with Labor Ministry officials and members of CODEH. During their whirlwind visit, they also consulted with representatives of multilateral development agencies, labor NGOs, and international human rights organizations for information on the "real situation" regarding child labor in Honduras and suggestions about rectifying the problem. Gap executives concluded that neither the Labor Ministry nor any of the Honduran labor unions were trustworthy or capable of policing the maquiladora zones. Meetings with the Labor Ministry in particular revealed problems of understaffing and susceptibility to bribes. My friend who spoke with the executives related, "The Labor Ministry was seen as not having a very good international reputation in terms of protecting workers' interests and preventing child labor."

From these meetings with both Honduran and non-Honduran consultants, Gap devised a couple of possible solutions to its problem. One was to commission a California-based labor-rights NGO as its monitoring agency in Honduras. In exchange for a contribution from Gap (and several other U.S. apparel multinationals with suppliers in Honduras), the NGO would keep tabs on the export processing zones and, if no violations were found, give Gap its seal of approval as a company that did not use child labor. The other option was to hire an independent monitoring consultant, an individual who would set up an office in San Pedro Sula and monitor the factories and report directly to the apparel companies should any flagrant violations of the law occur. Gap decided on the latter option, believing this approach would compel their contractors in Honduras to follow the rules.

What is interesting about Gap's decision is that Honduran government agencies were largely made peripheral to the process. The globalizers assumed the main role. Transnational business, in the form in this case of a single company, had chosen to engage in political negotiations related to its operations primarily with members of international development organizations and international NGOs.

The sidelining of Hondurans in the important national matter of enforcing labor codes in Honduras throws light on the transnational character of the politics surrounding this issue. How labor practices in the export processing zones would be monitored and laws enforced had in effect been left to non-Honduran institutions—in this case the multinational corporation Gap. The Honduran government and local labor unions and NGOs would of course continue their monitoring and enforcement and thus ensure their participation in making certain Honduran employees at the factories received fair treatment from their transnational employers; but, labor conditions in the zones would now be under the purview of a hodge-podge coalition of local Honduran *and* international organizations—subject, in short, to global governance. Furthermore, within this global coalition, the Gap corporation (through its hired independent consultant) would be the major player in the policing process, the probable wielder of the real power (through its mechanisms of surveillance) to ensure the local contractors obey the codes of conduct of their U.S. apparel buyers. If, for example, Gap received word from its consultant that one of its suppliers had been found in violation of the rules, Gap could terminate the contract and put the contractor out of business. This is swift justice compared to the meager fines and lengthy lawsuits the Honduran Labor Ministry might threaten.

Although such monitoring and enforcement would normally be the responsibility of the Honduran government and its Labor Ministry, global interests variously represented by the U.S. Congress, international labor organizations, and the transnational businesses themselves deemed these local political institutions incapable of preventing abuses (and their consequent negative publicity). Transnationals such as Gap and Liz Claiborne, therefore, circumvented the local political institutions in favor of independent monitors (sometimes truly independent, other times on the payrolls of the TNCs) vested with the authority to monitor compliance to Honduran and international labor laws. These independent monitors became a new cadre of globalizers in Honduras upholding the new global agenda of protecting Honduran workers against labor abuses and saving the TNCs using these workers the public relations embarrassment of being criticized as exploitative or inhumane. By means of their political activities the globalizers protect global economic interests: the sweatshop controversy momentarily threatening one global agenda—the development of Honduran export processing zones—is transformed instead into another global agenda—ensuring the protection of Honduran workers.

Garnering Consent for Maquiladoras

The sweatshop controversy of the 1990s has largely subsided in Honduras and elsewhere. Today there are a number of NGOs in Honduras engaged in independent monitoring on behalf of TNCs and international labor and human rights organizations.[49]

Whose consent, then, is being garnered? And for what agenda? What is happening here, in my view, is that the globalizers are working on political solutions to a global economic problem. Offshore production presents new problems for both Honduran workers, whose consent must be in place if the maquiladoras are to be saved from the damaging effects of worker protests, and consumers in donor countries, whose consent must be garnered if they are to continue buying clothing manufactured in the export zones. The political work being done is of benefit to the large donor-country corporations (Liz Claiborne, Gap, Wal-Mart, Disney, and others) that have created (with initial help from such globalizers as USAID) offshore assembly plants in Honduras and elsewhere and that face questions of legitimacy related to these new global economic arrangements. Enter the globalizers (again inserting themselves): to conduct surveillance and gather accurate information about the working conditions in the export processing zones; to facilitate political dialogue in order to create new policies and new agendas to ensure decent labor conditions; to provide funds and create programs to address the problem; and, ultimately, to serve as an international police force monitoring export processing plants to the satisfaction of those concerned about the child labor problem. The globalizers are garnering consent among Hondurans (especially Honduran workers, who might now feel they have a recognized way of raising grievances and getting a response) and transnational consumers.

SUMMARY:

What the Rise of the Maquiladoras in Honduras Tells Us

I have described how the globalizers participated in the creation of free-trade zones in Honduras in the 1980s and later became involved in their legitimization in the 1990s. The story of maquiladoras in Honduras illustrates the mechanisms of power the globalizers wield in the global governance of Honduras. USAID development workers took the lead in the initial creation of the export processing zones. USAID poured millions of dollars of U.S. government development assistance into Honduras as a way of inserting itself into the Honduran political process and connecting the global agendas of free-trade reform and the promotion exports to donor-country markets with the local agendas of particular Honduran business interests. To develop the most effective plan of action, it also engaged in surveillance of Honduran economic conditions. Finally, it garnered the consent of the Honduran government and public for its plan by (1) obtaining the government's formal agreement to the plan (with the promise of a large payoff down the road); (2) drafting the legal reforms and getting them through the Honduran legislature; and (3) setting up a Honduran institution, FIDE, to be the agent of developing the export processing zones. The USAID globalizers, with their Honduran counterparts, thus permanently transformed the Honduran economic landscape; export processing zones soon became a familiar way of life to Honduran workers and to the country's citizens in general.

These zones became familiar to U.S. workers and citizens, too. For once the maquiladoras were up and running, problems emerged for the globalizers to solve. At first, these problems (e.g., the *Sixty Minutes* allegation USAID was contributing to the loss of U.S. jobs) appeared to threaten the very global agenda USAID sought to promote. Nevertheless, the maquila industry continued (and continues) to grow and thrive, even without USAID support. The problems also spurred other international groups to action on behalf of other global agendas, in this case those related to the regulation of the maquiladora industry and the protection of labor rights. This second group of globalizers managed not only to insert themselves into the political debates surrounding the new maquiladoras and monitor and survey them to advance their own agendas, but also, by linking with important Honduran constituents (unions and Honduran human rights groups in particular), they established a new independent monitoring agenda and new opportunities for themselves as its global agents. These NGOs and their employees are poised to benefit economically from a new transnational political arrangement whereby they will be financed by donor countries (or TNCs directly) to carry out the political work that would normally be the province of the Honduran Ministry of Labor and Honduran legal system. It is a matter of speculation as to who will fill these new posts as "maquiladora monitors," but I would predict they will be members of an NGO or development organization hired on the basis of having some degree of professional expertise and, for that reason, are more likely to be non-Honduran than Honduran (it seems likely donor countries and the TNCs will hire their fellow citizens to supervise this work).

In terms of the five central themes of this book, the rise of the maquila industry in Honduras clearly demonstrates the following: First, it is apparent the global agendas won out over local agendas. USAID's plan for export processing zones succeeded where the original Honduran government plan did not. In addition, the global system of maquiladora monitoring was favored, and likely will ultimately prevail, over the Honduran government's system of legal monitoring and enforcement.

Second, only those local agendas able to tie into global agendas succeeded. The Honduran business interests that formed CONADI and FIDE and worked with the globalizers were the beneficiaries of the emergence of the export processing zones. In addition, Honduran labor organizations that mobilized global connections and networks to advance their cause were successful in bringing the world's attention to the sweatshop issue, thus achieving political gains for Honduran labor not otherwise likely had they not taken their case to the U.S. Congress and the global media.

Third, there were highly publicized benefits that Honduras as a whole *did* receive from the USAID export promotion project. Tens of thousands of jobs and millions of dollars in revenue were created as a result of establishing maquiladoras in Honduras. Highly touted by powerful groups in both Honduras and the United States, these benefits remain the big story. Honduras also enjoys better working conditions because of the activities of international human rights and labor organizations than would have been the case had they never exposed the poor working conditions in many of the factories in the first place. This is one of the benefits often pointed to by globalizers such as Art from USAID, who insist the maquiladoras provide, first and foremost, good-paying jobs to underemployed Hondurans.

Fourth, there were also, however, real negative consequences for Honduran citizens that came with the establishment of these factories. The exploitation in many maquiladoras was never a concern of the original USAID or Honduran promoters of the plan. Such negative consequences were overlooked or ignored. But these exploitative conditions (the undermining of Honduran collective bargaining laws, child labor, forced overtime, health problems) were so widespread that Honduran workers found need to take drastic measures to call attention to the problems. And, notably, most of these problems remain to some extent today. Furthermore, it should be kept in mind that, even though the international organizations solved some these problems to the benefit of Honduran workers, there are unacknowledged negative consequences for Honduras as well. There has been the loss in particular of local control over the monitoring of labor conditions. The solutions of the international community made no provision whatsoever for fostering local government capacity to regulate the maquiladoras operating within its borders. The authority of the Honduran Ministry of Labor, the most important local government agency in this case, was undermined by the new independent international monitoring system preferred as the most viable and so imposed by the globalizers.

Fifth and last, the possible reason for this is that the greater benefits of the export processing zones go to the donor countries in general and to powerful interests in the donor countries in particular. The growth of the Honduran export processing zones has meant great profits for U.S. transnational manufacturers and retailers such as Liz Claiborne, Gap, and Wal-Mart. One can assume that the benefits enjoyed by these global giants far outweigh the increased revenues of Honduran businessmen who invested in, built, and leased out the factory space inside the export processing zones. They certainly outweigh the economic gains of the Honduran workers who make a subsistence wage so that these TNCs might thrive.[50] In addition, since almost all the clothing is manufactured for the U.S. market, the United States is the major beneficiary of the export promotion development project; its citizens gain the availability of cheaper commodities. The TNCs and USAID economists claim the creation of maquiladoras throughout the developing world, including of course Honduras, gives U.S. and other donor-country consumers access to inexpensive clothing that would otherwise be markedly more expensive. The standard economic argument thus asserts these gains for the U.S. consumer even outweigh the job losses caused by shipping U.S. industrial jobs overseas.[51] Finally, U.S. citizens, as a result of the creation of maquiladoras in Honduras, might in the future be able to fill jobs as labor monitors.[52]

The relationship between globalizers from Honduras and the United States has been the focus of this chapter. Although other international agencies from other donor countries were involved in the creation and legitimation of maquiladoras in Honduras, U.S. globalizers had the most important role. In the next chapter, however, all the globalizers from all donor countries get involved: coordinating the large-scale effort to rebuild Honduras after the devastation caused by the second most powerful hurricane in recorded history, Hurricane Mitch.

Tegucigalpa residents look at some of the homes destroyed by a mudslide on Cerro El Berrinche, November 3, 1998. The mudslide was triggered by heavy rains from what was Hurricane Mitch.

Photo: Yuri Cortez/AFP/Getty Images

CHAPTER TEN

Rebuilding after Hurricane Mitch

It was the deadliest hurricane in recorded history. In late October 1998, Hurricane Mitch devastated Central America, killing 9,633 people. Honduras bore the brunt of its destruction, with over 7,000 dead, 12,000 wounded, and 2 million left homeless.[1]

The hurricane formed as a tropical storm in the western Atlantic Ocean on around October 23, 1998, and quickly grew in force. The storm headed straight toward the Bay Islands off Honduras's north coast. By October 27, Mitch had become a category five hurricane; it hovered over the Honduran island of Guanaja, battering its inhabitants with maximum force winds of 180 mph. Barometric pressure in the eye of the hurricane reached 906 millibars, the second lowest on record.[2]

Following the normal pattern, the hurricane was projected to continue moving west and north, but it just stopped off the coast of Honduras, where it remained for two days, bombarding the Bay Islands with high winds and rain. And then it did something that no other hurricane had ever done before: it took a sharp turn southward, heading straight into the heart of Honduras. Its winds abated as the eye of the hurricane traveled over the El Cajón dam watershed zone[3] and on toward the *maquiladoras*[4] in central Honduras, but its rains increased. On October 30 and 31, the eye moved directly over Tegucigalpa. Picking up moisture as part of the system reached out over the Pacific, Mitch dropped forty inches of rain in just forty-eight hours.

Most of the damage and loss of life resulted from these heavy rains. Just outside Tegucigalpa, the deluge proved to be too much for two dams—Los Laureles and La Concepción—which fed a pair of rivers flowing into the city. At approximately the same time, these two dams overflowed, causing a high flow release of water. Residents reported hearing a sound "like a jet" in the middle of the night as a wall of water came crashing through the city. Slamming into each of the city's eleven bridges—destroying three and damaging five others—the huge wave of water flooded the prison, the market, the central hospital, and many government offices located near the rivers. Even worse, the massive flow of water triggered major landslides. Two Tegucigalpa hillside neighborhoods—El Berrinche and El Chile—simply slid down into the swollen river, carrying cars, homes, and sleeping families in a cascade of liquefied dirt and debris.

Flooding elsewhere in the country was just as severe. In Choluteca, dozens died from mudslides and swollen rivers. In Pespire, forty-one people drowned in the town's rising river. By November 1, when Mitch had died down to a tropical depression and headed west into Guatemala and Mexico, the country was in ruins (table 4): roads and highways had been washed out, bridges destroyed, crops flooded, and hundreds of thousands left homeless. President Carlos Flores Facussé declared, "We have before us a panorama of death, desolation, and ruin."

The Honduran government disaster agency, COPECO (Comisión Permanente de Contingencias), was "completely unprepared" for Mitch and seemed

Table 4. *Consequences of Hurricane Mitch in Honduras*

- 7,079 dead (9,000 throughout Central America)
- 171,378 homes destroyed
- 1,960,000 homeless
- Thousands of water systems destroyed/damaged
- 17% of schools damaged
- 103 bridges destroyed; 75 heavily damaged
- 80 km of road networkd destroyed
- 80–90% of banana crop destroyed
- $3.3 billion total damages (60% of GDP)

Source: Gass, 2002.

incapable of handling such a disaster.[5] The immediate concern was conducting search and rescue missions. Faced with media questions regarding the ability of Honduran institutions to respond to the crisis, popular Tegucigalpa mayor César Castellanos Madrid told the press confidently that Hondurans could "handle the crisis" and that Honduras would be "rebuilt by Hondurans." The boost of confidence many Hondurans felt after the mayor's statement was, however, short-lived. The day after his press conference, Castellanos, attempting to get an early assessment of the city's damage, was killed when his helicopter crashed.[6]

Although the international development community was also surprised by the damage wrought by Hurricane Mitch, they were not unprepared. Many development agencies put disaster relief teams into action even as the rains were still falling. When the sun came out and the extent of the damage to the country became apparent, every development organization and international agency in the country dedicated itself to the task of rebuilding Honduras.

I explore in this chapter the extent to which international development professionals became involved in *governing* Honduras in its moment of crisis.[7] I should emphasize at the outset that the degree of their involvement was unprecedented. Unlike the cases of El Cajón and the maquiladoras, involving only several development agencies in one or two segments of Honduran society, Hurricane Mitch is the story of *full engagement* by the globalizers. Every single bilateral and multilateral agency working in the country became involved in managing the crisis; every international nongovernmental organization (NGO) played a part in the reconstruction, and every development professional shifted the focus of his or her work onto the new concerns. Furthermore, as development assistance and relief aid poured in from previously unknown sources, the work of the globalizers expanded to a scale never before seen in Honduras prior to the hurricane. The story of Honduras's recovery after Mitch is one of donor coordination and the solidification of the structures of global governance.[8] The nascent global political structures involved in the building of El Cajón and the emergence of maquiladoras gave birth, with Mitch, to a truly global government in Honduras.

Insertion: The Operations Center

The international development organizations inserted themselves into the disaster in two ways. First, they went out on their own to conduct early relief efforts, assess the damage, and coordinate action plans. Second, as Honduras was flooded with international aid, they were called upon to coordinate and administer this relief and recovery assistance.

With regard to the first, David, who worked for the World Bank (WB), had the following story to tell:[9]

> We decided to form a team that Friday before the crisis. So we called a meeting with USAID [United States Agency for International Development], Canadian CIDA [Canadian International Development Agency], the IDB [Inter-American Development Bank] . . . just nine or ten people. And we decided we would all wait out the storm over the weekend and have another meeting on Monday to figure out our response. We said we would make the arrangements. We said, "Sure, World Bank can host it and AID can chair it." They said they would pull together some of their people in the U.S. embassy, the army—they were already preparing to do rescues—and we'd all get together to figure out what to do. Well, by Monday, as you know, all hell broke loose. The phones were down—no water, no electricity. The highways were washed out, so there were no roads in or out of the city. Trucks and vehicles couldn't make deliveries. We were cut off.
>
> Well, a few other people had heard about the meeting, twenty more or so. So I told AID . . . we better get a room at one of the hotels. The hotels have generators. They had a room available. UNDP [United Nations Development Programme] called and said, "Can we come?" Then the Honduran government called and asked if they could participate. So on November 2, about ninety people crammed together in a small hotel room to figure out what to do. It turned out to be the only meeting in town! It was standing room only. Eight government ministers were there. They each gave a report on the damage. Several ministers were crying. Never had anyone seen destruction like this before. They were not prepared, they said; COPECO was unprepared and had no funds. It was unable to perform at all.
>
> But then the meeting ended up being the focal point. We decided to form sectoral groups: water, health, transportation, and so on. So we set up working tables for the following three days. Only the highest-ranking officer from each agency would participate. In addition, there would be a high-ranking officer from the government at each table—usually the minister. It became the operations center.

David's story shows how the globalizers immediately inserted themselves, without hesitation, into the Hurricane Mitch crisis. In cooperation with local

Honduran institutions, the major international development agencies set about the work of governing the country in the early days of the crisis. Believing the Honduran government was unprepared to cope with the challenges, David placed his organization at the center of the emergency meeting.

When I asked him why the government did not run the operations center meeting, David replied, "Well, we had taken the leadership role on Friday, and so I think people didn't mind that we were running it. And once it got started, it took on a life of its own. Also, at the time, the government was mostly shut down. The Ministry of Finance was flooded to the second floor. Their office was dead. The minister was using our offices to send faxes. Education and Health [Ministries] didn't have any offices either."

Although the flooded government buildings clearly figured into the WB's hosting of the meeting, it is likely the arrangement had much more to do with the relative disparity in institutional resources between the Honduran and transnational agencies. For example, the day after the meeting, the WB arranged for a helicopter flight across the country to assess the damage. Tomas Lozano, the Honduran minister of public works and member of the president's National Emergency Commission, went along. The mission was to gather, as a first step, accurate information regarding damage as quickly as possible. David explained, "Our priority was to put together a quick assessment of the damage. It would have been chaos trying to figure out what to do without some sort of report. We needed to see [the damage] for ourselves in order to put together a damage assessment right away."

From David's recounting of the events,[10] it is clear how the globalizers provided immediate institutional support for the management of the crisis, and created, in a time of potential chaos, a space where the complexities of the crisis could be aired and a plan of action developed. His description of events also makes clear the globalizers had wholly inserted themselves into the planning discussions regarding Mitch at the highest level.

Hurricane Mitch also left in its wake a huge amount of the world's attention on the small country of Honduras. Hondurans soon became familiar with the international nature of relief assistance as daily newspaper and television reports highlighted the visits of foreign dignitaries, celebrities, and emergency aid missions. U.S. First Lady Hillary Clinton and Tipper Gore arrived only two weeks after the hurricane, along with French prime minister Jacques Chirac. Many others—Bill Clinton, George H. W. Bush, the leaders of Ireland and Sweden—followed bringing words of encouragement and pledges of economic support. German supermodel Claudia Schiffer attracted a lot of press coverage when she visited the country and pledged to purchase 112 homes for those displaced by the hurricane. Even the mayor of Toledo, Ohio, received a guided tour and a meeting with Honduran president Flores, who was photographed almost daily welcoming well-wishers at Tegucigalpa's suddenly very busy airport.

The foreign relief brigades came in droves. The U.S. military sent fifty-five hundred troops to carry out search and rescue missions, fumigation for disease control, and emergency infrastructure repairs, including several "bailey" bridges that were quickly installed to much public fanfare. Mexico sent in a corps of volunteers who, at the expense of the Mexican government, took care of bulldozing, demolition, and cleanup of muddy downtown Tegucigalpa. The very popular "brigadas Mexicanas" also ran several refugee centers throughout the country. Cuba immediately sent four medical teams to Honduras, one of which worked in the remote regions of the Mosquito Coast treating hurricane victims that the Honduran government had been unable to reach. The Cuban doctors treated hundreds of people for free and were so popular that, five months after their arrival, the Honduran press urged the Cuban teams to "stay for good."

Hundreds of NGOs and religious charities trucked in containers of food, clothing, and medicine and pledged to build houses in the country by the thousands. So many foreign missions came to Honduras in the immediate aftermath of the hurricane that it actually created some burdensome logistical difficulties. On November 10, for example, a Japanese mission brought two planeloads of volunteers to Tegucigalpa to provide cleanup assistance and set up a hospital capable of treating two hundred patients daily. Unable to find room for both planes at the crowded airport, the Honduran government sent one (carrying youth volunteers) to Texas, where it waited for a week before being given the green light to land in Honduras.

Besides the individuals and groups that came to Honduras from all over the world, international pledges of official government assistance began to arrive as well. The U.S. ambassador pledged $2 million in immediate disaster relief and promised hundreds of millions more for reconstruction. Canada, Great Britain, France, Germany, and Japan each pledged millions of dollars in support and called for a moratorium on Honduras's debt obligations. Some donors even called for a complete cancellation of its debt. Such countries as China, Ireland, and Kuwait pledged their economic support. Sweden, a country that had previously given little aid to Honduras, made the headlines with a $200 million pledge. Multilateral organizations such as the WB and the United Nations' World Food Program announced plans to begin major relief and reconstruction efforts amounting to hundreds of millions of dollars.

Coordinating all of this global assistance quickly became a problem of its own. The globalizers were aware of the problem and, even in the early stages, discussed ways to create what they referred to as "donor coordination." Glen, a USAID employee who attended the first emergency meeting and the subsequent sectoral group meetings conducted by the WB, explained the problem:

> I think it's important . . . to understand that we were working on donor coordination before the hurricane. Before Mitch, we were really counting on having more donor coordination and that the UNDP would play that role . . . because a bilateral agency like us really can't. And so we were really hoping UNDP would play that role following the hurricane, but they never really did. The person they had then as the director was not the type of leader to bring groups together. We were waiting for the UNDP to really organize this thing, and they weren't really willing to do this at that time, and then the World Bank came. And, of course, they got all these groups down here organized. They [the WB] were not the organization I was looking for, but they got [the donor coordination] started. Then, later, the IDB played the main role.

Glen's mention of the WB and IDB as leaders in coordinating the hurricane crisis management efforts was echoed by what other globalizers told me. David, from the WB, recalled, for example, that the issue over who was going to convene and coordinate the impromptu planning meetings became a touchy issue in the midst of everything else that was going on during the first weeks of the crisis:

> [Another WB officer] and I really did most of the coordinating of those early planning meetings. But everybody pitched in. The teamwork was tremendous. Everyone came together for a common goal. We weren't really thinking about whether AID should lead or the UN or . . . the World Bank . . . After the first three days of meetings, the president called and asked everyone that had participated to have a meeting at the presidential office. Even though we had all his ministers participating at each working table, he wanted to call this meeting to make sure our group coordinated with the group that he had assembled in his offices. So we went to meet the president, but somehow UNDP wasn't invited. Somehow,

they didn't get the message that they were supposed to come. That created a lot of tension because, of course, they should have been there. It made perfect sense to be working and talking together, but we weren't used to it. We had to feel each other out. So we had to start from scratch, and we were asked to have another meeting. This time CABEI [Central American Bank for Economic Integration] offered the space and we all got together again.[11]

Several international development organizations were vying for the role of central coordinating agency after Mitch—the UNDP, USAID, the WB, the IDB, and CABEI. Some intentionally opted to downplay their role (recall Glen's statement about USAID, as a bilateral agency, not being in a position to assume the role), and out of this "feeling out" process, eventually the IDB settled into the position. When I asked David how the IDB became the central coordinating agency for the reconstruction effort, he replied,

Well, I think they had played that leadership role more than we [the WB] had in the past. I mean, before Mitch, the World Bank didn't have as significant a presence in Honduras as we do now. We didn't have a country office, for instance; they did. There was never a reason for us to have a country office in Honduras before Mitch. We handled everything from Washington. Honduras's portfolio was getting bigger, and we probably would have eventually moved here, but Mitch instigated the process. When Mitch hit, we jumped right in. . . . The bank is not supposed to do disasters, but in this case we did . . . and we were thanked by the Honduran government for doing it, and so we just kept working on it. The government even asked us to convene the [donor coordination meeting]. At that point, the IDB was miffed . . . they wanted to hold the meeting. They felt they had a longer working relationship with the donor community on the ground in Honduras and that, because they have more of a Latin America focus, they had greater legitimacy in bringing the various countries affected by Mitch—Nicaragua and Guatemala—together with the donors. So I think that was the main issue. Which was fine with us. So they made the announcement inviting everyone to Washington.

On November 9, 1998, just ten days after the hurricane, the IDB announced in a press release: "IDB to host meeting of Emergency Consultative Group regarding Hurricane Mitch." The announcement invited "countries and bilateral and multilateral agencies of the international donor community" to a meeting that would take place in early December to "establish an Emergency Consultative Group . . . to help Central America recover from one of its worst catastrophes." The press release made clear how the decision to hold the meeting had been made:

> The initiative was launched after a series of meetings and discussions held over the past week. IDB President [Iglesias] met . . . with USAID Administrator [Atwood] and representatives from the World Bank and the United Nations Development Programme to discuss their plans for cooperation with Central America. They agreed to set up a permanent coordination committee, to which other international organizations will be invited. Over the next few days Iglesias was in continuous communication with the Central American presidents, who supported the proposal for the emergency consultative group.[12]

In other words, while David and Glen (and other development workers) were conducting emergency meetings in Tegucigalpa with Honduran ministers and President Flores, their higher-ups back at headquarters in Washington were making the larger decisions regarding how the international hurricane relief aid would be coordinated at the international level.

At its December meeting in Washington, D.C., the IDB brought together government representatives from all the Mitch-affected countries and representatives from the donor community.[13] At this meeting, the global governing structure was put into place for laying out the time line for reconstruction and establishing the organizational framework for coordinating assistance to Central America.

The time line gave each Central American country five months to develop a reconstruction strategy, a master plan detailing the costs of the hurricane-related damage and specifying the projects for restoring each nation to normal functioning. The donor countries would then examine the proposed plans and, coordinating their assistance so as to match donor-agency strengths with the reconstruction needs of each country, make decisions regarding which projects to fund.

One of the first orders of business at the IDB meeting was establishing an organizational framework, El Grupo Consultivo (Emergency Consultative Group for Central American Reconstruction and Transformation). The original group consisted of representatives from the five donor countries present in Washington: the United States, Sweden, Spain, Germany, and Canada. Japan and the Netherlands joined later. Such multilateral agencies as the IDB, WB, UNDP, and the International Monetary Fund (IMF) also became members of the group. Defining the consultative group as a "forum for coordinating international development assistance among donor country government representatives, bilateral aid authorities, and international financial organizations," the group would hear master plan proposals from the five countries affected by Mitch and then, through a coordinated process, divide the programs and projects among themselves in order to carry them out in a way that avoided logistical problems, corruption, and duplication of services. In sum, the donors wanted to have one, coordinated forum in which the needs of the hurricane-affected countries would be presented, assessed, and matched with donor strengths and interests. The leadership in the consultative group would rotate every six months among all participating donors. Spain was in charge of its leadership first, followed by Sweden, the United States, Canada, Germany, and Japan.

The consultative group (also referred to as the "donor group" or the "technical group") would also provide technical assistance to each country for assessing damage and estimating the costs of reconstruction. As a part of this, the donor agencies encouraged their experts in Central America to continue utilizing the various working groups that had been established in the Tegucigalpa hotel room immediately following the hurricane. In all, thirteen subgroups were established, representing every social sector affected by Mitch: education, health, water and sanitation, bridges and roads, housing, agriculture, energy, macroeconomic policy, watershed management and environment, microbusiness, transparency, decentralization/municipalities, and justice. Together, these thirteen groups would become responsible for governing post-Mitch Honduras.

In addition to the consultative group, the IDB meetings in Washington called upon each recipient country to establish an official government institution that would be responsible for drafting the master plan to be submitted to the donor countries. In Honduras, President Flores established the Gabinete de la Reconstrucción Nacional (National Reconstruction Cabinet) and appointed to it top government officials from various ministries. The reconstruction cabinet would receive input and assistance from several international agencies, including the European Union (EU), USAID, the WB, and the UNDP. The UNDP, in fact, created a special technical assistance fund of $25 million and put it at the disposal of the cabinet to pay for any equipment, travel, or personnel needed as it went about formulating the Honduran master plan.[14]

Technically, the consultative group and the reconstruction cabinet had distinct roles and represented different political agendas. The consultative group was the authority deciding how aid would be disbursed on behalf of the donor countries, whereas the reconstruction cabinet was assigned the role of establishing Honduran national priorities. In practical terms, however, the two worked in direct relation to each another. For instance, all the Honduran ministers and government officials in the reconstruction cabinet participated in the discussions and activities of the thirteen working groups advising the consultative group. From the point of view of the Honduran government representatives, each working group was being "coordinated by the respective Honduran minister."[15] At the same time, all the donor agency representatives sitting on the consultative group participated in the formulation of the reconstruction plan by providing technical assistance and support directly to the reconstruction cabinet members. USAID, the UNDP, WB, and the IDB were in regular contact with the reconstruction cabinet and offered ongoing input into its discussions and decisions. This arrangement was, as will become evident below, a cause of some concern among members of the Honduran government and civil society.

Once the globalizers had inserted themselves into the political process of governing after Mitch, this bi-institutional arrangement—the donors' consultative group and the Honduran reconstruction cabinet—became the global forum making the crucial policy decisions regarding how Honduras would be rebuilt. The important point here is that the consultative group and the reconstruction cabinet, working closely throughout the reconstruction process, together formed the official global government in Honduras following Mitch. Later, as NGOs and citizens' groups became partially involved in the policy discussions, the structure of global governance would become tri-institutional.

The outcome of the Washington meetings was a clear statement from the donor countries and institutions that they expected a clearly laid-out plan for how their aid money was to be spent. The donors also stipulated that such a plan had to include input from civil society. Although these civil society groups were not yet a part of either the consultative group or the reconstruction cabinet at the end of December 1998, they would become increasingly involved in the broad political debates that emerged during the following period in which the Honduran master plan for reconstruction was developed.

This plan was to be presented in, of all places, Stockholm, Sweden. The Swedish government had offered to host the donor summit in May 1999 and provide airfare and lodging to any delegations that might require assistance. From that point on, all discussions related to reconstruction in Honduras took place with Stockholm in mind and, for the larger Honduran public, all roads for the future of the country went through "Estocolmo."

Surveillance: Damage Assessment

In order to respond adequately to the crisis, the global policy makers needed information. How does one take stock of an entire nation? This was the central question on the minds of the globalizers in the days immediately following the hurricane. The international development experts and the Honduran president believed getting damage estimates was the number one priority. In response to this urgent need, the WB announced on November 5 that it was taking immediate action to assess the damage caused by Mitch: "the World Bank office in Honduras has mobilized a special team of experienced staff, including specialists in disaster management, transportation, relief work, agriculture and water supply to assess the most urgent needs facing Honduras."[16]

Many institutions, global and local, were trying to find out how Mitch had affected the country, but the first *official* damage assessment report was put together by the WB. When I asked David why the first official damage estimates reported to the press had come from the WB instead of the Honduran government, he explained,

> Well that was our number one priority. And the government asked us to do it. They were trying their best, but many of their offices were shut down. So we always had the view that in these working group meetings, we should be trying to build an initial damage assessment report since you really can't do any planning until you know what you're looking at. At that point, we were blind. We needed information. So we put together our initial report over that first weekend after the hurricane. The World Bank actually wrote the report but it was based upon the input we had gotten during those three days at the working-group tables. Early that next week we took what we had to the government. Our preliminary investigation found that we had about $800 million worth of damages. But they thought that our report's estimates were too low. They never said it explicitly, they just thought the numbers "looked low" and suggested we meet again to look them over more carefully.

David's description of events reveals the extent of government-globalizer interaction in the days following the hurricane. It also highlights the globalizers' taking on the role of surveillance. David's account is echoed in that of a Honduran minister, who reported,

> During that first week, all the ministers were receiving reports from all over the country, and we would take this information to the working group meetings. The international organizations were also bringing information in, and we were trying to make a preliminary damage report. We thought the initial damage would be about $3.8 billion, but the international aid organizations said it wasn't that high. The World Bank said it was only about $1 billion. We had a press conference with the World Bank announcing what they had found, but we also told them that we needed to have another meeting to figure this out.

Representatives from the international aid agencies and government ministers met again on November 12 (this was the CABEI meeting) to try to resolve the highly political issue of the discrepancy between the two figures. David insisted the WB figures were correct:

> We knew our numbers were right, but the government thought we were leaving some things out. So we all got together again to review the figures and we double-checked and triple-checked. Was the damage underestimated? Did we leave anything out? There were minister-level people from the government at each table going through all the data again. And we came up with the same figures. We all—including the government—stood by the original figures. The only thing we changed were our figures for the private sector. Our view was that most of the private sector would be reimbursed through their insurance, but the government wanted the private sector included. So we "revalidated" our data and added about another $1 billion in private sector damages.

The report, a copy of which David gave me, was released on November 19, 1998, one week after the meeting. At the top of the cover page was a Honduran government logo and the title "Preliminary Estimates of the Damages Caused by Hurricane Mitch to the Public Infrastructure and the Costs of Recuperation."[17] The cover also included four photographs taken by the WB employees who wrote the report: a picture of the flooded Choluteca River taken from a helicopter, a group of children sitting outside a refugee center, mud and debris on a downtown Tegucigalpa street, and a photo of several of the working groups meeting in the hotel. At the bottom of the cover was the statement,

"Prepared by the World Bank on behalf of the Government of Honduras with the participation of various international entities." I flipped to the results page, where damages were listed at approximately $2 billion: $457 million for transportation; $180 million for water and sanitation; $56 million for health and education; and $51 million for energy and telecommunications. There were also columns for housing ($275 million), agriculture and environment ($400 million), and the private sector ($600 million); David indicated that these three columns were for the $1 billion added to the report.

David also mentioned there had been some discussion about whether the WB logo would go on the cover or not. He explained,

> Originally, we weren't going to put our logo on the cover of the report. We thought it should be the government's report. But [the government] said, "No, you did the work on this. You should put the World Bank's name on the report." So we put it on there. They still thought the $2 billion was too low. They thought it should be more like $4 billion. In the end, we had a tacit agreement that the report should be distributed. But they didn't want to distribute it. We were told not to distribute the report. But we wanted to get the report *out*. So I went and hand delivered the report to every government minister. But the report was never released to the public.

In the end, David said, the report became the basis for much of the initial relief and reconstruction planning leading up to the December meeting in Washington. Clearly, however, the Honduran government did not consider the WB report the final say on the matter. Indeed, while WB representatives stood by the report's validity, the Honduran government was negotiating with the UNDP to conduct a more intensive evaluation of damages related to Mitch.

Referring to this case of two reports, the Honduran minister explained it in the following manner:

> We were happy with the World Bank report because it gave us some preliminary information. But it also lacked certain issues that we had not realized in those early moments. We were thinking mostly about roads and bridges and how to prevent disease. But soon we began to realize there was going to be much more to the reconstruction than that. We began to talk about rehabilitation and transformation. In other words, we began to discuss how much of the damage caused by Mitch was due to prior shortcomings that needed to be addressed. We couldn't just rebuild Honduras the way it was, because the way it was is part of the

problem—we can't have rivers without flood controls; we can't have neighbor-hoods existing on precarious hillsides. So we needed to make a broader assess-ment of not just recuperation but also rehabilitation and transformation. Many of the donors like Sweden and Spain agreed with us on this point. They were talking more about "national transformation," not just reconstruction . . . so we decided to get together with UNDP and CEPAL [Comisión Económica Para America Latina y El Caribe] to do another damage report. [This report] used a different methodology and added the rehabilitation aspect, and the estimate went to $5 billion. And that is the report we took with us to the first IDB meeting.

Thus, the first several months of surveillance by the globalizers resulted in two damage reports. The first, the one by the WB, came out within a month after the hurricane; the second appeared two months later and was prepared by CEPAL, a UN affiliate that was contracted by the UNDP at the Honduran government's request.[18] The UNDP-CEPAL report was created through a spe-cial UNDP project (RLA/98/020), "Evaluation of the Socio-economic Impact of Natural Disasters (Hurricane Mitch)." For its investigation, CEPAL assem-bled an "interdisciplinary mission" that "visited [Honduras] from November 15 to 21" to "evaluate the larger environmental and macroeconomic effects of the hurricane." The investigators "developed a quantitative methodology which took into account the direct and indirect costs of the hurricane for Honduras on the macroeconomic level."[19] This second report, preferred by the Hon-duran government because it took the larger, indirect economic consequences of the hurricane into account, was released to the public.[20]

The two reports differed not only in their monetary estimates of the dam-age but also in terms of content. The CEPAL report, for example, placed hous-ing and the social sector as the number one priority, even over infrastructure; the WB report, by contrast, put housing at number six and infrastructure at number one. Whereas the CEPAL report devoted an entire section to enu-merating the costs of restoring the natural environment and included the problem of balance of payments and foreign debt exacerbated by the eco-nomic crisis caused by Mitch, the WB report left the larger macroeconomic is-sues indirectly related to Mitch unexamined; it looked only at direct effects.

What should be emphasized is that both reports were created by interna-tional development professionals working in cooperation with the Honduran government and not by the Honduran government itself. The official story of the damage suffered by Honduras because of Hurricane Mitch was born of an interactive process between the globalizers and their Honduran counterparts. This product of global governance would become the sole basis for official policy making leading up to the Stockholm summit. The Honduran government's reliance as a primary source of information on the surveillance and investigations undertaken by the WB and UNDP/CEPAL when it began to assemble its own plan for reconstruction and rehabilitation in the following months only underscored the extent of this collaborative arrangement.

Setting the Agenda: The Master Plan

Garnering Honduran support for disaster assistance was, in certain regards, an easy thing for the globalizers to do: Hondurans wanted and needed the help. But the international donor community wished the assistance to be administered in a certain fashion, and they took measures to ensure their relief money would be used in accordance with various global agendas. The first of these measures involved setting the agenda through the development of a master plan.

Although technically the master plan was the sole responsibility of the Honduran government's special reconstruction cabinet, the globalizers helped make sure the government did it the right way. To this end, the globalizers conducted various technical assistance missions with the reconstruction cabinet. The UNDP, for example, held a special seminar on risk management for members of the cabinet. The UNDP felt risk management techniques "should be part of the government's master plan presented at Stockholm."[21] The EU sent four "expert missions in health and education" to evaluate Mitch damages and help the government "define plans and priorities for the 'master plan.'" According to Sophia Schlette, one of the EU experts, "We are going to ask to see the reconstruction plan of the government and then we will see if it is in accord with the objectives [defined] by the European Union donors [coming to Stockholm.]"[22] This statement makes it plain that it was the donors who were largely setting the agenda for the Honduran reconstruction plan.

Such organizations as the UNDP, EU, and USAID worked directly with the Honduran reconstruction cabinet, while others engaged in activities with certain government ministries that had consequences for the cabinet. Nonetheless, "everyone was working on the master plan," as Glen from USAID reported, "whether they were working closely with the cabinet or not. All the agencies were helping by providing advisers to the government to help develop the plan. But our advisers were working very closely with the government at all levels."

When I asked Glen to describe how this interaction between development agencies and the government functioned, he mentioned "three levels"—the diplomatic/ambassadorial level, the donor level, and the working group level:

The first level, of course, is the ambassadorial level. Our ambassador and the ambassadors of the other major donors meet primarily with the Honduran reconstruction cabinet. That cabinet is headed by Gustavo Alfaro, the right-hand man—the minister—of the presidency. Gabriela Nuñez, the minister of finance is there. Moises Starkman from SETCO [Secretaría Técnica y de Cooperación Internacional] is there. FHIS [Fondo Hondureño de Inversión Social] is there. The president of the Central Bank is there. Lozano, the head of SOPTRAVI [Secretaría de Obras Públicas Transporte y Vivienda]—public works—is there. So that's the reconstruction cabinet. And, of course, they report directly to President Flores, so there was a very close connection at that level. . . . Then there is the "technical assistance level," which is formed by the heads of the development agencies: AID, GTZ [Deutsche Gesellschaft für Technische Zusammenarbeit], the AECI [Agencia Española de Cooperación Internacional] of the Spaniards, ACDI [L'Agence Canadienne de Développement International] of the Canadians, the JICA [Japan International Cooperation Agency] of the Japanese. We did a lot of work with the technical group setting up indicators: what does it mean, this transformation? what are we going to measure in order to say if we are successful or not at doing this reconstruction? So they brought in a consultant, and we worked very closely with the [Honduran government agency] UNAT [Unidad de Apoyo Técnico] on this as well. So there was this effort of moving together, working together at the technical level. And then, at the lower level, AID continued to work on these working groups. Our director said that we needed to stay involved in these sectoral group meetings that started right after the hurricane came; we needed to keep our people involved that are working on education, health, the transparency group. There was a transparency group because the IDB was pushing a transparency project that we were interested in supporting. The agricultural group, the natural resources group—there's a water and sanitation group, there's a roads and bridges . . . there were thirteen groups there.

Glen's description is a telling illumination of the structure of global governance that came about in Honduras in response to Mitch. It was a multi-level division of labor among the international development organs and Honduran institutions constructed to put together what would become a detailed and complex national reconstruction master plan. Some agencies, such as USAID, had a major role at each level; others were more or less involved at the diplomatic, technical, or sectoral levels. These levels were arranged hierarchically, and smaller donors (such as Great Britain or Mexico) did not participate as much at the higher levels; likewise, many international agencies operating in Honduras that were not affiliated with the major donor countries participated only at the sectoral level. International NGOs such as CARE and Save the Children fell into this category, and so, although they participated in some of the sectoral groups, they were not formal participants in the creation of the master plan at the higher levels such as the president's reconstruction cabinet.

The reconstruction cabinet became the focus of much public attention owing to its assuming responsibility for the entire hurricane recovery plan for the nation as a whole. The leading figures in the press reports were Gustavo Alfaro, President Flores's minister of the presidency and chair of the cabinet; Moises Starkman, head of SETCO (which coordinated foreign aid on behalf of the Honduran government); Gabriela Nuñez, minister of finance; and Tomas Lozano, chief of SOPTRAVI. These four ministers, and to a lesser extent their colleagues in the cabinet, became the official government spokespeople responsible for making statements to the press regarding the plan as it was being developed.

In terms of the globalizers, it made sense that these four should be at the center of attention: Alfaro, because, as chair of the cabinet, he was primarily responsible for coordinating the massive undertaking of pulling together all the international input into one central plan; Starkman, because he was the one in charge of accounting for billions of dollars of foreign assistance; Nuñez, because she had to negotiate with the IMF and WB (primarily) in connection with balance of payment problems and debt mitigation or rescheduling schemes; and, finally, Lozano, because his ministry was in charge of roads, bridges, and housing, the main targets of assistance. The immense task of putting together the plan and taking it to Stockholm completely absorbed each of the ministers' lives. One minister told the press, "We are working fourteen to sixteen hours a day, even on weekends."[23] The ministers also had to face increasing public scrutiny regarding their statements and growing speculation that they were benefiting personally from the hurricane-related assistance.[24]

The foreign development workers, however, were less subject to press scrutiny and criticism and did not face accusations of corruption. Indeed, the globalizers were presented as "authorities" giving a "lesson" to Honduran government officials or scolding them for something they had failed to do. A February visit by EU parliamentary president Jose Maria Gill Robles, for example, led to some negative press for the Honduran reconstruction cabinet. Robles had told journalists that "Honduras better hurry up if it wants to be ready for Stockholm. . . . They are a little behind."[25] Robles's statement disclosed an awareness of the master plan's status, and suggested perhaps he had even seen a draft (which was considered top secret). The event further indicated the subordinate position of the Honduran government vis-à-vis the globalizers.

Generally, the public image of the globalizers was framed in the discourse of helping. Dozens of articles recounted visits by various functionaries of the international agencies as they "came to see for themselves" how the reconstruction was going and what more needed to be done. In late February 1999, for instance, a delegation of WB advisers arrived in Honduras to "see if their help was effective." Related press articles described the "pleasant meeting" that took place between the executive directors of the WB and the Honduran president. It chronicled the "tour" of WB executives to meet government officials and see schools, markets, refugee centers, and other areas affected by the hurricane.[26]

In the WB's view, however, the visit was much more about negotiating (and setting) the agenda; in particular, the advisers were interested in assessing whether the Honduran government was satisfied with the support the WB was willing to give. David explained,

The executive directors came down because we were working on various projects already and we wanted to make sure that the Honduran government was satisfied with these projects, number one. But also, the directors wanted to see if anything else needed attention . . . even before Stockholm. I mean, we already had done some pretty amazing work. We had immediately installed some bailey bridges. We gave half a million dollars to the Ministry of Health and PAHO [Pan American Health Organization] to buy the chemicals and tanks and trucks to immediately start fumigation campaigns. All the rats and bugs after Mitch really concerned us in terms of typhoid and cholera. The fumigation was 100 percent successful. Another thing we did is the director of the World Bank decided that we would suspend all payments on existing loans. . . . In November, we also decided to give a $200 million emergency loan. It was here by January—$200 million, deposited directly into the Banco Central, where they could use it to buy necessities. This $200 million injection literally saved the country. It also balanced the economy and kept the lempira stable. There wasn't even a blip on the exchange rate. So we wanted to make sure the government felt good about these things as well and see if we could do anything else before Stockholm.

Such visits were common among all international aid donors, and they were more than a ceremonial or symbolic acknowledgment of the intensive working relationship operating behind the scenes between the international donors and Honduran government representatives. Although symbolism is important for agenda setting and garnering consent, the aim of these visits was political: to ensure the negotiations were going well for the upcoming Stockholm meetings. Donors had specific priorities and agendas in mind, and they used the visits to clarify their agendas and expectations with the Honduran government. Sometimes discussions centered on projects—building bridges or roads—the donor country was interested in carrying out.[27] And the government needed to know what to put in its master plan; the visits gave it the opportunity to negotiate the details of the plan with the globalizers.

In terms of what it was like negotiating these interactions—the intense working relationship between the Honduran and foreign authorities—the globalizers themselves described the relationship most often in warm, glowing terms. Glen at USAID called it "very constructive;" "I think the interaction has been a very constructive interchange of ideas," he explained, "and it's not a forcing thing . . . we don't force them. They have similar goals. Sometimes there [can be] difficulties, like when there are disagreements or when they have problems with the [Honduran] congress."

Echoing Glen's sentiments, David at the WB agreed, "It's a great relationship. And I think Mitch made the relationships stronger. I'm best friends with [a minister]. The president calls me by my first name. It's like we've been through this horrible thing together and now we're closer than before."

The Honduran government view was also usually couched in positive terms, but there was also a wariness expressed regarding negotiating the relationship. One of the Honduran ministers I interviewed explained:

I think it is a healthy relationship. The consultative group was incredible! They were not a burden, they were a support. I mean these are top people. But we always tried to make it clear that Hondurans needed to be the ones to define how this support is used. The consultative group understood this. They never tried to govern the country. They pushed certain things . . . but in a very easy way. They support, they don't dictate. At the same time, there were "suggestions" and there were "*suggestions.*" You learn to figure out when they are suggesting and when they are *suggesting.* . . . I would say that it's still Hondurans who are steering the course, but in this case we needed all the help we could get, and so we had to be willing to be flexible and take their suggestions into account.

Clearly, although all sides viewed the negotiations as a "healthy interaction," Honduran government officials were sometimes required to tactfully negotiate the donor countries' wishes. It is important to point out that all of this agenda setting took place out of public view. The master plan was top secret; only the Honduran reconstruction cabinet and the globalizers were aware of its contents. This represented a problem for both groups as they tried to build public support for the reconstruction agenda. In addition to working with the government on developing the master plan, therefore, the globalizers began to work on building a broad public consensus before Stockholm.

Garnering Consent

Coping with the "Social Mitch"

Although the political processes of donor cooperation and foreign technical assistance were going relatively smoothly among the globalizers, garnering consent among the larger Honduran population proved to be more difficult because of the major social disruption caused by the hurricane. This difficulty emerged in early 1999 and came to be known as "La Mitch Social."

The phrase referred to a broad range of social problems caused by the hurricane: disease, crime, and general social conflict and political instability. It was coined by the head of the Swedish aid organization International Development Cooperation Agency (ASDI) Pierre Schori during his visit to the country. He characterized the devastation he witnessed as "worse than Sarajevo" and declared that the "social Mitch" was potentially as devastating as the hurricane itself. Theorizing about the causes of the situation, he pointed to "the possible social instability generated by impatience, the government's attitude, or by the miserable conditions of life brought upon thousands of families" by the hurricane. "To ignore it," he asserted, "would be suicide."[28]

By early January 1999, four months before Stockholm, social unrest among the Honduran public was growing. Thousands of refugees had been living in makeshift shelters since the hurricane, and, for many, there seemed to be no signs the government was doing anything to facilitate the construction of more permanent living facilities. Some of these refugee shelters (called *albergues* in Spanish) were so large and housed so many families they became neighborhoods unto themselves and were called *macroalbergues*—megashelters. Not only were the megashelters home to rampant crime, gang activity, and unsanitary conditions, but there were also rumors the government was planning to keep families in the shelters permanently, that these shelters *were* the housing provided by the government with the foreign assistance received thus far. The rumors triggered widespread protests and demands from the refugees for better living conditions. On January 7, 9, and 20, 1999, news of the protests in Tegucigalpa and Choluteca appeared in the press alongside pictures of police in riot gear and families holding signs saying, "We want our homes back." In several episodes, police used tear gas and billy clubs, resulting in serious injuries. The violence with which the protesters were met only inflamed the rumors that the government had already absconded with the foreign aid and had no intention of helping the hurricane victims.

The government responded with a series of statements attempting to dispel the rumors and clarify that the reconstruction process was going to take time. "There is no reason for the protest," claimed Choluteca mayor Juan Benito Guevara, "We already have an agreement with the Spanish government for the construction of sixteen hundred homes right in the middle of the city. That is more than enough for the 1,456 displaced families we have registered."[29] In Tegucigalpa, representatives from the mayor's office came out and spoke directly with the protesters, emphasizing that "the city is not going to give land to anyone. In the first place, because we don't have land to give. In the second place, because the government has decided to build new housing complexes and give homes only to those people who really lost their houses [in the hurricane.]"[30]

The globalizers also became directly involved in the attempts to quell the rising social unrest. The international aid agencies began paying more attention to public relations and placed ads in the newspapers highlighting the projects that had been initiated. Guillermo, a Spanish aid worker I interviewed, said, "We realized that people really didn't see a lot of the aid that was coming in. So we had to make a concerted effort to publicize what we were doing." Appearing first in early 1999, the ads detailed the amount of aid being given for various projects and their beneficiaries in terms of specific neighborhoods. Eventually, each newspaper in the country was running a special weekly section of the paper publicizing the Mitch-related projects under way. The Tegucigalpa paper *La Tribuna* titled its weekly insert "Transformación Nacional" and regularly featured there optimistic statements from President Flores and the foreign donors whose projects were being presented. These inserts later became a forum for ads from all sorts of international contractors and agencies hired to build bridges, repair roads, and audit the aid funds.

In addition to spending money on a very assertive public relations campaign, the globalizers also worked on garnering the consent of specific citizens' groups. One of the stipulations of the Washington donor conference, it will be recalled, was that the governments from the affected countries had to take "civil society into account" in the development of their master plan. From the donors' point of view, input from local NGOs and other citizens' organizations was mandatory. Yet, no NGO or citizens' group sat in the reconstruction cabinet. The official Honduran government position, as related to the press, was "this is government business . . . though we will consult with civil society." But, perhaps in response to the growing social unrest, the government established, in January 1999, the Foro Nacional de Covergencia (FONAC, the National Convergence Forum). Appointed by the president and the reconstruction cabinet, its members included representatives from the military, business leaders, members of congress, and several religious charities. The cabinet met with FONAC several times as it prepared the master plan, and several FONAC members even publicly criticized the cabinet. President Flores called the criticism important because "the international community demands that the projects [in the master plan] involve everyone. They want a plan that captures not just the government's perspective and that of the international technical advisers but also that includes a broad dialogue with civil society."[31]

Although Flores may have thought a group of handpicked representatives from government and civil organizations would do the trick, he was quickly corrected by the international community that this was not the civil society it had in mind. Commenting on the growing problem, Stephan, a Swedish aid worker, explained to me:

The government thought that having the military and businesspeople and members of congress giving some advice to the reconstruction cabinet was the same thing as "NGOs." But this is not civil society in our view. The preparation of the master plan was very closed, I think, although the government considers that there was participation. I think it was perceived by the donor community and also by civil society that it was a very closed group . . . preparing the master plan; it wasn't open. And to a certain extent, I think that is normal in an emergency situation. I think the local governments wanted to act very rapidly and they thought they knew everything. So we said, no . . . you have to consult with the community. What are their priorities? So I think that we played a role in this one big issue . . . we fostered civil society participation.

In an attempt to resolve the issue, the Swedish ambassador met with the president and the reconstruction cabinet and explained to the Honduran government that civil society participation in the creation of the master plan was a requirement of the donor community; he asked the government to name the Honduran NGOs they were going to bring to Stockholm. When the Honduran government gave the Swedes a list naming government-affiliated agencies and members of FONAC, the ambassador made it clear it did not represent civil society and insisted other NGOs be included.[32]

The Swedish government also began sponsoring workshops on the master plan and invited "any group from civil society" to participate.[33] This was intended, as Stephan explained it, to gather a list of potential NGOs to invite to Stockholm and enlarge civil society participation in the reconstruction process despite the Honduran government's reluctance:

> [Real civil participation] was a major fear for the Honduran government. They believed civil society would only be interested in criticizing and wrecking their reconstruction and transformation plan. They questioned whether [NGOs] had the right to take part in writing this document. Of course, we couldn't get so much into that, but we could at least sort of work towards larger civil society participation *in Sweden,* which might foster civil society here. And so the solution was the Swedish government gave money to [Swedish NGOs] to organize a pre-meeting [in Stockholm] and ask the IDB and other donors if they would support the NGOs to come to the meeting that way. We also were able to find money to conduct some workshops here in Honduras that, I think, brought together some civil society groups that were excluded from the process.

Supported by the Swedish aid agency ASDI, the February 1999 workshops led to the formation of Espacio Interforos, a broad coalition of Honduran

NGOs that included the two largest NGO umbrella organizations (Foro de Organizaciones Privadas de Desarrollo de Honduras, FOPRIDEH, and Asociación de Organismos No Gubernamentales de Honduras, ASONOG), the Honduran Human Rights Commission (Comisionado de Derechos Humanos de Honduras, CODEH), and other citizens' groups previously involved in a variety of initiatives throughout the country. Seeking greater participation in the national reconstruction dialogue between Honduran government officials and foreign experts, this diverse group of organizations felt perhaps that by linking its local agenda to the global agendas of international NGOs and the Swedish aid agency, it could earn a seat at the table in Stockholm.

A member of Interforos I interviewed explained how the NGOs became more involved in the Hurricane Mitch reconstruction dialogue:

We had been working on various citizens' initiatives prior to Mitch: police reform, judicial reform. We had even broadened this and had a campaign devoted to "building democracy." Our goal has always been to increase citizen participation in government . . . something the government has been very unwilling to take seriously. Well, when Mitch came, we began to envision how this was an opportunity for a transformation of the country . . . but the government didn't even have an adequate plan. So we started making public statements criticizing the inadequacy of the government. The government reacted very negatively through the press, which they control—"Who are you to criticize the government?" "Who elected you to say anything?" Well in January, we started to get together with other NGO groups—CODEH, Fundación Ebert. It was a voluntary thing . . . we had a nonhierarchical structure. And we started making public statements criticizing FONAC, the group the president had formed to represent civil society. We said, "You don't need to make a new group. Civil society already exists. We are right here." But they criticized us in the press again. We were called malcontents and troublemakers. And that's when the international aid groups became interested: the Swedes, the Dutch, the Spanish . . . they came to us and asked what we were up to and if they could help. They were worried that the government really didn't have a broad plan for the transformation of the country . . . only a plan of reconstruction, a list of projects to reconstruct what damage had occurred. They wanted something broader. . . . They talked about citizen participation, and transparency . . . decentralization, justice. We wanted these things, too; we always had. But then, when we started to feel more support from these [international aid] groups because of Mitch, we felt like this was very promising. And so an association began to form between civil society here in Honduras and the international community that hadn't been as strong before. That's how we were invited to the workshops where Interforos was formed.

Asking if Interforos would have formed, in the view of this member of the coalition, without the support of international aid groups, the response was:

I don't think so. Not our group, anyway. I think FOPRIDEH and CODEH and some of the other NGOs that joined Interforos had this kind of support from international aid groups, but we never did. But because of Mitch and the Stockholm meeting, the international funding agencies demanded that the government include even the most belligerent organizations from civil society in the process. Because of this, we decided to participate. Of course, we were always aware of the two faces of international aid.

When I asked what was meant by "two faces," the person replied:

The two faces is like two different attitudes that the international aid agencies have in Honduras: one towards the government and one towards society. They act one way with us and say, "We want democratization and justice. . . ." and "We want to make sure the government is not corrupt as well . . . and we need to keep an eye on them." But then, they also work with the government, with the reconstruction cabinet; they support the government, too. So who knows what they're saying to [the government] about us? But we still felt it was worth participating.

This statement reveals that, although members of the NGOs were suspicious of the globalizers' intentions, they took advantage of the opportunity the globalizers provided. During the early spring of 1999, not long before the May meeting in Stockholm, the Honduran NGOs made their presence felt. Every week in February, March, and April, front-page news stories chronicled the NGOs' criticisms of the government's response to Hurricane Mitch, and the president and the reconstruction cabinet began to feel the heat. In March, for example, Leo Valledares, head of CODEH, held a press conference announcing that his organization had conducted its own social audit of the humanitarian aid coming into the country and found evidence of corruption. Valledares cited seventeen instances of "government irregularities" resulting in a number of problems, including the disappearance of several containers of donated goods. He also suggested some of the works being contracted by the government were going to government officials' family members and that the costs of the works were "overvalued."[34] Valledares raised the specter that was on everyone's mind: corruption. Was the aid pouring into the country being mismanaged or embezzled by corrupt government officials?

Such accusations were not new by the time Valledares made his report. The newspapers had reported stories of donations that had disappeared; some containers of food and medicine were found "rotting" in government warehouses and at the Honduran port.[35] The stories only confirmed the popular belief in Honduras of government corruption and became a problem for the globalizers in terms of garnering consent.

These accusations of corruption were almost always leveled against Honduran government officials; rarely, it should be noted, were they made against the international aid community. Nevertheless, the international donor community quickly realized that something needed to be done to address the public perception that the billions of dollars they were pledging to the country were being misused. How could the donor community guarantee accountability and garner the consent of Honduran NGOs and civil society at large? More importantly, how could the donor community guarantee accountability to the citizens from the donor countries? And how could they ensure that the aid would not be wasted?

When I posed these questions to Glen at USAID, he said the problem of corruption had been taken into account early on in the process: "We knew that corruption was the three hundred pound gorilla sitting in the room that no one wanted to talk about. So we were working on ways to cope with this problem early on. In our case, it was really the U.S. Congress that set the tone. They said, 'You will have to conduct auditing on how this money is spent.' But I think every donor agency . . . and the multilaterals, too . . . knew that there would have to be tight controls put in place."

David from the WB echoed this concern:

Accountability became a big concern. The IDB was concerned about accountability. AID had to deal with it. The [U.S.] Congress stipulated that a program of controls be put in place to ensure that the money would really go where it was supposed to go. Our position at the World Bank was always about avoiding corruption through transparency. We always have told governments, "Look, we trust you. But allow us to verify as well." . . . [These concerns] caused a big debate among the donors. The IDB and AID came up with an auditing plan that would cover every Mitch project coming out of Stockholm. It was daunting.

They called it the "umbrella." We said we would sign on but that we thought it was too much. They were putting more money into the controls than the relief! AID wanted to send in audit inspectors with the power to stop any project if there were problems. We said that would be perceived as too cumbersome and even as a threat to the Hondurans. The IDB said, "Well, this is a major issue," and we came up with a compromise— a second "umbrella" plan. It was cheaper and was not as intrusive. But it still had teeth and was a good system of checks and balances. And I think it has worked well. I would say 99 percent of the money went to where it was supposed to go. We have had constant supervision and audits. We've had audits on top of audits. I'm sure someone got rich off of Mitch but probably not on World Bank money.

The system of auditing and accounting controls the donor community created was already decided upon and established prior to Stockholm and had nothing to do with the Honduran reconstruction cabinet's work in formulating its master plan. Moreover, this system of controls was publicized and discussed openly in the Honduran press early in the process. This occurred, I believe, because of the globalizers' need to garner the consent of the broad Honduran public and the donor countries' public prior to Stockholm; they wanted to assure these constituencies the aid would be effectively administered. It also corresponded with the global agenda of transparency that the donor countries had promoted in Honduras prior to Mitch.

As early as January 1999, USAID announced it was spending 4.5 million lempiras for the "auditing of reconstruction efforts . . . to assure that reconstruction works will be supervised by foreign firms."[36] Later, in March, the IDB announced that it, too, would be soliciting contracts from several accounting firms to conduct "monitoring of aid" related to Mitch.[37] Three large accounting firms, Price Waterhouse Coopers, KPMG-Peat Marwick, and Deloitte and Touche, were selected to carry out these audits. The Honduran government also believed these controls were necessary, because of the "high volume and diversity of sources of the aid and in order to guarantee transparency in the national reconstruction process."[38]

For the audits to take place, however, a special provision had to be made in Honduran law allowing foreign firms full access to government offices and files. The government agreed to the provisions as a condition of donor assistance. Although these announcements were presented favorably in the Honduran press—the audits were labeled "corruption repellents"[39]—some journalists questioned members of the reconstruction cabinet whether the "foreign inspectors" posed a threat to Honduran sovereignty. Government officials responded, "We shouldn't be offended. This supervision is part of an attitude today among the donor community in order to create internal support for aid in those countries so that they know it is well administered."[40] The Honduran inspector general, who signed the contracts with each foreign firm in a special ceremony, explained, "contracting the international firms will guarantee that the government of President Carlos Flores will utilize [the funds] honestly."[41] By hiring these international firms, the donor community garnered the consent of everyone, in Honduras and in the donor countries, and at the same time reinforced the international governance being established in Honduras.

The globalizers' master plan came to encompass everything: bridge repairs, housing construction, water and sanitation for the new housing, road repairs and improvements, new schools, extensive public health initiatives, repairs to damaged government buildings, agricultural assistance, telecommunications, energy, microenterprise loans, macroeconomic projects, and extensive auditing. Practically every sector of Honduran society would get a chunk of the proposed assistance, and, as Stockholm neared, tensions mounted regarding who was going to get a piece.[42]

Members of the NGO groups—Interforos, in particular—had never been formally invited to participate in any of the reconstruction cabinet activities. Because civil society groups had been excluded from the dialogue, they were elaborating their own reconstruction and transformation plan for Stockholm. These groups had, in fact, been invited to a parallel NGO conference in Stockholm organized by international NGOs from the donor countries. Regarding the Honduran NGOs' announcement they would present their own plan in Stockholm, an Interforos representative explained, "Because we have not been allowed appropriate participation in the development of the master plan, . . . fourteen representatives of various NGOs will make a separate presentation at Stockholm."[43]

Newspaper headlines in the following weeks—"NGOs Will Present Their Own Plan,"[44] "Representatives of Civil Society Will Also Travel to Stockholm!"[45]—called attention to the growing conflict between the government's reconstruction cabinet and the NGOs. In an attempt to quell the growing controversy, Gustavo Alfaro maintained the NGOs had chosen to exclude themselves from the process: "[The donors] invited various NGOs to join the official

Honduran delegation to Stockholm so that their concerns could be presented as a part of the government's statement, but apparently they want to do it on their own."[46]

But the situation was not as Alfaro had characterized it. As mentioned earlier, the Swedish government had encouraged the Honduran government to include members of the various Honduran NGOs in the official delegation to Stockholm. It had even found European NGOs willing to cover the costs of the additional members.[47] The Honduran government agreed to allow the NGOs to join their delegation but refused to allow Interforos to make a presentation during the actual master plan presentation. An Interforos member I interviewed recalled the decision not to join the government delegation:

> We received an invitation from the government to go to Stockholm, but it was a farce. They wanted to use us as "ornamentation." They said that we couldn't speak but that they would include our comments in their presentation before the donors. We decided to decline their invitation because we couldn't have the government presenting our views. How were they going to present views that criticize the government? We wanted to criticize their plan. We were proposing new policies, a new way of doing things, not new projects. So we stayed with the idea of going to the parallel conference because we knew we could present our concerns openly there.

So there were two delegations going to Stockholm. Civil society and the government were at an impasse.

The reconstruction cabinet under President Flores had other critics as well. As the deadline for submission of the master plan neared, the cabinet prepared for a presentation before the Honduran congress. The congress was under the leadership of National Party member and former president Rafael Callejas. Callejas and the National Party, President Flores's political opponents, had been strongly critical of the manner in which the president had managed the creation of the master plan, agreeing in particular with the other groups that public debate over the plan had been curtailed because of the secrecy attending its promulgation. When Callejas learned that congress would not be allowed to view the actual plan before it was submitted to the donor community, he protested, charging that the reconstruction cabinet had "no interest in hearing suggestions or submitting to a discussion about the plan with the congress." When the cabinet entered the parliamentary chambers to present its "summary of the plan," Callejas and the other National Party members walked out in protest over the cabinet's "lack of dialogue with members of parliament." En masse, they "left the chambers and stayed inside a closed office while the Reconstruction Cabinet presented its plan in top secret."[48]

The remaining members of congress were the "last to approve" the master plan before it was formally submitted. The next day's front-page news told the story of to whom it had been submitted: "The Master Plan Is in IDB's Control."[49] IDB representative Fernando Cossío was the official recipient of the Honduran master plan documents. The document transfer was commemorated in a special ceremony captured by photographers. The pictures showed reconstruction cabinet coordinator Gustavo Alfaro handing the official copy of the plan to a smiling Cossío as the two exchanged a warm handshake. "We are very satisfied with the plan," Alfaro announced, "The plan addresses all the relevant issues and will allow for a complete recuperation from the tragedy in both the short and long term."[50]

Asked if the IDB would make any changes to the document, Cossío replied, "That is not our role. We will be taking the document and translating it into various languages so that it can be distributed to all the delegations from the donor countries participating in Stockholm. We think it is an excellent proposal." Cossío's statement revealed what everyone might have guessed: the international donors had already seen the "top-secret" plan. He left no room for doubt when he stated, "[the IDB] will not be making any modifications because [the cabinet] has already received technical assistance from various international agencies and consultants [whose] views have already been incorporated in the elaboration of the plan."[51]

But the Honduran public had not even seen the plan yet. Not until four weeks had passed were the details of the $3.9 billion plan revealed to the public. Their release triggered a new wave of criticism toward the government. Several civil society organizations spoke out against the plan: "The master plan is inherently flawed because it never included a broad range of groups," declared a representative from a large Honduran farmers' NGO. "It was put together by a centralized cabinet. We do not see anything in this plan that will be of benefit to us."[52]

The criticism also revealed a degree of public suspicion regarding the activities of the globalizers. One area of criticism was directed at most of the bridge-building contracts going to construction firms from the donor countries and not to Honduran companies. Sweden, for example—the host of the donor conference and advocate of NGO participation—was undertaking a large percentage of the bridge repairs (along with Japan, the United States, and Great Britain), and the Swedish transnational corporations Sveco and Skanska would receive the lion's share of the contracts. Responding to the criticism, Gustavo Alfaro explained it was a matter of "efficiency": "Sweden is giving us bridges. They are going to hire the contractors and they will build them and then turn them over to us. This is more efficient because our ability to do them would be very slow and cumbersome. They will build them very quickly."[53]

As the Stockholm meetings drew near, suspicions about the international donors and the Honduran government being in cahoots became grist for speculation and editorializing in the Honduran press. An "anonymous source" from "within the government" articulated the growing suspicions in one such article: "I don't think they've included all the proposals from the different sectors in Honduras. What is most surely included are the concerns of the international agencies because they're providing the money. I've even seen reconstruction project salesmen come in to meet with the cabinet as the plan has been developed."[54]

Suspicions were heightened when a controversial report from the international NGO Transparency International made its way into the Honduran papers. It stated Honduras was "one of the most corrupt" governments in the world. Reconstruction cabinet member Moises Starkman responded to questions concerning the Transparency International study by refocusing attention on the broader NGO criticism of Honduran government institutions and what it meant for Stockholm: "The divergence between government and civil society could put the aid we are requesting at Stockholm at risk."[55]

As the "historic date in Stockholm"[56] grew closer, President Flores took some last-minute measures to mitigate the NGO problem.[57] Whether acting at the behest of the international agencies or the ambassadors from the donor countries, President Flores convened a meeting on May 21—just three days prior to the Honduran delegation's departure—with representatives of the Interforos NGOs.[58] One Interforos member I interviewed told me,

> The meeting lasted four hours. They presented their plan to us in a very humble manner and asked us to present ours, which we did. Some of the groups were more critical of the government than others. They said that they would like to invite five people to join their delegation in Stockholm and would we reconsider our decision not to participate. We wanted more to go. We were twelve different

organizations. So we finally settled on eight. It seemed to us that they needed us. It was going to be a "show." We knew that, but we also knew this would be an opportunity to present our ideas, our visions. And the international community was going to hear them. The thing that was more significant was that the government promised us that we could participate on the working groups that would be formed during the reconstruction . . . that we could observe the projects being implemented and offer our ideas at that point. It was too late to change the plan. So we were not optimistic about changing the master plan; we knew we couldn't change that. But we decided the compromise was worth it and we signed the declaration with the reconstruction cabinet saying we supported the government's plan.

The news that the NGOs had "signed a joint statement of approval of the master plan" created an air of optimism in Honduras as its delegation left for Sweden. The NGOs, for their part, felt "vindicated"[59] and "looked forward to greater dialogue in the future with the government."[60] The president also was "in good spirits": "We are confident that we will find much success in Stockholm. We have prepared everything and we have a strong proposal that includes recommendations from all sectors of Honduran society."[61]

In terms of garnering consent, it is important to keep in mind that the conflict between Honduran civil society and the government in developing the master plan took place in a global context. By requiring Honduras to submit a master plan for reconstruction that included civil society, the globalizers ensured that broad political support for the plan would be garnered—at least on the level of public, formal appearances (in the form of, e.g., declarations and delegations). That the international donors were the target audience of the formal document and also its public presentation in Stockholm meant that Honduran society at large—governmental and nongovernmental institutions alike—was put on a particular path. To receive the aid money, Hondurans had to demonstrate a unified consent; anything less than wide consent for the master plan would put the assistance in jeopardy. The globalizers thus created a highly effective mechanism for garnering Honduran consent for the Hurricane Mitch reconstruction and transformation plan.[62]

Stockholm

The Honduran papers called it a "historic appointment" and "moment of truth."[63] On May 24, 1999, hundreds of Central American officials and hundreds more international development agency representatives traveled to Stockholm for the "Inter-American Development Bank Consultative Group Meeting for the Reconstruction and Transformation of Central America."

The presidents of Guatemala, Nicaragua, Honduras, and El Salvador were there to present their reconstruction plans; government ministers and officials from all Mitch-affected countries were also in attendance. They were also accompanied by business leaders and citizens' organizations representing civil society. The Central American delegations were met by the directors of bilateral assistance organizations from each donor country: Sweden, the United States, Japan, Spain, Canada, the Netherlands, Germany, Italy, Norway, Switzerland, Great Britain, and Austria. The regional and in-country directors of the multilateral organizations and international NGOs were also there. Over the course of four days, these delegations would hammer out the details of the global assistance effort relating to the damage caused by Hurricane Mitch.

The reaction of a Honduran government minister I interviewed who was a member of the official delegation to Sweden clearly conveyed the momentousness of the event:

> Going to Sweden was such a marvelous experience. I kept the newspaper clippings because I want to tell my grandchildren someday that I was in Stockholm with the Honduran delegation. It was such a stimulating environment to be in. It was very intense but also very satisfying. Everybody thought so. Even the friction with the civil society groups was diminished. I think we were able to open up some major spaces for discussion there. The civil society [groups] said, "Enough is never enough," but we really did our best and maybe they saw that there. We went to all of these events together. We were on the radio. We would drop off things for them to read and they would leave things for us. It all just felt very chic. The fashion was to be working on Mitch.

On the first day of the meetings, delegates were greeted by Swedish prime minister Göran Persson and UN secretary-general Kofi Annan. Each of the Central American presidents also made an inaugural speech. That afternoon, Central American presidents and their government ministers attended special workshops on ecological vulnerability, transparency, and decentralization. These workshops were coordinated by the donor agencies and gave a good indication of what the core values of the donor community were with regard to Hurricane Mitch relief assistance: In the ecological vulnerability workshops, the donors emphasized the importance of flood management, urban planning, risk management, and disaster mitigation strategies. Message: there is a reason the death and destruction were as severe as they were. The transparency and decentralization workshops sent an equally clear message to the Central American government representatives in attendance.

On the second day of the meetings, each Central American country presented its master plan to the donors. Honduras went first and had the largest portion of time for its presentation. From 8:00 A.M. to 1:30 P.M., the Honduran president and his ministers from the reconstruction cabinet laid out their plan for discussion with representatives of the international organizations and donor countries. Seated at the head table, the Honduran ministers were faced with forty-six representatives of governments and agencies of foreign aid. Members of the Honduran delegation equated the experience of being questioned by the international community to a "doctor's examination." The Honduran press referred to it as an inquisition. The representative from Japan, for example, asked the Honduran delegation why it was "asking for donations for businesses but loans for poverty programs. Shouldn't it be the other way around? Isn't this a contradiction?" Germany asked, "What makes you certain that these programs will continue in the next administration? This is a very ambitious program. Do you think it is realistic? Or does it exceed the capacity of your government?" Particularly painful were the questions regarding the inclusion of civil society groups in the development of the master plan: "Why were organizations such as Interforos kept outside the process?" a UN representative demanded. When Gustavo Alfaro, who had been fielding most of the questions, pointed to the Honduran representative from FONAC (the hand-picked National Convergence Forum already mentioned), the only nonminister at the table, and suggested that FONAC could best answer the question, the Japanese representative interrupted, "I am sorry, sir. But you are not civil society."[64]

The ministers expressed surprise at the level of questioning from the donor countries. Were the donors unhappy with the responses? Did this critical questioning mean that the donors were not in favor of Honduras's master plan? Back in Tegucigalpa, the newspapers variously speculated what the outcome of the Honduran presentation in Stockholm would be. *La Tribuna* reported the five hours of questioning was "as expected." A little more dramatically, *El Heraldo* stated, "The Master Plan for Reconstruction and Transformation presented by the Government of Honduras today received some praise but also . . . criticisms of the execution, feasibility, coherence, and above all the top-heavy nature of the plan." Both papers suggested that perhaps the Honduran delegation had not done as well as it might have and that the results were "uncertain."[65] Hondurans would have to wait until the following day, when the donors presented their commitments, to find out.

As to the purpose of this public grilling, I believe it was ultimately about garnering the consent of the recipient governments to the donor country agendas. Through their questioning, the donor countries emphasized the core principles of transparency, decentralization, and accountability that they had been stressing all along. It was not enough to give the Central American governments the relief assistance for them to do with as they chose; the donor countries insisted that the posthurricane reconstruction be about something *more* than just reconstruction: it had to be about transformation, too. Transformation of what? one might ask. Although the donor countries framed the discourse of transformation in terms of Honduran society and the mechanisms available to it to more effectively manage such natural disasters in the future, I believe the donor countries were really working on the governance of Honduras: they wanted to transform the Honduran state. They wanted to emphasize, and establish if possible, a different manner of governance, what many at the conference referred to as "good governance." The donor countries thus saw the hurricane relief assistance as a means to achieve other, broader political ends in Central America, such as democratization, civil society participation, transparency, and accountability. And in Stockholm, they made certain that the recipients of Mitch-related assistance danced to the proper tune. Although it would be difficult to quarrel with these ends in the abstract— all are fine, worthwhile goals—and though they were the very goals Honduran NGOs such as Interforos were struggling to establish in an authoritarian Honduran political space, we should not lose sight of the global power dynamics that provided what I consider to be the central lesson of Stockholm: You are going to do it our way.

On the last day of the conference, all participants signed the Stockholm Declaration and so gave their consent to the core principles heralded by the globalizers. The declaration proclaimed that "the governments of Central America and the international community ... [establish] *a long-term partnership* guided by the priorities defined by the Central American countries and based on the following goals and principles."[66] These priorities, goals, and principles were not defined by the Central American countries alone but, as has been made clear, were also products of the aid-offering international community. As an illustration of the globalizers' political principles to which Honduras and the other Central American nations (to varying degrees) acquiesced, they are worth examining in their entirety:

- To reduce social and ecological vulnerability in the region
- To reconstruct and transform Central America on the basis of an integrated approach through transparent management and good governance
- To consolidate democracy and good governance, reinforcing the process of decentralization of governmental functions and powers, with the active participation of civil society
- To promote respect for human rights as a permanent objective. The promotion of gender equality, the rights of children, of ethnic groups, and other minorities should be given special attention
- To coordinate donor efforts, guided by priorities set by the recipient countries
- To intensify efforts to reduce the external debt burden of the countries of the region.[67]

Perhaps of more interest than the political guidelines laid out by the declaration was the $9 billion aid package to Central America the conference produced: $5.3 billion in multilateral aid from the WB and IDB and $3.7 billion from the bilateral donors. Honduras received $2.76 billion, a full 70 percent of what the Honduran master plan had requested. President Flores called it an "excellent result." When asked what he thought the delegation's success could be attributed to, he responded, "The NGOs . . . Honduras's credibility before the international community was fortified by the participation of the representatives from civil society."[68] The "show" had worked. Back in Honduras, Stockholm was considered a great success. The "long-term partnership" that some feared but many had hoped for was finally born.

Hurricane Mitch and Global Governance in Honduras

The stories of the hurricane recovery efforts following Mitch reveal the truly global nature of governance in Honduras. The immediate response to the crisis was coordinated by international working groups made up of Honduran government officials and international development professionals who had immediately inserted themselves into the crisis. The relief and recovery efforts aimed at taking care of the dead and wounded, cleaning up the flooded areas, and attending to the immediate health needs was done largely through foreign aid in conjunction with local Honduran authorities. The official damage reports that became the basis for official governmental policy regarding the priorities of reconstruction following Mitch were written through a cooperative process of surveillance by international development professionals and Honduran government officials. These priorities then became codified in the Honduran government's master plan, which, likewise, was drafted in a coordinated transnational process. Even though the plan was ultimately presented by Honduran government officials, the process of its creation involved international and local agencies operating in a transnational space. The plan served the purpose of garnering the consent of the Honduran government and civil society to the priorities uppermost in the global agendas of the donor countries.[69] Finally, this garnering of consent continued at the meeting between donors and recipients in Stockholm. Formally, legally, and symbolically, the conference solidified the international partnership of governance that would be responsible for carrying out, managing, and auditing the multibillion dollar reconstruction effort. Even the site of the meeting itself makes plain the transnational nature of post-Mitch governance.

How did the reconstruction effort fare? According to the development workers and Honduran government officials I interviewed in 2001, the Hurricane Mitch reconstruction is largely considered a success. The most successful reconstruction initiatives are consistent with what Robinson's theory of the transnational state (TNS) suggests they would be. First and foremost, the international assistance effort gave Honduras financial stability at a time of crisis. The WB's $200 million emergency loan to the Central Bank of Honduras, according to David, "literally saved the country. It kept the lempira stable . . . there was not even a blip in the exchange rate." This is consistent with Robinson's model positing macroeconomic stability as the number one priority of the TNS. In relation to number two priority of the TNS, "to provide the basic infrastructure necessary for global economic activity," the rebuilding of damaged roads and bridges is also viewed as having succeeded. The repairs were quickly carried out by contractors from the donor countries (primarily Sweden and Japan), allowing transportation links to be effectively reestablished. In regard to the third priority of the TNS, maintaining "social order and social stability through coercive as well as consensual mechanisms of social control (democracy and development)," the "social Mitch" many globalizers feared was mainly avoided. In the area of health, the initial fumigation was amazingly effective; despite the early problems with water and flooding, there were no epidemics as a consequence of Mitch, avoided thanks mainly to international aid. In terms of housing, however, the story is not as good: Many displaced by the flooding never received assistance. A lot of the housing projects built by NGOs, mission groups, and some official donors were heavily criticized. Much of the criticism related to building houses on land whose ownership was unclear or the lack of a provision of infrastructure with the housing (e.g., plumbing, electricity, and sanitation, but also schools, health clinics, and parks). Some donors—Sweden, for example—did a better job in this regard than others. Nevertheless, reconstruction problems related to the hurricane persist to this day. Just as El Cajón Dam and the maquiladoras created new problems and opportunities for the globalizers to work on, Hurricane Mitch reconstruction will also likely raise new problems requiring the attention of the globalizers as they govern Honduras.

Which brings me to the central question: How did the globalizers fare? I address this question according to the central propositions of globalization that have guided this book.

First, once again the agendas of the donor countries won out over local agendas regarding the Hurricane Mitch reconstruction process. Representatives from the donor countries and international development agencies on the ground in Honduras presented their views early as to how the disaster should be handled. In bringing their global experience with disaster management to the table, they set up the rules of the game. Framing the root causes of the disaster as underdevelopment, the globalizers created the basic design of the reconstruction efforts. As the globalizers analyzed it, Honduran poverty forced Hondurans to live in ecologically precarious situations without modern safeguards such as emergency management organizations, river-monitoring and flood-control technologies, and state-of-the-art road and bridge engineering. Not only did Honduras need to be rebuilt, therefore, but this was also an opportunity for more development, better development. And since developing countries often have difficulty affording such expensive safeguards and technologies, the Mitch-affected countries would be given official development assistance for achieving these goals. With this assistance, Honduras could put into place the proper technologies and institutions deemed necessary to mitigate such crises in the future. Macroeconomic stability, infrastructure, and social order were the main targets of this assistance.

Hurricane Mitch also afforded donor countries the opportunity to promote other global agendas not directly related to repairing storm damage. Since the donor countries would be providing unprecedented amounts of aid for the reconstruction efforts, why not encourage the Honduran government to participate more with civil society groups, nudge it to decentralize its authority to municipalities and, most importantly, prod it to open up its practices (and files) to foreign inspection in the name of "transparency"? The globalizers built these agendas right into the Mitch reconstruction plan signed in Stockholm. The agendas—democratization, decentralization, and transparency—also directly corresponded with those of certain Honduran citizens' organizations and NGOs that, prior to Mitch, had had limited success in making their criticisms of the state's antidemocratic tendencies widely known.

Second, local agendas were able to succeed insofar as they were tied to the donors' agendas. The first Honduran beneficiaries were the government institutions themselves. The administration of President Flores faced a catastrophe as a result of the hurricane. The Honduran ministries and institutions were ill-prepared for the crisis—especially the emergency organization COPECO—and the ministers expressed grave doubt they had the wherewithal to adequately cope with a disaster the scale of Mitch. If the world were one where countries lived in complete isolation from one another, President Flores, in particular, and the Honduran state, in general, forced to meet the crisis alone, would have faced calamitous social and political upheaval. One can only speculate about the extent to which economic stagnation, famine, disease, crime, and civil unrest would have overwhelmed the Honduran political establishment in such an imaginary world. But, fortunately for President Flores and his ministers, our world is a globalizing one, and, therefore, their agendas of political stability and (even) political achievement were bolstered by an infusion of international relief and assistance. The globalizers shored up the Honduran government so much that President Flores and his ministers came back from Stockholm as heroes.

Other local agendas also managed to achieve success from globalizer support—Honduran NGOs whose initiatives toward democratization, transparency, and civil society participation were in alignment with globalizer interests, for example. Interforos, in particular, gained support from the Swedish assistance efforts that placed a high priority on local NGO involvement. Its NGO members, many of which had been kept on the Honduran political periphery, were, as a result, launched into the public political debate about the master plan and were able to ride the wave of globalizer support directly into the president's office and on to Stockholm. This support even landed them a permanent place at the political table. Today, the thirteen working groups monitoring the progress of the Mitch reconstruction have NGO representation.[70]

Third, Honduras as a whole certainly won benefits from the Stockholm conference. These benefits continue to be highly touted by the international donor community.[71] The country was able to buy, with the $2.7 billion, a lot of new things: bridges, roads, houses, clinics, schools, flood control technologies, and more. The assistance also brought broad political and social benefits to particular Honduran constituencies that would otherwise not likely have come about. The country's qualification for special debt-relief assistance as a result of the Mitch process is just one example.[72]

Fourth, Honduras nonetheless had to bear some costs. These costs were downplayed by the globalizers when the project was being promoted. Although the reconstruction was by no means the swindle El Cajón was (in part because the economic aid contained more donations than loans), Hondurans still paid a price for the aid. The most lucrative construction contracts, for instance, went to foreign firms, from Sweden, the United States, and Japan, rather than to Honduran enterprises. There were also the political costs shouldered primarily by Honduran government institutions and their personnel, who bore the brunt of most of the media criticism (especially compared to their globalizer counterparts) and who had to endure public reprimands in Stockholm and abdicate much of the decision-making authority to the donor nations.

Finally, there were the benefits to the donor countries. The many lucrative bridge-building and road-repair contracts they won were considered by many donors to be the prizes of their aid efforts. There were also the jobs and research opportunities made available to the hundreds of globalizers called into the country to assess the damage, formulate plans, and evaluate the results. The greatest benefit to the donor countries, however, was deeper penetration into the Honduran political and social space. The long-term effects of this penetration are, as yet, unclear. But certainly Hurricane Mitch offered yet another opportunity for extending Honduran integration into the global system. I examine in the final chapter the future of this global system in the light of the role of the globalizers.

G8 Summit Meeting, 2003, Evian, France
Photo: French Ministry of Foreign Affairs, Photo Unit

Maintaining Global Governance

How does understanding the activities of the globalizers shift one's view of globalization? My argument throughout this book has been that globalization has *agents* who actively create, promote, and sustain the global agendas responsible for bringing the remote places of the planet closer together economically and socially. Globalization is not a mechanistic superforce beyond human control; it is the product of human beings operating within institutions they themselves have invented. The individual globalizers tend to be highly trained, professional experts whose education and technical experience are increasingly valued in the postindustrial information age. Their particular skills give them legitimacy and job opportunities throughout the developing world. The institutions they work for—international development institutions—have been created by the world's wealthiest nations. These donor countries use their vast economic resources to foster and expand the activities of these agencies for the purpose of advancing their agendas on a global scale in general and in the developing world in particular. Globalization is thus not a neutral force; it is shaped largely by donor-country interests.

The major claim of this book is that globalization is first and foremost a *political* phenomenon. The agents of globalization work in powerful institutions that promote global agendas with long-term economic and social consequences. A look behind the beneficent veneer of development clearly reveals the power the globalizers possess. Globalization is about the exercise of power by institutions operating on a global scale as well as the clashes and convergences between what I have called "global agendas" and "local agendas." To clarify this political process and its future direction, I return to the five propositions that have framed this book.

First, I think it is clear that, in the developing world, global agendas will continue to win out over local agendas most of the time. The social institutions in developing countries such as Honduras simply do not have the technical or financial capacity to directly oppose or stay the global agendas advanced by the globalizers. Only through massive social protest can the agendas of the globalizers be directly challenged or stopped. I did not find evidence of protest on this scale in Honduras, and, I would cautiously add, it is not commonplace in much of the developing world. Rather, as seen in the case of Honduras, local institutions must confront and negotiate the globalizers' powerful agendas in an attempt to shape or steer them in a way that also advances some local interest.

Second, local agendas will succeed primarily to the extent they are capable of linking into the global agendas. I have described cases of local Honduran groups working directly with the globalizers in order to advance their own local agendas. The Honduran electricity company "went global" linking with the international development banks and European dam builders in the construction of El Cajón. Some sectors of the Honduran business community went global as they linked with the United States Agency for International Development (USAID) and private foreign investors to build industrial parks. Honduran nongovernmental organizations (NGOs) went global by hooking up with bilateral aid agencies and international NGOs, enabling them to take their local agendas all the way to Stockholm. This important dynamic of local institutions increasing their power by linking to global agendas is *inconsistent* with the simplistic view of globalization as pure domination. It highlights the cooperative side of global power dynamics and suggests that the ability to act in concert is also part of the globalization process. As Hannah Arendt might remind us, there are reasons in addition to coercion, false consciousness, and hegemony for local interests in the developing world to participate actively and willingly in advancing the global agendas of the donor countries.

Third, the benefits institutions in the developing world receive and will continue to enjoy from participating in the globalization agenda should not be underestimated. ENEE (Empresa Nacional de Energía Eléctrica, the National Electrical Energy Company), Honduran business leaders, and the Honduran state have all benefited from their cooperation with the globalizers, receiving, respectively, a 300 megawatt generating dam, profitable industrial parks, and a $2.7 billion reconstruction package. Other Honduran groups have realized gains as well. Mainly because of these benefits the globalizers are able to garner consent for their global agendas.

Fourth, the negative consequences or potential drawbacks of development projects are often downplayed or ignored. Although international development agencies may insist that project risks occupy a more prominent place in their development project proposals today than they did when El Cajón was built, this is only because official attention to these risks were almost completely absent then. These risks continue to be downplayed by the international development profession. For example, a discussion of long-term costs was largely absent from the Honduran master plan after Hurricane Mitch.

Finally, the greater benefits of international development assistance will continue to accrue to the donor countries. These benefits are the raison d'être of the international development profession, though they are mostly hidden from view. Were these benefits to subside, the globalizers would recede from the developing world. This is not, however, likely to occur. Indeed, the activities of the globalizers in Honduras are expanding and becoming more entrenched. Is the same trend occurring worldwide? To answer this question, it is necessary to move beyond these propositions to look at how the international development profession seeks to maintain its role in the world.

Saving a Place in the World

The globalizers have put down deep institutional and political roots in developing countries such as Honduras, and they are engaged in many activities designed to maintain and extend these roots. They seek, in particular, to preserve and expand their power and legitimate their future role in the world. Although this study has focused on the Honduran case, I suspect that the dynamics of global governance are operating in a similar fashion in other aid-recipient countries. The precise configuration of the transnational state apparatus, I assume, varies from country to country, and I would predict that the power of the development industry in those countries that are heavily aid dependent (e.g., Honduras) is going to be much greater than in larger, less dependent countries (e.g., Mexico). Nevertheless, I believe the case of Honduras provides a good indication of how global governance operates throughout the developing world. Although future comparative analysis would be necessary to reveal the extent to which this model holds for other aid-recipient nations, I believe such an analysis would find a great deal of consistency regarding how the globalizers operate throughout the world.

Irrespective of the generalizability of the Honduran case, what does this study of the globalizers in Honduras lead us to conclude in terms of their future? Are the globalizers temporary fixtures of the current globalization moment? Or are they destined to become a permanent feature of the coming global age? I would argue that the latter is more likely since (as has become evident) the international development profession has proven to be well able to maintain its position in the center of the transnational state apparatus. The globalizers in Honduras have demonstrated their capacity to deal with opposition to their activities in ways that have strengthened their position. They deflect criticism of their activities to reinforce their position in the global government; each problem the international development profession has faced has been recast as a problem for these professionals to solve. In order to make this capacity more apparent, I briefly examine below four current criticisms of the international development profession that have the potential to threaten its existence and legitimacy. In each case, the globalizers have been adept at developing strategies for confronting these criticisms, individually and institutionally, and in fact bolstering their legitimacy and hegemony in the developing world.

The Question of Incompetence

International development organizations are often criticized for being wasteful and inefficient. There are so many donor countries and international agencies represented in Honduras, for example, that their services often overlap and duplicate one another. Recall the turf wars discussed by Julia in chapter 4, the conflict between her organization and another over which was going to deliver a health project in a particular community. As development agencies vie for position in governing a country, program duplication frequently results, and this can create problems for local communities forced to negotiate between them. The development workers themselves in some cases point to the bureaucratic waste in the profession. Elaine (chap. 3), for example, criticized the high salaries paid United Nations bureaucrats in Chile who "did nothing but write meaningless reports."

Countering this perception of inefficiency, the globalizers highlight their competence. At the individual level, the globalizers respond to the criticism by asserting their professional ability and qualifications. Many development workers I interviewed emphasized their professional training and justified their relatively high salaries by arguing that "they were worth it" because of the unique and much-needed technical skills and expertise they brought to the country.

On an institutional level, international development agencies similarly deflect criticism by pointing to the expertise of their personnel. In addition to claims of professional expertise, the international development profession increasingly emphasizes the business model and its focus on customer service and results. By demonstrating that their organizations are achieving quantifiable goals and performance outcomes, the globalizers fend off criticism that international development assistance is a waste of money. Recall Greg Lamar's vision in chapter 1 of a potential future in which development programs that cannot show results will have their funds taken away by globalizers elsewhere in the world who can show results. Furthermore, to avoid a duplication of services, the globalizers actively pursue donor coordination, which, as shown in the case of Hurricane Mitch, not only defuses criticism of development project repetition but also strengthens the structure of global governance by establishing a formal system of working groups made up of development workers and their government counterparts. Finally, the development profession maintains an elaborate evaluation apparatus constantly on the lookout for development project problems and mistakes. With an ongoing evaluation of their activities, the globalizers are not only able to keep tabs on the extent to which they are successful, but they can also turn any failure into a future development project. Recall, for example, how the globalizers used the leak in El Cajón Dam and the depleted watershed as targets for new interventions. In this way, the globalizers build their future into the very structures of the international development profession. The cycle of insertion, surveillance, agenda setting, and garnering consent will likely repeat itself again and again.

"We Aren't Forcing Anybody to Do Anything"

A second major criticism of the globalizers is that they are imposing a foreign way of life in developing countries. Often accused of being "foreign agents," they have also been labeled as "agitators" or "outside meddlers" from a belief their activities undermine local political sovereignty. They are also frequently viewed as agents of cultural imperialism, threatening local cultural integrity and contributing to patterns of dependency.

As individuals, development workers respond to these concerns in two ways. First, claiming they are simply doing a job they have been asked to do, they emphasize the apolitical nature of their professional role. More importantly, they claim they have no ability to force anything upon anyone. Although this denial of power is part of their cloak of beneficence, it nevertheless allows them to deflect the criticism that they are operating under ulterior motives. They say they are simply doing what the recipient country has asked them to do. Second, development workers downplay their allegiance to any particular nation as they carry out their work in developing countries. In countering accusations they are agents of a foreign government, they are more likely to claim an international allegiance and say that they are citizens of the world.

At the institutional level, development organizations deal with the problem by making good use of the mechanisms of consent. The signatures of local government organs on formal contracts, agreements, and treaties with the globalizers demonstrate local governments "have asked" for the projects. Strong institutional bonds are created between the globalizers and local authorities, ensuring there is always a local government counterpart involved offering consent, or not, to any plans under consideration. The 1987 export processing law that established the *maquiladoras* in Honduras and the Honduran government's master plan for Hurricane Mitch reconstruction illustrate the extent of local government acquiescence, approval, and cooperation in globalizers' undertakings. The globalizers have even made it a priority to transform the local national state to function more smoothly with the international development assistance apparatus. This "long-term partnership" is a global institutional arrangement that makes old debates about foreign imposition and erosion of local sovereignty irrelevant. The locals are no longer sovereign (they have not been for a long time); the globalizers (in partnership with the locals) are.

Secrecy and Transparency

Secretiveness is another criticism frequently leveled at development organizations. The World Bank (WB) and the other large international development institutions in particular have been singled out. The old way of confronting this criticism, claiming the information was private and the sovereignty con-

ntal Governance 307

cerns of the borrowing country had to be respected, has largely been abandoned, and international development organizations tend now to subscribe to a strategy of transparency with claims the details of their operations are readily available to public scrutiny.

Individual globalizers, on the other hand, have remained secretive about their activities and the benefits they receive from their jobs. The globalizers' preference for not talking about the salary gap between expatriate and local development workers illustrates this. When the subject does come up, the globalizers use a strategy of rationalization: their high salaries are needed for expenses "back home." This strategy asks their Honduran coworkers to understand that the international nature of their jobs involves certain high costs that should be taken into account. It remains to be seen if this deflection will resolve the potential conflict between the expats and locals.

On an institutional level, development organizations are increasingly opening up their records and files in order to maintain, and even enhance, their legitimacy. Transparency has become a new global agenda, and, to promote it without hypocrisy, international development organizations are beginning to make their archives available to public scrutiny. Many of the documents I refer to in this book were not available in 1995 when I began my project. In 2001-3, however, I had access to them thanks to mechanisms USAID, the WB, and other agencies have established to make their project documents available to the broader public.[1] In addition, the globalizers have gotten wired. Every development organization operating in Honduras cited in this book, for example, now has a Web page presenting limited information to the public regarding its activities. This opening up also serves the purpose of garnering public consent in favor of their activities since much of the information has public relations value. As one development worker claimed, "If people really saw what we did, I think we would have greater support for what we do."[2]

Democracy and Questions of Accountability, Local Control, and Citizen Participation

Finally, the globalizers face a criticism common to all governments. They have been accused of being too "top-down," "unaccountable," of not allowing for enough local control and citizen participation. The very question, "To what extent are the globalizers held accountable for their actions?" presupposes they are involved in governance. Throughout this book I have presented cases where the globalizers' accountability is low; El Cajón is the most significant and clear example of donor failure in this regard. But the question of accountability in the international development profession applies more broadly than just the cases of failure; the question is just as relevant in cases of success.

As individuals, the globalizers confront a situation of mixed accountability. They feel accountable to their own agency, the donor country providing the funds, and, in this case, to the Honduran government and the Honduran people. In my view, this mixed accountability poses a problem for international development professionals: The globalizers are ultimately accountable to the donor countries because they are the ones paying their salaries and holding the power to hire or fire them. But if the international development profession really wants the recipients of their projects to be the test for accountability, then they should give them the power to determine their salaries and to hire or fire.

In the meantime, the individual globalizers I interviewed coped with the problem of individual accountability primarily by emphasizing the "feel good" stories in their work. These tales from their work experience are particularly poignant or touching to the development workers. They typically involve some "unfortunate person" who has touched their hearts. Elaine's story (chap. 3) of the children she encountered who had to walk five hundred meters uphill for water, for example, served to assure her that her work mattered. Such stories solve the crisis of accountability in development workers' minds by making them accountable to an ideal; what the globalizers are doing in the world, the stories tell them, is right and good.

At an institutional level, international development organizations have addressed the issue of accountability by incorporating NGOs into the structures of global governance. NGOs are now largely working within the donor-country agendas; they are the globalizers, too. By inviting NGOs to the table, official aid agencies from the donor countries have institutionalized public participation. In particular, by subcontracting the implementation of their global agendas to NGOs, the donor countries guarantee local participation, legitimate their activities as democratic, and garner the consent of any who might criticize them. The "NGO boom" has, in short, shored up the activities of the globalizers and, in so doing, shored up the economic politics of capitalist, donor-led globalization. For those who believe that NGOs are the most hopeful solution to the top-down approach of official development organizations, this could be cause for concern. And it should be. I think my examination of the role of NGOs in Honduras in the context of the international development profession raises some difficult questions regarding the extent to which so-called NGO agendas like workers' rights and human rights have become incorporated into the practices of official development agencies and, thus, buttress (rather than undermine) the ability of these agencies to carry out donor-country interests in the developing world. But it is not necessary to be too pessimistic, either. Rather, the question to ask is whether NGO participation in the donor-driven agendas of the globalizers is a situation of cooptation or cooperation. Are the powerful interests of the Group of Seven (G7) nations driving the activities of the NGOs, or are the NGOs driving the powerful interests of the G7 nations?

This question is relatively easy to answer if it is understood that most influential NGOs come from the donor countries. This is why I think there is reason to be wary of NGOs being presented as a panacea. It is also why many developing countries are wary of the NGOs as well. Whose globalization agendas are being promoted by the international NGOs? Feminism, democracy, and human rights are worthy ideals, but to what extent have their agendas, in practice, been shaped by those at the bottom of the global ladder? And are there other agendas that are being left out?

There is much about the international NGO movement that, I would agree, is promising. But at the same time, my experience of examining the globalizers in Honduras has led me to question how much the veneer of beneficence is distorting my view. I think it is important to keep in mind that, in looking at NGOs and development organizations, we see their activities as aid; we view what they do as helping. And we tend to believe they will "make a better world." Recall the original Peace Corps slogan: "you can make a difference in the world." Yet, what this is really about is power. Stripping away the shiny veneer of beneficence and looking at the international development profession, what do we see? I have shown in this book that development workers certainly can, and do, "make a difference." But their activities also have other consequences and, ultimately, the lesson of the globalizers in Honduras is that these individuals with the best of intentions are, nevertheless, participating in a global institutionalized practice from which they receive benefits. With the polished veneer removed, development work shows itself to be not about aid but about power. It is about the benefits the globalizers bring to the *donor countries* of the world.

Notes

INTRODUCTION: The Globalizers in Honduras

1. Using Foucault, Ferguson argues that "development" is ultimately an exercise of power (Ferguson, 1994, 255–56).

2. Ibid., xvi, 260.

3. See, e.g., Giddens, 2000, and Stiglitz, 2002.

4. Whether this is a new development or the continuation of an old one is the source of debate within world-systems theory. For advocates of the former, see Robinson, 1996a; and Boswell and Chase-Dunn, 2000.

5. See, e.g., Albrow, 1996; and Sachs, "One World," in *The Development Dictionary*, 1992.

6. Bourdieu, 2001, 2; emphasis added.

7. Perhaps because so many scholars now interested in globalization have backgrounds in the field of economic development, development organizations are often portrayed in the literature as familiar and widely understood entities. Although discussions of the structure and nature of the global economy are extensive and detailed, those on global political institutions are usually abbreviated and general. See, e.g., Sklair, 1995, 68–74; Albrow, 1996, 123–28.

8. None of the scholars previously referred to, for instance, mention international development agencies as primary agents of globalization. Although official development aid (especially as it is disbursed through large institutions such as the WB or the UN) is often alluded to in these works, most theories of globalization place such agencies low on the list of institutions engaging in global practices and have not fully explored the role of development institutions in promoting globalization. Some accounts dismiss the significance of these institutions inasmuch as they fail to constitute the authority of a true world state (e.g., Barnet and Cavanaugh, 1994). Others imply that the activities of many of these agencies are "distinctly marginal" relative to the practices of TNCs and the TCC (Sklair, 1995, 69). The work of the world polity school (e.g., Boli and Thomas, 1997b) and that of William Robinson (1996b; 2001b) are notable exceptions. As I hope to make clear in this analysis, what appears to be a "world state" from the Honduran point of view (from the bottom up) might be quite different from what these authors have concluded looking from the top down.

9. The institutions of global governance that are the subject of this book are different from both the colonial apparatus that operated in Honduras prior to independence from Spain and the neocolonial apparatus operating in Honduras in the nineteenth and early part of the twentieth century. USAID, the UN organizations, the WB,

and what we now call the "NGO community" simply did not exist prior to World War II. A historical comparison between the current institutions of global governance and the earlier colonial and neocolonial "globalizers" is beyond the scope of this analysis. Thanks to Walter Goldfrank for drawing my attention to this important point. For a discussion of Honduran dependency in historical perspective, see Schulz and Schulz, 1994.

10. See, e.g., Sklair, 1995.

11. Benjamin Barber calls this engine the "market imperative of 'McWorld'" (the word *imperative* connoting his view of the unstoppable, larger-than-life nature of globalization). Anthony Giddens refers to it as the "economic processes" of transnational corporate expansion. For Thomas Freidman, it is the "Lexus" (as opposed to the "Olive Tree") driving globalization forward. And William Robinson's "new epoch" of "capitalist globalization" is primarily the consequence of the actions of the transnational capitalist class.

12. See Giddens, 2000; Friedman, 2000; and Grieder, 1997.

13. See, e.g., Brecher, et al., 2000.

14. Ibid.

15. See, e.g., Sassen, 1988.

16. See, e.g., Fox and Brown, 1998. Of particular relevance to this point, see the discussion of the Narmada campaign in India on pp. 61–65.

17. The term *globalization* seems often to be followed by "and its discontents;" three recent publications use this phrase in their titles: Burbach, Nuñez, and Kagarlitsky's *Globalization and Its Discontents: The Rise of Postmodern Socialisms* (1997); Sassen's *Globalization and Its Discontents: Essays on the New Mobility of People and Money* (1992); and Stiglitz's *Globalization and Its Discontents* (2002).

The debate about democracy in the context of globalization is a central concern of those who examine globalization from below. For some (e.g., Barber, 1992), democracy is unlikely under a future global system. For most, democracy is something that must be constructed by civil society as it challenges the power of transnational capital (e.g., Giddens, 2000). Yet for others (Robinson, 1996a; Boswell and Chase-Dunn, 2000), democracy is antithetical to the globalization agenda of the transnational capitalist class and is only possible under a new economic order.

18. This is Thomas Friedman's "Olive Tree." For Benjamin Barber, it is the "jihad" that clashes with "McWorld." For Anthony Giddens, it is the "fundamentalism" that opposes the "cosmopolitanism" of globalization. For William Robinson, it is the "counter-hegemonic" clash of antiglobalization forces with the "hegemony" of the transnational capitalist class; a clash that, in his words, amounts to a "world war."

19. Phillip McMichael (1996) refers to this agenda as the "globalization project."

20. I believe the globalizers themselves are somewhat responsible for this oversight because their role has been obscured by the language of "helping" and "aid." The image of development workers as do-gooders rather than advocates of capitalism or globalization has perhaps shielded them from the critical gaze of globalization scholars. This veneer of beneficence is discussed later in this chapter.

21. Boli and Thomas, 1997b.

22. Much more effort is going into the promotion of tourism in Honduras, for example, than into promoting solar power. Both "the promotion of tourism for national development" and "the use of solar energy as an alternative fuel in rural areas" are

global scripts currently being advanced by various groups in the development profession. The former, however, is having a much greater impact on Honduran society. Development professionals employed to promote the tourism industry in Honduras are likely to find themselves working on "big-time" projects involving millions (or even billions) of dollars, whereas those promoting solar energy are working on projects involving a much smaller number of constituents and resources.

23. OECD, 2001.

24. These twenty-two donor countries, in the order of the average net ODA provided to the developing world in 1999 and 2000, are: Japan, the United States, Germany, Great Britain, France, the Netherlands, Sweden, Canada, Denmark, Italy, Norway, Spain, Australia, Switzerland, Belgium, Austria, Finland, Portugal, Ireland, Greece, Luxembourg, and New Zealand (OECD, 2001).

25. For an overview of this convergence, see "The Rise of the Globalization Project," in McMichael, 1996, 147–77.

26. Net ODA to the developing world in 2000 was $53.7 billion (OECD, 2002).

27. The research of the many critics of development organizations is too vast to summarize here. For a critical look at the WB specifically, see Rich, 1994. For other Bretton Woods institutions, see Bandow and Vásquez, 1994; Bello, 1994; Osterfeld, 1994; Payer, 1982; and Stiglitz, 2002. For critical analysis of USAID, see Maren, 1997. For a critical assessment of the UN system, see Hancock, 1989. For criticism of development in general, see Attwood, Bruneau, and Galaty, 1988; Escobar, 1995; Hayter, 1971; Paddock and Paddock, 1973; Sachs, 1992; Smillie, 1991 and 1995; and Tendler, 1975. Finally, for a critique of the discourse of "helping," see Marianne Gronemeyer's "Helping," in Sachs, 1992.

28. Sachs, 1992, 51.

29. Average net ODA to Honduras in 1999–2000 was $633 million a year.

30. Cuba is an example of a developing country that largely eschews development assistance.

31. Jonathan Fox and L. David Brown (1998) define accountability as "the process of holding actors responsible for actions." This is of course relevant for developed countries as well.

32. Slogan can be found on the WB Web page, www.worldbank.org.

33. I agree with Wolfgang Sachs and his colleagues, who, in the *Development Dictionary*, write, "The idea of development stands like a ruin in the intellectual landscape . . . its shadow obscures our vision" (Sachs, 1992, 1). In this book, I attempt to shift attention away from the chimera of "development" to the reality of globalization.

34. I do not intend to oversimplify here by implying that donor countries have a monolithic set of interests; class dynamics are also at play. Donor countries' interests are dominated by certain groups within those donor countries (in particular, the globalizing transnational capitalist class). These groups largely determine the political process in donor countries and use the international development apparatus for their own purposes (and though they are the most powerful, they are not the only ones). This process is brought into sharper focus in the second half of the book. In particular, I offer specific examples of how certain corporations in the donor countries have benefited from development projects in Honduras (e.g., maquiladoras benefiting Gap, hydroelectric dams benefiting U.S. and European engineering firms, bridge construction following Hurricane Mitch benefiting Japanese and Swedish construction companies, etc.). The Honduran class dynamics are just as complex.

35. Sweden, for example, has become one of the top ten donor countries to Honduras. In chapter 10, I describe how this aid has allowed Swedish engineering firms to garner lucrative construction contracts in Honduras.

36. See, e.g., Schulz and Schulz, 1994, on the strong influence of the United States on Honduras.

O N E : The Institutions

1. According to the OECD, the "Organisation for Economic Co-operation and Development was set up . . . [to] promote policies designed to achieve the highest sustainable economic growth and employment and a rising standard of living in Member countries while maintaining financial stability, and thus *to contribute to the world economy . . .*" (OECD, 1966, ii; emphasis added).

2. Many globalization scholars have posited the UN and the Bretton Woods institutions (the WB and the IMF) as the key international institutions giving rise to the global economy. The OECD has received much less attention as an international institution of global governance; yet, it may be just as significant in this regard.

3. The twenty-two donor nations making up the Development Assistance Committee of the OECD are: Australia, Austria, Belgium, Canada, Denmark, Finland, France, Germany, Greece, Ireland, Italy, Japan, Luxembourg, the Netherlands, New Zealand, Norway, Portugal, Spain, Sweden, Switzerland, the United Kingdom, and the United States.

4. OECD, 1995, 249.

5. Ibid.

6. These figures have been adjusted to reflect the value in 2002 dollars. Figure 2 shows the total amount of net ODA in terms of grants and loans from bilateral and multilateral donors that has flowed into Honduras each year from 1960 to 2002. Sources: OECD 1966; 1975; 1984; 1995; 2002; OECD database: *http://new.sourceoecd.org*; accessed December 15, 2004.

7. SECPLAN, 1993.

8. SECPLAN, 1995.

9. AECI, 2001, 34, 57–61.

10. Upon arriving in Honduras, I initially tried to gather information regarding the finances of all development NGOs with headquarters in Tegucigalpa. Most were reluctant to share such information with me. In 1994, The UNDP attempted to gather similar information (through a survey) for its own appraisal of NGOs in Honduras; it met the same reluctance: few NGOs were willing to give the UNDP any indication of the size of their operations, the projects they were carrying out, or the size of their budgets. A UNDP employee told me, "They don't have to volunteer this information to anyone but their donors. What we discovered [when we tried to gather this information] is that NGOs are secretive . . . and they're suspicious . . . but with good reason. They don't want the government to intrude upon their work." In the end, I decided to abandon the idea of compiling such information.

11. Edwards and Hulme, 1996; Smillie, 1995

12. Norsworthy and Barry, 1993, 121.

13. Hayter, 1971; Norsworthy and Barry, 1993.

14. Smillie, 1995.

15. Ibid.

16. Giddens, 2000; McMichael, 1996; Robinson, 1996a; Schaeffer, 2003.

17. Robinson, 2001b.

18. Tegucigalpa grew tremendously in the seventies and eighties, from around 100,000 people in 1970 to over 1 million by 1995.

19. All individual names in this chapter are pseudonyms.

20. In 1995, when this episode took place, Internet access had just arrived in Honduras; USAID was one of the first organizations to be connected.

21. In 1995, the World Wide Web was still somewhat new. Many of the organizations I was studying at that time had either just established a Web page or were in the process of constructing one. Most of these Web pages are now much more developed.

22. In 2000, the U.S. government spent approximately $16.5 billion on international assistance out of a total federal budget of $1.8 trillion. Of this, $9.4 billion was for bilateral assistance, the majority of which is channeled through USAID.

23. When I asked Greg whether USAID supported agricultural co-ops, for example, he responded that USAID had supported co-ops for "a long time" but that currently they were trying to "promote more of a business model among these communities."

24. This legal reform was part of the agricultural component of USAID's 1984 "Export Development and Services" project, discussed in chapter 8.

25. Hayter, 1971; Norsworthy and Barry, 1993.

26. President Reina was so concerned about the poll that he held a press conference a few days later at which he reassured the country that *he* was in charge, not Ambassador Price.

27. The importance of networks as a unit of analysis has been highlighted by numerous social theorists (e.g., Castells, 1996) attempting to define the characteristics of postmodern society.

TWO: **The People**

1. See, e.g., Barnet and Cavanagh, 1994, 288; Stiglitz, 2002, 3; Bourdieu, 2001, 4; McMichael, 1996, 299; and Robinson, 2001b, 20. For exceptions to this tendency to underexamine these individual experiences, see Escobar, 1995; Ferguson, 1994; Maren, 1997; and Klitgaard, 1990.

2. I leave religious missionaries (who may or may not promote development as a part of their mission) outside my analysis of the globalizers in this book. I do so because I do not believe religious missionaries fit the definition of globalizer as I have formulated it (see also note 9 below). I have limited my study to development workers and organizations that are either secular in nature (official aid organizations and NGOs) or whose mission excludes proselytizing (e.g., Catholic Relief Services).

3. Sources: "Fact Sheet," and "Two Years after Mitch: Status of the USG Reconstruction Effort," U.S. Agency for International Development, Press Office, personal copy collected in Tegucigalpa, July 2001; and "La Cooperación Internacional No Reembolsable: Memoria 1999," SETCO, personal copy. These projects are discussed in more detail in chapter 10.

4. New in the sense that it is based on certain space-time compressing technological developments of the past twenty or so years such as international jet travel, and global communication channels such as fax, e-mail, and the Internet. These technologies allow

more fully for the "establishment of networks across space" (Portes, Guarnizo, and Landolt, 1999).

5. Portes, Guarnizo, and Landolt, 1999; see also Bamyeh, 1993.

6. Portes, Guarnizo, and Landolt, (1999) argue that transnationalism comprises various types of activities (economic, political, or cultural) and levels of institutionalization (from informal or grassroots institutions up to more established and powerful ones). Although their work focuses primarily on the experiences of what they call "third world immigrant groups" in the "first world" (and how these immigrant communities maintain cross-border networks), their theoretical framework does suggest that transnationalism can also be seen in the activities of first world professionals working in developing countries in the economic (entrepreneurs, for instance), political, or cultural realm. Development professionals work in all three areas and operate within institutions of some power and influence.

7. Ibid., 217.

8. I use the terms *globalizer* and *development worker* interchangeably throughout this book; they should be considered synonymous. Although I use the two labels, no one I interviewed referred to him- or herself as a globalizer; they all called themselves "development worker." Thus, although I am essentially redefining what they do, development workers/globalizers themselves still view their activities within the ideological frame of development as opposed to globalization.

9. This definition excludes entrepreneurs, soldiers, and religious missionaries as globalizers. Although all these groups engage in extensive international travel and promote global agendas similar to the development professionals discussed in this book, they are not, I believe, agents of globalization as much as they are agents acting globally. Entrepreneurs are not globalizers according to this definition because, although they may advise or consult with development professionals in making economic policy in various settings, they are employed by institutions whose primary mission is to make a profit for a limited group of shareholders (not the globe as a whole). As to whether TNCs and entrepreneurs can be globalizers, they can; but, in my view, only inasmuch as they engage in the economic politics of globalization as Bourdieu defines it (a similar qualification can be made regarding soldiers). Entrepreneurs are not, however, primarily concerned with building the political institutions of globalization (they leave that to the globalizers). Entrepreneurs are, on the other hand, more heavily involved in international institutions devoted to free trade (such as the WTO or NAFTA, two institutions that do not figure significantly in my story). In addition, as many of my case studies in later chapters illustrate, entrepreneurs often work as subcontractors for the globalizers, and in that capacity, they become globalizers as I have defined them. Soldiers are not globalizers because, although they are occasionally involved in humanitarian assistance projects, they are employed by institutions whose primary mission is to advance the military interests of one government (rather than the entire globe) over another. Similarly, although religious missionaries might carry out extensive development projects as part of their work, they are employed by institutions advancing the beliefs and practices of their members (not the globe as a whole) and so are not globalizers.

10. Many world-system scholars, such as Andre Gunder Frank, argue that there is really nothing new going on in the world that we can call globalization as distinct from the ongoing spread of the capitalist world economy that began around 1500 (or earlier).

I place myself among those scholars who disagree with this point of view. Not only are the globalizers in this book different from the earlier missionaries, colonizers, viceroys (and other agents of colonization in the period of European expansion and colonialism) in terms of their skills and ideological outlook (the globalizers are highly trained modern professionals who adhere to the universal goals of development, whereas the colonizers of earlier epochs had no training in the modern professions and simply adhered to the particular goals of the motherland); but the globalizers also operate within global institutions that are truly transnational in nature as opposed to operating within colonial institutions that were subsumed under the governing apparatus of one or another nation-state. They are neither purely colonialist nor neocolonialist (though many certainly take on these roles as well as they pursue the interests of one particular nation-state); they are globalist. They are agents of this new age of globalization. I refer in this study to the current epoch of globalization articulated by scholars such as Robinson and Giddens. For Robinson (1996a), this epoch began around 1970. For Giddens, this "major period of historical transition," which "has no parallels in earlier times," dates back "only to the late 1960s" (Giddens, 2000, 27–28). Others (such as Barnet and Cavanagh, 1994) believe it began slightly earlier in the postwar period with the advent of the UN and Bretton Woods institutions circa 1945. All of these time frames are consistent with the rise of development organizations in the 1960s and the subsequent turning on of aid flows from donor countries to developing countries that resulted. The rise of ODA to Honduras (see chap. 1) illustrates, for example, how the globalizers discussed in this book have been operating in Honduras only since the 1960s and really took hold during the 1970s and 1980s.

11. I used a purposive and snowball sampling design that allowed me to interview a total of twenty-eight NGO employees (fourteen from small/local NGOs, fourteen from large/international NGOs), nineteen bilateral agency employees, seventeen employees from multilateral agencies, and five Honduran government officials (including two ministers) who worked closely with international development professionals. Eighteen of those interviewed were Honduran and fifty-one were expatriate development workers. Of the foreign respondents, twenty-four were from the United States or Canada, twenty were from Europe or Japan, and seven were from other Latin American countries. I interviewed forty men and twenty-nine women whose ages ranged from twenty-five to sixty-four. All interviews were semi-structured and were tape-recorded for subsequent transcription and analysis. They were conducted in English or Spanish, based on the interviewee's preference. I use pseudonyms in the book for all respondents to protect their anonymity. For more details on methodology, see Jackson, 1998.

12. Perkin, 1996, 1

13. I am referring here to the vast academic literature filling the curricula of university courses on third world development throughout the world. In particular, I allude to the modernization perspective of scholars such as Walt Rostow, who theorize about the various stages all countries go through in a process of socioeconomic evolution known as development. For accounts of the schools of thought (modernization theory, dependency theory, etc.) and development models that have emerged out of this fifty-year-old field of scholarship devoted to understanding the processes whereby certain countries have become "developed" and others remain "developing," "less developed," "underdeveloped," or "undeveloped," see So, 1990; McMichael, 1996; and Jaffee, 1990. For a critical analysis of this literature, see Sachs, 1992; and Escobar, 1988, 1992, 1995.

14. For a historical analysis of this sociology of knowledge problem, see Said, 1979. For an application of Said to the contemporary Latin American context, see Jackson, 1993.

15. Foucault, 1979.

THREE: The Expats

1. Anthropologists Elizabeth Colson and A. F. Robertson were among the first social scientists to argue that international development workers constitute a global community with its own customs, values, and practices (Colson, 1982; Robertson, 1984). In a speech given at Berkeley in 1982, Colson asserted that development "has its own culture": "We are dealing with a close-knit international network that transcends the boundaries of the voluntary, bilateral and multilateral agencies" (Colson, 1982, 20). She postulated that the conferences attended by development personnel serve a "ritualistic function": "The workshops and conferences which float from one city to another provide the occasion for face-to-face encounters, but they are also ritual events which speak to the value of the development community. They bring together and remind its dispersed members that they are linked in a common endeavor and share in the same goals" (p. 23). She also proposed a "multinational nature" (I would say global) of the development community, the self-interest of development personnel in maintaining their jobs, and the tendency for development workers to travel to the third world at opportune times of the year to take advantage of "development tourism." My research gives empirical support to most of Colson's ideas. Her description of international development workers as a community is right on the mark when it comes to Honduras.

2. USAID employees, of course, are also effectively sponsored by the U.S. government since they are federal employees. As in the Dutch program, entry-level professionals at USAID are paid professional salaries. The difference is that the Dutch program allows its professionals to work in any number of organizations (such as the UN) sponsored by the Ministry of Development Cooperation (as is the case for many European countries). To my knowledge, the U.S. government does not have a similar program to train and pay the salaries of U.S. professionals working in development aid organizations not directly affiliated with U.S. foreign assistance.

3. Emphasis added.

4. Additionally, I discovered later that the meeting with Elaine involved a Japanese project for a new master health plan on behalf of the Honduran government. The final plan (discussed briefly in chap. 5) held up the UNICEF community water project as a successful model of making potable water available to low-income communities (System Science Consultants, 1996).

5. Perkin, 1996.

6. Many development workers I spoke with had access to elite social circles. The social prestige associated with being a foreigner and a professional enabled development workers to establish contacts, networks, and even friendships with Honduras's elite. Willis, for example, was a European volunteer making only $1,000 a month. In the development profession, he was not among those at the highest level; yet, his everyday experience included participation in elite social circles. His prestige seemed to be based primarily on his European identity and relatively high salary (by Honduran standards). He was able to afford to travel throughout the country and visit Tegucigalpa on week-

ends, where he would often "hang out" with his international friends (including the German ambassador).

7. It is important to point out here that development workers from less powerful or less influential donor countries tended to have more limited access to these powerful social networks, though not always.

FOUR: The Locals

1. I learned in my interview with Anita, an administrator in charge of payroll for a European bilateral organization, that these salaries are often determined by development agencies in conjunction with one another.

2. Cooperation vs. cooptation is developed further in relation to power in chapter 5.

3. This interview was in Spanish and has been translated from the Spanish transcript into English by the author.

4. According to UNESCO, in 1983 only 3.3 percent of the Honduran population had some postsecondary education. Currently, according to the WB, for every hundred Honduran students who enter first grade, fewer than eight finish twelfth grade (World Bank, 2000). So the proportion earning a college degree is probably less than 1 percent of the total Honduran population. According to the Honduran government, between 1990 and 1994 approximately eight thousand college degrees (bachelor's or master's) were awarded per year (SECPLAN, 1995).

5. The exception to this general observation is the community volunteers I interviewed who work advancing the agendas of development organizations in their (usually impoverished) communities. Although they are not considered professional employees of development agencies, they are local Honduran agents whose work promotes various projects throughout the country. These community volunteers are almost always from poor backgrounds.

6. This fact has even become the subject of current development projects in Honduras. The Japanese, for example, have funded a project designed to improve the training of nurses in the country. The project includes trips for Honduran nursing professionals to Japan to study Japanese nursing programs and Japanese nursing consultants coming to Honduras for the improvement of its nursing training.

7. "Household livelihood security" is defined in CARE manuals as "adequate and sustainable access to income and resources to meet basic needs. These needs may include adequate access to food, potable water, health facilities, educational opportunities, housing, time for community participation, etc." (CARE-International Honduras, "Long-Range Strategic Plan 1995–2000"; personal copy).

8. Marcos interview, spring 1996, from field notes.

9. The exchange rate in early 1996 was approximately 12 lempiras to U.S.$1.

10. Sociologist Patricia Hill Collins might suggest that Julia's "outsider within" position allows her to see power dynamics to which those in dominant positions are often blind (Collins, 1991).

11. Whether or not this is the case awaits an empirical demonstration. I was unable, from Honduras, to ascertain the national composition of employees of the international development agencies included in this study. To determine the extent to which development professionals from developing countries are employed at the highest

level of management in international development agencies, it would be necessary to study the professional makeup of their regional and international headquarters.

12. This was the case for CODEH, the Honduran Human Rights Commission; see chapters 9 and 10.

13. One Honduran development worker I spoke with, for example, told me she often took her organization's vehicles home to use over the weekend, though her job description included no such entitlement. When her foreign boss approached her about what he believed to be the misuse of organizational resources, she feigned ignorance of the organization's policy.

FIVE: Global Governance

Epigraph: Roy, 2001, 27; italics in original.

1. Arturo Escobar refers to this process as the "institutionalization and professionalization" of development activities in the developing world (Escobar, 1995).

2. Outhwaite and Bottomore, 1994, 504.

3. Giddens, 1985, cited in Jary and Jary, 1991, 378.

4. Foucault, cited in Outhwaite and Bottomore, 1994, 504.

5. Foucault, 1977, 187.

6. Perkin, 1996. See also Said, 1979.

7. Russell, 1938, and Weber, 1921, cited in Outhwaite and Bottomore, 1994, 504.

8. Parsons, cited in Outhwaite and Bottomore, 1994, 504.

9. Ibid.

10. Outhwaite and Bottomore, 1994, 505.

11. Ibid.

12. Ibid.

13. Poulantzas, cited in Abercrombie, Hill, and Turner, 1994.

14. Arendt, 1970, cited in Outhwaite and Bottomore, 1994, 505.

15. Dahl, cited in Jary and Jary, 1991, 379.

16. Outhwaite and Bottomore, 1994, 505.

17. Although I side with Robinson's perspective (Robinson, 2001b), it is not an uncritical acceptance. Robinson's model tends to ignore the role of international development organizations, per se, in transnational governance. Furthermore, his theoretical orientation (drawing as it does primarily on a Marxian definition of the state and Gramsci's concept of hegemony for its understanding of power) fails to fully take into account the role of knowledge systems (professions, expertise, and the mechanisms of surveillance and agenda setting highlighted in this book) in the transnational state apparatus. For these reasons, I draw upon other theoretical work (Bourdieu, 2001; the world polity school, e.g., Boli and Thomas, 1997b; Foucault, 1979; Escobar, 1995; and Perkin, 1996) to complement my use of Robinson's TNS.

18. Robinson, 2001b, 165.

19. Ibid., 158.

20. Ibid., 160. Robinson's main interest is accounting for what he calls "transnational structural formations" that accompany economic globalization. He uses a Marxian definition of the state in his analysis, according to which states themselves are not historical actors; rather, social classes and groups acting in and out of states (and

other institutions) "do" things as collective historical agents. States, therefore, are an instrument reproducing and enforcing class relations and practices.

21. Ibid., 165–66; italics in original.

22. Ibid., 166. Robinson calls these the "twin dimensions of the transnationalization of the state."

23. Ibid., 167.

24. They are a "managerial elite that controls the levers of global policy making," according to Robinson (2001b, 175).

25. Ibid., 167. Robinson argues that this elite cadre of transnational policy makers is largely in the hands of the global rich and powerful; in particular, the emerging transnational capitalist class (TCC). Although I agree with Robinson that this pattern is mostly true in the case of Honduras, I would also argue that the structures of global governance are more contingent than that: these structures may not be as firmly under the control of the TCC as Robinson suggests. This is an empirical question, but my study demonstrates, I believe, that global policy is more porous. There are spaces in the current transnational state for groups and classes other than the capitalist elite to influence global policy making. Although these spaces are subordinate, or, in Robinson's model, "counter-hegemonic," to the dominant procapitalist TCC, they are, nevertheless, important. In these cases, it seems clear the globalizers are involved in a multiplicity of agendas, not simply those benefiting the TCC.

26. Ibid., 188.

27. Interviews with Anita and Art, 1996.

28. "Winter vegetables," referring to crops out of season in the wintertime in the United States or Europe, reveals the global character of their promotion. Builders of Honduran agricultural projects often try to identify such windows of opportunity in the U.S. or European market and encourage Honduran farmers to adjust their planting and harvesting in order to take advantage of these market niches. My interview with Milton made apparent the global dynamics of such projects.

29. Interviews with Milton and Francisco, spring 1996. "Exotic" refers to specialty vegetables used mainly in Asian food restaurants in the U.S. and Europe.

30. Beef and shrimp are two of Honduras's larger exports. Their ecological costs are of concern to Honduran and international environmental groups. "Swine" refers to a Japanese project attempting to establish factory pork farms in Honduras.

31. Honduran agriculture has been subject to outside intervention for centuries. Colonialists promoted and managed agricultural production (of cotton, peanut and palm oils, sugar, etc.) throughout the third world. In earlier periods, however, these initiatives were undertaken primarily by employees of foreign-owned companies or by the colonial authorities themselves in pursuit of profit for the foreigners. Now (at least since the 1960s) the development organizations have taken on and expanded this work. They have done so as largely autonomous institutions of professionals buttressing the activities of the TNCs in order to support transnational capital regardless of its origin (for globalist as opposed to nationalist reasons) and in pursuit (discursively, at least) of local national development.

32. World Bank, 2000, 14.

33. Until recently, outsiders researching the international development profession found it difficult to come by such documents. Most development organizations (and

NGOs) produced these plans for internal use only and kept their contents shielded from public scrutiny. They argued that such documents contained sensitive information and certain contractual obligations and understandings that were, therefore, not appropriate for public examination. The current trend, however, is away from such secrecy. Although many organizational representatives were at first reluctant to share their internal documents with me, most finally agreed to give me copies.

s I x : Building Dams

Epigraph: Loker, 1998, 115.

1. World Bank, 1989, iv.

2. The report states that the El Cajón Dam would be the "least-cost solution . . . compared with the second-best alternative of thermal plants." World Bank, 1980a, 20.

3. Raphael, 1986.

4. In 1980, the year the $800 million El Cajón project was approved, the Honduran annual GDP was U.S.$1.48 billion. Honduras's central government receipts in 1979 were approximately $209 million (World Bank, 1980a).

5. Each of the four Francis turbines used in El Cajón were imported from Switzerland at an approximate cost of $3 million at the time the dam was built. In 1986, when one of the turbines was damaged and needed to be replaced, the cost was $5.5 million.

6. Sklar and McCully, 1994, 12.

7. Ibid., 5.

8. Ibid. See also Rich, 1994; and Ugalde and Jackson, 1995.

9. *The Wapenhans Report,* cited in Sklar and McCully, 1994, 13.

10. In June 1994, for example, 2,154 NGOs from forty-four different countries signed the Manibeli Declaration, named in honor of the village of Manibeli, India, whose inhabitants have resisted the building of the WB-funded Sardar Sarovar Dam. The declaration calls for a moratorium on WB funding of large dams until it fully addresses environmental and resettlement issues from past projects.

11. For an outline of these environmental costs, see Sklar and McCully, 1994; and Dorcey, 1997. Dam advocates point out that these costs must be analyzed in comparison to other power-generating technologies such as thermal or nuclear, which may be even more environmentally problematic.

12. There was one person staffing this department (Rich, 1994; Sklar and McCully, 1994, 26).

13. Sklar and McCully, 1994, 6.

14. World Bank, 1994, "Resettlement and Development," cited in Sklar and McCully, 1994, 5.

15. World Bank study cited in Sklar and McCully, 1994, 14.

16. The literature on the human activity of building dams is too vast to summarize here. Anthropologist Marvin Harris argues that the state was born as a mechanism for resolving human political conflicts over the regulation of water resources in the form of dams and canals (Harris, 1977, 233–50). Social scientists currently emphasize the important role of political structures in the creation of dams; see, e.g., Scudder, 1997.

17. Of course, it is more complex than this. There are many examples of dam projects with private interests in mind. My point is that most dams are constructed with the stated objective of providing a public good.

18. I was not able to verify whether the Harza study was financed in conjunction with development assistance. The first official development assistance loan or grant for energy purposes I was able to find occurred in 1959 when the WB loaned Honduras $1.45 million for an interim power project (Loan 226-HO). The WB gave ENEE another six loans for power projects, totaling approximately $100 million, between 1960 and 1978, including the construction of three relatively small hydroelectric dams (the 30 megawatt Canaveral Dam in 1960; the 46 megawatt Rio Lindo Dam in 1968, expanded to 86 megawatts in 1975; and the 22.5 megawatt Nispero Dam in 1978) (World Bank, 1989, 51).

19. ENEE, 1982, 2.

20. See "Administración del proyecto," in ENEE, 1982, 12.

21. Ibid.; author's translation.

22. Ibid.; author's translation.

23. World Bank, 1980b, 72.

24. They also examined the possibility of locally available building materials.

25. Arriviallaga and Kreuzer, 1981a, 38: "As the short observation period is insufficient for establishing a reliable reservoir operation study, a 50-year synthetic runoff sequence was generated by the Monte Carlo method including both dryer and wetter years than the observed ones."

26. Sklar and McCully, 1994; see also Dorcey, 1997, 77.

27. Arriviallaga and Kreuzer, 1981a, 39.

28. Loker, 1998, citing 1976 Motor Columbus study, 106.

29. The WB first instituted a policy on involuntary resettlement in 1980 (Sklar and McCully, 1994, 19). It has, in recent years, acknowledged its past mistakes and instituted a broader range of policies on the resettlement issue; see, in particular, World Bank, 1994, "Resettlement and Development," cited in Sklar and McCully, 1994, 5. Critics argue that despite these policies the WB record on resettlement remains highly suspect (Loker, 1998; Sklar and McCully, 1994; Rich, 1994; Dorcey, 1997). WB's own study found only three cases (out of hundreds) where resettlement was successful (Sklar and McCully, 1994, 20).

30. World Bank, 1980b, 27.

31. Loker, 1998, 106.

32. Unpublished INA report, 1979, "Informe sobre el levantimiento catastral, avaluo y promoción realizada en el Proyecto Hidroeléctrico El Cajón," cited in Loker, 1998, 106. Loker argues that this number (1,848) was "almost certainly an underestimate."

33. Loker, 1998, 107.

34. Ibid.

35. Ibid., 106.

36. IDB Loan ATF/SF 1460-HO, cited in World Bank, 1980a, 18, 72.

37. "The EBASCO study actually considered some 20 alternative generation installation sequences to find the optimum hydro-thermal generation mix. In addition to El Cajón—at various dam heights, with and without staged construction—these sequences included the installation of other hydroelectric projects in line with their feasible construction schedule." World Bank, 1980a, 38; see also World Bank, 1989, 4–5.

38. World Bank, 1980a, 40.

39. World Bank, 1980b, 20.

40. The 1989 WB evaluation of El Cajón repeatedly uses the words "optimistic" and "over optimistic" in its assessment of the economic evaluation undertaken by EBASCO and approved by Motor Columbus (World Bank, 1989).

41. The two factors were cited in both WB and ENEE documents as principal reasons why El Cajón should be built. See, e.g., World Bank, 1980a; ENEE, 1982.

42. El Cajón project documents cite the "1973 increase in world petroleum prices" as having "deteriorated" ENEE's financial performance (World Bank, 1980a, 29).

43. The IDB was just one of the international development institutions arguing in favor of Central American economic integration. The El Cajón project was likely viewed as contributing to this agenda as well, which may explain some of the optimism it evoked among the globalizers.

44. The WB concluded that "export sales are not necessary to justify the construction of El Cajón" (World Bank, 1980a, 17).

45. "Because of its large size compared to Honduras's home market, the Government has always considered El Cajón to be a project of regional interest. Negotiations have therefore been conducted with both Guatemala and Nicaragua with a view to selling any possible surpluses available." World Bank, 1980a, 17; see also ENEE, 1982, 1.

46. World Bank, 1989, vi and v, respectively.

47. Ibid., 5.

48. The WB's original appraisal report states, "Undertaking a hydroelectric project of the size of El Cajón involves a substantial financial risk for Honduras. Such projects are subject to considerable uncertainties . . . [including] . . . major fluctuations in exchange rates." (World Bank, 1980a, 37). EBASCO's computer programs did not, nonetheless, consider such potential fluctuations.

49. The evaluation states that the possibility of lempira devaluation "appears not to have been perceived" by the EBASCO study and that "indeed, the experience of El Cajón raises the unpleasant question of whether or not the analytic technique was substituted for judgment."

50. See the World Bank, 1980b, 20, which presents the results of this economic analysis. Nowhere in the results are the costs of lost economic revenue related to agricultural production in the region listed. Only the direct costs of construction and relocations and land acquisition (i.e., cash indemnification payments made to people displaced by the reservoir) are considered. The importance of including net agricultural losses in the economic calculations regarding the feasibility of dams is emphasized by dam critics today (see, e.g., Dorcey, 1997; Sklar and McCully, 1994).

51. The 1989 WB Operations Evaluation Department assessment is unequivocal in this regard: "With the benefit of hindsight, it would seem that the Bank placed too much reliance upon the results of the economic justification exercise. . . . The records and recollections are clear: The Bank was preoccupied by El Cajón's size, and yet it nevertheless relied upon a flawed analytic technique whose guidance was contrary to intuition, common sense, and experience. It seems clear in retrospect that reliance was placed on a mechanistic calculation, rather than upon judgment" (World Bank, 1989, 9–10).

52. Ibid.

53. These are the WB's own words; see note 51 above.

54. World Bank, 1989, 5–6.

55. ENEE, 1982, 1–2. Twenty years was the same as the amortization period of most of the project loans.

56. Ibid., appendix, 5; see also World Bank, 1980b, 22.

57. The WB documents (1989) state, "The work force required to complete the Project engineering and administration has been calculated to aggregate 1,455 expatriate and 9,240 local staff months. The average foreign consultant base line cost (excluding travel and subsistence) is US$8,500/staff months."

58. Guifarro, Flores, and Kreuzer, 1996; Gerodetti, 1981; Schulthess, 1985.

59. See, e.g., Arriviallaga and Kreuzer, 1981a, 1981b; Gerodetti, 1981; Schnitter, 1984; Schulthess, 1985; Raphael, 1986.

60. Schnitter, 1984; Raphael, 1986.

61. Raphael, 1986, 1278.

62. These were El Cajón's rankings at the time it was built. Currently, it is the fifth largest dam in the Western Hemisphere and sixteenth tallest in the world.

63. ENEE, 1982, 1.

64. Lopez's tenure was briefly interrupted between 1971 and 1972, when Hondurans elected Ramon Ernesto Cruz as their first civilian president since 1957. Lopez resumed power after leading the military overthrow of Cruz in 1972 and retained it until his ouster by Colonel Juan Alberto Melgar Castro in 1975.

65. There is, in fact, no reference to military rule at all, just the "Honduran government."

66. Sklar and McCully, 1994, 17.

67. World Bank, 1989, ii.

68. The Venezuelan Investment Fund actually provided a total of $55 million in credit. Much of this went directly to ENEE, through the government of Honduras, to cover some of Honduras's contributions to the project's cost.

69. The information in this paragraph has been assembled from various sources, including ENEE, 1982, appendix, 5; World Bank, 1980a, ii, 1; World Bank, 1980b, 72; and World Bank, 1989, 55–60.

70. The Honduran public debt at the time of project approval was approximately $917 million (World Bank, 1980b, 27). El Cajón thus increased the Honduran debt by 85 percent (almost double) to approximately $1.7 billion.

71. ENEE, 1982, 1.

72. World Bank, 1980b, 1.

73. *La Prensa*, June 10, 1994, "Desde que empezó a operar habían fallas en El Cajón."

74. World Bank, 1989, 2–3.

75. The WB report states, "El Cajón, as feared by many *ex-ante*, is, indeed, *ex-post* too big" (World Bank, 1989, vi; emphasis in original).

76. Myton's statement and background are taken from Gollin, 1994.

77. Loker, 1998, 115.

78. World Bank, 1989, 3. It is important to recall that the El Cajón project was the *eighth* power project loan given by international development agencies to ENEE. In other words, ENEE had been working with the globalizers since its inception in 1957. The WB (along with the IDB, USAID, and others) had already coordinated and financed the installation of two small hydroelectric dams, various diesel-powered thermal generators, and transmission/distribution systems throughout the country (World Bank, 1980b, 28). All these projects were coordinated in relation to a larger energy policy framework designed on the basis of ongoing consultant studies (such as those by Harza and Motor Columbus); El Cajón was simply the next step. The decision facing

ENEE and the international development consultants was not so much whether to build El Cajón, but when. Ultimately, the decision was made on the basis of the economic calculation made in the EBASCO study discussed earlier.

79. World Bank, 1989, 3.
80. Ibid.
81. World Bank, 1980b, 12.
82. Ibid., 37.
83. World Bank, 1980a, 18.
84. This is one thing that worked well for the El Cajón builders: final project cost overruns were only 6 percent.
85. World Bank, 1980b, 13.
86. World Bank, 1989, 2.
87. The WB concluded that it was able to achieve "considerable success" in this regard citing, "77% of the costs coming from foreign financing including concessional-term operations by IDA, IDB (Fund for Special Operations), Japan," and others. Nevertheless, the overall package, with a grant element of only 14 percent, did not meet the OECD 25 percent grant-element requirement to qualify it as ODA. In strict terms, it was only partially a development loan. This only strengthens the argument that the international development banks are operating behind a shiny veneer of beneficence. El Cajón was always presented as a "development project"; yet, its cost reveals it was in no way "aid" to Honduras. Honduras paid close to what could be considered full market price for the dam, and the financial institutions providing the credit received profits as a result.
88. World Bank, 1989, 1.
89. Ibid.; emphasis added.
90. ENEE, 1982.
91. Schnitter, 1984.
92. Cited in Loker, 1998, 106.
93. Loker writes that Bajo Aguán was cited as "the most problematic because of bad living conditions in the region, including poor health, educational, and sanitary facilities, low-quality housing, and general neglect of the area by government authorities" (Loker, 106).
94. Loker, 1998, 108.
95. Twenty-seven individuals received approximately 75 percent of the total cash payments actually intended for five hundred families (Loker, 1998, 108–9).
96. The remaining 25 percent reported "some benefits," such as fishing (12 percent) and transportation (6 percent) (Loker, 1998, 109–10).
97. From approximately $2 a day to $1.16 a day, according to Loker's study (Loker, 1998, 110).
98. Loker, 1998, 105.
99. See, e.g., Arriviallaga and Kreuzer, 1981a, 1981b; Raphael, 1986; Schnitter, 1984; Schulthess, 1985.
100. ENEE, 1982, 8.
101. Mangurian, 1997.
102. *El Heraldo*, "Complejo El Cajón recibe el nombre del ilustre procer Centroamericano 'General Francisco Morazán,'" February 19, 1992.

103. Ibid. I assume among these "foreign diplomats" were included some of the representatives from the international development banks and consulting agencies that helped build the dam.

104. Ibid.; translation by author.

105. Ibid.

106. World Bank, 1989, v.

SEVEN : Fixing Dams

1. *Tiempo,* "Inevitable racionamiento de energía a partir de 93," June 25, 1992.

2. *La Prensa,* "Desde que empezó a operar habían fallas en El Cajón," June 10, 1994.

3. *Tiempo,* "Inevitable racionamiento," June 25, 1992.

4. *La Prensa,* "Desde que empezó," June 10, 1994.

5. *La Prensa,* "En peligro la firma de Carta de Intenciones por crisis energética," June 9, 1994.

6. The dam level was 247 m.a.s.l. and falling. El Cajón was therefore contributing only 225 megawatts per day to the Honduran electrical grid. Four older (and smaller) hydroelectric dams in the country were contributing a total of another 121 megawatts. A privately owned power plant was producing 34 megawatts, and ENEE had managed to start four of their older diesel plants, which added another 86 megawatts, for a total of 466 megawatts. The daily Honduran electric demand at the time was 460 megawatts per day.

7. *Tiempo,* "Seguirán racionamientos de la ENEE," February 10, 1994.

8. *El Periódico,* "Aprobar incremento de tarifas pide la ENEE al Congreso," April 20, 1994.

9. *El Periódico,* " 'Bombazos' de la ENEE están acabando con electro domésticos," June 27, 1994.

10. Ibid.

11. *La Tribuna,* "Días y meses a oscuras le esperan a hondureños," April 9, 1994.

12. This paragraph is a brief summary of the extensive research conducted on the El Cajón river basin subsequent to the construction of the dam, most of it funded by the WB and IDB. For a brief account of this research, see Gollin, 1994, and Loker, 1998. For a detailed discussion of these complex hydrological and ecological issues, see Mahmood, 1987.

13. *El Heraldo,* " 'Transcaso' eléctrico será igual al de Callejas: ENEE," April 6, 1994.

14. *El Periódico,* "500 dólares la hora ganarán técnicos que verán El Cajón," April 19, 1994.

15. Ibid.

16. *Tiempo,* "Se nivel de embalse sigue bajando, en dos meses dejará de funcionar represa El Cajón," April 22, 1994.

17. *El Periódico,* "Nada que hacer con El Cajón," April 22, 1994.

18. Ibid. There may have been other consultants as well, including IDB engineer Rolando Yon-Siu, who appeared in the IDB newsletter article, and the original Swiss dam designer, Harald Kreuzer, who coauthored an article on the repair in 1996 (see n. 23 below).

19. Mangurian, 1997, 7.

20. Ibid.
21. Ibid. 6, 7.
22. Ibid.
23. Guifarro, Flores, and Kreuzer, 1996.
24. Ibid.
25. I have not been able to ascertain just how high the rate was. According to original dam hydrological data, the average inflow to the reservoir was 110 cubic meters per second. But during periods of low inflow (during dry months such as April), it was 17 cubic meters per second. It is likely that these original flow rates were overestimated considering the flaws discovered in these data as part of the IDB watershed study referred to earlier (see n. 12). If these data are nevertheless considered to be accurate (in order to make a conservative guess), then the reported leakage rate in 1993 of 1.6 cubic meters per second could be defined as insigificant (in comparison with average inflow, it represents a leakage rate of approximately 1 percent) or significant (in comparison with low inflow, it indicates a rate of about 10 percent). I do not know the rate of water inflow required to run the turbines, but this figure would tend to increase the relative significance of the leak in comparison to both numbers. When I asked a hydraulic engineer (with no experience with hydroelectric dam reservoirs) at the University of Mississippi what he thought, he responded, "That sounds like a pretty big leak." The description of the repair by Guifarro, Flores, and Kreuzer (1996) seems also to support that conclusion.
26. Guifarro, Flores, and Kreuzer, 1996, 2.
27. See note 25 above. These hydrological data are reported in Arriviallaga and Kreuzer, 1981a; and Guifarro, Flores, and Kreuzer, 1996.
28. Guifarro, Flores, and Kreuzer, 1996, 2.
29. Was the low reservoir level itself caused by the leak? Apparently, this would be a difficult thing to establish without detailed hydrological data from the El Cajón basin. According to the hydraulic engineer at the University of Mississippi I interviewed, one would have to consider numerous variables to make this calculation, including the precipitation and evaporation rates within the reservoir catchment area over the period of time in question as well as the amount of outflow required to run the turbines.
30. Guifarro, Flores, and Kreuzer, 1996, 2.
31. David Mangurian's wording; see Mangurian, 1997, 7.
32. Ibid.
33. Ibid.
34. *Tiempo*, "Reina declara emergencia energética," April 22, 1994; *Tiempo*, "Si nivel de embalse sigue bajando, en dos meses dejará de funcionar represa El Cajón," April 22, 1994; *El Periódico*, "A cinco horas sube racionamiento de electricidad," April 25, 1994.
35. *Tiempo*, "Gobierno emite Decreto de Emergencia ante crisis: Autoriza a la ENEE para que adopte cualquier medida que permita superar crisis, menos aumento a tarifas," April 22, 1994.
36. *El Periódico*, "A cinco horas," April 25, 1994.
37. *El Periódico*, "Nada que hacer con El Cajón," April 22, 1994.
38. *Tiempo*, "Comisión de Emergencia ya tiene alternativas para superar la crisis energética," April 29, 1994.

39. *El Periódico*, "Empresa privada promete energía a maquiladoras," April 28, 1994. This is consistent with the global agenda of privatization.

40. *La Prensa*, "Lps. 20 millones diarios pierde economía del país por apagones," May 5, 1994.

41. *El Periódico*, "Reina, único responsible por la crisis energética," April 28, 1994.

42. *La Prensa*, "Varias veces descargaron El Cajón intencionalmente, revela Reina," July 11, 1994.

43. *La Prensa*, "El Cajón llega a su agonía," May 26, 1994.

44. *La Prensa*, "Ni un diluvio salva a El Cajón," May 27, 1994.

45. *La Prensa*, "ENEE racionará energía también en la madrugada," May 26, 1994.

46. *La Prensa*, "Lps. 20 millones diarios," May 5, 1994.

47. *El Periódico*, "Hay que rezarle a la Virgen para que llene 'El Cajón,'" April 26, 1994.

48. *El Nuevo Día*, "El Cajón se paralizará si no llueve en 15 días," June 23, 1994.

49. *La Prensa*, "A 9 metros del caos," June 9, 1994.

50. *El Periódico*, "Un pueblo en tinieblas," June 30, 1994.

51. *La Prensa*, "Norteamericanos inician el bombardeo de nubes," June 27, 1994.

52. *Tiempo*, "En doce días deja de funcionar El Cajón," June 23, 1994.

53. *El Periódico*, "Un pueblo en tinieblas," June 30, 1994.

54. *Tiempo*, "Pararán de un momento a otro una turbina de El Cajón," July 1, 1994.

55. *El Periódico*, "¡PARALIZADA! Primera turbina," July 2, 1994.

56. *La Prensa*, "Paralizada turbina de El Cajón por bajo volumen de agua," July 2, 1994.

57. *Tiempo*, "Renuncia el gerente de la ENEE," July 22, 1994.

58. *La Prensa*, "Hoy nos devuelvan la luz," December 14, 1994.

59. *La Prensa*, "El fin del reino de las velas," December 14, 1994.

60. *El Periódico*, "Más de 120 millones de dólares de pérdidas," December 15, 1994.

61. *El Nuevo Día*, "Sequía y racionamiento eléctrico, mayores causantes en baja del PIB," March 28, 1995.

62. Guifaro, Flores, and Kreuzer, 1996, 43.

63. IDB press release, "IDB and Honduras Sign Contracts for $36.82 Million for Energy Program," PR2012, NR-033/95, February 15, 1995.

64. Fox and Brown, 1998, 12.

65. Although these engineering firms are private companies, inasmuch as they are subcontracted by the development banks and engaged in the economic politics of the development organizations, they are globalizers as I have defined them.

66. Loker, 1998, 114–15.

67. Ibid., 116.

68. Some dam activists have argued that the legal doctrine of "odious debts" (based on a 1900 treaty between the United States and Spain) may provide a mechanism for redress. The doctrine "frees citizens of a country from obligation to repay debts incurred without their consent for purposes contrary to their interests" (see Sklar and McCully, 1994, 17, citing Patricia Adams, *Odious Debts*).

69. I would like to thank my brother and civil engineer Chris Jackson for helping me understand the contractual obligations in place in the Milwaukee case and how they might relate to El Cajón.

70. Cited in Rich, 1994.

71. This raises the question of accountability. The issue has been the subject of much scholarly attention in recent years, but I believe the case of El Cajón indicates the need for further sociological analysis of emergent transnational legal frameworks that might be used by the recipients of development assistance when making contractual agreements with international development agencies to avoid getting burned by flawed development projects. Just as local communities in developed regions of the world build guarantees into their public works contracts at the local or national level, so too might there be the possibility for developing countries to build safeguards into the negotiations and contracts they make with international development agencies. Much research is being conducted in the area of international legal contracts with transnational businesses and how those contracts are being created and enforced in the new global political economy. Similar attention should be paid to the creation of international contracts in the public sector.

72. McMichael, 1996; Sklair, 1995; Robinson, 1996a.

73. Loker, 1998, 114.

74. This is another example of how my framework differs from William Robinson's model of the transnational state. His model would not include the development professionals discussed in this chapter as part of the institutions of global governance; these development professionals are much more important than Robinson's model would suggest.

EIGHT: Making *Maquiladoras*

1. In my undergraduate sociology class at the University of Mississippi, I assign students the task of examining twenty items of clothing from their closets to illustrate the global assembly line. Approximately 90 percent report possessing at least one item with the label "Made in Honduras" or "Assembled in Honduras."

2. See, e.g., Sklair, 1995, 108 ("introducing"); Barnet and Cavanagh, 1994, 254 ("setting up plants"); and McMichael, 1996, 88 ("moving").

3. Nissan's decision to locate an assembly plant in Jackson, Mississippi, for example, followed consideration of alternative sites in other states. Each state government put together a team of public officials who negotiated with Nissan, and Nissan made its decision based on the most attractive tax-incentive package. Such tax-incentive packages can be granted only by political institutions. The state of Mississippi offered a $295 million incentive package that clinched the deal ("Nissan Incentive Package a Good Deal, Musgrove Says," *Commercial Appeal,* June 20, 2002).

4. For general information on the history of export processing zones, see Sklair, 1995, 108–19; McMichael, 1996, 92–96; and Schaeffer, 2003, 134–35.

5. For information on offshore assembly practices of U.S. manufacturing firms such as Nike, see Barnet and Cavanaugh, 1994 (pp. 325–29 in particular); and LaFeber, 1999.

6. As indicated in chapter 5, this is consistent with Robinson's second global agenda promoted by the transnational state: "foster broad economic policies which promote macroeconomic stability, foreign investment, and export-oriented economic growth."

7. Following the 1984 passage of the CBI, U.S. assistance to the region increased by 40 percent, with the majority of this aid going to private sector development programs;

see "Aiding and Abetting Corporate Flight: USAID in the Caribbean Basin," *Multinational Monitor* (January/February 1993), 40.

8. See House Subcommittee on International Economic Policy and Trade of the Committee on Foreign Affairs, *Foreign Assistance Legislation for Fiscal Years 1984–85, Part 6*, 98th Cong., 1st sess., Bureau of Private Enterprise, Trade and Development Program, March 9, 1983, 7.

9. These initiatives were labeled "investment promotion" activities; see House Subcommittee on International Economic Policy and Trade, *Foreign Assistance*, 11. Also significant in this process was the U.S. government's Trade and Development Program (TDP), which, along with USAID and the Overseas Private Investment Corporation (OPIC), make up the U.S. government's International Development Cooperation Agency. The TDP was instrumental in advancing the new policy focus of the U.S. government, which emphasized "leveraging private funds" and fostering "private enterprise" in promoting development goals throughout the third world. Although the activities of TDP and OPIC are relevant to the Honduran case (both carried out work in relation to the development of export processing zones), neither body is as important as USAID, and so I focus only on USAID's projects in this chapter.

10. House Subcommittee on International Economic Policy and Trade, *Foreign Assistance*, 22.

11. Ibid., 51–52.

12. Ibid.

13. "Aiding and Abetting Corporate Flight," *Multinational Monitor*, 40.

14. GAO, 1993.

15. USAID, 1983.

16. GAO, 1993.

17. Ibid.

18. Petersen, 1992.⎫
19. Ibid., 13.   ⎬⎰

20. Ibid. USAID promotion of offshore assembly zones in these countries was actually even more significant than in Honduras.

21. Casco, 1996; Moncada Valledares, 1995.

22. Casco, 1996.

23. Ibid.

24. CONADI is another example of a Honduran institution formed in association with a USAID initiative. USAID and the IDB provided development assistance grants and loans to CONADI members (entrepreneurs and local business elites) to encourage them to invest in export-oriented businesses. In 1993, CONADI was involved in a huge scandal when it was discovered that many of the entrepreneurial projects it had initiated were, in fact, nonexistent. Apparently, some of the entrepreneurs had simply pocketed the money. The scandal also affected the Honduran government since the IDB loan to CONADI had to be repaid from Honduran public revenues. The press portrayed the CONADI businessmen as "crooks" who had gotten rich off public monies. See Moncada Valledares, 1995, 4–5.

25. The information in this paragraph is taken from USAID project documents, in particular the "Evaluation of FIDE" conducted by Cole, Hurwitz, and Shroy, of Nathan Associates, Inc., August, 18, 1986, 34; personal copy.

26. See House Subcommittee on International Economic Policy and Trade, *Foreign Assistance*, 6, where BPE assistant administrator Elise DuPont states, "From the outset, the Bureau [BPE] has established a series of relationships with American businesses and business organizations. Through these links, AID is able to capitalize on the management experience, technical/technology skills, and other resources to implement private sector strategies requiring business expertise not otherwise available to the Agency."

27. These institutions are specified in USAID, "Project Paper, Honduras: Export Development and Services (Project No. 522-0207)," August 6, 1984, annex F.1, p. 12; personal copy . The project paper also mentions "a whole array of other public and private sector institutions in the U.S. and in other countries of Europe and Latin America." Although it cannot be ascertained that these business organizations were part of the original reconnaissance teams that traveled to Honduras in the early 1980s, it seems clear that, upon its creation, FIDE was to establish linkages with these institutions. The specific mention of these institutions in the 1984 project paper suggests these agencies were likely aware of FIDE's potentially significant role in promoting exports in Honduras. Some, such as the IESC, were mentioned in the congressional hearings at the time as being centrally involved even before 1984; see House Subcommittee on International Economic Policy and Trade, *Foreign Assistance*, 8, 143.

28. According to USAID documents, GEMAH "was created as an AID project" and received almost all its funding from USAID at the time FIDE was founded. HAMCHAM had received two USAID grants as of 1984. ANDI and ANEXHON both worked closely with USAID and had received its financial support to carry out their work; they also participated in USAID seminars and trainings geared toward promoting free-trade zones and export promotion in the early 1980s; see "Evaluation of FIDE," 20–23.

29. From USAID, "Project Paper, Honduras," annex F.1, p. 1.

30. See "Evaluation of FIDE," annex 1, p. 1.

31. The likelihood USAID had envisioned FIDE as the main channel for its promotion of the export processing zones seems high because most project documents refer simultaneously to the establishment of FIDE and the goals of the export promotion project. The 1994 evaluation of FIDE (again by Nathan Associates) states, "The purpose of the Export Development and Services (EDS) project was to promote economic growth and employment through promotion of nontraditional exports, both manufactured goods and agriculture. The Foundation for Research and Business Development (FIDE) was established in February 1984 *to implement the component of the project concentrating on nontraditional manufactured exports.*" See Boles and Rourke, Nathan Associates, Inc., "Final Evaluation for Fundación de Inversiones y Desarrollo de Exportaciones (FIDE)," October 1994, USAID document, personal copy; emphasis added.

32. These studies are cited along with several others in USAID, "Project Paper, Honduras," 56.

33. Ibid., annex F.2, p. 37.

34. USAID's plan included industrial and agricultural exports; however, this chapter focuses only on the industrial aspects of the project. Nevertheless, a similar process was used by the globalizers in promoting agricultural exports. For example, USAID advocated and eventually passed through the Honduran government's legislative process

the Agricultural Modernization Law of 1992. It also financed and supported, as with FIDE, the activities of the Federation of Agricultural Export Producers of Honduras for the promotion of agricultural exports (USAID, "Project Paper, Honduras").

35. Abstract for "USAID Project Paper, Honduras: Export Development and Services," USAID Development Experience Clearinghouse System, *http://www.dec.org/search/dexs*; accessed September 25, 2003. The final agreement signed by the government of Honduras was also unequivocal: "The GOH will modify its export policies which at present favor import substitution industries and impose important disincentives and practical constraints to the development of non-traditional exports. The GOH will implement the following policy changes needed to improve the environment for exporting: 1. reduce the costs imposed on export operations . . . [by] the need to obtain . . . permits . . . 2. support legislation which will authorize the temporary importation, without payment of taxes or charges of any kind, of raw materials, machinery, and equipment needed to produce products for export to areas outside Central America . . . 3. speed up the process for obtaining government permits of natural resource exploitation . . . 5. examine the potential for expansion and use of industrial parks and free trade zones to encourage the development of labor-intensive industries. . . ." *Project Agreement between the Republic of Honduras and the United States of America for Export Development and Services*, Tegucigalpa, Honduras, August 31, 1984, 3; personal copy.

36. The project document reads: "The Export Policy Advisor will assist the GOH to completely review its export policies and develop a revised set of export incentives." Other advisers, it states, "will help the Ministry of Economy to plan its program of training for GOH . . . representatives and develop its information system to support those representatives on a continuing basis. He is expected to be a PASA employee from the Department of Commerce Foreign Commercial Service [a U.S. government agency]." USAID, "Project Paper, Honduras," annex F.2. pp. 2–3.

37. Abstract for "USAID Project Paper, Honduras."

38. Ibid.

39. Ibid.

40. House Subcommittee on Western Hemisphere Affairs of the Committee on Foreign Affairs, *Foreign Assistance Legislation for Fiscal Year 1985, Part 6, Review of Proposed Economic and Security Assistance Requests for Latin America and the Caribbean, Recommendations of the National Bipartisan Commission on Central America*, 98th Cong., 2nd sess., Feb. 8, 21, 22, 23, Mar. 1, 1984, 93.

41. The *Project Agreement* (p. 13) stipulated, for instance, that any shipping services required under the project grant funds had to go to cargo ships sailing under the U.S. flag and any vehicle purchased for the project had to be of U.S. manufacture.

42. Author's calculations based on USAID, "Project Paper, Honduras," 19, 52–53; annex F.1, p. 10; annex F.2, pp. 5–7, 18. Some examples include an "export policy adviser" to be hired for two years at $100,000 per year; a "new products development adviser" at approximately $80,000 per year; and a "labor-intensive industries adviser" at $131,000 per three-month rotation. For the agricultural exports component of the project (not discussed in this chapter), there were "cocoa development specialists" ($100,000/year), "citrus development specialists" ($100,000), and "short-term vegetable advisers" ($12,500/month). Ibid., 53; annex F.2, pp. 2–17.

43. Abstract for "USAID Project Paper, Honduras."

44. As with any development loan, this loan was to be paid back on highly conces-sional terms: over the course of forty years at 2 percent interest for the first ten years, 3 percent after that; *Project Agreement,* 1.

45. The *Project Agreement* reads: "[certain] legislation [required by the project] will be enacted prior to the disbursement of Project funds. Regulations and implementa-tion procedures for this legislation will be put into effect prior to initiating disburse-ments under the Project."

46. See GAO, 1993.

47. Ibid.

48. Ibid., 25–26.

49. This conclusion is further supported by the inclusion in the original USAID project documents of a copy of one such "anteproyecto" (USAID, "Project Paper, Hon-duras," annex G.2, pp. 1–17).

50. This information is found in the 1986 "Evaluation of FIDE," cited above (see n. 25), 19. Mr. Bendeck later became president of COHEP; see *La Tribuna,* "Empresa privada suspende pláticas con obreros," June 7, 1996.

51. Interview with Greg Lamar, fall 1995 (see chapter 1). In addition, according to the NLC, CADERH received over $13 million from USAID between 1984 and 1990 (NLC, 1992, 8).

52. See Mas Dinero, "FIDE Brings Jobs to Honduras," *Honduras This Week,* Janu-ary 13, 1996. See also GAO, 1993.

53. Ad cited in Moncada Valledares, 1995, 15.

54. FIDE information packet; personal copy. After calling one of the numbers in a FIDE ad, I received a packet of information in spring 1998.

55. Echoing the requirement in USAID project documents that such a "one-stop" center be established (*Project Agreement,* p. 5).

56. FIDE information packet.

57. Boles and Rourke, "Final Evaluation," 4. The conclusion reads: "roughly 35,000 new jobs . . . The employment generation attributed to FIDE's efforts has served to alleviate poverty. Nearly half of the new hires (63% of the women) for the export ap-parel operations were previously unemployed. . . . On average, earnings for apparel in-dustry workers are 80% higher than their previous earnings level and run 20–30% over the current minimum wage. Surveys undertaken in 1992 and 1993 in communities where the apparel assembly operations are located also show significant improvement in quality of life indicators." I was unable to locate copies of the surveys referred to here. As the next chapter tells, these conclusions are the subject of much debate.

58. See Joel Millman, "Bienvenidos, Tigers! Modern Capitalism Is Coming to Central America, and Who Is Bringing It? Koreans and Chinese," *Forbes,* May 27, 1991, 190–91.

59. Ibid., 190.

60. Ibid., 191.

61. Global Fashions' work for Wal-Mart's Kathie Lee Gifford clothing line became embroiled in a major controversy in the United States in 1996; see chapter 9 for details.

62. Moncada Valledares, 1995.

63. See Moncada Valledares, 1995. They were: ZIP Búfalo, ZIP Choloma #1 and #2, ZIP San Miguel, ZIP Villanueva, ZIP Buenavista, ZIP Continental, ZIP San Pedro Sula,

ZIP El Progreso, ZIP Puerto Cortés, and ZIP Tegucigalpa. In addition, there were six "free trade zones" (subject to different regulations): Zona Libre La Ceiba, Zona Libre Tela, Zona Libre Puerto Cortes, Zona Libre INHDELVA, Zona Libre Galaxy, and Zona Libre Empresas Independientes.

64. "Honduran Apparel Manufacturing Industry," *Destination Honduras 2001* (San Pedro Sula: ABC Publicaciones de Centroamérica, Grupo Nación, 2001), 56.

65. Banco Central de Honduras, Departamento de Estudios Económicos, "Actividad económica de las empresas maquiladoras en Honduras (zonas libres y de procesamiento industrial), 1990–1994," Tegucigalpa, M.D.C, September 1995.

66. "Honduran Apparel Manufacturing Industry," 56; according to the Honduran Manufacturers Association, during 2000–2003 employment in these zones ranged between 107,000 and 125,000 (*El Tejedor,* AHM online magazine, *http://ahm_honduras.com/ tejedor_english/estadisticos.html*).

67. Banco Central de Honduras, Departamento de Estudios Económicos, "Actividad económica de las empresas maquiladoras en Honduras (zonas libres y de procesamiento industrial), 1990–1994," Tegucigalpa, M.D.C, September 1995.

68. House Subcommittee on International Operations and Human Rights of the Committee on International Relations, *Child Labor,* 104th Cong., 2nd sess., June 11, July 15, 1996, 31.

69. FIDE, "Honduras: For Profitable Investment and Gracious Living," 7; personal copy; U.S. Department of Commerce, "TradeStats Express: National Trade Data," *http://tse.export.gov*; accessed December 12, 2004.

N I N E : Legitimating *Maquiladoras*

1. *La Tribuna,* "No queremos que se vayan maquiladoras de Honduras," June 20, 1996.

2. Of the approximately 50,000 maquila workers employed in over 175 factories located within the new export processing zones by 1995, there were sixteen registered unions representing 7,500 members; see Moncada Valladares, 1995, 49.

3. Ibid., 45–48.

4. *El Heraldo,* "Vandalismo!" February 13, 1996.

5. CODEH received funds from many European ODA agencies as well as international human rights and labor rights organizations. In the years of the maquiladora scandal in Honduras, CODEH enjoyed support from the ILO, NLC, and the Spanish government; see, e.g., Moncada Valledares, 1995; and *La Tribuna,* "Con proyecto financiado por españoles: Obreros lucharán por sus derechos en maquiladoras," January 22, 1996.

6. This study is cited in Charles Kernaghan's congressional hearing presentation, Senate Subcommittee on Labor of the Committee on Labor and Human Resources, *Child Labor and the New Global Marketplace: Reaping Profits at the Expense of Children?* 103rd Cong., 2nd sess., September 21, 1994, 69.

7. Larry Rohter, "Hondurans in 'Sweatshops' See Opportunity," *New York Times,* July 18, 1996, A14.

8. FIDE pointed out, for instance, that whereas in 1985 Honduras occupied eighteenth place in terms of exports to the United States, by 1992, it had risen to number seven, ahead of Argentina, Venezuela, Jamaica, Bahamas, Peru, El Salvador, Chile,

Trinidad and Tobago, Uruguay, Haiti, Panama, Bolivia, and Paraguay (Moncada Valledares, 1995, 13). In 2003, it was number three.

9. Ibid., 1995.

10. This is likely because all of the major newspapers in Honduras are owned by wealthy businessmen who are unsympathetic to the union's perspective on this issue and would be unlikely to present their foreign ties as problematic.

11. *Multinational Monitor,* "Women and Children First" (January/February 1993), 30–32; Rohter, "Hondurans in 'Sweatshops' See Opportunity"; *Business Week,* "Cleanup at the Maquiladora," July 29, 1996, 48.

12. "Hire Rosa Martinez!" *Sixty Minutes,* September 27, 1992, transcript, 14–20.

13. Ibid., 18–19

14. *Senate Consideration of HR 5368,* 102nd Cong., 2nd sess., *Congressional Record* 138 (September 30, 1992), H. 28938.

15. Public Law 102–391, Section 599, passed October 6, 1992.

16. The GAO report (1993, 42) stated, "AID and other U.S. agencies have made a contribution to the growth of these industries—through policy dialogue, export processing zone financing, and other programs—but this support was not the deciding factor in company investment decisions. . . . As illustrated by the growth of Mexico's maquiladora industry, U.S. foreign assistance funds did not have to be expended to support growth in production sharing—U.S. companies are well acquainted with the concept. U.S. government support may, however, have helped countries popularly perceived as less desirable locations to benefit from the growth in offshore assembly."

17. The sociological literature on NGOs is too vast to summarize here. For a general discussion of NGOs as a part of the international development profession, see Fox and Brown, 1998; Edwards and Hulme, 1996; and Fisher, 1998.

18. This is an important fact regarding development projects. Especially if they are successful, they tend to thrive even after international support has subsided and the globalizers have moved on to promote another global agenda.

19. USAID continued to defend its promotion of the maquiladoras in Honduras, citing the economic benefits of the project to Honduras and U.S. businesses. Their argument hinged on the claim that U.S. businesses were already well aware of offshore assembly as an option and that their activities in no way caused any U.S. business to shut its doors in the United States and move to Honduras. The GAO came to a similar conclusion in its 1993 report in connection with the 1992 congressional amendment curtailing the USAID program. Nevertheless, USAID was never again involved in promoting export processing zones in Honduras.

20. Interview with Charles Kernaghan, from Kathy Jones, "The Guy Who Made Kathie Lee Cry," *Albion Monitor,* no. 21, p. 1, *http://www.monitor.net/monitor;* accessed August 26, 2003.

21. Ibid., 3.

22. Senate Subcommittee on Labor, *Child Labor and the New Global Marketplace.*

23. Lesly's testimony is available in its entirety in ibid., 5–7.

24. Ibid., 7, 72.

25. That the same U.S. Congress which ten years before had been emphatic in its approval of the project paving the way for the maquiladoras in Honduras and else-

where was now in part condemning them reveals the complexity of the advancement of global agendas.

26. See, e.g., *Business Week*, "Cleanup at the Maquiladora," July 29, 1996.

27. Charles Kernaghan claimed to have counted 130 workers under the age of fourteen in just one of the Honduran plants he visited; see Jones, "The Guy Who Made Kathie Lee Cry," 7.

28. See Rachel Sylvester and Joe Smith, "Exposed: Shame of Gap's Child Labour Sweatshops," *The Electronic Telegraph*, January 22, 1996, *http://www.telegraph.co.uk*; accessed July 16, 1997; and Rachel Sylvester and Joe Smith, "Credibility Gap: How a Politically Correct Clothes Company Uses Cheap Child Labor," *The Electronic Telegraph*, January 22, 1996, *http://www.telegraph.co.uk*; accessed July 16, 1997.

29. During his testimony, Kernaghan also leveled accusations against Walt Disney in connection with its use of child labor in the production of Pocohontas T-shirts in Haiti (House Subcommittee on International Operations and Human Rights of the Committee on International Relations, *Child Labor*, 104th Cong., 2nd sess., June 11, July 15, 1996, 48).

30. "Human Rights Group Hits Kathie Lee Collection," *Women's Wear Daily*, April 30, 1996, 171, no. 84, 3.

31. House Subcommittee on International Operations and Human Rights, *Child Labor*, 49.

32. Ibid.

33. Ibid., 70.

34. Ibid. Some voices in the apparel industry, e.g., the trade magazine *Bobbin*, criticized Gifford's decision to testify as "naïve" and expressed concern such tactics resulted in a "gross distortion of the actual working conditions in maquila factories offshore." These critics claimed that Gifford was being manipulated by labor activists and that, though other celebrities such as Michael Jordan, Jaclyn Smith, and Cheryl Tiegs had chosen to ignore or rebut the media attacks, only Gifford "rose to the bait" (*Bobbin*, October 1996, 82).

35. This according to Charles Kernaghan, who was present at the meeting and reported these statements before the U.S. congressional committee on June 11, 1996 (House Subcommittee on International Operations and Human Rights, *Child Labor*, 34–35).

36. Jones, "The Guy Who Made Kathie Lee Cry," 1.

37. House Subcommittee on International Operations and Human Rights, *Child Labor*, 35. The Gifford episode highlights the role of the globalizers in building global political arrangements. Gifford is not a globalizer as I have defined this term; but she is participating in a new global political space. The globalizers in this case are the international labor NGOs (such as Kernaghan's organization) that put the Honduran maquiladora labor conditions under the spotlight. These organizations prompted the creation of the international political nexus through which transnational garment corporations and Honduran maquiladora workers could negotiate new international rules and standards regarding transnational labor practices. It is notable that this global political nexus was largely created in Washington, D.C., in the form of U.S. congressional debates and subsequent legislation. But this nexus extends transnationally to Europe, Asia, and Central America as well. And, as becomes clear below, it is not the

U.S. Congress that implements solutions to the labor problems in Honduras; it is the NGOs stepping in to legitimate the maquilas.

38. House Subcommittee on International Operations and Human Rights, *Child Labor,* 31–33.

39. Ibid.

40. Ibid., 45.

41. Ibid., 46–47. Representative Moran later chastised Canahuati for the reports he heard that Wendy Díaz was being labeled a "traitor" in the Honduran press for testifying before the U.S. Congress in a manner that might hurt the Honduran apparel industry. He said, "I am sure Mr. Canahuati is going to rectify this situation and make sure that Ms. Díaz is appreciated . . . and that she is not punished. I am sure that you are going to tend to that, Mr. Canahuati" (p. 49).

42. Carl and Mark, two USAID employees I interviewed in 1996, for example, both expressed approval for the actions of the anti-sweatshop NGOs.

43. Testimony of U.S. Department of Labor administrator Maria Echaveste before Congress; see House Subcommittee on International Operations and Human Rights, *Child Labor,* 17, 20.

44. Ibid., 28.

45. Ibid., 15. Miller said, "You have a whole series of contractual relationships that are really there to camouflage what is really taking place. [The companies] have created a whole system of deniability."

46. Senate Subcommittee on Labor, *Child Labor and the New Global Marketplace,* 35.

47. This account is based on discussions I had while in Honduras with several individuals who attended meetings with the Gap executives.

48. Personal interview, spring 1996.

49. Interview with Dennis Smith, founding member of the Central American labor NGO COVERCO, spring 2003.

50. I know of no available data that could be used to compare the relative benefits that TNC apparel companies and U.S. consumers receive compared to Honduran investors and Honduran workers. Although such an economistic calculation is beyond the scope of this study, I assume the asymmetrical interdependence between TNCs and their Honduran counterparts in the international offshore assembly production process yields far greater profits (in absolute terms) to the TNCs.

51. Recall interview with Milton, USAID, Honduras, spring 1996 (see p. 233–34).

52. Such was the case for my friend mentioned in connection with the Gap visit. She later found a job as director for a prominent labor rights monitoring NGO in the United States.

TEN: Rebuilding after Hurricane Mitch

1. Gass, 2002, 4.

2. Hurricane Camille recorded 905 millibars in 1969.

3. One of the few benefits of Hurricane Mitch is that it filled the El Cajón reservoir. Despite some concerns regarding its holding capacity, the dam held and is considered responsible for saving numerous downstream towns and cities from the

destructive flooding that swamped Tegucigalpa and Choluteca. In addition, the filled reservoir restored the dam to its full generating capacity of 300 megawatts, a boon at a time when electrical energy in much of Honduras was shut down and petroleum for diesel-powered generation was not easily transported because of washed-out roads. These economic and social benefits provided by El Cajón during the Mitch crisis would have to be added to the ongoing tally regarding its overall benefits and costs to Honduras. Unfortunately, on February 13, 1999, only four months after the hurricane, El Cajón experienced a major fire in its powerhouse. The fire completely destroyed one of the four transformers and damaged the high voltage transmission cables of all four generating units. The plant was completely shut down for repairs and Honduras was again forced to undergo energy rationing until mid-June 1999, when 100 megawatts of new thermal plants came on line and most of El Cajón's turbines were reactivated. The damage assessment and transmission cable repairs were conducted by ALCATEL of Canada with funding from Sweden and the WB. Currently, all the turbines have been reactivated and the dam is functioning at full capacity. (Information taken from a WB report, "Visit by the World Bank Executive Directors," February 23–26, 1999; personal copy.)

4. The maquiladoras, for the most part, did not sustain hurricane damage. Although several were closed for one or two days as workers faced difficulty getting to work, most maquiladoras were running normally in a matter of days; see "Mitch Leaves Nation in Ruins," *Honduras This Week*, November 7, 1998, 5.

5. COPECO was a Honduran military institution created after Hurricane Fifi in 1974. This description of COPECO was common among the globalizers I interviewed as well as in the press (see, e.g., *La Tribuna*, "La necesaria reorientación de COPECO," February 1, 1999).

6. "Mayor Castellanos Killed in Copter Crash," *Honduras This Week*, November 7, 1998.

7. This chapter is based on twenty in-depth and twenty-six informal interviews conducted by the author in July and August 2001 with development workers and Honduran government officials who had worked on projects related to Hurricane Mitch. These interviews included seven key players from major development organizations (e.g., USAID, GTZ, ACDI, AECI, and the WB) who were in Honduras at the time of the hurricane and who participated in the consultative group meetings that directed much of the reconstruction process. They also include two pivotal Honduran government ministers who were members of the Honduran president's reconstruction cabinet and involved in presenting the Honduran master plan to the donor countries in Stockholm. These interviewees also provided me with hundreds of documents, photographs, reports, press clippings, and videos documenting in detail many aspects of the Hurricane Mitch reconstruction process.

8. The importance of the international development profession in Honduras was only strengthened following Mitch because of the overwhelming need for this assistance. In addition, whereas prior to Mitch the international organizations working in Honduras tended to operate somewhat independently from one another, after Mitch development assistance became coordinated in a formal structure of donor cooperation that, along with the Honduran government counterparts, assumed a full-fledged international governing body.

9. Although the real names of many individuals involved in the Hurricane recovery appear in this chapter (based on press clippings or publicly available reports), my interviewees (e.g., David) are given pseudonyms to protect their anonymity.

10. David's perspective on the crisis should not be taken as the only one held at the time of the events. A Honduran minister I interviewed, for example, told a slightly different version of events in which the president and the government were presented as the catalysts for the original planning meeting at the hotel; according to the government, it was in control. The foreign globalizers seemed happy to go along with this version of reality, even as they may have had greater influence than such a construction implies.

11. The group David is referring to was the president's National Unit for Technical Support (Unidad de Apoyo Técnico, UNAT), basically a presidential advisory board. In response to Hurricane Mitch, the president later set up the National Reconstruction Cabinet, discussed later in the chapter.

12. IDB press release, "IDB to Host Meeting of Emergency Consultative Group Regarding Hurricane Mitch," November 9, 1998; personal copy.

13. The countries were Honduras, Nicaragua, Guatemala, El Salvador, and Costa Rica.

14. UNDP, "Project Budget HON/98/029: Support to Civil Society's Effort to Initiate Reconstruction of Honduras"; official project document, personal copy. The funds were particularly designated to support civil society initiatives.

15. This was the perspective of one of the Honduran ministers I interviewed, July 2001.

16. "World Bank Announces Immediate Actions," *Honduras This Week,* November 14, 1998. The announcement was made at a press conference on November 5, 1998.

17. *Estimaciones preliminares sobre daños causados por el Huracán Mitch a la infraestructura pública y costos de recuperación,* November 19, 1998; personal copy.

18. United Nations/ CEPAL, 1999.

19. Ibid., 1.

20. The CEPAL report was released to the public on January 12, 1999. *El Heraldo,* "'Mitch' ocasionó pérdidas por $4,364.8 millones a Honduras," January 12, 1999.

21. *El Heraldo,* "Prevención y ordenamiento territorial piden expectos," April 16, 1999.

22. *El Heraldo,* "U.E. diseñará plan para reconstruir a Honduras," February 10, 1999.

23. This was finance minister Gabriela Nuñez; *La Tribuna,* "Falta de dinero limita labor de Gabinete de la Reconstrucción," February 24, 1999.

24. Lozano in particular faced accusations of corruption; Lozano's family owned a road-construction business that received some road-building contracts related to Mitch.

25. *El Heraldo,* "Honduras está atrasada con su plan de reconstrucción," February 20, 1999.

26. *La Tribuna,* "BM quiere saber si su apoyo es efectivo," February 24, 1999.

27. According to David, for example, donors were already eyeing the bridge-building possibilities: "The bilaterals were interested in the roads and bridges early on. They wanted to do those."

28. *El Tiempo*, "Tegucigalpa es peor que Sarajevo: Ministro sueco," January 7, 1999; *La Prensa*, "Urgen soluciones al 'Mitch Social,'" January 9, 1999.

29. *La Tribuna*, "Batalla campal entre policías y damnificados," January 20, 1999.

30. *El Heraldo*, "Pollo, carne y terrenos piden 300 damnificados en protesta," January 7, 1999.

31. *El Heraldo*, "Elaboran plan de reconstrucción que llevarán a Estocolmo, Suecia," January 22, 1999.

32. July 2001 interview with Swedish aid worker who participated in these discussions.

33. *El Heraldo*, "El CATIE y la sociedad civil diseñan reconstrucción regional," January 13, 1999.

34. *La Tribuna*, "Informe del comisionado denuncia irregularidades en entrega de ayuda," March 17, 1999.

35. *El Tiempo*, "Se arruinan donaciones en bodegas de 'La Mesa,'" January 23, 1999. The government claimed, in some cases, to have lost track of the containers in the midst of the overwhelming task of coordinating all the humanitarian assistance coming into the country immediately following the hurricane. In others, the containers had been addressed to organizations that simply never came to pick them up; in these cases, it was usually NGOs (and less often Honduran government agencies) that either did not know the containers had arrived or were unable to pick them up.

36. *La Tribuna*, "EUA dona Lps. 4.5 millones para auditaje de la reconstrucción," January 27, 1999; *La Tribuna*, "Más de $500 mil dispone la AID para contratar empresa auditoría," March 11, 1999.

37. *El Heraldo*, "El gobierno ya tiene auditorías internacionales: Gustavo Alfaro," March 11, 1999.

38. *La Tribuna*, "Tres firmas internacionales fiscalizarán manejo de ayudas," May 14, 1999; *El Heraldo*, "El gobierno ya tiene auditorías internacionales: Gustavo Alfaro," March 11, 1999.

39. *La Tribuna*, "Repelente contra corrupción . . . ," May 14, 1999.

40. *La Tribuna*, "Anunciada supervisión de ayuda de los EEUU no debe ofendernos," March 11, 1999.

41. *La Tribuna*, "Repelente contra corrupción . . . ," May 14, 1999.

42. Honduran business organizations were among the most vocal in expressing their concerns regarding the top-secret plan. Leaders from the Honduran Council of Private Enterprise (COHEP) were part of FONAC and used their meeting with the reconstruction cabinet as an opportunity to make sure their concerns were heard. COHEP urged the cabinet's master plan give priority to infrastructure. The business leaders believed these concrete measures—building bridges and ports, restoring the country's road and telecommunications networks—were the most vital for restoring the Honduran economy.

43. *El Tiempo*, "Organizaciones de la sociedad civil harán propuesta de reconstrucción," March 12, 1999.

44. Ibid.

45. *El Tiempo*, "Representantes de la sociedad civil también viajarán a Estocolmo," March 25, 1999.

46. *La Prensa*, "Gobierno busca consenso entre ministros sobre plan maestro de reconstrucción," March 13, 1999.

47. These NGOs were, according to newspaper accounts: Diakonía, Forum SID, Radda Barnen, and the Swedish Cooperative Center (*ibid.*).

48. *El Heraldo,* "Diputados son los últimos en conocer Plan de Reconstrucción," March 31, 1999; *La Tribuna,* "$3 mil 900 millones requiere plan de reconstrucción, según diputados," March 31, 1999.

49. *El Heraldo,* "Plan Maestro está en poder del BID," April 5, 1999.

50. Ibid.

51. Ibid.

52. The NGO was Organizaciones Campesinas de Honduras (COCOCH); *La Tribuna,* "Plan de Reconstrucción tiene 'pecado original,'" May 4, 1999.

53. The statement was made before the names of the contractors were revealed; *El Heraldo,* "El gobierno ya tiene auditorías internacionales," March 11, 1999.

54. *La Prensa,* "Estocolmo: Una esperanza que tiene paralizada a Honduras," April 11, 1999.

55. *El Heraldo,* "Divergencia gobierno: Sociedad civil pone en peligro ayuda de Estocolmo," April 10, 1999.

56. *El Heraldo,* "La cita histórica," March 22, 1999.

57. Claiming, "If the NGOs' plan is to criticize the government, it could be destructive and we might not get as much aid"; *La Prensa,* March 30, 1999.

58. My interviews made it clear the international donors were pressuring the Honduran government to more fully include the NGOs in their Stockholm presentation. Development workers from the Swedish aid agency ASDI and from USAID, in particular, referred to this in general terms. However, whether this suggestion was seen as a *suggestion* by the Honduran president and whether this is what caused him to call the meeting to negotiate with Interforos is something I was unable to establish.

59. My interviewee told me, "The press was surprised. They had been paid to attack us for all this time and then the president has a meeting with us and we sign an agreement. So we were vindicated some."

60. *La Prensa,* "Foro Ciudadano y gobierno sellan acuerdo con declaración conjunta," May 21, 1999.

61. Ibid.

62. This process of bringing about a consensus might actually have exacerbated the tensions between the Honduran government and civil society. The extent to which social fracturing may be a product of the globalizers' involvement in the governance of the country (with their "two faces," as the NGO interviewee referred to it) is a question that begs future research.

63. *El Heraldo,* "La cita histórica," March 22, 1999; *El Heraldo,* "Empieza la hora de las verdades en Estocolmo," May 25, 1999.

64. This interrogation was covered in detail by the Honduran press. See, e.g., *El Heraldo,* "Las incómodas preguntas de la comunidad internacional," May 27, 1999; *El Heraldo,* "Comunidad internacional cuestiona el Plan Maestro de Reconstrucción," May 27, 1999; and *La Tribuna,* "Sólo poner en evidencia su división fueron malos hondureños a Estocolmo," May 28, 1999.

65. Ibid.

66. Stockholm Declaration, May 28, 1999; emphasis added.

67. Stockholm Declaration, May 28, 1999.

68. *El Heraldo*, "Honduras logró financiar el 70% de sus proyectos: Flores," May 30, 1999.

69. Perhaps at the same time it fractured Honduran society, thus allowing a new form of governance to commence (see note 62 above).

70. Interforos, for instance, has a representative in each group. In the follow-up meeting on national reconstruction and transformation ("Reunión de Seguimiento de la Reconstrucción y Transformación Nacional") that took place in March 2001, there was civil society participation in each of the thirteen working groups (Gobierno de Honduras, Memoria, Reunión de Seguimiento, 28–29 de marzo, 2001; personal copy). This is not to imply, however, that the participation was (or is now) on equal terms. One representative I interviewed in Honduras told me that the NGOs have little power in these committees and are often relegated to the role of observer; and yet, even as observers they are not granted access to "sensitive" project documents. The government and international donors, in contrast, have full access to project documents and audits regarding the reconstruction.

71. While in Honduras in July 2001, I noted almost every development institution I visited had glossy pamphlets, booklets, and reports—even CD-ROMs and videos— celebrating the Mitch reconstruction. Among other things, Mitch represented a golden opportunity for these organizations to polish the shiny veneer of beneficence.

72. This is the WB's Highly Indebted Poor Country (HIPC) initiative, for which Honduras qualified in 1999.

CONCLUSION: Maintaining Global Governance

1. USAID, for instance, has established a Development Experience Clearinghouse that makes USAID records available for a small processing fee. The WB and IDB offer similar, albeit slightly more restricted, services.

2. Interview with Milton, spring 1996. Whether or not this will be the case is an important question for future research.

Bibliography

Abercrombie, Nicholas, Hill, Stephen, and Turner, Bryan S. 1994. *The Penguin Dictionary of Sociology*. 3rd ed. New York: Penguin.

AECI. 2001. *Ayuda Española a los países centroamericanos afectados por el Huracán Mitch*. Madrid: Agencia Española de Cooperación Internacional.

Albrow, Martin. 1996. *The Global Age*. Stanford: Stanford University Press.

Arriviallaga, A. D., and Kreuzer, H. 1981a. "The El Cajón Hydro Project in Honduras: Part One." *Water Power & Dam Construction* (February): 37–40.

———. 1981b. "The El Cajón Hydro Project in Honduras: Part Two." *Water Power & Dam Construction* (March): 37–39.

Attwood, Donald, Bruneau, Thomas, and Galaty, John, eds. 1988. *Power and Poverty: Development and Development Projects in the Third World*. Boulder: Westview Press.

Bamyeh, Mohammed. 1993. "Transnationalism." *Current Sociology*, 41, no. 2 (Autumn): 1–78.

Bandow, Doug, and Vásquez, Ian, eds. 1994. *Perpetuating Poverty: The World Bank, the IMF, and the Developing World*. Washington, D.C.: Cato Institute.

Barber, Benjamin. 1992. "Jihad vs. McWorld." *Atlantic Monthly* (March): 53–63.

Barnet, Richard J., and Cavanagh, John. 1994. *Global Dreams: Imperial Corporations and the New World Order*. New York: Simon & Schuster.

Bello, Walden. 1994. *Dark Victory: The U.S., Structural Adjustment, and Global Poverty*. London: Pluto; Oakland: Institute for Food and Development Policy (Food First).

Boli, John, and Thomas, George M. 1997a. "World Culture in the World Polity: A Century of International Non-Governmental Organization." *American Sociological Review* 62: 171–90.

———, eds. 1997b. *World Polity Formation since 1875: World Culture and International Non-Governmental Organizations*. Stanford: Stanford University Press.

Boswell, Terry, and Chase-Dunn, Christopher. 2000. *The Spiral of Capitalism and Socialism*. Boulder: Lynne Rienner Publishers.

Bourdieu, Pierre. 2001. "Uniting to Better Dominate." *Items and Issues*, 2, no. 3–4, (Winter): 1–6.

Brecher, Jeremy, et al. 2000. "Globalization from Below." *The Nation*, December 4, 19–22.

Casco, Oswaldo. 1996. "El desarrollo de zonas francas para la exportación: Caso de Honduras." In *Zonas francas en Centroamérica: Antología*, ed. Luis Rodríguez Pérez and Ana Lissette Amaya. Managua, Nicaragua: Editorial Ciencias Sociales INIES

Castells, Manuel. 1996. *The Rise of the Network Society*. Cambridge: Blackwell Publishers.

Caufield, Catherine. 1996. *Masters of Illusion: The World Bank and the Poverty of Nations*. New York: Henry Holt and Company.

Collins, Patricia Hill. 1991. *Black Feminist Thought: Knowledge, Consciousness, and the Politics of Empowerment.* New York: Routledge.

Colson, Elizabeth. 1982. *Planned Change: The Creation of a New Community.* Berkeley: Institute of International Studies.

Departamento de Estudios Económicos, Banco Central de Honduras. 1995. *Actividad económica de las empresas maquiladoras en Honduras (Zonas libres y de procesamiento industrial),* 1990–1994 *y perspectivas para* 1995. Tegucigalpa: M.D.C., Septiembre.

Dorcey, Tony, ed. 1997. *Large Dams: Learning from the Past, Looking at the Future.* Workshop proceedings, Gland, Switzerland. April 11–12, 1997. IUCN/World Bank.

Edwards, Michael, and Hulme, David, eds. 1996. *Beyond the Magic Bullet: NGO Performance and Accountability in the Post–Cold War World.* West Hartford, Conn.: Kumarian Press.

ENEE. 1982. *Proyecto hidroeléctrico "El Cajón."* Tegucigalpa: Empresa Nacional de Energía Eléctrica.

Escobar, Arturo. 1995. *Encountering Development: The Making and Unmaking of the Third World.* Princeton: Princeton University Press.

———. 1992. "Imagining a Post-Development Era? Critical Thought, Development and Social Movements." *Social Text* 31/32.

———. 1988. "Power and Visibility: Development and the Invention and Management of the Third World." *Cultural Anthropology* 3, no. 4: 428–43.

Esteva, Gustavo. 1992. "Development." In *The Development Dictionary: A Guide to Knowledge as Power,* ed. Wolfgang Sachs. London: Zed Books.

Ferguson, James. 1994. *The Anti-Politics Machine: "Development," Depoliticization, and Bureaucratic Power in Lesotho.* Minneapolis: University of Minnesota Press.

Fisher, Julie. 1998. *Nongovernments: NGOs and the Political Development of the Third World.* West Hartford, Conn.: Kumarian Press.

Foucault, Michel. 1979. *Discipline and Punish: The Birth of the Prison.* New York: Vintage.

Fox, Jonathan A., and Brown, L. David, eds. 1998. *The Struggle for Accountability: The World Bank, NGOs and Grassroots Movements.* Cambridge: The MIT Press.

Friedman, Thomas. 2000. *The Lexus and the Olive Tree.* New York: Anchor Books.

GAO. 1993. *"Foreign Assistance: U.S. Support for Caribbean Basin Assembly Industries: Report to Congressional Requesters."* Washington, D.C.: General Accounting Office. December.

Gass, Vicki. 2002. *Democratizing Development: Lessons from Hurricane Mitch Reconstruction.* Washington, D.C.: WOLA.

Gerodetti, M. 1981. "Model Studies of an Overtopped Rockfill Dam." *Water Power & Dam Construction* (September): 25–31.

Giddens, Anthony. 2000. *Runaway World: How Globalization is Reshaping Our Lives.* New York: Routledge.

Gollin, James D. 1994. "Trees Down, Lights Out in Honduras." *Christian Science Monitor,* November 15, 1994, 12.

Grieder, William. 1997. *One World, Ready or Not.* New York: Simon & Schuster.

Guifarro, R., Flores, J., and Kreuzer, H. 1996. "Francisco Morazán Dam, Honduras: The Successful Extension of a Grout Curtain in Karstic Limestone." *The International Journal on Hydropower and Dams,* 3, no. 5: 38–43.

Hancock, Graham. 1989. *Lords of Poverty: The Power, Prestige and Corruption of the International Aid Business.* New York: The Atlantic Monthly Press.

Harris, Marvin. 1977. *Cannibals and Kings.* New York: Vintage Books.

Hayter, Teresa. 1971. *Aid as Imperialism.* Harmondsworth, UK: Penguin Books.

Jackson, Jeffrey T. 1998. "Doing Development: Global Planners and Local Policy in Honduras." *PhD diss.*, University of Texas at Austin.

———. 1993. "The Decline in the Latin American Critique of U.S. Sociology: A Critical Examination of Latin Americanism." *Master's thesis*, University of Texas at Austin.

Jaffee, David. 1990. *Levels of Socio-Economic Development Theory.* Westport, Conn.: Praeger.

Jary, David, and Jary, Julia. 1991. *The HarperCollins Dictionary of Sociology.* New York: Harper Perennial.

Klitgaard, Robert. 1990. *Tropical Gangsters: One Man's Experience with Development and Decadence in Deepest Africa.* New York: Basic Books.

LaFeber, Walter. 1999. *Michael Jordan and the New Global Capitalism.* New York: Norton.

Loker, William. 1998. "Water, Rights, and the El Cajón Dam, Honduras." In *Water, Culture and Power*, ed. John Donahue and Barbara Johnson. Washington, D.C.: Island Press.

Mahmood, K. 1987. *Reservoir Sedimentation: Impact, Extent and Mitigation.* World Bank Technical Paper XX: 70.

Mangurian, David. 1997. "Ingenuity Saves Dam." *The IDB* 24, no. 8: 6–7.

Maren, Michael. 1997. *The Road to Hell: The Ravaging Effects of Foreign Aid and International Charity.* New York: The Free Press.

McMichael, Phillip. 1996. *Development and Social Change: A Global Perspective.* Thousand Oaks, Calif.: Pine Forge Press.

Mills, C. Wright. 1956. *The Power Elite.* New York: Oxford University Press.

Moncada Valledares, Efraín. 1995. "*Las dos caras de la maquila en Honduras.*" Draft document, Tegucigalpa: POSCAE

NLC. 1992. *Paying to Lose Our Jobs.* New York: National Labor Committee Education Fund in Support of Worker and Human Rights in Central America. September.

Norsworthy, Kent, and Barry, Tom. 1993. *Inside Honduras: The Essential Guide to Its Politics, Economy, Society, and Environment.* Albuquerque: The Inter-Hemispheric Education Resource Center.

OECD. 2002. *Geographical Distribution of Financial Flows to Aid Recipients.* Paris: OECD.

———. 2001. *Geographical Distribution of Financial Flows to Aid Recipients.* Paris: OECD.

———. 1995. *Geographical Distribution of Financial Flows to Aid Recipients.* Paris: OECD.

———. 1984. *Geographical Distribution of Financial Flows to Developing Countries.* Paris: OECD.

———. 1975. *Geographical Distribution of Financial Flows to Developing Countries.* Paris: OECD.

———. 1966. *Geographical Distribution of Financial Flows to Less Developed Countries: 1960–1964.* Paris: OECD.

Osterfeld, David. 1994. "The World Bank and the IMF: Misbegotten Sisters." In *The Collapse of Development Planning*, ed. Peter Boettke. New York: New York University Press.

Outhwaite, William, and Bottomore, Tom, eds. 1994. *The Blackwell Dictionary of Twentieth-Century Social Thought*. Oxford: Blackwell.

Paddock, W., and Paddock, E. 1973. *We Don't Know How: An Independent Audit of What They Call Success in Foreign Assistance*. Ames: Iowa State University Press.

Payer, Cheryl. 1982. *The World Bank: A Critical Analysis*. New York: Monthly Review Press.

Perkin, Harold. 1996. *The Third Revolution: Professional Elites in the Modern World*. New York: Routledge.

Petersen, Kurt. 1992. *The Maquiladora Revolution in Guatemala*. New Haven: Orville H. Schell, Jr. Center for International Human Rights at Yale Law School.

Portes, Alejandro, Guarnizo, Luis E., and Landolt, Patricia. 1999. "Transnational Communities. Introduction: Pitfalls and Promise of an Emergent Research Field." *Ethnic and Racial Studies*, 22, no. 2 (March): 217–37.

Raphael, Jerome M. 1986. "Hoover Dam Plus Fifty Years Equals El Cajón Dam." In *Water Power '85: Proceedings of an International Conference on Hydropower*, ed. Michael J. Roluti. New York: American Society of Civil Engineers.

Rich, Bruce. 1994. *Mortgaging the Earth: The World Bank, Environmental Impoverishment, and the Crisis of Development*. Boston: Beacon Press.

Robertson, A. F. 1984. *People and the State: An Anthropology of Planned Development*. New York: Cambridge University Press.

Robinson, William I. 2001a. "The Debate on Globalization, the Transnational Capitalist Class, and the Rise of a Transnational State." *Paper presented at the American Sociological Association Meeting*, Anaheim, August 18–21, 2001.

———. 2001b. "Social Theory and Globalization: The Rise of a Transnational State." *Theory and Society*, 30: 157–200.

———. 1996a. "Globalisation: Nine Theses on Our Epoch." *Race & Class*, 38 (October–December): 13–31.

———. 1996b. *Promoting Polyarchy: Globalization, US Intervention, and Hegemony*. Cambridge: Cambridge University Press.

Roy, Arundhati. 2001. *Power Politics*. Cambridge: South End Press.

Sachs, Wolfgang, ed. 1992. *The Development Dictionary: A Guide to Knowledge as Power*. London: Zed Books.

Said, Edward. 1979. *Orientalism*. New York: Vintage Books.

Sassen, Saskia. 1998. *Globalization and Its Discontents*. New York: Norton.

———. 1988. *The Mobility of Labor and Capital*. Cambridge: Cambridge University Press.

Schaeffer, Robert. K. 2003. *Understanding Globalization: The Social Consequences of Political, Economic, and Environmental Change*. 2nd ed. Lanham, Md.: Rowman & Littlefield Publishers.

Schnitter, N. J. 1984. "El Cajón Arch Dam." *Concrete International* (August): 7–13.

Schulthess, D. 1985. "Vortex Tower for the El Cajón Spillway Intake." *Water Power & Dam Construction* (July): 27–30.

Schulz, Donald E., and Schulz, Deborah S. 1994. *The United States, Honduras, and the Crisis in Central America*. Boulder: Westview Press.

Scudder, Thayer. 1997. "Social Impact of Large Dams." In *Large Dams: Learning from the Past, Looking at the Future*, ed. Tony Dorcey, 41–68. Workshop proceedings, Gland, Switzerland. April 11–12, 1997. IUCN/World Bank.

SECPLAN. 1995. *Plan de acción nacional de desarrollo humano, infancia y juventud.* Tegucigalpa: SECPLAN. Personal copy.

———. 1993. *Presupuesto del gobierno hondureño.* Tegucigalpa: SECPLAN. Personal copy.

Shannon, Thomas R. 1996. *An Introduction to the World-System Perspective.* Boulder: Westview Press.

Sklair, Leslie. 1995. *Sociology of the Global System.* 2nd ed. Baltimore: Johns Hopkins University Press.

Sklar, Leonard, and McCully, Patrick. 1994. "*Damming the Rivers: The World Bank's Lending for Large Dams.*" Working Paper 5, International Rivers Network, November.

Smillie, Ian. 1995. *The Alms Bazaar: Altruism Under Fire—Non-Profit Organizations and International Development.* London: Intermediate Technology Publications.

———. 1991. *Mastering the Machine: Poverty, Aid and Technology.* London: Intermediate Technology Publications.

So, Alvin Y. 1990. *Social Change and Development: Modernization, Dependency, and World System Theories.* Sage Library of Social Research 178. Newbury Park, Calif.: Sage.

Stiglitz, Joseph E. 2002. *Globalization and Its Discontents.* New York: Norton.

System Science Consultants, Inc. 1996. *Estudio sobre las estrategias y planes para el mejoramiento de la situación de la salud en la República de Honduras.* Personal copy.

Tendler, Judith. 1975. *Inside Foreign Aid.* Baltimore: Johns Hopkins University Press.

Ugalde, Antonio, and Jackson, Jeffrey T. 1995. "The World Bank and International Health Policy: A Critical Review." *Journal of International Development,* 7, no. 3: 525–41.

United Nations/CEPAL. 1999. *Honduras: Evaluación de los daños ocasionados por el Huracán Mitch, 1998.* Naciones Unidas, 26 de enero. Personal copy.

USAID. 1983. *Free Zones in Developing Countries: Expanding Opportunities for the Private Sector.* A.I.D. Program Evaluation Discussion Paper 18 (November), PN-AAL-024.

World Bank. 2000. *Country Assistance Strategy of the World Bank Group for the Republic of Honduras.* World Bank Document, Report 20072-HO, January 27.

———. 1989. *Project Performance Audit Report. Honduras. El Cajón Power Project* (Loan 1805-HO and Credit 989-HO). World Bank Operations Evaluation Department Report: Report 7901, June 30.

———. 1980a. *Report and Recommendation of the President of the International Bank for Reconstruction and Development and the International Development Association, to the Executive Directors on a Proposed Loan to the Empresa Nacional de Energía Eléctrica with the Guarantee of the Republic of Honduras and a Proposed Credit to the Republic of Honduras for the El Cajón Power Project.* World Bank Document, Report P-2710-HO, February 20.

———. 1980b. *Staff Appraisal Report: Honduras, El Cajón Power Project.* World Bank Document, Report 2388a-HO, Projects Department, Latin America and the Caribbean Regional Office, February 21.

Index

Numbers in *italics* denote illustrations.

accountability, xiii, xiv, 14, 110, 201, 285, 294, 307–9, 330n71; definition of, 194, 313n31. *See also under* development worker(s)
Africa, ix, 1–2, 113, 152, 211, 247
agency, human, xi–xii. *See also* globalization, agents of
Agency for International Development (AID). *See* USAID
agenda setting. *See under* power, mechanisms of
agriculture, 6, 41, 48, 112, 139, 217, 315n24, 321n31, 332n34; and Mitch reconstruction, 268, 272, 275, 287. *See also* cooperatives, agricultural; exports
agronomists, 64, 112–13
aid, x, xi, 66, 115, 261; bilateral, 11, 24, 25–26, 30; as helping, 89, 277, 309, 313n27; institutional structure of, 135; multilateral, 11, 24, 26–28, 30; two faces of, 284; tying, 221–22; unofficial private flows, 31, 314n10. *See also* development organizations; food aid; official development assistance; technical assistance
aid-dependent countries, 5, 63, 304
Albrow, Martin, 311nn5&7
Annan, Kofi, 130, 291
anteproyecto (draft legislation), 52, 223, 334n49
anthropology/anthropologists, 149, 159, 163, 168, 322n16
apparel, 207, 209, 228, 230, 241, 242, 243, 254, 330n1; Honduran exports to U.S., 230, 335n8
APSO (Agency for Personal Service Overseas–Ireland), 27, 35
Arendt, Hannah, 134, 302
Asia/Middle East, ix, 91, 152, 247, 337n37; APEC (Asia-Pacific Economic Cooperation), 136;

China, 27, 31, 192, 230, 264; Hong Kong, 228; India, 44, 91, 131, 247, 312n16, 322n10; Kuwait, 27, 264; Middle East, ix; Pakistan, 228, 247; Sri Lanka, 74, 75, 76, 90; South Korea, 27, 35, 227–28, 241, 243, 246

banking. *See* development organizations, banks; Honduras, government of, Central Bank
Barber, Benjamin, 312nn11&17
Barnet, Richard, 311n8, 315n1, 317n10, 330nn2&5
beneficence, shiny veneer of, 12, 17, 66, 76, 93, 124, 126, 204, 302, 306, 309, 312n20, 326n87, 343n71
Boli, John, 9, 311n8, 312n21
Boswell, Terry, 311n4, 312n17
Bourdieu, Pierre, 3, 8, 311n6, 315n1, 320n17
brain drain, internal, 107, 125
bridges, 70, 138; Bailey-style, 264, 277; contracts for building, 289, 299, 340n27; and Mitch reconstruction, 268, 272, 276, 287, 290, 296, 299, 340n27

campesinos, 100, 102, 197, 202
Canada, 11, 31, 73, 165, 166, 172, 203, 264, 292, 339n3
Canadian International Development Agency (CIDA), xix, 27, 35, 37, 50, 165–66, 262, 275, 339n7
capitalism, x, 3, 7–8, 9, 135, 201, 308, 312n11; bureaucratic nature of, 320n17, 330nn71&74; epochs of, 3, 316–17n10; integration into, 8, 141; logic of, 3. *See also* entrepreneurs; transnational capitalist class; transnational corporations; world economy; world system, capitalist

CARE (NGO), 5, 31, 38, 54, 55, 105–11, 118–21, 141, 145, 276, 319n7; description of, 98–99; location in hierarchy, 35; power of, 106; and World Health Organization (WHO), 104

Caribbean Basin Initiative (CBI), 210–11, 330n7

Catholic Relief Services (CRS, NGO), 5, 31, 35, 38, 108, 110, 315n2

Cavanaugh, John, 311n8, 315n1, 317n10

Central America, 160, 176, 211, 214, 225, 235, 240, 241, 243, 259, 267, 291, 293–95, 324n43, 337n37; Costa Rica, 27, 176, 211, 215, 340n13; El Salvador, 176, 211, 215, 340n13; Guatemala, 211, 214, 260, 266, 292, 324n45, 340n13; Nicaragua, 160, 176, 177, 266, 292, 324n45, 340n13; Panama, 172, 176, 211

Central American Bank for Economic Integration (CABEI), 28, 35, 139, 152, 158, 163, 165, 192, 266, 271

Chase-Dunn, Christopher, 311n4, 312n17

child labor, 229, 239, 241, 243–45, 247–49, 251, 252, 337nn27–29; U.S. Department of Labor study on, 249–50. *See also maquiladoras,* and sweatshop scandal

children's rights, 7, 10, 82

citizens, Honduran, xiii, 222, 283, 308

civil society, 8, 14, 32, 33, 312n17; and Mitch reconstruction, 269, 281–82, 285, 287, 288, 292, 294, 295, 298, 342n62; and social fracturing, 342n62, 343n69. *See also* NGOs

class, 134, 135; dynamics in donor countries, 313n34. *See also* transnational capitalist class

colonialism, 4, 311n9, 317n10, 321n31

Colson, Elizabeth, 318n1

community participation, local, 82, 119, 197, 199

consultants, 42, 112, 162, 252

cooperatives, agricultural, 49, 315n23

corruption, 46, 79, 162, 277, 284–85, 290, 331n24; international audits as solution to, 285–86. *See also* transparency

Covenant House (NGO), 5, 35

Dahl, Robert, 134, 320n15

dams, 131, 322n16; authorities, 154–55; Canaveral, 323n18; costs of, 151, 155; critics of, 324n50, 329n68; development bank role

in, 152; ecological consequences of, 155, 322n11; Hoover, 149; industry, 151, 152–53, 302; large, 152; Los Laureles, La Concepción, 260; Narmada, 131, 312n16; political aspects of, 154–56, 322n10&16; private, 154; Rio Lindo, 150, 323n18; Sardar Sarovar, 322n10. *See also* El Cajón; NGOs, opposing large dams

debt: Honduran, 150, 193, 195, 200, 264, 295, 299, 325n70; "odious," 329n68

decentralization, 142; and Mitch reconstruction, 268, 283, 292, 293, 294, 295, 299

democracy, 7, 10, 14, 295, 296, 298, 308, 312n17; as a global agenda, 138, 294, 309

dependency, Honduran, 5, 306

developing countries/world, ix, 12, 13, 64, 65, 152, 201, 203, 204, 208, 221, 240, 248, 268, 302

development, 6, 107, 296, 297; as academic field, 66, 67, 103, 311n7, 317n13; as chimera, 16–17, 313n33; as converging paradigm, 12; critics of, 12, 313n27, 317n13; as discourse, 76, 197–98; economic aspects of, 139, 175; as ideology, 16–17, 67, 149, 317n10; industry/apparatus, 1–2, 5, 33; social aspects of, 81, 140. *See also* beneficence, shiny veneer of

development organizations, x, xii, 1–2, 62, 99, 131, 136, 173, 194, 195, 239, 250, 252, 261, 275, 301, 307, 309, 311nn7&8, 313n27, 319n11; administration of, 111; banks, 28, 54, 55, 80, 105, 131, 150, 152–53, 157, 192, 195, 200, 302, 327n103; bilateral, 25–26, 27, 37, 136, 165, 261, 265, 266, 285, 302; bureaucratic nature of, 78, 110; conflict between, 110, 119–20, 127, 265–66, 304; contributing to global inequality, 94; coordination of, 116–18, 127 (*see also* donor countries, coordination); donor control over, 117–18; evaluation apparatus, 305; hierarchy of, 33–35, 39, 120, 126, 276; in Honduras, 23–24, 141–42; as immune to criticism, 17, 39; inefficiency and waste in, xiv, 80, 111, 304–5; inequality within, 114; local control over, 119, 307; location of, 36–39; multilateral, 26–28, 37, 136, 165, 261, 265, 285; network of, 54–55, 114, 315n27; at nexus between rich and poor countries, 8; power of, 50–51, 105–7, 118; as providers of experts, 64–65; relationship with Honduran government, 118, 136, 201; socialistic models in, 53; ties between, 78, 84, 108, 110; top-down nature of, 144, 307; ubiquity of, 6. *See also specific organizations*

development profession, international, x, xii, xiii, 1–2, 3, 6, 19, 62, 97, 126, 209, 249, 308–9, 339n8; adventure and fun of, 69, 90–91; birth of, 6, 317n10; as career, xii, 89, 120–21, 124–25; critics of, 109, 117, 304, 305–6, 307, 313n27; entering, xiii, 90, 104–6, 122; exchange programs and, 66; game of, 78–79; glass ceiling in, 124; legitimacy of, xii, xiv, 14, 94, 121, 123, 304, 307 (*see also* beneficence, shiny veneer of); lingo, 40, 46; maintaining, xiv, 118, 126, 301, 303–9; as metaprofession, 68; mission of, 82, 101, 102, 144; pay gap within, xii, 86–88, 93–94, 113–15, 124, 307; problems of, xii; propaganda and public relations of, 40, 99, 281, 307, 343n71; responding to criticism, 94, 304–9; reward structure within, xii, 68–69, 87–88, 93–94, 98; sense of purpose in, 69, 307; socialization practices, xii, 67, 91–92, 98, 103; subculture, xii, 46, 62–63, 67, 318n1

development projects, xii, xiii, 1–2, 109–10, 116–17, 138, 336n18; compensation for failure of, xiii, 14; and donor countries, 12, 198; largest, 150; mechanisms for redress, 197; negative consequences downplayed, 16, 197. *See also* agriculture; bridges; education; El Cajón; energy; health; housing; Hurricane Mitch reconstruction; infrastructure; *maquiladoras;* road projects; telecommunication

development worker(s), ix, x, xii, 8, 63, 78, 195, 248, 261, 273, 277, 296, 308, 320n13; access to power networks, 69–70, 84, 94–95, 98, 105–7, 121, 318–19nn6&7; accountability of, 85–86, 308; cross-cultural skills/experiences of, 66, 68, 101; definition of, 61, 316n8; dual life of, 92, 100, 101; evaluation of, 84; as example of transnationalism, 60, 316n6; experiences abroad, 58, 74, 90, 100; family and friends of, 91–92, 99–101; first experiences of, 75–76, 90, 102; Honduran views about, 111–13; international identity of, 92, 101, 306; lifestyles of, 41, 62, 69, 86–87, 93, 220, 318–19n6; middle- or upper-class position of, 100; pro-globalization worldview of, 67–68, 90, 307; public

perceptions of, 183, 277; salaries of, 68, 86, 93, 105, 111, 114–15, 218, 220, 333n42; socialization and education of, 67–68, 91–92, 98, 100, 103, 104; top-down viewpoint of, 144; views about Honduras, 89; working for Honduran government, 103–5. *See also* experts, professional; globalizers

development worker(s), expatriate, ix, xiii, 62, 68, 73–74, 86–95, 101, 102, 115, 120, 126, 138, 144; hardships, 68, 75; perks and benefits, 86–87, 114, 307; rationalizations of, 307

development worker(s), local Honduran, ix, xiii, 68, 93, 97–126, 138, 144, 307, 319n5; benefits, 123–24; as cheap labor, 123; exploitation of, 114, 124–25; patronizing views toward, 87, 113; role of, 84, 113, 121–22. *See also* Honduran counterparts

diesel-powered plants. *See* thermal plants

disaster management, 261, 297

"discontents," 7, 312n17

division of labor, international, 65

documents, ix, 63, 307, 321n33, 324n41, 327–29, 339n7. *See also under specific organizations;* methodology; press

donor countries, ix, xi, 8, 11, 26, 65, 126, 141, 152, 165, 247, 266, 268, 286, 290, 292, 294, 296, 298, 301, 307; agendas of (*see* global agendas); aid rationale, 115–16, 303; Australia, 27; Austria, 27, 91, 292; Belgium, 27, 73, 90; benefits to, xi–xii, 17–18, 60–66, 70–71, 95, 98, 122–23, 201, 203, 220, 237, 257, 303, 309, 333n41: —economic, 18, 70, 156, 165, 203–4, 211, 299; —economic, to TNCs in, 154, 165–66, 203, 211, 257; —political, 18–19, 70, 211, 239, 294, 299; citizens in, 88, 237, 254; coordination between, 305, 339n8 (*see also under* Hurricane Mitch reconstruction); Denmark, 27, 92; Finland, 27; France, 11, 27, 263; Ireland, 27, 31, 263; Italy, 11, 27, 163, 165, 166, 172, 174, 185, 186, 203, 292; legal agreements with, 145, 164, 221, 222; the Netherlands, 27, 75, 77, 88, 267, 283, 292, 318n2; Norway, 27, 292; as serving own interests, 12, 154, 201, 204, 213, 249, 309; United Kingdom, 11, 27, 31, 165, 166, 264, 276, 292. *See also* Canada; G7; G22; Germany; Japan; Spain; Sweden; Switzerland; United States

ecology/ecologists, 155, 168, 181

economics/economists, xi, 50, 64, 80–81, 161, 163, 257

education, 6, 9, 47, 108, 140, 319n4; and Mitch reconstruction, 268, 272, 275, 287, 299

El Cajón, xiii, 149–51, 156–77, 259, 261, 297, 299, 302, 303, 305, 307; administration of, 157, 169, 185; construction of, 172; costs related to, 150, 151, 161, 165–66, 175, 193, 326n84, 339n3; description of, 149–51; design for, 162–64, 165, 194; as development project, 150, 326n87; economic feasibility of, 159–62, 170, 323n37, 324nn40–44, 48–51; environmental assessments of, 158; experts and, 157, 171, 180, 181, 182–83, 186, 194, 195, 327n18; feasibility studies for, 156, 157–59; height/size of, 149, 163, 325n62; historical context of, 153, 156–57, 164; Honduran opposition to, 150, 166–68; loan agreement, 164–65, 198–99, 326n87; "lumpiness" of, 167, 170–71, 202; Mitch reconstruction and, 338–39n3; name/naming ceremony, 172, 175–76, 326n102; origins of, 156–57, 323n78; as ripoff, 196. *See also* dams; electrical power; energy, 1994 crisis of; engineers/engineering. *See also under* ENEE; globalizer(s); IDB; power, mechanisms of; USAID; World Bank

El Cajón, builders of: A. Diaz Arriviallaga, 163, 323nn25&27, 326n99; Jorge Flores, 163, 185, 186; foreign consultants, 151, 174, 182, 185, 187, 194, 200; Dr. F. Gallavresi, 185; M. Gerodetti, 163, 325n59; Ramon Guifarro, 163, 186, 325n58, 328nn23,26–28,30; Honduran, 172, 181, 186, 187; Harald Kreuzer, 163, 185, 323nn25&27, 325nn58–59, 327n18; Giovanni Lombardi, 184, 185; Andrew Merritt, 184, 185; Jerome Raphael, 163, 322n3, 323nn59–61, 324n99; Nicolas J. Schnitter, 163, 325nn59&60, 326n99; D. Schulthess, 163, 325n59, 326n99

El Cajón, contractors, 165–66, 329n65; ABG Telefunken, 166; ALCATEL, 339n3; ASEA, Inc., 166; Astaldi, 166, 172; Ateliers de VEVEY, 165; Brown Bovey, 165; Canadian Wire, 166; Cimentazoni e Sondaggi, 166, 175; Codelfa, 166, 172; Colcrete, 166; Colenco

Power Consulting, 185, 193; CONRODIO, 186, 193; EBASCO, Inc., 159–62, 170, 202, 323n37, 324nn48&49; El Cajón Consortium (CECLA), 172; El Cajón International Consortium (CONICA), 172; Harza Engineering, 156, 323n18; Impregilo, 166, 172; Ishikawa Heavy Industries, 165; Jacob Associates Construction Engineers, 171; Losinger, 165, 172; MARKHAM, 166; MONENCO, 160, 166; Motor Columbus, 156–57, 158, 159, 160, 163, 165, 172, 175, 185, 323n28; Rodio, 166; Sedgwick Forbes, 171; SVECA, 166; Swissboring, 165; Züblin, 166, 172

El Cajón, features (physical): capacity, 150, 164; dam wall, 149, 163, 165, 166, 172; flood control, 163–71, 203, 338–39n3; Francis turbines, 150, 164, 165, 172, 184, 191, 193, 322n5; generators, 166; grout curtain, 158, 163, 165, 166, 172, 174–75, 181, 184, 185–86; high-tech design, 150–51, 163, 174; powerhouse, 149, 163, 165, 166, 172, 175, 184–85; spillway tower, 151, 163; transmission lines, 166, 172

El Cajón, features (reservoir): geology of riverbed, 158, 184; rainfall/hydrological data, 156, 158, 323n25, 328n27; sedimentation, 159, 181, 196; watershed, 166, 179–80, 193, 196, 327n12

El Cajón, problems with: bad data, 158, 196; bad studies, 161–62, 170; damaged turbines, 174, 191; deforestation, 159, 181–82, 193, 196–97; depleted reservoir, 151, 180, 182, 191, 192–93; drought, 182, 189–90; energy crisis (*see* energy crisis of 1994); leak, 174–75, 182, 183–87, *188*, 328nn25&29; lending to military government, 164, 198, 325n65; powerhouse fire, 338–39n3; resettlement, 154, 159, 172–74, 197, 323nn29&32, 324nn93–97; watershed mismanagement, 180

El Cajón, repairs, 174, 175; cloud seeding, 190; costs of, 193; emergency loans related to, 182, 185, 186; of leak, 185–87, 188; toy ball solution, 187, *188*

electrical power, 138, 149–50, 156, 160, 164, 169–70, 174; private production of, 189, 193, 194. *See also* dams; El Cajón; ENEE; energy; thermal plants

ENEE, 150, 157, 159–62, 163–64, 166, 167, 172, 173, 175, 176, 177, 188, 189, 190, 191, 192, 195, 202, 302; documents, 324n41, 325nn63, 69&71; as El Cajón loan recipient, 164; employees, 179, 180, 183–84, 186, 191, 194; employees' union, 167; finances of, 171, 180, 195; Raúl Flores Guillén, 179–80; inviting foreign consultants, 182, 184; origin of, 156; public perception of, 180, 189; purchasing energy, 182, 193, 194; responding to public criticism, 189, 191; role in energy crisis, 179–80, 188; Jerónimo Sandoval Sorto, 191; Federico Travieso, 176; Jorge Valle, 189, 191. *See also* El Cajón

energy, 6, 201, 268; Honduran need for, 151–52, 155; and Mitch reconstruction, 268, 272, 287; solar, 141, 312n22

energy crisis of 1994, 150, 151, 179, 203, 327n6; aftermath, 192–94; causes of, 194; consequences for Honduran citizens, 188–89; costs of, 189, 191, 192–93, 203; end of, 191–92; origins of, 179–81; rationing, 188, 189, 192; responsibility for, 194–97; tariff increases, 180, 189. *See also* El Cajón

engineers/engineering, 64, 88, 151, 157, 158, 163, 204; civil, 59, 74, 75, 166; expertise, 152, 163, 297; Honduran, 152, 163; school, xi. *See also* El Cajón, builders of

entrepreneur(s), 6, 140, 155, 208, 214, 234, 316n9

environment, 10, 49, 153; and Mitch reconstruction, 273, 292–93, 295. *See also* ecology/ecologists; El Cajón, features (reservoir)

environmental movement, 7, 70

Escobar, Arturo, 313n27, 315n1, 317n13, 320n17

Europe, 30, 163, 196, 319n1, 337n37

European Union (EU), 28, 35, 37, 74, 77, 78, 136, 268, 274, 277

Executive Service Corps, International (IESC), 216, 219

expatriates (expats). *See* development worker(s), expatriate

expertise, xi–xii, 64, 89, 95, 100, 112, 162, 220, 255, 305; global supply and demand of, 65, 115; local, 112–13, 114, 115, 121, 122–23, 317n4; production of, 65, 100, 319n6. *See also* knowledge, systems of

experts, 64–65, 131, 270, 274, 283, 301; apolitical role of, 306; export of, 64–66. *See also under* El Cajón; *maquiladora* promotion

export processing zones. See *maquiladoras;* free trade, zones

exports, Honduran, 4, 48, 139, 228, 230, 321nn28&30, 332–33n34; bananas/coffee, 4, 139; non-traditional, 139, 217; vegetables, 139, 238, 321nn28&29. *See also* agriculture; apparel

feminism, 70, 305

Ferguson, James, 1–2, 311n1, 315n1

FIDE, 216–17, 218, 210, 224–28, 255, 256, 331n27; advertisements, 225, 233, 236; arranging tours, 226, 236; assisting investors, 228; documents, 334n54, 335n69; evaluation of, 219–20, 227; founding of, 216, 332n31; growth after U.S. support ends, 240; offices abroad, 220, 225; promotional materials of, 225–27, 233; role in export promotion, 218, 220, 224–28; and sweatshop scandal, 233, 234–35, 236; USAID financing of, 216, 225, 227. *See also maquiladoras*

finance. *See* macroeconomic stability

Food and Agriculture Organization, UN (FAO), 26, 28

food aid, 98–99, 107, 108, 109, 213

foreign direct investment, 140, 201, 221

foreign service nationals, 42. *See also* development worker(s), local Honduran

forestry, 6, 18, 49–50, 139, 140, 217

Foucault, Michel, 71, 132–33, 135, 311n1, 318n15, 320nn4,5&17

Foundation for Investment and Development of Exports. *See* FIDE

Fox, Jonathan, 194, 312n16, 313n31, 329n64, 336n17

Frank, Andre Gunder, 316n10

free trade: reforms, 210; zones, 210, 214, 235, 238, 254, 330n4. See also *maquiladoras*

Freidman, Thomas, 312nn11,12&17

G7/G8 (Group of Seven/Eight), ix, 11, 136, 201, 300, 309

G22 (Group of Twenty-two), 11, 136, 313n24, 314n3

Gap, Inc. See *maquiladoras,* TNCs using

garnering consent, 79. *See also under* power, mechanisms of

GDP/GNP, Honduran, 25–26, 192

Germany, 11, 26, 31, 53, 116, 141, 154, 165, 166, 172, 203, 213, 264, 267, 292, 293

Giddens, Anthony, 132, 311n3, 312nn10,11,17&18, 315n16, 317n11, 320n3

Gifford, Kathie Lee, 243–45, 334n61, 337nn34&37

global agendas, xii, 3, 8–9, 10, 11, 70–71, 81, 97–98, 106, 109, 122, 138–41, 146, 201, 208, 235, 253, 255, 274, 286, 296, 297, 301, 302, 337n25; accommodation and resistance to, 13; benefits to local for participating in, 15, 170, 202–3, 256, 299, 303; conflicts between, 10, 248, 249; conflict with local agendas, 14, 145; convergence of, 6, 11–12, 313n25; dam building as, 155–56; development organizations as main promoters of, 10; development worker negotiation of, 10, 81, 106; hierarchy of, 10–11, 81, 312–13n22; local cooperation with, 98, 319n2; *maquiladoras* as, 210–15, 222, 224; multiplicity of, 9, 62; NGOs and, 33, 235, 239, 255, 309–10; protests against, 302; risks of, downplayed, 172, 196, 203, 256–57, 299, 303; as superceding the local, 15, 123, 126, 201–2, 239, 256, 297–98, 302. *See also* local agendas

global cultural scripts, 9–10, 312–13n22

global economy, 135, 250, 254; management of, 136. *See also* world economy

global governance, ix, xi, 127, 132, 141–42, 157, 301–9, 311n9, 314n2; cyclical nature of, 146, 197, 239, 249, 255, 297, 304, 305; and El Cajón, 157, 192; features of, xii; and *maquiladoras,* 235, 238, 239, 247, 248, 253, 254; and Mitch reconstruction, 261, 274, 276, 295; NGOs and, 239–40

global government, x, 1, 23, 36, 141–42, *143,* 261, 269, 339n8. *See also* transnational state

globalization, x, 1, 2, 3, 6–8, 12, 55, 74, 94, 135, 301–2, 308, 312n17; as advancing interests of wealthy countries, 8, 203, 301; agents of, xi, 2, 3, 57, 62, 74, 126, 201, 239, 248, 301–2, 311n8, 314n1; architecture of, 3, 62; civil society and, 7, 308–9, 312n17; critics of, 7–8, 239;

cultural aspects, 3; current epoch of, 317n10; definition of, 3; and development, 16–17; economic aspects, 2, 7, 135, 227, 312n11, 320n20; as "economic politics," 3, 8, 308, 316n9, 329n65; "from above/below," 7–8; lack of local control over, xiv; logic of, in development, 6; and nation-state, 14, 33; political aspects, x, xii, 135, 302, 311n7, 320n20; "project," 19, 132, 201, 312n19; resistance to, 7–8, 302, 312n18; and rise of ODA, 33; scholarship on, xii, 2–3, 6–8, 9, 33, 57, 61, 207, 239, 311nn7&8, 312n20, 314n2; technological aspects, 1, 315–16n4 (*see also* expertise, professional); TNCs as main force behind, 7, 321n25; as unstoppable force, 2, 7, 312n11

globalizer(s), x–xiii, 2, 6, 13, 14, 55, 65, 90, 138, 139, 140–41, 162, 172, 301–3, 304–9, 329n65, 337n37; and dam building, 152; definition of, 62, 126, 315n2, 316nn8&9; and El Cajón, 157, 162, 181, 182, 184, 194; Honduran criticism of, 183, 289–90; local Honduran, 97, 115, 138 (*see also* development workers, local Honduran); location of, 36–39; and *maquiladoras,* 208, 220, 227, 230, 239, 247, 248, 250, 252, 253, 254, 257; and Mitch reconstruction, 261, 262, 263, 265, 270, 273, 274, 277, 278, 279, 280, 284, 297–99; power of (*see* power, mechanisms of). *See also* development profession; development worker(s); globalization, agents of

global law, 10, 330n71

global politics/polity, xi–xii, xiii, 136, 230, 249, 253, 337n37. *See also* world polity

global society, 7, 10–11, 247

GTZ (Germany), 5, 26–27, 37, 50, 53, 136, 139, 275, 339n7; location in hierarchy, 35

hand-me-down equipment, 38, 99

health care, 6, 9, 47, 54, 103–4, 108, 117, 119, 140–41; and Mitch reconstruction, 268, 272, 275, 297, 299

hegemony, xiv, 134, 302, 304, 312n18, 320n17

Honduran counterparts, x, 54, 68, 104, 110, 112, 137, 141, 157, 184, 220, 255, 274, 305, 306. *See also* development worker(s), local Honduran

Honduran institutions: Agricultural Investment Fund (FHIA), 41; Agricultural Modernization Law, 50, 53, 333n34; Agricultural

Policy Development Project (PRODEPAH), 51–53; Association of Nongovernmental Organizations (ASONOG), 283; Chamber of Commerce (HAMCHAM), 216, 224, 235, 332n28; CONADI, 215, 256, 331n24; Council of Private Enterprise (COHEP), 189, 192, 224, 334n50, 341n42; Forestry Commission (CODHEFOR), 49, 166, 181, 196; Forum of Private Development Organizations (FOPRIDEH), 32, 48, 55, 283, 284; Foundation for the Rehabilitation and Integration of the Disabled (FUHRIL), 35, 73, 141; Human Rights Commission (CODEH), 234, 235, 240, 241, 243, 247, 248, 249, 250, 252, 283, 284–85, 314, 320n12, 335n5; Interforos, 282–84, 287, 288, 290–91, 293, 298, 343n70; Management Association (GEMAH), 216, 224, 332n28; Manufacturers Association, (AHM), xix, 229, 234, 245–46, 335n66, 338n41; National Agrarian Institute (INA), 159; National Association of Exporters (ANEXHON), 215, 224, 332n28; National Association of Industrialists (ANDI), 215–16, 224, 332n28; National Convergence Forum (FONAC), 281, 282, 283, 293, 341n42; Social Investment Fund (FHIS), 29, 38, 275; Society of Civil Engineers (CIMEQH), 166, 167, 179, 202

Honduras, 4, 210, 292, 304; Bay Islands, 4, 259; Choluteca, 271, 280; history of, 4–5, 311n9; integration into global system, 3–4, 8, 141, 299; lempira exchange rate in, 319n9; legal system, changes in, 51, 140, 218, 223–24, 286–87; map of, 4; under military rule, 102–3, 164; Pespire, 260; political climate in, 101, 102; Puerto Cortés, 228; San Pedro Sula, 195, 218, 243, 252; U.S. influence in, 4–5, 30, 314n36. *See also* citizens; civil society; debt; methodology, Honduras as case study; press, Honduran; Tegucigalpa; United States, and Honduras

Honduras, government of, xii, 28; Agricultural Sector Planning Unit (UPSA), 51–53; Central Bank, 219, 221, 275, 296, 335n67; Colonel López Arellano, 102, 164, 325n64; conflict with NGOs, 283, 287–88, 290–91, 342nn57–59; congress, 51, 52, 175, 180, 187, 191, 192, 278,

281, 287–89; control over development organizations, 116–19; criticism of, 289, 290; and development organizations, 38–39, 47, 50–54, 103–4, 136, 278–79, 298; and El Cajón, 150, 166, 195, 309; Emergency Contingency Commission, Permanent (COPECO), 260, 262, 298; Emergency Energy Commission, 182, 189; Labor Ministry, 234–35, 250, 251–52, 253; location of, 37–39; and *maquiladoras*, 215, 217, 221, 246, 252, 255; military, 140, 164, 281; ministers, 221, 271, 276, 298, 339n7; ministries, 50–51, 104, 109, 117, 140, 157, 192, 218, 263, 268, 298; Ministry of Public Works (SOPTRAVI), 275; Ministry of Water and Sanitation (SANAA), 82–83, 139; and Mitch reconstruction, 260, 262, 263, 266, 270–72, 277, 285, 286, 298; new institutions of, created through aid, 29, 33; officials, x, 27, 50, 94, 140, 157, 175, 192, 214, 245, 296; presidency/presidents, 29, 51, 270, 277, 325n64: —Azcona, 176; —Callejas, 175, 176, 180, 189, 288; —Facussé, 260, 264, 268, 275, 276, 281, 287, 290–91, 293, 295, 296; —Melgar Castro, 164, 325n64; —Reina, 51, 180, 184, 187, 189, 192, 314n26; reform of, 140; SECPLAN, 53–54, 116–17, 314nn7&8; SETCO, 29, 38, 275, 276; transformation of under globalization, 33, 141, 294, 306; UNAT, 38, 275, 340n11. *See also* ENEE

housing, 35, 140; and Mitch reconstruction, 268, 273, 276, 280–81, 287, 297

Houston International Airport, 58–60

human rights, 7, 10, 39, 70–71, 81, 251, 295, 309; and El Cajón resettlement, 174; organizations, 124, 235, 239, 240, 250, 252, 254, 335

Hurricane Mitch, xiv, 25, 59–60, 70, 192, 203, 257–58, 259–300, 303, 306; damage caused by, 259–60, 271; damage reports, 262, 263, 270, 271–74, 296; dignitary visits, 263–64; early relief efforts, 261–62, 263, 264, 295; economic consequences of, 270, 272; people displaced by, 260, 264, 271. *See also* Honduras, government of; IDB; National Convergence Forum; Hurricane Mitch reconstruction; Stockholm; UNDP; USAID; World Bank

Hurricane Mitch reconstruction: Consultative Group, 266–68, 269, 274, 278–79, 292; disease fumigation, 277; donor coordination, 261, 262–63, 265–66, 267, 279, 295, 339n8; donors, 267–68, 269, 274, 281, 282, 285–87, 289, 291, 292, 294; early pledges, 264–65; flood control, 273; Honduran businesses and, 281, 292, 341n42; master plan, 267, 268, 274, 276, 278, 279, 282, 287, 288–89, 293–94, 296, 306; National Reconstruction Cabinet, 268, 269, 274–75, 278–79, 282, 288–89, 293–94, 299, 340n11: —Gustavo Alfaro, 279, 280, 291–92, 293, 294, 297; —Tomas Lozano, 263, 275, 276, 340n24; —Gabriela Nuñez, 275, 276, 340n23; —Moises Starkman, 275, 276, 290; overall aid package, 295; refugee shelters, 271, 277, 280; results of, 296–97; the social Mitch, 179–80, 296; social unrest and, 280; TNC contractors and, 286, 289, 290, 296; transformation vs. reconstruction, 272, 294; working group meetings, 268, 271, 275, 291, 299, 343n70. *See also* IDB; Stockholm
hurricanes, 158, 180, 338n2
hydroelectric dams. *See* dams; El Cajón

IDB, 26, 28, 37, 108, 141, 234, 267; documents, 329n63, 340n12; and El Cajón project, 150, 155, 157, 159, 164–65, 167, 172, 175, 177, 181, 182, 186–87, 189, 192, 194, 196, 197, 198, 199, 200, 324n43; location in hierarchy, 33, 35; and Mitch reconstruction, 262, 265, 266–67, 273, 282, 285–86, 289, 292
ILO. *See* Labor Organization, International, UN
IMF (International Monetary Fund), x, 11, 28, 108, 136, 199, 267
imperialism, 51, 306
indigenous groups, 7, 167
industrialization, 175, 332n34
infrastructure, 108, 138–39, 150, 155, 201–2; as a global agenda, 138; and Mitch reconstruction, 273, 296, 297, 341n42
insertion. *See under* power, mechanisms of
Inter-American Development Bank. *See* IDB
Internet, 42, 307, 315nn20&21
interviews/interviewees (*pseudonyms*), 41–54, 63, 74–90, 98–121, 124, 223, 237, 296, 339n7;

expatriate, 90, 91, 92, 93, 94, 248, 256, 280, 281, 318n6, 319n1, 321n27, 337n51, 338n42, 341n32, 342n58: —David, 262–63, 265–66, 270–72, 277–78, 340nn9–11, 340n27; —Glen, 264, 266, 274–76, 285; —Greg Lamar, 41–54, 223, 305, 334n51; —Milton, 237–38, 248, 321nn28&29, 243n2; —Elaine Van Royan, 74–90, 114, 125, 126, 305, 309, 318n4; local, 73, 99, 100, 104, 105, 106, 112–13, 271, 272–73, 278, 283–84, 288, 290–91, 292, 319n8, 321n29, 340nn9,10&15, 342n59, 343n70; —Julia Navarro, 98–121, 125, 126, 304, 319n10; —Miguel, 167, 179, 195–96, 197, 199–201

Japan, 11, 26, 30, 31, 84, 116, 117, 154, 165, 172, 213, 264, 267, 290, 292, 293, 296, 299, 318n4, 319n6, 321n30
Japan International Cooperation Agency (JICA), 5, 26–27, 37, 136, 138, 139, 140, 275; location in hierarchy, 35
journals, professional, 163, 174, 195, 325n59, 326n99

Kernaghan, Charles, 235–36, 240–41, 243–45, 247, 250, 335n6, 336n20, 337nn27, 29&35
knowledge: accumulation in donor countries, 71, 95, 318n14; local (*see* expertise, local); scientific, xi, 64–66; systems of, xi, 71, 133, 135, 144, 320n17; transfer of, 124, 152, 219 (*see also* technical assistance)

labor: child (*see* child labor); laws, 233, 243, 245, 252, 253; movement, 7, 70; organizations, 240, 247, 250, 335n5, 337n37, 338n49, 338n52; rights, 309; unions (*see* unions, labor)
Labor Committee, National (NGO), 234, 235–36, 240, 247, 248, 249, 250, 251, 335n5
Labor Organization, International, UN (ILO), 234, 247, 250, 251, 335n5
language, 66, 68, 101, 208
Latin America/Caribbean, ix, 113, 152, 210, 215, 247, 267, 318n14; Argentina, 27, 335n8; Brazil, 199; Chile, 27, 74, 79, 335n8; Colombia, 100; Cuba, 264, 313n30; Dominican Republic, 215; Guyana, 74, 77–79; Haiti, 210, 211; Jamaica, 211, 212; Mexico, 5, 27, 31, 100, 189,

190, 192, 193, 209, 215, 230, 260, 264, 276, 304;
Venezuela, 27, 100, 165, 325n68. *See also*
Central America
local agencies and institutions, 145, 195. *See
also specific agencies*
local agendas, xii, 13, 156, 235, 302; conflict with
global agendas, 145, 269; cooperation with
global agendas, 14, 98, 99, 102–3, 106–7, 123,
255, 257, 269, 283, 298, 302, 306, 309; suc-
ceeding as linked to global, 15, 124, 202, 234,
239, 256, 298–99, 302
local participation, 82–83, 144. *See also* development workers, local Honduran
Loker, William, 149, 168, 173–74, 197, 203,
323nn28,31&36, 326nn92–98

macroeconomic stability, 139–40; as a global
agenda, 138; and Mitch reconstruction, 273,
278, 287, 296, 297
maquiladora promotion: advertising, 218,
334nn53&54 (*see also under* FIDE); business
coalitions, 214; cheap labor, 207, 208, 225;
experts, 218, 219, 333n36; experts' salaries,
220, 333n42; Export and Development
Services Project, 217–21, 315n24; foreign
company needs, 214; legal reforms, 214, 218;
observation trips, 217, 218, 332n27; regulatory environment, 208; start-up financing,
214, 219; taxes/tariffs, 208, 214, 223, 225, 229;
training, 214, 218, 220, 225; transportation,
208. *See also* USAID, and *maquiladoras*
maquiladoras, xiii, 17, 140, 207–57, 222, 227,
245, 248–49, 253, 260, 261, 297, 306; benefits
of, 229, 249; consequences of, 228, 229, 230,
245, 334n57; construction of, 220–21; criticisms of, 229, 249; definition of, 207, 209;
feasibility studies for, 217, 221; growth in,
228–29, 230, 240; Honduran businesses
and, 215–16, 218, 224, 234, 235, 247, 302;
Honduran government attempt to create,
215; independent monitoring of, 250, 251–53;
industrial parks, 228, 334–35n63; investigation of, 234, 235, 241, 244, 245; law creating,
221–24, 306, 333n35, 334nn44&45; legitimating, 233, 239, 249–54, 257; making, 207, 239,
257; and Mitch reconstruction, 339n4; ZIP
plants 228, 234, 243

maquiladoras, and sweatshop scandal, 230,
233, 239, 244, 247, 254; donor country
concerns in, 239; Honduran government
inability to address, 250, 252, 253; origins of,
241; solutions to, 250–51, 252
maquiladoras, TNCs using, 207–8, 209, 337n37,
338n50; Cheil, 243; Disney, 254, 337n29; Dong
Bang, 228; Fruit of the Loom, 228; Galaxy
Industries, 234, 241, 243; Gap, Inc., 207, 243,
251–53, 254, 257, 337n28, 338n47; Global Fashions, 227–29, 234, 243–45, 334n61; Guess, 209;
Hanes, 207, 228; JC Penney, 228; J. Crew, 241;
K-Mart, 241; Kathy Lee Gifford Collection,
243, 334n61; Kellwood, 228; Levi's, 209, 241; Liz
Claiborne, 207, 241, 242–43, 251, 253, 254, 257;
Macy's, 242; Mi Kwang, 243; number of, 228;
Olga, 228; Oshkosh B'Gosh, 241; Polo, 203,
228; Sara Lee, 228, 241; subcontractors, 241,
253; Tommy Hilfiger, 207; Trans Pacific Garments, 228; True Form, 228, 241; U.S.-owned,
228; Van Heusen, 241; Wal-Mart, 228, 243,
244–45, 254, 334n61; Wrangler, 241
maquiladora workers, 225, 228, 229, 241, 247,
252, 253, 254, 337nn27&37; child labor and
(*see* child labor); congressional testimony
of: —Wendy Diaz, 244–45, 246; —Lesly
Rodríguez, 241–42, 251, 336n23; exploitation
of, 229, 239, 256; interviews with, 241; number of, 229; protests, 231, 234; rights of, 229,
233; salaries of, 225, 229, 241, 244; union percentage, 233; working conditions of, 233,
234, 235, 241–42, 246, 248
Marx, Karl, 134, 320nn17&20
master plan(s), 141, 144, 156. *See also* Hurricane
Mitch reconstruction, master plan
McMichael, Phillip, 312n19, 313n25, 315nn1&16,
317n13, 330n72,2&4
McNamara, Robert, 153, 160, 166, 170–71
mechanisms of power. *See* power, mechanisms
of
methodology, ix–x, 57, 63, 317n11; documents
(*see* documents); generalizeability to other
countries, 303–4; historical time frame, 5,
312n9; Honduras as case study, 5, 63, 131, 303,
310; interviews (*see* interviews/interviewees)
migration, 7, 60, 210; international, 60–61; to
U.S., 210, 211, 237

Milwaukee, deep tunnel sewer project, 198, 329n69
mining, 18, 139, 217
missionaries, 58, 315n2, 316n9, 317n10
modernity/modernization, 3, 175
Morazán, Francisco, 175–76; Complejo Hidroelectrico General. *See* El Cajón

NAFTA, 7, 136
nation building, ix, xi, 141
nation-state, 14, 33, 135; neoliberal, 138; reorganization of, 136, 137, 141–42
natural resources, 18, 139
neocolonialism, 4, 311n9
neoliberalism, 9, 12, 39, 108, 116, 201, 210, 239
NGOs (nongovernmental organizations), xiv, 5, 7, 25, 31–33, 35, 55, 75, 90, 94, 105, 116, 117, 298–99, 302, 308–9, 312n9, 336n17, 342n47; becoming a part of donor countries' agendas, 33, 39, 239–40, 255, 298, 308–9; boom in, 31, 33, 308; in donor countries, 282, 287, 288, 309; and El Cajón (*see* Honduran institutions, Society of Civil Engineers; Rivers Network, International); finances of, 314n10; as globalizers, 308, 337–38n37; local Honduran, 32, *34,* 235, 247, 283, 302, 342; location of, 36, 38; and *maquiladoras,* 235, 239, 243, 248, 251, 252, 255 (*see also* Honduran institutions: Human Rights Commission; Labor Committee, National; Labor Organizations, International, UN; unions, labor); and Mitch reconstruction, 261, 276, 281–84, 285, 287 (*see also* Honduran institutions: Interforos, National Convergence Forum; Stockholm); number of, 31–32; official support of, 29, 31–33; opposing large dams, 153–54, 322n10; ties to USAID, 31, 45, 48; as Trojan horse, 31; working with TNCs, 251, 252, 255. *See also* civil society

OECD (Organization for Economic Cooperation and Development), 11, 24, 136,313nn23& 24, 314nn1–6; member nations (*see* G22)
official development assistance (ODA), xii, 1, 5, 165, 202, 210, 213, 261, 264, 297, 313nn24&26, 314n6; as boon for donor countries, 18–19; definition of, 24; globalization and, 33,

317n10; Honduran coordination of, 29, 33, 265, 276; to Honduras, 2, 25–26, 29, 33, 313n29, 323n18; loans, 24; sources of, 29–31, *30;* transnationalization of, 30, 33. *See also* aid
offshore assembly/manufacturing, 9, 139, 215, 240, 250, 254, 330n5; history of, 208–9; Honduras as a major site, 227, 230; pilot programs, 211. See also *maquiladoras*
OPEC, 28, 165

Pan American Health Organization (PAHO), 28, 35, 54, 159, 173
Parsons, Talcott, 133, 320n8
Peace Corps, 77, 90, 102, 309
Perkin, Harold, 64, 133, 317n12, 318n5, 320nn6&17
Petersen, Kurt, 214–15, 331nn18–20
petroleum, Honduran dependence on, 156, 160, 169–70, 193, 195, 324n42
population control, 44, 140
Portes, Alejandro et al., 316nn4–7
postindustrial age, 64, 301
poverty, 16, 90, 101, 118, 140, 203, 227, 297, 334n57
power: definitions of, 132–34; elegant exercise of, 13; on global scale, 132, 134, 135, 146, 294, 302
power, mechanisms of, x–xii, xiii, 142–46, 239, 254; cyclical nature of, 146, 197, 239
—agenda setting, xiii, 133, 144–45; and El Cajón, 162; and *maquiladoras,* 217; and Mitch reconstruction, 274, 277, 279, 296. *See also* master plan(s)
—garnering consent, xiii, 134, 145–46, 303, 306, 307, 308; and El Cajón, 164, 171, 185; and *maquiladoras,* 221–22, 224, 254, 255; and Mitch reconstruction, 274, 279, 281, 285, 291, 294, 296
—insertion, xiii, 132, 142; and El Cajón, 156, 181–82; and *maquiladoras,* 215, 217, 235, 240, 247, 255; and Mitch reconstruction, 261, 262, 269, 295
—surveillance, xiii, 132–33, 142–44; and El Cajón, 157, 162, 164, 182, 184, 202; and *maquiladoras,* 215, 217, 240, 241, 247, 250, 253, 255; and Mitch reconstruction, 270, 271, 273, 296
press, Honduran, 151, 175, 179–81, 183, 189–90, 240, 264, 276, 280, 286, 287, 291, 293–94,

336n10; *Destination Honduras,* 335n64; *El Heraldo,* 293, 326n102, 327, 335n4, 340, 341, 342; *El Nuevo Dia,* 329; *El Periodico,* 183, 327, 328, 329; *Honduras This Week,* 334n52, 339, 340n16; *La Prensa,* 325n73, 327, 329, 341n46, 342; *La Tribuna,* 281, 293, 327, 334n50, 335, 336, 337, 338, 339; *Tiempo,* 327, 328, 329, 341

press, international, 240–41, 244; *Bobbin,* 225, 337n34; *Business Week,* 225, 336n11, 337n26; *Donahue,* 240; *Forbes,* 334n58; *Guardian,* 235; *Latin Finance,* 225; *Multinational Monitor,* 213, 331, 336n11; *New York Times,* 335n6; *Nightline,* 240; *Sixty Minutes* (see *Sixty Minutes*); *Telegraph,* 243, 337n28; *Wall Street Journal,* 225; *Women's Wear Daily,* 337n30

private enterprise, 49, 140, 211

professionals, 64–66, 126, 133, 317n10; Honduran, 65, 319n4. *See also* expertise; experts

religious groups/charities, 58, 264, 281, 314n2. *See also* missionaries

resettlement. *See* El Cajón, problems with; World Bank

Rich, Bruce, 313n27, 321n8, 323n29, 329n70

river(s): flooding, 260, 271; Humuya, 149, 156, 174; impounding for dam, 154, 174; monitoring technology, 297, 299

Rivers Network, International (NGO), 153, 164, 166

road projects, 60, 138; and Mitch reconstruction, 268, 272, 275, 276, 287, 296, 299

Robertson, A. F., 57, 318n1

Robinson, William I., 134–38, 296, 311nn4&8, 312nn11&17, 315nn16,17&1, 317n10, 320nn17–20, 321nn21–26, 330nn72,74&6. *See also* transnational state

Roy, Arundhati, 131, 141, 320

Russell, Bertrand, 133, 320n7

Sachs, Wolfgang, 311n5, 313nn27,28&33, 317n13

Said, Edward, 318n14

Sassen, Saskia, 312nn15&17

Save the Children (NGO), 5, 38, 55, 110, 276

secrecy, 306, 322n33. *See also* transparency

Sixty Minutes, CBS's, 236–37, 238, 240, 241, 255, 336n12

Sklair, Leslie, 311nn7&8, 312n10, 330nn72,2&4

social welfare programs, 108–9, 140; as a global agenda, 138, 140

sociology/social science, xi, 109, 132–34

sovereignty, xiv, 13–14, 287, 306

Spain, 26, 186, 267, 280, 283, 292, 335n5

Spanish Agency of International Cooperation (AECI), xix, 26–27, 29, 35, 37, 73, 141, 275, 314n9, 339n7

Stiglitz, Joseph, 311n3, 312n17, 313n27, 314n1

Stockholm, 269–70, 274, 276, 277, 279, 282, 283, 287, 288, 290, 296, 302; declaration of, 294–95, 342nn66&67; meeting in, 291–95; NGOs and, 287, 290–91, 295

structural adjustment, 29, 108–9

surveillance, 132. *See also under* power, mechanisms of

Sweden, 31, 84, 90, 263, 264–65, 267, 281, 283, 287, 289–90, 291, 292, 296, 297, 298, 299, 314n35, 339n3; ambassador of, 282; NGOs from, 342n47; TNCs from, 290. *See also* Stockholm

Swedish International Development Cooperation Agency (ASDI), 26–27, 35, 279, 282, 283, 342n58

Switzerland/Swiss, 154, 156, 163, 165, 172, 174, 175, 185–86, 203, 292, 322n5; Development Agency (COSUDE), 5, 27, 73

technical assistance, 219, 268, 274, 275, 279

technology, 1, 139 152, 297

técnico, 42, 46

Tegucigalpa, xii, 36–39, 58, 62, 73, 138–39, 218, 225, 260, 264, 271, 280, 293; growth in, 315n18; mayor killed, 261; neighborhoods, 37, 63, 73, 258, 260

telecommunication, 138, 287

thermal plants, 156, 160, 170, 176–77, 180, 189, 191, 193

Thomas, George, 9, 311n8, 312n21, 320n17

tourism, 140, 312n22

transmigration/migrants, 61, 92

transnational capitalist class, x, 3, 7, 311n8, 312nn11&17, 313n34, 321n25

transnational corporations (TNCs), 3, 7, 8, 207, 239, 251, 253, 254, 257, 311n8; American Power International, 193; Bechtel, Burns &

transnational corporations (*continued*)
  Roe, Fluor, 212; development aid and, 154;
  Nike, 330n5; Nissan, 330n3; Stromberg
  Carlson, 213. *See also under* El Cajón,
  contractors; *maquiladoras,* TNCs using
transnational institutions, 9, 136, 240, 320n17
transnationalism, 60–61, 315n4, 316nn5–7; dual
  life and, 92
transnational state (TNS), xiii, 5, 132, 136, 296,
  303, 304; Robinson's model of, 134–38, *137;*
  —additions to, 135, 320n17, 330n74; global
  agendas of, 138, 330n6
transparency, xiv, 268, 275, 283, 285, 286, 290,
  292, 293, 294, 295, 298; as global agenda, 307

UNDP (United Nations Development Programme), 5, 26, 28, 53, 55, 139, 267, 314n10;
  and Mitch reconstruction, 262, 265–66, 270,
  272–74
UNICEF (United Nations Children's Fund), 5,
  26, 28, 54, 55, 73, 74, 82–87, 103–4, 145, 249,
  250, 318n4
unions, labor: Honduran, 233–35, 242, 248,
  250, 253, 255; international, 250
United Nations (UN), x, 10, 11, 26, 28, 37,
  79–89, 105, 108, 110, 111, 136, 293, 311n9,
  313n27; CEPAL, 273–74, 340n18; documents,
  340nn14&18; location in hierarchy, 35;
  support of NGOs, 32
United States, 11, 26, 31, 43, 91, 152, 163, 174, 185,
  190, 196, 210, 221, 230, 263, 267, 292, 299,
  318n2; aid from, 315n22; aid rationale, 21;
  businesses, 154, 211, 236, 248, 290; Child
  Labor Elimination Act, 251; congress, 44, 60,
  211–13, 221, 238, 243, 244, 247, 248, 253, 285,
  337n25, 338n37; congressional hearings,
  241–43, 244–47, 249–50; congressmen,
  211–12, 246–47, 250, 338nn41&45; documents,
  331nn8–10, 332n26, 333n40, 334–38; Economic
  Support Fund (ESF), 213, 221–22; Foreign
  Assistance Act, Section 599, 236–37; GAO,
  221–22, 237, 331, 336n16; in Honduras:
  —ambassador, 51, 246, 264; —economic
  assistance, 30; —embassy, 40; military,
  18–19, 30; National Endowment for Democracy, 250; presidents, 210, 240, 263; senators,
  236, 241, 242; State Department, 43, 44; tax-

payer dollars, 236, 240. *See also* Peace Corps;
  USAID
universalism, 3, 10, 317n10
universities, xi, 65, 66, 75, 77, 91, 100, 101, 112,
  140
USAID (United States Agency for International Development), xix, 5, 26–27, 37, 59,
  90, 98, 99, 108, 136, 138, 139, 140, 141, 145, 209,
  239, 302, 307, 311n9, 313n27, 315nn22–24,
  331n9; Bureau of Private Enterprise, 211, 212,
  213, 216, 332n26; documents, 210, 307, 315n3,
  331nn15&25, 332nn27–34, 333nn35–42, 334,
  343n1; and El Cajón, 156, 196; employees of,
  42, 46–47, 318n2; institutional structure,
  45–50; location in hierarchy, 33; and Mitch
  reconstruction, 262, 265, 266, 270, 274, 275,
  285–86, 339n7; PL-480 (food for peace)
  program, 99 (*see also* food aid); power of,
  50, 51; re-engineering in, 43–45; and Honduras: —government relationships, 47,
  50–54; —role in changing law, 51–52, 214;
  —strategic objectives in, 43–44; subcontracting, 31–32, 45, 48, 51–52, 54, 99, 224–25,
  334n51; technical divisions, 46–50; tour of,
  40–54; Trade and Development Program,
  212, 213, 331n9; as Trojan horse, 51; in
  Washington, 42, 44, 267
USAID, and *maquiladoras,* 209–11, 213–28, 229,
  235, 248, 249, 250, 251, 254, 256; creating
  FIDE (*see* FIDE); Elise Dupont, 211, 332n26;
  Export Development and Services Project,
  217–21; export promotion, 215, 216; exposé
  of, 235–36, 240; as global agenda, 210; Christian R. Holmes, 212–13; key role in, 208, 229,
  254–55; legal reforms, 214, 218, 221, 222–24;
  loan package, 221; private contractors:
  —Arthur D. Little, 217; —International
  Finance Corp., 221; —International Parks
  Inc., 217; —Manchester Associates, 217;
  Nathan Associates, 219, 221, 227, 332n31; —
  Price Waterhouse, 217, 219; Private Enterprise Initiative, 213; role curtailed, 236–38,
  240, 336n19; working with Honduran
  businesses, 215

vehicles, development organization, 6, 38,
  320n13

volunteering, 66, 68, 90; symbolic importance of, 76

Washington Office on Latin America (WOLA), 124, 251
water and sanitation, 75, 82–84, 139, 141; as human right, 81; and Mitch reconstruction, 268, 272, 287
Weber, Max, 133, 320n7
women's rights, 7, 10. *See also* feminism
World Bank (WB), 5, 10, 11, 27, 28, 37, 47, 71, 108, 135, 138, 139, 140, 239, 250, 251, 267, 307, 311n9, 313n27; Country Assistance Strategy, 145; and criticism, 167–68; delegation visit, 277–78; documents, 145, 167, 169, 196, 307, 321n32, 322–27, 340n17; and El Cajón, 150, 156, 157, 158, 160, 161, 165, 172, 177, 182, 184, 185, 186, 192, 194, 195, 196, 197, 198, 199, 339n3; environmental concerns, 151, 156; HIPC initiative, 193, 339n72; history of, 152–53; loans: —internal pressure for, 153, 169; —to military government, 164, 168–69; location in hierarchy, 35; and Mitch reconstruction, 262, 265, 266, 268, 270–72, 273–74, 277–78, 285–86, 339n7; and resettlement, 159, 173; slogan, 17, 313n32; support of NGOs, 32. *See also* dams; development organizations; McNamara, Robert
world economy, 3, 24, 135, 314n1, 316n10. *See also* global economy
World Food Programme, UN (WFP), 28, 119–20, 265
world polity perspective, 134, 311n8, 320n17
world state, 311n8. *See also* global government; transnational state
world system, capitalist, 5, 135, 316–17n10; world systems perspective, 134, 311n4, 316n10
World Trade Organization (WTO), 7, 11, 136, 199, 239
World Vision (NGO), 5, 35, 38, 108

Printed in the United States
91235LV00003B/100-117/A